In Pursuit

OF Plants

In Pursuit of Plants

OF Plants

Experiences of nineteenth &
early twentieth century plant collectors

PHILIP SHORT

TIMBER PRESS
Portland · Cambridge

First published in North America and the United Kingdom in 2004 by
Timber Press, Inc.
The Haseltine Building
133 S.W. Second Avenue, Suite 450
Portland, Oregon 97204-3527, U.S.A.

Timber Press
2 Station Road
Swavesey
Cambridge CB4 5QJ, U.K.

Catalog records for this book are available from the
Library of Congress and the British Library.

Cover: A view of Kangchenjunga from Singtam, Sikkim, based on a sepia drawing by Joseph Hooker and completed by the artist Walter Hood Fitch (1817–1892) for publication in Hooker's *Himalayan Journals*. (Source and copyright: Royal Botanic Gardens, Kew)

Produced by Benchmark Publications Pty Ltd, Melbourne
Consultant editors: Jan Anderson Publishing Services, Melbourne
Designed by Colorperception P/L
Typeset in Sabon
Printed by BPA Print Group, Australia

CONTENTS

INTRODUCTION vii

EDITORIAL NOTES xiii

ACKNOWLEDGMENTS xv

AFRICA 1
  J. R. T. Vogel (1841) 3
  R. W. Plant (1851–1852) 9
  C. Barter (1857–1859) 19
  F. M. J. Welwitsch (1860) 27
  J. T. Baines (1861) 31
  W. G. Milne (1863–1865) 37

ASIA 45
  J. Arnold (1818) 47
  G. W. & A. W. Walker (1833) 51
  J. D. Hooker (1847–1848) 57
  R. Fortune (c. 1850–1855) 70
  J. Motley (1855) 77
  F. W. Burbidge (1878) 90
  H. O. Forbes (1878–1883) 100
  G. Forrest (1905, c. 1931) 107

AUSTRALIA & NEW ZEALAND 117
  R. W. Lawrence (1833) 119
  J. Drummond (1839–1853) 124
  W. Colenso (1845) 137
  F. W. L. Leichhardt (1844–1845) 150
  F. J. H. Mueller (1855–1856) 161
  W. E. P. Giles (1872–1874) 167
  D. Sullivan (1882) 181
  W. B. Spencer (1894) 184
  F. J. Gillen (1894) 190
  M. Koch (1899–1925) 192
  W. A. Michell (1903) 196

EUROPE 197
  P. E. Boissier (1837) 199
  J. H. Balfour (1844) 206

NORTH AMERICA   215
    T. Drummond (1825–1827)   217
    D. Douglas (1825–1831)   229
    A. Gray (1841)   238
    C. Geyer (1843–1844)   248

CENTRAL AMERICA & SOUTH AMERICA   261
    G. U. Skinner (1837–1841)   263
    F. W. Hostmann (1838–1843)   269
    T. L. Bridges (1844–1845)   279
    R. Spruce (1852–1854)   285

OCEANS & ISLANDS   295
    J. D. Hooker (1841–1842)   297
    W. G. Milne (1855–1856)   305
    B. C. Seemann (1860)   312

APPENDICES   321
    Plant names   323
    Herbaria   326
    The Wardian Case   329

REFERENCES & NOTES   335

INDEX   345

INTRODUCTION

In 1792, David Burton died of gunshot wounds on the banks of the Nepean River, near Sydney, in Australia. In 1833, Robert Lawrence, just twenty-six years old, was found dead in his bed. Two years later, Richard Cunningham died of spear wounds. In 1844, Franz Sieber ended his days in a lunatic asylum and, in the following year, John Gilbert was fatally speared in the neck. In 1848, Ludwig Leichhardt disappeared in the interior of Australia and in 1874, at Barrow Creek Overland Telegraph station in Central Australia, Ebenezer Flint and his colleagues were attacked by Aborigines. Although wounded in the thigh, Flint survived the attack whereas the stationmaster, mortally wounded by a spear thrust into his groin, could do no more than tap out a farewell message to his family in Adelaide.[1]

All of these men left a common legacy. At some stage in their lives they had collected plants in Australia; seeds and living plants destined for European gardens, or dried specimens sent to botanists for formal naming and description.

Those of us who spend their time classifying, describing and giving scientific names to plants are known as taxonomists, and many of us spend most of our research time studying a particular group of plants. My particular speciality is the daisy family (the Compositae or Asteraceae). Many species inhabit the arid areas of Australia and some years ago, driving north along the Stuart Highway to Alice Springs on a collecting trip, I initially found much of the surrounding countryside was devoid of flowering herbs. However, the pock-marked landscape surrounding the opal-mining centre of Coober Pedy was in full bloom. But, it was not the daisies that caused me to stop; instead it was the plants of Sturt's desert pea that carpeted the ground. The grandeur of this pea has never failed to impress me and my admiration was obviously shared by others, as was evident from the numerous footprints which encircled the plants. How lucky we are to be able to drive in comfort to such places. It is a far cry from the problems and suffering encountered by early explorers, many of whom were in the habit of collecting plants, and by their animals. Francis Gregory, leader of an exploratory journey to the Hamersley Ranges in 1861, recorded:

> I cannot omit to remark the singular effects of excessive thirst upon
> the eyes of the horses; they absolutely sunk into their heads until

there was a hollow of sufficient depth to entirely bury the thumb in, and there was an appearance as though the whole of the head had shrunk with them, producing a very unpleasant and ghastly expression.[2]

The following extract from Colonel Peter Egerton Warburton's journal, written when his party were struggling to traverse the sandy deserts of north-west Australia in the 1870s, is possibly as compelling:

Having no water, to halt upon obliged to move on ... On reaching camp at eighteen miles the advance party had found a splendid well, or rather had made one in a good place — we have reason to be thankful as this well saved us from going back over the stiff sandhills we have crossed. The country has not improved as I had hoped; I shall resume a west course tomorrow. My riding camel has completely broken down, and could not bring me into camp today. She lay down, and we could only get her on her legs again by lighting some spinifex under her tail; but it was no use, she could not travel, so I tied her to a bush and walked in. Sent a man to lead in my camel. It is quite clear I must give up day travelling; the camels will be ruined by it.[3]

Taxonomists need to know a great deal about when, where and by whom different plants were first collected. I was already aware that Sturt's desert pea was first collected by English buccaneer William Dampier in 1699 — indeed it is sometimes referred to as Dampier's pea — and that several early Australian explorers such as Edward John Eyre, not just the plant's namesake Captain Charles Sturt, had commented upon it in their journals or had collected specimens. Francis Gregory provided one of the more vivid descriptions of the species:

While on shore today several new and very beautiful plants and flowers were observed, amongst them one in particular, which, without exception, is the handsomest shrub I have ever seen in Australia; in form the plant resembles a large chandelier, with a series of branches springing from a centre stem in sets of five each; on these are short erect stems a few inches apart, carrying five beautiful deep crimson dragon flowers, nearly three inches in length, grouped like lustres, producing a very gorgeous effect; the leaves of the plant are elegantly formed, like those of the mountain ash, and are of a rich green.[2]

Settled again in my car, I resolved to make available to a wider audience both published and unpublished articles and letters

Sturt's desert pea, Swainsona formosa *(synonyms:* Clianthus formosus, Willdampia formosa*), an annual or short-lived perennial, is the floral emblem of South Australia but is found throughout much of arid Australia. Commonly flowers, which are c. 5–8 cm long, are predominantly red with the standard petal having a black, central boss as pictured here.*

containing accounts by early collectors of their experiences when gathering plants. The work would not be parochial but contain accounts of overseas collectors, highlight minor amateur collectors as well as major professional collectors, and include those who primarily gathered plants for scientific naming and study, not just for horticulture.

This was decided before I arrived at Alice Springs, where Ebenezer Flint was for some time the senior stationmaster of the Overland Telegraph station. It was during his time there that Flint seems to have collected plant specimens, in 1882 leading a small exploratory party to the east of the settlement. Unlike me, he was never to leave Central Australia. In 1887, just thirty-three years old and recently married, he succumbed to rheumatic fever.

Francis Gregory's expedition party to the Hamersley Ranges included two plant collectors, Permberton Walcott and Maitland Brown. The latter's collections included Ptilotus rotundi-folius. The genus Ptilotus, a member of the family Amaranthaceae, contains c. 100 species and all but one is confined to Australia. This species may be up to 1.5 m tall and the flowers are grouped in cylindrical inflorescences which are 8–12 cm long.

That, essentially, was the origin of this book. Nothing happened for quite some time, taxonomic research and flora-writing taking up official work hours. However, I did familiarise myself more with the many letters published in assorted nineteenth-century botanical journals, particularly those edited by Sir William Hooker of the Royal Botanic Gardens, Kew, in England. Not all such letters were strictly botanically orientated. Interspersed with the more mundane accounts of drying and transporting specimens, and lists and descriptions of plants, were accounts as diverse as witchcraft in west Africa and vampire bats in Surinam. In short, some accounts were highly entertaining or, at the very least, interesting records of the activities and prejudices of a lost world. Added to this, the fact that a number of nineteenth-century collectors published their own accounts of their travels, I decided to concentrate on presenting the activities of collectors from that century and the early part of the twentieth century.

This is a broad scope as throughout the world, safely locked away in herbaria and their associated libraries, there must be a massive collection of published and unpublished documents relating the activities of collectors. It would be a near-impossible task to obtain and read more than a small fraction of them. Hence, collectors covered here were often associated in some way with Kew. This partly reflects which journals are available to me in Australia but is also a result of my having spent twelve months working at the Herbarium, Royal Botanic Gardens, Kew, during 1991–1992. During my stay there I was able to spend time in the Kew archives, sifting through original letters for material of interest. In many cases it was possible to view the original letters which were edited and published by Hooker and when available it is these, not the previously published versions, that are used here.

This may suggest a narrow range of material for a book in which the principal aim is to introduce readers to the difficulties, and sometimes, life-threatening situations encountered by plant collectors. However, Kew was, and still is, a major hub of plant taxonomic research and was frequently involved in the introduction to Britain of what are today commonly cultivated plants. Furthermore, there is a limit to the number of tales of near-starvation, life-threatening diseases and loneliness which can be included in a work such as this! It would also be too easy to repeat similar accounts of more practical problems encountered by collectors, whether they were problems with transport, lack of paper for plant presses, or the loss of specimens to floods, fire and insect pests.

The fact that only one woman is included in this compilation possibly requires comment. The absence of women is primarily due to the fact that the social constraints of the time did not permit women to travel widely, at least not by themselves. Furthermore, married women, often with large families to care for, had limited opportunities even to step out into the local bush and spend time collecting. This lack of opportunity is reflected in the proportion of men and women who collected for herbaria. For example, a tally of collectors who were born before 1901 and collected in Australia showed that for every woman there were at least seven men who had collected herbarium specimens.[4] Of the women who did collect, either no correspondence pertaining to their activities was found — and this is the norm for most collectors, both men and women — or I rarely found applicable material. Unfortunately, when I did find records, as for example for Marianne North and Ellis Rowan — both of whom collected plants but were essentially flower painters — I felt that these women had had either plenty of recent exposure in other publications or that the accounts by some men were more interesting and more suitable for the purposes of this book.

It will be apparent from some extracts that I was occasionally sidetracked from reading about experiences of collectors to reasons given for collecting plants. That many collectors simply enjoyed botanical pursuits, with or without travel to exotic localities, is hardly surprising. However, until I read one of Max Koch's letters, I did not appreciate that the money obtained from the sale of specimens was, for some collectors, such an important supplement to the normal family income. Reading further on the topic, it became evident that Koch was not alone. For example, it is highly likely that for at least some members of Ferdinand Mueller's network of Australian collectors — some of whom belonged to pioneering, farming families with low incomes — payment for plant specimens would have been very welcome.[5] I was also intrigued to learn that Daniel Sullivan began to collect plants as a way to alleviate the monotonous routine of village life. However, he too was not alone in finding plant-collecting an escape from daily chores. One of Australia's earliest women collectors, Mrs Georgiana Molloy (1805–1843), recorded that for her a plant-collecting trip with her husband and children was delightful as it freed her from the cares of the household.[6]

Another aim of this book is to alert readers to the fact, alluded to above, that botanical journals and unpublished letters from botanists sometimes contain vivid descriptions of places and activities that are by no means related to plants. As a devotee of both natural history writing and travel, I was fascinated by many of these records and have occasionally incorporated some non-botanical matters in this compilation.

From the outset I never seriously considered presenting a synthesis of the letters and articles that came to hand. I prefer to let the collectors speak for themselves, albeit that those articles taken from published accounts and not original letters may have been rigorously edited before publication. However, biographical information about each collector, subheadings to highlight various features of the extracts and, sometimes, additional notes about the plants they gathered, are provided. In the Appendices there are also notes on plant names, herbaria and the development of the Wardian Case, which was developed to transport plants long distances without their dying.

EDITORIAL NOTES

Names of localities and organisms have often changed since the collectors' accounts were written and, when I've felt it useful to do so, some names have been updated. Such changes are indicated by the use of square brackets. These are also used if words in original manuscripts are unclear, and in some cases I have inserted a question mark within the brackets to show that I have endeavoured to interpret a word or a meaning.

As noted in the Appendices, it is common practice in scientific papers to follow the scientific name of a species (the binomial) with the author(s) of that name. This is not done here. It is unnecessary in a book of this nature, and to most readers would be no more than an irritating distraction from the main text. However, when used in an extract, authorities are left in.

In some letters, particularly those of Milne, grammatical errors, spelling mistakes and an almost total absence of punctuation are common. In strictly historical documentation it is desirable that such letters are reproduced with all mistakes indicated. However, a procession of square brackets can be extremely disruptive to readers. Therefore, unless they are proper names, spelling errors are usually corrected without indication. Similarly, no indication is given for minor changes or additions to punctuation, all such changes having been made only when I was confident that they would not alter the meaning of a statement. However, grammatical changes are indicated by square brackets.

Some abbreviations are also standardised; for example, 'etc.', not '&c.'. I have also standardised the spellings of some words; for example, 'wagon', not 'waggon', and 'botanised' not 'botanized'.

Two collectors, Milne and Hooker, are mentioned in more than one section: Milne in 'Africa' and 'Oceans and Islands', and Hooker in 'Asia' and 'Oceans and Islands'. Their biographical notes have been split between sections, depending on their relevance to the quoted extracts.

In the Contents and chapter headings, the years accompanying each collector's name represent the expeditions that are described in this book. Although I would have liked to have also included the years of birth and death for each collector, this was not always possible — regardless of extensive database searches. They were simply unavailable.

Regarding the content of the Appendices, many books have been written on plant naming, taxonomy and herbarium practice. Thus, although the notes on these topics should answer many questions that come to mind when reading the main text, not all may be answered. Many large public libraries and university libraries stock texts that elaborate on these topics and all sizeable botanic gardens and herbaria should have staff to assist with enquiries.

ACKNOWLEDGMENTS

My initial reading and compilation of articles occurred while I was employed at the National Herbarium of Victoria, Royal Botanic Gardens, Melbourne. That the book was written is largely due to the fact that during 1991–1992 I was the Australian Botanical Liaison Officer at the Royal Botanic Gardens, Kew, a position funded by an Australian Biological Resources Study grant.

The following written material is used with permission: an extract from a letter by Max Koch (permission of the Royal Botanic Gardens, Melbourne); extracts from letters that are part of the Director's Correspondence at Kew (permission of the Trustees of the Royal Botanic Gardens, Kew); an extract from a letter by George Forrest (permission of the Scottish Rock Garden Club); and an extract from a letter by Francis Gillen (permission of the Pitt Rivers Museum, Oxford). Of the many primary sources of information used in writing this book, it is understood that a large number are now out of copyright and therefore do not need further acknowledgment.

One or more illustrations were published with the permission of the Royal Botanic Gardens, Kew; the Royal Botanic Gardens, Melbourne; the National Library of Australia, Canberra; the Department of Infrastructure, Planning and Environment, Northern Territory; and the School Council of Moyston, Victoria. Several individuals also provided illustrations, for which I am most appreciative.

The following people have kindly assisted with the compilation of this work: at the Royal Botanic Gardens, Kew, Dr Dick Brummitt and Professor Bob Johns of the herbarium and past and present library staff, particularly Cheryl Piggott, Sylvia Fitzgerald, John Flanagan, Marilyn Ward and Dor Duncan; at the Royal Botanic Gardens, Melbourne, Professor Jim Ross, Dr Roger Spencer, Helen Cohn and Jill Thurlow. Others who have kindly helped in some way include Robyn Barker, James Burke, Robert Gadsdon, Dr Willem de Wilde, Dr W. Wüster, and Emma, my wife.

Acknowledgment of the help I received from Dr E. Charles Nelson deserves a separate paragraph. In 1991, Charles drew my attention to, and provided photocopies of, some letters from William

Grant Milne to David Moore. Subsequently he read and commented on a copy of the near-final manuscript and provided various references. I thank him for his meticulous attention to detail.

Having acknowledged those who helped in the compilation of the manuscript, it would be remiss of me not to mention the staff of University of Western Australia Press, particularly Dr Jenny Gregory, Maureen de la Harpe and Sam Wilson, through whom this project has reached fruition. We never met but frequently corresponded and I greatly appreciated the prompt and cordial manner in which matters were dealt with. Similarly it has been an enjoyable exercise working — again solely by correspondence — with Janine Drakeford of Benchmark Publications and Jan Anderson of Jan Anderson Publishing Services. Jan handled the bulk of the copy-editing and I much appreciated her constructive comments, gentle queries and obvious diligence. Some final matters were handled similarly by Brenda Hamilton.

AFRICA

J. R. T. VOGEL (1841)

Born in Germany, J. R. Theodor Vogel (1812–1841) received the degree of Doctor of Philosophy from the University of Berlin, his thesis being a study of the plant genus *Cassia*. In August 1840, Vogel became acquainted with the London-based African Civilisation Society, formed for the express purpose 'of extending civilisation amongst the natives of Western Africa, and putting an end to the slave trade'. In May 1841, he departed for Africa, the British Government having fitted out three steamers to travel up the Niger River. Vogel was Botanist to the expedition.[1]

Free Town, Sierra Leone

On entering the river at Free Town, the shore, on which the town stands, is bordered at a short distance by a range of hills, which make a very pretty appearance with their gentle swelling summits and insolated lofty trees. A rich vegetation stretches from the shore upwards, which captivates the eye by its soft bright green, such is only seen in the tropics, and gives the whole an incomparably charming character. I rushed eagerly into these woods ... When I return laden with plants, I have no where to prepare them; and when they are dry, the damp insinuates itself to such a degree, that I am compelled to redry them. This is very troublesome; and on board a ship, especially a man-of-war, there is no especial place for preparing or preserving plants. I am quite a nuisance to my messmates when I unpack them, and so is the servant who announces breakfast, lunch, etc., for the table must be cleared. I must be off, and then I try to work on deck; but there the wind and rain attack me, so that I have to contend with all the elements. I am here quite amongst the Negroes, for there are few white persons in the town, and during my excursions I frequently do not see one, during the whole day. I cannot, however, say that this seems altogether strange to me, for on our voyage outward, we had many black sailors in our ship, and their number has gradually been increased in the course of our progress.[2]

Soaked bedding

Last night, without any remarkable wind, there was so strong a rocking of the ship, that I scarcely slept a wink. I was up late for the first time, namely after eight o'clock, and was not present at the morning prayers, which a German Missionary, from Sierra Leone, the Rev. Frederick Schön, performs from half past seven to eight. Breakfast comes between eight and nine; today we had ham and yams, and as usual, coffee without milk. The atmosphere was so thick that we could not see half a mile, though when there was for a moment a clear sky, we descried the mouth of a river, which we took for the Nun [Niger], therefore we anchored about six miles from the shore. The rain came down in torrents, and the whole of the gun-room was flooded. I betook myself to my cabin, from the window of which I let down the shutter, to enable me to see; but the cabin and bedding were soon so soaked from the entrance of the rain, that I was obliged to fly to the deck in my mackintosh. The awning is not waterproof, and the water stood in many places two inches deep; nevertheless, I tried to while away the time there till dinner. This takes place between two and three, and, thanks to preserved meats, yams, pastry, etc., is very comfortable. Afterwards, the carpenter was in requisition to make my cabin watertight. The window-shutter was closed and the bed dried, as well as circumstances permitted. The stove was again placed in the gun-room, so that we had the pleasant warmth of 87° Fahr. There was enough to occupy me till tea in putting my cabin to rights. At six o'clock we have tea, without milk, and sea-biscuit. At half-past seven, evening prayers. The rain having somewhat abated, my companion and I sought for a tolerably dry place, where wrapped in my cloak, I might smoke a cigar; and then I took a seat in the gun-room, where I am writing this letter. The violent rolling of the ship, however, still continues, and its effect is evidenced in my more than ordinarily bad writing.[3]

Baobabs and 'horned devils'

At Iddáh, the country which was before low and flat, begins to be elevated and rises in mountains 2,000 feet high, which with occasional interruptions, extend to this place, where they are confined to the right bank of the river. Here and there, spots occur, which remind one of the Rhine; the bed of the river is, however, too broad (generally above half a mile) to be picturesque, and is often broken and enlarged by various islands. The mountains are bare, without any sign of human industry; only once I saw a village on the top of a hill which appeared very pretty. Mount Patteh, in whose neighbourhood we lie, is a quadrangular mountain on the right bank, rising precipitously on all sides about 1,200 feet high, with many patches of forest, and thickly clothed everywhere with plants. At its foot grow many slender oil-palms, so that the whole picture, painted with the fresh green which the rainy season has produced, is very lovely. As I sit under the awning on the quarter deck, and look towards that spot, I cannot help being pleased with the view, beholding in the solitary baobabs, and the oil-palms, though familiar to me now for weeks, forms which still interest me from their novelty.

The natives, who come to us from far and near, behave extremely well; they have never shown the slightest sign of enmity, on the contrary, they are rather too confiding. They are not of that deep black hue which is observable in other Africans, and in this neighbourhood they have often very good features. They understand spinning and making cloth; they know how to work in iron, to manufacture knives, sabres, nails, etc.; they cultivate also the fields with some degree of skill. It is sad, however, to think, that they have possessed the same aptness for these arts, probably from an almost inconceivable time, without making any improvement; they want that spiritual energy, which renders every acquisition a step to further advancement. We have a daily market on the shore, whither the inhabitants of a neighbouring village resort in great numbers, to sell or barter what they possess. Small looking-glasses, framed in paper, meet with very ready purchasers, and I shall never forget the joy which beamed in the eyes of many, when they first beheld their own faces in a mirror. The women, especially, cannot be satisfied with gazing on themselves, smeared with the powder of a red wood and their short hair standing upright in little tufts, so that they appear more like horned devils than human beings. In general, however, they prefer what is useful to trifles, provided the latter be not too dazzling and enticing; as for instance, a bright red cap edged with gold.

There is a peculiar custom in the whole of Africa, called 'dash'. Before a person deals with a stranger, a present is given, called in African-English, 'dash'. As the Africans expect that strangers or Europeans give far more than they receive, this system is a sort of indirect impost, and unpleasant to those who are not prepared for it, and I have seen many a silk handkerchief given away in this manner for nothing. The cotton ones, which I had bought, have done me good service in this way.[4]

Island of Fernando Po

We were desirous of proceeding farther when the tropical fever, which we had long feared, but at last considered as left behind, broke out with such a degree of virulence, that in a short time almost all the Europeans were seized, and most of them suffered severely. On the same evening on which I wrote my last letter [18 Sept.] I fell ill of the fever, which assumed a serious aspect. The sea air being considered the best remedy against the malady, we went all together down the river to this place. First, the *Soudan* with the sick; then our ship, the *Wilberforce*; and lastly, the *Albert*, after it had proceeded up the Niger for some days, was finally compelled to return, and to bring all the Europeans with her ... They brought me on shore in a very high fever, and I have been now almost three weeks here. The fever, which on my way was almost always upon me, has left me for the last week and a half, and I am now, as I believe, out of all danger.

Of the Island of Fernando Po [Bioko Is.] itself I can say little; I have not yet been in a condition to look round me. Yet it seems rich in plants, and I hope especially that the examination of the mountains may prove productive; for they are mainly covered with thick woods, and the highest point is above 10,000 feet high. The accommodations are but limited and poor. All the houses are merely made of boards, knocked together, and are raised on strong posts, which are obliged to be frequently renewed to keep off the vermin, and to facilitate the current of air. They are constructed, principally, with a view to airiness; the windows, that is the shutters, do not close; the roof is seldom watertight, and in the walls and floors are great holes, so that during a heavy rain, such as prevailed yesterday, our chamber is almost flooded, and it is merely the holes in the floor which, allowing the water to escape, give some relief. The German Mineralogist, belonging to the Expedition, who is somewhat more advanced than myself towards recovery, will remain here, and we have clubbed together for our housekeeping; but even this is expensive. Anything in the shape of a kitchen is out of the question. To the open space under the house, which is beaten hard like a barn-floor, the cook brings every day his iron grate, and prepares, with a monstrous consumption of wood, in four or five iron pots, everything that can be procured for food. There is, however, no great choice. We have fowls, and beef when ships come, but only then, and occasionally fish. Yams never fail, and they are excellent, so that I prefer them by far to our potatoes. What a pity that there is no possibility of introducing this plant at home! We can have them every day; indeed the poorer people live almost entirely upon yams. Add to this, rice, which however is not cultivated here; and it is almost all that the country can afford to set a poor invalid on his legs again; and it is little enough! If anything else be wanted, it must be procured from Europe. For our domestic affairs, we are obliged to have two servants, of whom one is cook. Each receives daily a shilling, so that the two cost above three pound sterling a month, and we have to keep them too. Both together do not accomplish in a day half so much as one European would.[5]

Bad servants and swarms of insects

Since I wrote last, there has been no great alteration. My recovery is tardy, but progressive; or, rather, I have been well for some time, only my strength returns very slowly. Yet I am able to undertake moderate excursions; longer ones I must defer, till the occasional rains cease entirely. I am most desirous of going to the mountains and to lead there for some time a really natural existence; for here there is a wretched mixture of artificial and natural. For these last five weeks, we have had everything in our domestic arrangements to superintend ourselves; otherwise we must have engaged more servants, and that is not only expensive, but we have quite enough to do to manage the two we have. An African servant will not listen to orders, but will do everything out of his own head, and if his taste does not agree with his master's, the master he thinks must comply with his. If I say to the cook, 'This must not be dressed so', he answers quietly, 'That is how I like it'; and if my servant, contrary to my directions, goes out for the whole evening, he says coolly, 'When you have got your meal, you have nothing more to do with me'. It is often difficult to procure anything for dinner; we have had no meat for two days, and there was none to be got for money. The same is often the case with bread, and if one has not a stock of ship biscuit, there is great difficulty about it. The light afforded by a palm-oil lamp is worse than that of the lamps which, in Germany, are allowed to servants, and this is very bad when we have any work to do in the evening. What I chiefly dislike is the host of ants, beetles, moths, etc., which swarm everywhere: they are very destructive to my collections, and I wage constant war with them. Besides the wasps, flies of all sorts, lizards, salamanders and rats pay us constant visits, so that a zoologist ought to rejoice in having so good an opportunity to make their acquaintance.[6]

Vogel never recovered his strength and contracted dysentery soon after the above letter was written. He died on 17 December 1841 and was buried alongside thirteen other participants in the expedition who had already succumbed to tropical diseases.[7]

R.W. PLANT *(1851–1852)*

Robert W. Plant was for some time a gardener at Kew, and a nurseryman at Cheadle, Staffordshire. In 1850, or 1851, he sailed for Natal. The following is his account of an excursion during 1851–1852, for the purpose of collecting objects of natural history, to the Zulu country of the interior.[1]

Miserly cupidity

Having forwarded the principal and heaviest portion of our luggage, such as provisions, boxes, paper, and ammunition, from Natal, by the wagon, we started on ox-back; pack-oxen entirely superseding horses for coast travelling, the frequently excessive heat and sour pasturage proving fatal to the latter. The usual equipage is one ox to ride and another, or sumpter-ox, to carry blankets and other necessaries for each person; and it is a matter of some moment to secure native or thoroughly acclimatised oxen, for should one or other of these two fail, there only remains one of the two alternatives, either to walk the rest of the journey or abandon the least valuable of the baggage.

At the Umvoti I got all the information possible of our intended route; and as this is the last mission station in the colony, on leaving it we bid adieu to civilisation *in toto*. Two days brought us to the Tugella [= Tugela River], the confines of the colony, and as the country wore a promising aspect I determined on staying a short time, both to rest the oxen and obtain an opportunity of looking into the flora. The country here, as in every other part, is hilly, but being well wooded the acclivities do not seem so great. The principal wood consists of two or three species of *Mimosa*, *Assagai*, and bastard-stinkwood; in the ravines, which are here numerous, many other trees and bushes are found; one of the latter, bearing no distant likeness to a *Laurustinus*, was blooming profusely and scented the air for many yards with its delicious aroma. A pretty pure white *Crocus* (?) ornamented the ground in patches, and large beds of *Gazania unicolor* were frequent. *Ipomoea nil*, or a species very like it, occurred often among the bushes, and pendent tufts of two lycopods were now and then seen hanging from the tops of trees. The river Tugella is a wide stream, and when full in the rainy season must present a formidable barrier; where we crossed there was about five or six hundred yards' width of water, but the banks must be near a mile apart, the intervening space being sand. We had been here four days and were just becoming interested in the place, when going one evening towards the river for the purpose of shooting ibis for dinner next day, I made my first acquaintance with the monarch of the forest — a lion was crouching within a few yards of my path: with nothing but small shot in the gun, I knew that the least hesitation might prove serious. This intelligence rendered a move next day indispensable, or the loss of an ox or two would be the probable result. Consequently next morning we entered the Zulu country. We had now eighty miles before us entirely uninhabited, and as the objects of my journey were not likely to be met with on the roadside, it became improbable that we should fall in with any party of traders. Great care was necessary to keep an accurate account of our course and to guard against any waste of provisions, for Kaffirs are the most improvident people I ever met with. They will continue eating while a morsel remains, though there was a certainty of starving the next day. They can however go without food for an amazing length of time, and, unlike most other savages, are not passionately fond of intoxicating drinks: a miserly cupidity is their ruling passion; they will drink anything given them, but they buy none. I have often seen them drink vinegar and water under the name of 'Jualo' (Kaffir-grog), with all the gusto imaginable — it costs nothing.[2]

A most cheerless night

On entering this range of country my intention was to proceed through it, as near to the sea as possible; and, from its general character and the fact that few if any had ever gone over it before, I had great expectations of meeting with new things. A few, very few nights' experience showed this route to be impracticable. The number of hyenas and tigers [sic] seemed to increase with each march, until they grew so bold that our fires would not keep them off, and three or four volleys were often necessary to drive them back. We therefore retraced our steps to the road, and the passage of two or three minor rivers brought us to the Umlilassi [= Mlalazi River], a noble stream, and decidedly the largest I have yet seen. From its size and proximity to the sea, we supposed it to be a tidal river, but night approaching, and wood being scarce on our side, we determined to push over at once. My sumpter-ox refused to take the water; not all the blows or jabbering of the Kaffirs could induce him to enter. It came on a cold rain, and as the rest were across, there was nothing left but to unload and lead him over in the middle of the stream. The water was breast high; the ox grew frightened, and with a plunge was bearing his leader off down the stream to the sea, so that the loss of both man and ox seemed inevitable, and to wade after them could not be done quick [*sic*] enough even if the depth of water would allow it. I was but a poor swimmer before I arrived in this colony, but my practice since proved of essential benefit in this instance; a few rapid strokes brought me before them, and by dint of shouting we got the ox round. The poor fellow who took the lead was nearly exhausted, being as often under water as above it, in consequence of the thong by which he had hold of the ox becoming entangled round his wrist. During this time the rain had come on heavily, wetting everything, and on coming to drink our coffee we found the water was salt; — so that this was the most cheerless night (with one single exception) I spent on the journey. Sleep was out of the question: we were close to the river and the sea-cows kept up a bellowing all night. The passage of this river was indeed most disastrous, and we had two days' journey before we should arrive at the place appointed for the wagon to leave our first lot of provisions; luckily the next day afforded us a good supply of meat, antelopes of two or three kinds being plentiful; the largest, or 'Eiland', is certainly the most graceful animal I know in this part of the world, and its flesh is the best eating of all the wild meats.

The country here began to assume a bolder appearance, the hills larger, backed in the distance by a range of mountains which we were evidently approaching, little or no bush on the left hand, while towards the sea the trees were gathered into dense forests. On the hills around us, whole acres of blue, pink, white, and yellow flowers occurred every mile or two, either in detached beds or mingled together in the most pleasant confusion. The fan-palms, which in Natal are but miserable stunted things, are here seen in native magnificence. Of the herbaceous plants, I may mention a large white *Aster*, two or three bright-yellow *Genista*-like dwarf plants, a very pretty little purple *Polygala*, a very dwarf deep blue and red *Cynoglossum*, the *Gazania* before named, and a larger one, several species of *Asclepias*, *Gladiolus psittacinus*, and a green variety of the

same, the dwarf hispid *Thunbergia*, a large white *Linaria*, two
or three terrestrial orchids, one of them remarkable for its large
chocolate-brown and yellow flowers, fully equal to the majority
of epidendrums, three or four gnaphaliums, and a very fine
white *Hyoscyamus*.[2]

Valuable articles for mere trash

In the afternoon of the second day from the Umlilassi, we crossed
the Umsatense, and at night arrived at our expected depot; great
indeed was our astonishment and disappointment to find the wagon
had passed on and left us nothing. We however procured mealies,
milk, and a goat from the Zulu kraal, with which we pushed on,
the country hereabouts offering but little inducement to stop.
Proceeding over a comparatively level country, in the forenoon of
the second day again we were somewhat startled by the sound of a
gong, apparently two or three miles off, and on observation noticed
the Zulus collecting on all sides towards the sound; a winding track
brought us suddenly in sight of an erection which in that position
caused no little surprise — it was evidently of corrugated iron; to
determine the matter we advanced, and found it a Mission Station,
and to our still greater surprise found it was Sunday morning (we
had lost a whole day in our reckoning) and that [the] service was
just commencing. We unloaded and took our seats on the ground
in the midst of some two hundred Zulus, who were here collected
by M. Schroeder, a zealous missionary, who alone in the midst of
this fickle people, and far from the support of civilisation, maintains
a position in the good will of those by whom he is surrounded.
We were hospitably entertained by him in the afternoon, and after
forcing upon us some acceptable presents and giving us much valuable
information as to our proposed route, we left him in the evening,
wending our way again towards the sea. As our wagon
was now far ahead of us, it was thought inadvisable to continue the
pursuit of it for the present, but rather to set to work at once and trust
to such supplies as could be drawn from the kraals around us.
Moreover our oxen required rest, and I longed to be getting my
collection together. A day and a half brought us into a thickly wooded
district nearly midway between the Umsatense and the Umgoa, and
here two oxen were soon loaded and despatched homewards.

Strange as it may seem, I could not tempt natives to assist me in
any way towards gathering insects, shells, etc.; they would not or

could not conceive any man so foolish as to give away such valuable articles as beads, etc., for the mere trash that I wanted. In natural disposition there seems little difference between these people and the Kaffirs; they are equally well made, light, active and vigorous when roused, but naturally prone to indolence; they set no value on time, and having nothing to care for except their cattle, do not wish to sell their lazy independence for the wages of a white man's servitude. A sense of past favours I am persuaded hardly exists among them, and either fear or the prospect of an advantage is the only motive to exertion. Like the Kaffirs they are mean, overreaching, and avaricious, yet they are honest and temperate; the females do all the work of the kraal, except attendance on the cattle; the young ones are many of them handsome, but in age they become wrinkled and abominably ugly. In person they are clean and fond of ornaments, but in many habits they are excessively dirty. They make extremely neat baskets and earthen pots to cook in; but the latter are clumsy things. Their own assagais [spears] and ornaments for the person, such as collars of beads, snuffboxes, etc., are also the work of their own hands; nor must I omit a three-legged stool for a pillow (cut out of solid wood), and the snuffspoon, generally of bone; it has three long teeth like a fork, to serve as a handle, and to fasten it in their woolly hair; the opposite extremity is furnished with a small bowl like that of a saltspoon, and with it they shovel up snuff by the handful, and perform all other necessary operations about the olfactory organ.

The district between the Umsatense and the Umgoa on the coast is very thickly populated; large quantities of Indian corn, sweet potatoes, tobacco, and Kaffir corn (a kind of millet) are grown for their own consumption. The Indian corn is broken in a kind of rough mortar, boiled and eaten with curdled sour milk. This is the staple food of the natives; to a European it is at first intolerable, but on acquaintance it becomes palatable, and indeed grateful in the overpowering heat felt in the middle of the day. Of the Kaffir corn they make a black bread, by grinding it between two stones and baking it on the ashes without leaves; and from the same corn brew a sharp, sour, and intoxicating beverage called 'jualo'; this corn, by distillation, yields a spirit very like the common brandy of the Cape. A sweet rush is also found on the banks of the streams, and eaten raw or boiled to sweeten their meals; and a small Labiate plant is cultivated to use as tobacco — this is probably a *Plectranthus*.[2]

Terrestrial and epiphytic orchids

The trees here assume a majestic stature, and many new forms are apparent. The *Mimosa* and stinkwood are still prevalent; the fan-palms are more frequent than before, and often attain a height of 50 or 60 feet, bearing fruit in abundance; two or three species of *Ficus* occur at intervals, and are usually very grotesque in appearance; strelitzias are scarce. But herbaceous plants are in great variety, and several new forms exist. I may mention the following genera as most prevalent: *Commelina, Justicia, Sparaxis* (several new ones), *Tritonia* (three species) wherever there are swamps, *Gladiolus* occasionally, *Chironia, Campanula, Lobelia, Rhus, Veltheima, Ornithogalum, Asparagus* (two beautiful kinds), *Aponogeton* in all the small streams, *Gnidia* (rarely), *Schottia, Oxalis* (frequent), *Hibiscus, Indigofera, Senecio* and *Cineraria*. The terrestrial orchids deserve more than a passing remark: they are numerous and very beautiful; in my opinion there are many here but little inferior to the most showy of the epiphytous kinds. I shall take care to forward a good parcel of roots, and then perhaps cultivators may have an opportunity of judging for themselves. In the meantime a description, however faint, may induce some to give them the attention they so well merit. Fancy then a plant with the general characteristics of an *Ophrys*, producing a spike of flowers as large and as thickly set as those of *Saccolabium guttatum*; often indeed measuring two feet in length, of a bright salmon-colour intermixed with as bright a yellow. Another with plaited foliage and a nodding head of some 20 bright yellow blossoms, having a deep stain of crimson on the cucullate lip, in the manner and of the size of a *Dendrobium*. Again, a species with fleshy persistent leaves and an erect stem of about two feet, supporting from 15 to 30 large yellow flowers, the lip blotched and lined with pale purple, bearing the aspect of some robust *Epidendrum*; and others whose white and pink blossoms at a little distance are easily mistaken for hyacinths ...

With regard to the culture of African terrestrial orchids I would observe that the soil I fancy the highest approach to their native medium will be found in the black alluvial mould of marshes or water-meadow, tempered with pure sand, which enters largely into the composition of all the soils here, where we have nothing like the peat-soil of England, nor is there much decaying vegetable matter present where these orchids are usually found. All these from the coast are subject to a long period of drought; and unless specially marked as the inhabitants of swamps, this fact will have to be borne in mind. The dry season commonly extends from April to October, and for two months towards the end of this period they may be said to be perfectly dry, and being in most cases but just beneath the surface, would be subject to extreme aridity were it not for the shelter afforded by the thick vegetation of herbs and grasses by which they are surrounded.

In October the rains begin at first but sparingly, dews however are frequent and heavy, and in November and December the ground becomes saturated; January and part of February dry weather usually prevails, to be succeeded by even more rain than before. Most of the terrestrial orchids bloom at the beginning of each of these rainy periods, and by the end of May the leaves of such as are deciduous, wither and die off. The mean temperature need not be high for them, as I frequently find the coast plants running back to an elevation of two or even three thousand feet, and at this height sharp frosts are very common in our winter season. I fancy that greenhouse treatment, with the help of a close frame at the commencement of their growth, will prove all that is needed, and to keep them rather *less* dry than is usual with bulbs, during the torpid season.[2]

Sickly oxen, warring tribes and loss of specimens

After despatching the two oxen before mentioned we crossed the Umgoa and found the country more thickly wooded than before; trees of a gigantic size being frequent, and the bush of several days' journey through. The *Bulimus kraussii* is here common, and a darker one, which I think differs essentially, is also tolerably plentiful. After a few days I found but little difference in the vegetation, and therefore pushed on, crossing the Umpongo [? = Empangeni River], whence three or four days' travelling made an immense difference in the aspect of the country. It here becomes flat, so much so that lagoons are frequent and the bush is scattered about in detached patches. Epiphytal orchids are decidedly on the increase, and if we can push some 50 miles further I think it probable some new forms in the family must result; but unfortunately our oxen show unmistakable symptoms of wearing out. We have now a good load, quite as much as they can get on with.

Leaving the cattle on the Umpongo to rest and refresh themselves, with two Kaffirs to take care of our effects, I set off to determine if possible the extent of this flat country, taking with me the rest of the Kaffirs to carry necessaries. Three days brought us to another considerable stream, and two more to the head of St Lucia's Bay. At starting I promised myself to reach this place, as I had heard some glowing accounts of the scenery, etc., and certainly it is not belied by the reality: the bay itself is about the size of that at Natal; the entrance is almost stopped by a bar, so much so that it is quite possible to wade across the mouth. The country falls back gradually to the highlands apparently some 30 or 40 miles distant; the intervening lands being either level or a very gradual slope. There is plenty of wood, but it is not so dense as near the Umgoa: the herbage is very rank, and the weather extremely hot and moist. Elephants seem in great plenty all over this district, as we frequently saw herds of them. There are but few inhabitants of this part, which argues but little for its healthiness, although the sea-breezes seem to temper the extreme heat in a very agreeable manner. Orchids, as I expected, are on the increase, and I feel extremely vexed at having to stop short where the objects of the journey seem to be increasing; but as the oxen do not come up, I can only suspect they are not improving in condition, and therefore the sooner we get them back to cooler latitudes the better. Some very handsome shells have rewarded two days' toil on the sea-coast, and with them we start back again tomorrow for the oxen. Somehow it seems impossible to keep a correct reckoning of the time. I have quite lost every idea of what day it is; but as the Kaffirs tell me we have been out nearly three months this must be about the beginning of September, and as the rains will shortly be setting in it will be good judgement to get over some of the larger rivers before they are too much swollen. Adieu, then, to the Bay of St Lucia.

On our arrival at the place where the oxen were left, I was grieved to find one dead and two others more sickly than when we parted; it became therefore necessary to abandon the least valuable of our collections, and, selecting such as could be procured nearest home, we loaded the remaining beasts. Despatching two more homewards with directions to look for the wagon, and if they fell in with it to leave the luggage and return to a rendezvous appointed; or otherwise, to make the best of their way to Natal; while with the remainder I followed the route to the hills. This we accomplished in a fortnight, and the relief from the oppressive heat of the coast was most seasonable both to men and beasts. I was induced to take this

Among the collections gathered on Plant's last trip was a new species subsequently named Stapelia gigantea. *The illustration shown here is by John Sanderson, also a collector of specimens for Kew. (Source and copyright: Royal Botanic Gardens, Kew)*

course as I wished if possible to catch the spring season on the highlands, and with the summer before me I could return gradually towards Natal. But while we had been quietly at work in Nature's laboratory, different was the occupation of our neighbours. We found on attaining the populated part of the country that a sanguinary war was raging between Pandu and some of the tribes on his frontier next to Drachenberg; we were unconsciously involved in the midst of the contending parties before we became aware of it; and now a second abandoning of the precious subjects of so much toil was pressingly necessary; but as I do not wish to dwell on this subject, suffice it to say that by dint of much skulking and some tact we got through with the loss of another ox (which we had to kill and eat), almost as empty-handed as when we entered the country. The fate of the two oxen previously started homewards also caused some alarm. The heaviest loss at this unfortunate crisis I estimate to be the insects, for as we had entered the Zulu country in the middle of winter, it was only at the latter end of the journey that I was able to make any additions of the least consequence; therefore all the best were with us at the time we were obliged to think only of saving our lives. We were, however, no sooner fairly clear of the belligerents than we set to work again, and as nothing else offered I had soon a goodly collection of bulbs, which are here both numerous and beautiful.

As we had crossed the Umpongo, and, to get up the most accessible way from the coast to the hills, [we] were obliged to double the head of St Lucia's Bay. I compute our most distant point on the Drachenberg Range to have been about 27°, and the average altitude at which we made collections about 5,000 feet: higher than this it was useless to go, for nearly all the time we spent in this we experienced sharp frosts at night, and in the day were often so completely enveloped in clouds that it was dangerous to venture far from camp; besides which, lions are here so numerous as to be a source of continued anxiety. Pursuing our way as rapidly as the ruggedness of the country would permit, we at length fell in with some natives, and from them learned we were near the source of the Tuzella and within a hundred miles of Pietermaritzburg. This lightened our spirits, which were by this time beginning somewhat to flag, and a seasonable supply of mealies and milk did quite as much for our bodies. I continued with the baggage till we came once more upon a high road, and then we made the best of the way homewards.[2]

A footnote to this notice records that the bulbs collected near the end of the excursion arrived safely in England. Many bulbs had been consigned for sale but a set was cultivated at the Royal Gardens, Kew.

Plant was the Curator of the Botanic Gardens, Durban, during 1854–1856. He subsequently farmed near Tongaat but persisted with natural history expeditions to Zululand and environs, and continued to forward living plant collections to England. In 1858, Plant ventured northward to Delagoa Bay. He contracted fever on the return journey and died at St Lucia Lake in March of that year.[1]

C. BARTER *(1857–1859)*

Charles Barter, after being employed under his father as a gardener, joined the staff of the Royal Botanic Gardens, Kew, in April 1849. Two years later he was employed as a foreman at the Royal Botanic Society in Regent's Park, a position he retained until 1857 when, following the recommendation of William Hooker, he was appointed Botanist to the Niger Expedition under William Balfour Baikie.[1] Up river, in September of that year, Baikie wrote to Hooker from on board the S. S. *Dayspring*.

Pleasing number of collections

I am highly pleased with Barter, who is most indefatigable and hard-working, and who never loses an opportunity ... We have now upwards of 700 species dried and labelled; all collected since leaving the sea, most of them got close to the river, or within five or six miles from it, as we have not yet made any long excursions into the interior. Several hills have been ascended, but none as yet exceeding 1,000 feet above the river; still each one has afforded some novelty. This very morning, during a couple of hours' walk on shore, he [Barter] brought off nearly 20 species new to our collection. We have also a considerable number of fruits, both dried and preserved moist, and a few living plants in Wardian cases [*see* Appendices on p. 329]. We have also purchased any vegetable preparations in use among the natives, either as medicines, dyes, or for commercial purposes, and we have collected native names, or native uses for plants, whenever in our power.[2]

Many of Barter's collections aboard the S. S. *Dayspring* were subsequently lost as reported in the following letter from Barter.

Loss of ship

Three weeks ago an effort was made to communicate with England overland by way of Abeokuta and Lagos. Letters were therefore intrusted to a native messenger with directions to proceed to the nearest missionary out-station distant seven days' journey from

Abeokuta. This person has returned, reporting that our letters are detained by the King of Ilorin, which refuses to let them pass (into the territory of another chief, with whom he has not friendly relations), unless a European be the messenger.

One of our party therefore leaves today, who if possible will convey the mail to Lagos, it being now essential that we should transmit home intelligence of the accident which has happened, viz., the loss of the ship, and such material as effectually stops the expedition. This happened Oct. 7th between Rábba and Boussa in latitude 9° 30' North, where the river becomes contracted by low mountain ranges. The channel here is much broken by huge rocks, some rising almost perpendicular from 400 to 500 feet, while smaller ones concealed under water, and a furious current rendered navigation extremely dangerous. On arriving here anchor was cast, and careful soundings showed a great depth of water in narrow channels. On attempting one of these the ship became unmanageable in the eddies, and had not sufficient speed on to make head against the stream, was thrown on a ledge of rocks under water, crashed in her bottom, and began immediately to fill. Efforts were made to get off, which only increased the danger; the ship heeled over rapidly. We therefore hastily abandoned it, reached the shore by various means, but luckily without any loss of life. Eventually the ship did not sink entirely, but going down head foremost left the stern on the rock and above water. Hence we have recovered many things which now render our life in the bush far from unpleasant. We have built two houses, each 30 feet by 40, sufficient to house all our people. These are built with native mats formed of the split petiole of [a palm] *Raphia vinifera* laid on rafters of the same entire, with upright posts of *Bassia parkii* [shea butter or *Butyrospermum paradoxa*]. Pens and houses for sheep, goats, and fowls which we purchased from the natives are also made. We have fortified our camp with a wall of stones, and planted the ship's guns on rocks which command the whole and all approaches to it.

The natives continue to bring us yams, sweet potatoes, rice, Indian corn, onions, ground nuts, sugar canes, two kinds of pulse, beer brewed from the Doura corn and sufficient to supply all our wants. For this they receive such goods as are saved, viz., cloth, beads, etc.

I regret to add many of my dried plants are lost. Those which I succeeded in getting on shore remained several days in water, and are therefore of trifling value. Nevertheless I have dried them all [again] in the sun to keep them if possible. Living plants, seeds, wood, and fruits on deck at the time were, for the greater part, swept away by the current.

We shall in all probability remain here two months longer. I have therefore time to collect the greater part of the vegetation of the adjacent country. The rainy season is over, hot weather is setting in; thermometer already ranges over 120° [Fahrenheit] in the open air. The harmattan has commenced blowing slightly. We have had much sickness in our party, but probably not more than is incident to expeditions of this character. Have lost two by river fever, the ship's mate and a colonial seaman. Of the Government party, Mr Davis, the surgeon, and Mr Dalton, naturalist, have been both ill some time, [the] climate not agreeing with [them]. They will return home the first opportunity for sending them down the river. Since being on shore all the Europeans but myself and the captain have been suffering from fever, but are now recovering. I may consider myself singularly fortunate, for although nearly always in the sun, and from my botanical rambles much exposed to the influence of malaria when visiting swamps, etc., yet I have enjoyed better health than when at home.

The surrounding country has a healthy appearance — low mountains and hills with huge masses of bare sandstone rock (in which I found fossil remains of a plant jointed like *Equisetum* and very abundant, but in one form only occurring); but in all valleys near the river swamps are prevalent, teeming with a rank vegetation and noxious forms of animal life. No true forests are met with. Scattered trees give a park-like appearance to the landscape. These consist of about 30 species amongst which I recognise *Bassia parkii* very abundant, *Inga biglumosa*, *Sarcocephalus esculentus*, wild tamarind, and a large [leguminous] tree, now white with blossom, which the Rev. Mr Crowther, a native of Yoraba, and well versed in the products of Western Africa, tells me is the tree from which gum copal is obtained. It yields a gum resin; but I have not succeeded in collecting any quantity. Other [sapotaceous] trees are common [and] several [legumes]. Oil palms are common near the river or in wet places. Wine palms are less so. *Borassus aethiopicus* [= *B. aethiopium*, another palm] is plentiful, but not in the immediate vicinity. The stem of it [is] always largest halfway from the base, resembling exactly the common rolling-pin used in pastry making, pardon my making such a simile. The oil palm never takes this form, so far as my observation extends. [Species of *Calamus*, another genus of palms], which abound in the lower parts of the river, do not occur here, or indeed scarcely any of those plants which delight in a moist climate. Terrestrial [orchids] are not uncommon, but none as epiphytes. Ferns I find none, even in favourably shady places under the rocks. Succulents are becoming numerous. Rocky places abound with a large *Euphorbia* ... [and] a leafless [asclepiadaceous] plant with sweet-scented white flowers covers the face of precipitous cliffs, with coral-like branches. Aloes are common — none of large size ...[3]

The S. S. *Sunbeam* was sent to replace the *Dayspring*. Meanwhile collecting continued and letters from both Barter and Baikie, outlining their activities, continued to arrive at Kew. The following extracts are from Barter's letters of July and September 1858.

High mortality of Europeans

We have been in the river one-year today; out of this time nine months in our camp. The steamer [*Sunbeam*] we expect now weekly, when it is proposed to go down to Fernando Po, and ascend again while the water is high to complete the work contemplated. The mortality in the *Dayspring*'s crew is unfortunately high, just half the number! viz., of eight Europeans four [are] dead; of four American seamen somewhat coloured, three dead; of two coloured stewards, one dead. But of 62 Kroomen natives only three, one of these deaths through accident. No death has taken place among our own party, six in number. But Mr Davis has left us, his health not permitting him to stay longer. I trust that in the future vessel few Europeans will be employed. We have abundance of evidence that this is no place for the white. My health is good; I have fits of ague [malaria] occasionally which readily yield to quinine, but at this moment feel as strong as when leaving England. [I] have neither impaired appetite, enlarged spleen, or anything to indicate debility from climate, yet I have worked much harder than I should do in England, and traversed in an open boat in all weathers some 1,000 miles of river. I do not mention this otherwise than to show that our health has been well cared for, and that we have the fullest confidence in Dr Baikie.[4]

Desertion and myriads of fireflies

We learn from the coast that the *Sunbeam* entered the river, but soon stuck fast, and that her Kroomen, afraid of the natives, seized the boats and deserted the ship. However this could have happened we cannot tell, unless all the Europeans were sick. Our people here, Kroomen especially, are very anxious to be home, from which they have been kept much longer than was originally intended; but we have had little cause to complain of them. Since Dr Baikie took [?absolute] control out of the hands of Mr Laird's people, these have never [?been a problem] with us. I trust a different class of men will come in the next ship. I mention one instance soon after we came on the shore here. The Kroomen one morning were all in a state of mutiny. A moment's hesitation would have been fatal. Most of them were dancing about with drawn knives. Lieutenant Glover seized the ringleader by the throat; a powerful man, three of us could not put him in irons. Yet out of eight people forming the remainder of the ship's crew, only one, the master, assisted us in the struggle; [the others] looked on with affected indifference. With such people I often wonder we have gone on so well. Strict discipline has been maintained since, and each trifling offence has been followed by punishment.

The routine of our life is not so monotonous as may be supposed. We rise at daybreak. I generally make some short botanical trip till nine or ten o'clock or we breakfast together at eight o'clock, lay out or shift my plants, write, or superintend some job at which the people are kept employed at out of doors; for occupation is undoubtedly the best plan to keep people from getting discontented. By the middle of the day we have a babel of tongues in the camp, some as visitors but chiefly people bringing provisions for sale, [the] greater part women who are the traders in Africa. We dine at three o'clock, afterwards a ride on horseback till sunset, or accompany Dr Baikie in the boat to visit some of the little towns on the river near us. Here, seated under a locust, baobab, or spreading tamarind tree, surrounded by romping groups of little naked children who generally manage to inspect our pockets of beads and cowries, we chat to the people either of our own country, a subject they never tire of listening to, or hear all the gossip of the house. Nupe politics [?are] trade and scandal — the latter as much a subject of conversation and agreeable comment in central Africa as at home.

The boys and girls delight to spend the evenings or sometimes half the night dancing to the rude music of a wooden drum, or vary their amusement when tired by singing songs. One does this extemporarily; all the others joining in the chorus at the end of the verse. They are quick at putting in this form any passing incident of the moment. By the soft tropical moonlight coming through the trees, we thread our steps over groups of little forms asleep in each other's arms on the ground; [?thus] many of them pass the night in this warm climate.

Coming home at night anywhere near the river or in low grounds a beautiful scene presents itself. The sky, though spangled with stars of great brilliancy in this clear climate, is rivalled with the myriads of fireflies, which dart their scintillating light over every object. I never saw them like it on the coast, either so numerous or so large. The jarring of cicadas, which seem to render the very soil tremulous, is perhaps less pleasant, but one becomes so accustomed to it that I almost fancy I could not sleep in stillness.

I am constantly picking up some new plants, but have nothing especially worth noticing. I am arranging my whole collection and in my next will give a summary of the species collected, which I hope now to be about 2,000. Insects are troublesome, but not moisture, although it rains now nearly every day. The climate is agreeable, the sky clouded till noon, after which the thermometer seldom rises over 90° in the shade. Much less rain has fallen this season than last. We find the swamp betwixt our camp and the river, through which we waded among nymphaeas nearly to the waist last year, is this [season] quite dry.[5]

After leaving the above camp, the expedition shifted its attentions to off-shore islands. The following account describes Principe.

Fine ornamental plants but few algae

We visited Prince's Island to purchase stock, and recruit the health of our sick people by a sea breeze. This island, unlike Fernando Po, has no very elevated land; it presents from the sea a number of peaks, an immense block of rocks (some conical, others flat-topped), with butting cliffs or perpendicular walls of sheer precipices more than 1,000 feet high, these bare of any vegetation, white and dazzling in the tropical sun. We steamed into West Bay amidst torrents of rain, which, clearing up, showed a number of pretty cataracts descending in streams down the precipitous sides of the little mountains ...

Much of my collecting was done in a boat, landing here and there whenever a footing could be obtained. Dr Baikie and I visited many of the small islets which lie just detached in these bays, generally with a thorough drenching. These are mere rocks rising 20 or 30 feet above the water; some of them were covered almost exclusively with *Oleandra nodosa*, full exposed to the sun and sea-breeze. The plants were 3 or 4 feet high, quite shrub-like in character, beautifully in fructification, and covered with lichens. On the steep sides of the larger rocks grew an abundance of a very large orchid, resembling a *Vanda* in habit, but, like too many of the African Orchidaceae, with small, yellow, insignificant flowers. Melastomaceae, as usual, were plentiful; one species, 12 or 16 feet high, with magnificent red flowers, would be a fine ornamental plant in our stoves at home. I have sent, in the cases, plants of another species, of small growth, rose-coloured flowers, and scorpioid inflorescences. Species of *Mussaenda*, with their conspicuous white bracts, were common; also a shrub with spikes of purple flowers, like a *Veronica*: this had a singular pair of white leaves at the base of each spike, rendering it a very showy plant. Ferns were not wanting — *Drymaria, Asplenium, Elaphoglossum. Polytrichum commune* I was much surprised to find occupying the moist hollows on the top of the rocks in dense tufts; with it, almost buried in the moss, grew *Trichomanes crispum*. In shady places a very pretty fern was growing, an *Asplenium* somewhat resembling *Darea cicutaria*, but of a still more elegant habit.

Whoever has an opportunity of visiting the quiet nooks in the bays about these islands will be struck with the exquisite beauty of the waters and the various forms which can be seen beneath them. At 50 or 60 feet, the eye penetrates with ease: the bottom is rocky and very irregular; the boat at one moment glides over masses of coral-bound rock many feet below, but on which many beautiful sponges and corallines can be seen; the rest reveals nothing but a cavernous depth of blue water, unless a shoal of those beautiful fish of the tropics dart across. The rocks and everything that is exposed to the alternate action of the tides are covered with the small mangrove oyster; below it, seldom exposed, grows a pretty crimson coral, with it a large *Flustra*. Gorgeous Actiniae, with the common *Echinus* and starfish of more northern climes, abound in all the little salt pools, on these rocks. The sponges are very large; but few are sufficiently soft to be fit for use. The waters are almost destitute of algae; I gathered but one species of Fucaceae, and that not attached; a small plant of confervoid growth alone represents the family.[6]

In a footnote to the above letter, Barter noted that he was in excellent health. A little more than six months later he was dead, having succumbed to the ravages of dysentery on 15 July 1859.[1] He was succeeded as botanist to the expedition by Gustav Mann, who remained in West Africa until 1862 and safely returned to Europe.

F. M. J. WELWITSCH (*1860*)

Friedrich Martin Josef Welwitsch (1806–1872) acquired an early interest in natural history when, as a boy, he walked with his father, the surveyor of a district in Corinthia in the Austrian Empire. He graduated in Medicine from the University of Vienna but continued to pursue his love of natural history. In 1853, with backing from the Portuguese Government, he commenced exploration of Angola and other parts of south-west Africa. He returned to Portugal in January 1861, having amassed an enormous herbarium, 'undoubtedly the best and most extensive ever collected in Tropical Africa'.[1] His most treasured botanical find was that of the bizarre plant, *Welwitschia mirabilis* (syn., *W. bainesii*).[2]

Discovery of Welwitschia mirabilis

My last journey to the southern districts of the province (Benguela, Mossamedes, and Huilla) was at first intended to extend over a few months, merely for the investigation of the littoral regions, as at that time I was still suffering from the effects of fever: only in case of the entire re-establishment of my health did I contemplate penetrating the interior to Huilla. I set out at the end of June 1859, from Loando for Mossamedes, calling at Benguela. The magnificent climate of Mossamedes was so delightful, and so speedily restored my shattered health, that after a stay of five weeks I had quite recovered, and felt myself a new man. I therefore gradually extended my excursions further and further — first northward, and southward along the coast to beyond Cape Negro and Port Alexander, then more and more inland; and as the month of October approached, with which, in this region, the spring sets in, I felt induced and encouraged, by the entirely new vegetation which the shores of Benguela and Mossamedes presented, in contrast to that of Loando, to visit the elevated plateau of Benguela, known under the name of Huilla, which rises at about a distance of 80 miles from the coast, and slopes to the east towards Quipungo, to the north and north-east towards Quilengues and Caconda. And I am indeed delighted and abundantly satisfied that I undertook this excursion; for I am

now convinced that I have seen the most beautiful and the most magnificent scenery that the tropics of South Africa can offer.

Before, however, I speak of the vegetation of the plateau of Huilla, which rises from about 5,800 to 6,000 feet above the sea level, allow me to tell you a little about the interesting flora of the coast between Mossamedes (i.e. Little Fish Bay) and Cape Negro ...

Several miles before reaching Cape Negro the coast rises to a height of about 300 to 400 feet, forming a continuous plateau, extending over six miles inland, as flat as a table. This tabular elevation, which is composed of calcareous tufa (tuf) and strata of clay, is scattered all over with loose sandstone shingle, and clothed with a vegetation which, though scanty, consists of plants of the highest interest; among them a dwarf tree was particularly remarkable, which, with a diameter of stem often of four feet, never rose higher above the surface than one foot, and which, through its entire duration, that not unfrequently might

Welwitschia mirabilis, *photographed in the Namib-Naukluft Park, about 50 km east of Swakopmund. This specimen, as with most specimens, has two leaves split into numerous segments. Occasionally three-leaved plants are found.*

exceed a century, always retained the two woody leaves which it threw up at the time of germination, and besides these it never puts forth another. The entire plant looks like a round table, a foot high, projecting over the tolerably hard sandy soil; the two opposite leaves (often a fathom long by two to two and one-half feet broad) extend on the soil to its margin, each of them split up into numerous ribbon-like segments. As I bring some specimens of this wonderful plant to Europe, together with flowers and fruit, and shall thus have the opportunity of presenting it *in natura*, it will suffice just now to append to the foregoing a short notice of it in technical language ... In the meantime I may intimate that this dwarf tree probably represents the type of a quite peculiar family of the South African tropics, of which a closer examination of the tract to the eastward, and the coast extending southwards, may lead to the discovery of more species.[3]

Welwitschia mirabilis is found in a narrow, 1200-kilometres-long strip between the Kuiseb River (in Namibia) and the Nicolau River

A winged seed from a female cone of Welwitschia mirabilis.

(in Angola). For much of its range the annual rainfall is less than 100 millimetres.

In *Welwitschia*, plants are either male or female, with the reproductive organs enclosed in small cones. Systematically it is placed with a group of gymnosperms, the Gnetophyta, which are commonly regarded as being the closest relatives of the flowering plants.

J. T. BAINES *(1861)*

Artist, explorer and botanical collector, J. Thomas Baines was born in King's Lynn, Norfolk, England, in 1820. He was involved in various explorations in southern Africa and was also a member of the North Australian Expedition of 1855–1856. In 1861, he joined James Chapman's expedition of 1861–1863 through Namibia, to the Victoria Falls.[1] The following extracts are from an article in which Baines described a journey in Damaraland, Namibia during which he painted a spectacular aloe, 'another marvel of the vegetable kingdom'.

More cartridges for the rifle

It was during the month of May, 1861, and about a fortnight after my first sight of the *Welwitschia mirabilis*, that I was privileged to behold another marvel of the vegetable kingdom, which I believe is not yet figured in any work available to the public in this country, nor contained in those which, by the kindness of Dr J. Hooker and Professor Oliver, I have been permitted to examine in the herbarium of the Royal Botanic Gardens at Kew.

Leaving Hykamkop on the 10th, and halting to send the cattle down the long ravine at Oosip, again to seek a little water in the Swakop River, we spanned out after a long night journey, near the Roode-berg, where, on the 11th, the rising sun showed that the soil began to be scantily veiled with small narrow-leafed white grass, which, though nearly invisible when we looked straight down upon it, showed, like the mirage, in greater strength when the eye glanced along the distant plain; and with the heavy dew sparkling upon it, reminded me in some degree of hoarfrost upon the fields in England. As the mist cleared off, we saw the bold outline of the Roode-berg, its peaks barren as they had appeared the day before, but its sides slightly tinted by scanty grass, dwarf aloes and bushes, scattered among the enormous boulders. We expected shortly to reach Tincas, the reputed headquarters of the lions, where at one time the spoor of as many as eighteen together had been seen, and at another a traveller had encountered a number, 'sitting across his path', and by no means too eager to get out of his way; and where, in sober reality, the drivers considered it unsafe to walk beside the wagon after dark, lest a lion following, in hope of picking up a disabled ox, should spring upon them. With so hopeful a prospect, I thought it as well to spend an hour or two in getting my hand in to the manufacture of cartridges for my rifle ...

At night, I believe a little farce was got up for the benefit of a couple of tradesmen going up from Cape Town; one of the Damaras personating a lion leaping and roaring in the bushes, and the rest of the party firing as wide of him as possible.[2]

Grappler

At Otjimbengue, formerly a station of the copper-mining company, and now the headquarters of the Rhenish mission, I found Mr C. J. Andersson, whose property it then was, preparing for an overland journey with cattle for the Cape market, and was hospitably received by Mr Henry Hutchinson, who walked out with me to the nearest hills. These were mostly of disintegrated granite, the large fissures in which were sometimes filled with light pink quartz, from six to ten inches thick, smooth, straight, and perpendicular as a well-built wall; while on others seemed to be an incrustation of limestone, sharp and unpleasant to the feet as well could be imagined. On the plain he called my attention to a small creeping plant which, somewhat later, bears a beautifully-marked pink or crimson flower, followed by that peculiarly thorny seed known as the Grappler, which, if its complicated arrangement of hooks, projecting at every conceivable angle, happens to catch the lips of a grazing animal, causes the poor creature to stand in helpless and painful entanglement, moaning piteously for assistance. The seed is frequently brought as a curiosity of the colony, and a resident there once purposed to plant a quantity around his orchard as a terror to barefoot urchin depredators. I am happy to add, however, that his project for its acclimatisation was never carried into effect. Among the mimosas we caught several brilliant butterflies and beetles, one of them of a rich emerald-green, with white longitudinal stripes on the wing-cases. Mr E. Layard, of the Cape Museum, supposed it to be new, and proposed to call it *Hutchinsonia*. The Elephant beetle, so named for its peculiar form, especially about the head and trunk, and of a dull black colour with red stripes, was also common; but the Rhinoceros beetle I did not see till afterwards.[2]

The grappler, or grapple plant, is *Harpagophytum procumbens*, a member of the Pedaliaceae. Its potato-like tubers are used in the treatment of arthritis and for dissolving kidney stones and gallstones. Native people of Botswana are recorded as using a decoction of the tuber for any infectious diseases and for the treatment of female infertility. In some parts of Namibia it is used to relieve stomach and post-natal pains, and as a treatment for diabetes.[3]

Gigantic aloe

On Saturday, May the 25th, we turned into Andersson's new road, which, though perhaps more rugged than the old, avoids the great detour to the south of the Roode-berg. In passing through a narrow poort, I saw, upon the hills, a small tree, bearing a marvellous resemblance to a stunted baobab. In fact, in the stem and branches, I could see but little difference; but the leaves, instead of spreading like those of the chestnut, from one stalk, were small, nearly round, and arranged in pairs opposite each other. It was, probably, one of the sterculias which abound here. In the distance I observed several trees, which reminded me of Humboldt's print, — familiar, I should think, to everyone, — 'the Dragon-tree of Orotava'. I found the wagons outspanned in the poort, under a pretty clump of kameel-doorns, beside a nameless and waterless sandy river; and the rough veldt being now covered with seeds like miniatures of the spiked balls on the clubs of Gog and Magog, I turned to repair my dilapidated boots, to replace the canvas slippers I had been obliged to wear. I saw a troop of ostriches, but, being armed only with light shotgun, I dropped out of sight as quick [*sic*] as possible, and ran back for my rifle. The noise of the coming wagons, however, had alarmed them, and as the singular granite peaks, called by the white people Wollaston's or Andersson's 'Ears', and by the Namaquas 'Anison', or the 'horned owl', were now before me, with two or three of the supposed dragon-trees standing boldly on an intervening ridge I stayed and made a careful sketch, allowing the wagons ... to pass me while I did so.

To observe its character more closely, I turned aside toward the largest tree, and, to my astonishment, saw that it was in reality a gigantic aloe. Kneeling down so as to bring my arms low enough to embrace the solid trunk, I found the circumference to be nearly twelve feet. Above this it divided into five stems, each of which, about four feet higher, was subdivided into four or five more; and

Found in Namibia and the north-west of South Africa, the quiver tree, Aloe dichotoma, *is commonly 3–5 m tall but is sometimes much taller. It produces spikes of yellow flowers which produce copious nectar. Baboons seeking this nectar may rapidly strip trees of their flowers.*

from these arose branches nearly as thick as my arm, and of uniform size, even to the very top, where each was crowned by the well-known star of aloe-leaves, short, thick, tapering to a finely-hardened point, and curving gracefully upward, and each surmounted by three or more magnificent spikes of yellow flowers, showing, with more than golden lustre, above the fresh green of the succulent leaves. The stems were smooth, round, and externally of a light cream-colour.

Upon the smaller branches, immediately below the leaves, thin annular flakes, easily detachable, marked, I suppose, the position of those that had been most lately shed; and near the base of the main trunk the bark seemed to burst and curl off as if very thin veneers of fine satin-wood had warped off the foundation they were laid upon.

The effect of this magnificent crown of leaves and flowers more than fifteen feet from the ground, and twenty in diameter, growing from sterile ridges of rough red rock, strewed with many-coloured pebbles and quartz crystals flashing back, like diamonds, the intense sunlight, was lovely in the extreme; so, choosing a position that commanded not only the best view of the tree, but also of a smaller one (with an upright stem, perhaps eight feet in height, as many inches thick, and having four already bifurcated branches), and of a small sterculia in the foreground, I made the sketch which, without more artistic licence than the interpolation of the solitary ostrich, is now placed in chromolithography before the reader.

It was with regret that I broke off a couple of branches about four inches thick, in order to possess myself of a specimen; for, indeed, I am never quite able to get over the idea that the wondrous products of nature ought to be admired rather than destroyed, and I am rather afraid that this feeling, more proper to an artist than to a sportsman, greatly contributed to the safety of the only two quaggas I saw during the day. My botanical specimen, with gun, sketching-folio, and appurtenances, proved too heavy a burden; so, after carrying it for some time, I sat down to sketch it, and, preserving only the flower-spikes, left it by the path. The stony character of the country in advance seemed now to force upon the euphorbias the necessity of enlarging their roots above ground till they looked like blocks of granite, as big as tables, with the thin green rod-like leaves growing abruptly out of them.

I found Onesimus already preparing supper, and, on my showing him my sketches, he remarked — 'Dit ist neit voor nicht dat onzen Heer zoo agter blyven' (he does *some* work when he stays behind). He recognised the tree, and, as I was anxious to secure another specimen, sent a Damara to seek for one in the rugged kloof near Wilson's Fountain. The Damaras called it 'Otjitumbo'; but that, I believe, is rather the general name for any stump-like tree, and is applied to many other aloes, as well as to the *Welwitschia mirabilis*, which is distinguished by the addition of 'Otjihooro', making it 'the stump with a head'; eventually, however, they gave it the name of 'Omontinde', though whether this applied exclusively to the gigantic aloe I could not learn.[2]

The giant aloe described and illustrated by Baines was not new to science; it proved to be *Aloe dichotoma*, the quiver tree. The common name for the species alludes to the fact that Bushmen used the soft branches to fashion quivers for their arrows.

Bleaching skulls of rhinoceros

Our path lay down a deep ravine, from whose dry sandy bed rose stifling dusty-clouds, which though the moon shone brightly, rendered even the nearest objects all but invisible. We passed the junction of the Onanies River with the Swakop; and, though the bed of the 'Father of Waters' showed only as a strip of desert sand, the roots of the 'kameel doorns' seemed to find moisture enough beneath to enable them to keep up a refreshing verdure in their spreading foliage and gracefully waving catkins, among which I found an opportunity of netting a few butterflies. 'The Reeds', as, from the coarse vegetation on which the oxen fed, our halting place was called, were varied by groves of thorns and tamarisks; and from the branches we brushed off, in passing, caterpillars against which Onesimus earnestly warned me, as the mere pricking of the skin with two or three of their bristly tufts was enough 'to make a man scratch himself to death'. Nevertheless, I have handled more formidable looking creatures of the kind in Kaffirland, and the only result has been a slight but long-continued irritation of the finger-ends, and a consequent vow against future contact with hairy caterpillars. Some of the trees were thickly covered with a kind of red-flowering mistletoe, from the berry of which bird-lime is sometimes made to strew in the path of guinea-fowl; — and the spoor of a solitary rhinoceros proved that the species was not yet 'shot out' from Damaraland, though the number of bleaching skulls would almost lead a traveller to think so.[2]

Between 1869 and 1872, Baines carried out two expeditions into Matabeleland. He died in Durban in 1875.[1]

W. G. MILNE *(1863–1865)*

After his 1850s voyage to the South Seas (*see* pp. 305–311), William Grant Milne worked for a time as gardener at Glasgow Botanic Gardens in Scotland but he soon ventured to West Africa to collect objects of natural history.[1,2] The following extracts are from letters dated June and July 1863.

Superstitions

I am fairly settled in the district of Old Calabar, exploring the creeks and corners of this majestic river [the Niger]. Africa is certainly rich in botany and other branches of natural history. Years must roll away before the botany of this vast continent is thoroughly investigated, and that will not be until Christianity is upon a more substantial basis. I will give you one extract from my daily journal to show the superstition which still exists amongst the people in Western Africa. While in the district of Ikorofiong, in passing through a large native town in the Ebebo country, I saw a straggling shrub belonging to Bignoniaceae. While in the act of pulling down some of the flowers, I was surrounded by some hundreds of men, women, and children, shouting and dancing like so many fiends. At first I was inclined to think they were about to hang me in front of their palaver house or heathen temple. On looking round I could see no way of escape, so I held my ground, determined to have some of the flowers; but they were as determined that I should not get them. At last they put me out of the town. On the following Sunday I accompanied the Rev. Zerub Baillie to several of the plantation villages, where he preaches once a week. We met the Ebebo chief. I wished to shake hands with him, but he would not come near. He said he was afraid of the strange medicine I was making, and told Mr Baillie that I was not to come to his town again.[3]

Bush medicines and Calabar chop

About a fortnight ago a man told me that if I went into the bush I would be shot: so you see it is not all plain sailing at Calabar. But I have an extensive field before me, and I am determined to make the best of it, in spite of the natives, as it will not do to let them have it all their own way. I will mention a few of the leading characteristics of the vegetation which have come under my own observation.

There are five species of *Melastoma*, six species of *Dracaena*, five species of *Amomum*, and several others belonging to Zingiberaceae. There are a number of species belonging to the Scrophulariaceae; and amongst them is a *Digitalis*, which is scattered over all waste ground. Euphorbiaceae and Cucurbitaceae are both extensive [families] here. Three species of *Amaryllis* are abundant — one in the river, and the other two spread all over the plantations. Solanaceous plants are numerous: there are two kinds sold in the market as purgatives and for bathing the sides of their faces when they have discharge from the ears. Anonaceae is another extensive [family]. According to the Rev. Mr Thomas there are 16 or 18 kinds. I have collected a number of Bignoniaceae and Cinchonaceae. I have also met with eight or nine species of *Convolvulus*, but there are more than that. Amongst the Labiatae is a large species of *Salvia*, which is used as medicine. There are three true mints used for seasoning; in fact, all this [family] is made use of as articles of food. A species of *Nymphaea* is frequent in the inland streams.

I think there are from 18 to 24 distinct orchids: one fine terrestrial species has a flowering stem six or seven feet high. There are two fine species of *Strophanthus*. One true *Verbena* and two clerodendrums are abundant. I have also observed two species of *Amaranthus*. 'Love-lies-bleeding' is one of them, but I am doubtful if this is indigenous, although the natives say so. Both kinds are used as vegetables in Calabar chop. One *Penstemon* is found by the margin of a small stream at Ikorofiong, but not plentiful. A *Phytolacca* and a *Polygonum* also occur at the same place. I have collected specimens of a *Loranthus* [mistletoe] from trees by the banks of the river. Two species of *Lonicera* are very common. Leguminous plants are very numerous. Amongst them is a sensitive *Mimosa*. The poison beans (*Physostigma*) are often used for deadly purposes. One species is largely cultivated for putting into the streams to poison fish, and another is sold in the markets for Calabar chop: one kind is very like our scarlet runner. The ripe pods are from six to eight inches long, and the fruit is beautifully spotted. Compositae are not so numerous as might be expected: however, there is a due proportion. A *Tillandsia* climbs up the palm trees. There is one fine species of *Calophyllum*, and a tree belonging to

Myrtaceae; also an *Aristolochia*, which I think is *A. gigantea*.
There are five different palms. One large species of *Juncus* is
abundant on the sides of the river at Creek Town; also another
smaller species. There are several Cyperaceae by the river, and
amongst the lowland plantations there are a number of Gramineae
sprinkled about. Eighteen varieties of yams and six varieties of
Colocasia are cultivated; the flowering stems of the latter, with
spathe and spadix, are sold in the market for putting into Calabar
chop. The corms are also boiled and used by the natives. There
are two kinds of cassava largely cultivated. There is only one true
banana with very small fruit, and eight kinds of plantains, sold in
the markets. There is a malvaceous plant cultivated; the fruit is
cut up into slices and put into soups. There are two species of
Agaricus [mushroom] sold in the markets. They are said to be very
nourishing, and to give a fine flavour to Calabar chop. The larger
kind is also put into rum as it is of an intoxicating nature. Calabar
chop is composed of the following ingredients: palm oil, yams,
mints of all kinds; flowering stems, leaves and corms of the
Colocasia; two species of *Agaricus*, the fruit of two leguminous
plants, the leaves of two kinds of *Amaranthus*. The rest consists of
monkey's flesh, dogs, rats, fish, goats, fowls, parrots, and birds of
all kinds; in fact everything eatable, whether animal or vegetable, is
put into this wonderful dish. It is a favourite dish among the natives,
and relished by Europeans, only they take nothing but palm oil,
fowls, and goat's flesh. I have only seen three species of snakes.
There is only one parrot, five species of monkeys, three rats, and
three mice, four or five land crabs, and a number of freshwater fish,
some sixty or eighty butterflies, and a host of beetles and other
insects. Amongst my collection I find twenty-four different ants.
Such is a very brief outline of the botany and the natural history
around Old Calabar.[3]

A murderous class

The natives are not such a murderous class, except amongst
themselves. For instance, there is not a day passes but they are
killing their twin children instantly after birth, and banishing the
unfortunate women to what they call twin villages, where they are
left to languish out a life of silent sorrow, and are denied all
intercourse with the rest of the world. Mrs Goldie, about seven
weeks ago, saved two of those little unfortunates. She remained by
the poor woman until she was confined, and then at the dead hour

of midnight she entered the mission house with a little boy and a girl rolled in her lap. The mother followed about six o'clock in the morning. They are all under the protection of the Rev. Mr Goldie. About a month ago the King of Creek Town had a sister whose daughter died of consumption. She sent for a number of her slaves to give them poison bean. Three women died, three more escaped by vomiting, and one girl took refuge in the mission house, under Mr Goldie, where she is now attending the school. These poor people were to be servants to her daughter in the future world.[4]

The following year, 1864, Milne made an attempt to reach and explore the Qua Mountains. The party reached the locality but with their lives threatened by hostile tribes, they had to return immediately to the coast. During the outward journey they had to pay tributes to tribesmen and 'having been despoiled of everything in the way of clothing, poor Milne had to make his way back in a nude state nearly 200 miles'.[1] Soon after this aborted expedition, Milne was attacked by a near-fatal fever. Once he had recovered, he went to Gaboon River. The following extracts come from a letter sent from Gaboon and written in March 1865.

Bamboo palm and other plants

I have just returned from a long and interesting cruise. Mr Latta, an enterprising young man, was kind enough to give me a passage. We were in the district of Fernan Vas. We had occasion to pass through some miles of creeks which formed a complete network. We entered those creeks at Cape Lopez and came out at Fernan Vas. There is what is called the bamboo palm, the petiole of which is used for building houses; the plant does not send out one direct stem, rather a mass of shoots, and capable of bearing fruit when not more than six feet high; while the foliage reaches the astonishing height of 90 feet. Nothing can be more graceful than to see their tops overhanging almost every other species. It differs greatly from what is called the bamboo at Old Calabar, but both belong to the genus *Raphia*. There are two species of *Pandanus* very plentiful along the margin of those creeks. As we approached Fernan Vas I saw several species of aquatic amaryllids, also along the sides of the creeks great patches of *Papyrus*, resembling *Papyrus antiquorum*. The stems are used by children for making baskets; it is not used otherwise. The *Clerodendrum thomsoniae* Balf. is very plentiful at Fernan Vas, more so than Calabar. It is also to be found at the head

of the Rembo River, bordering on the Backina country. A large
species of *Juncus* is plentiful on the Rembo. I saw the same species
of aquatic plants which I found at Calabar, with the exception of
one which was new to me. I also saw two species of very small
waterlilies (Nymphaeaceae); one is yellow, which I would say is a
Nuphar, and the other a *Nymphaea*; independent of the two in
question there is a third, the widely diffused large white one.[5]

The penalty for witchcraft

When leaving Viti [Fiji] I thought I had forever left the land of
cannibalism and barbarism. Such has not been the case. On our
return from Fernan Vas we halted for a night at Cape Lopez.
On the following morning I saw a party of people coming along the
beach, beating drums, and in the midst was a woman, her body all
painted over and her hair ornamented with feathers. I soon found
that she was about to go through the ordeal of drinking poison for
witchcraft, and followed the party to a freshwater stream. By order
she sat down upon a bank. At this time I went amongst them and
used all my influence to save the poor woman. They promised that
she should not die; but I had no sooner turned my back than they
gave her the poison. It brought on shivering, and in a few moments
she was a corpse. A large fire was now kindled; her legs, arms, and
head were severed from the body and burned to ashes. Her body
was opened, her heart taken out and held up to public gaze, and the
executioner crying out to all parties to look upon the witch. Such is
the present state of Africa.[5]

After leaving Gaboon, Milne went to Fernando Po [= Bioko]. On
28 June, he wrote of his experiences from Cameroon River. In this and
the next letter Milne refers to both the general region of Cameroon
and its mountains (as 'the Cameroons') and to Mount Cameroon (as
both 'Cameroons Mountain' and 'Cameroon Mountain').

A wet blanket to keep you warm

You will see that I have taken another jump; in fact I was forced.
I have camped on the mountain of Fernando Po for 18 days [at]
9,000 feet and exposed to heavy tornadoes and fearful thunder
storms. The consequence was as soon as I got upon the lowlands
I caught fever and to save my life I went with the mail to [the]
Cameroons. But to return to the mountains, at 9,000 feet nothing
existed but long grass and a scant, scrubby vegetation and my boys

had to carry water five miles. I shifted my camp to 6,600 feet close to a freshwater spring. Let me tell you something about a collector's camp. Fancy that you see [a] temporary hut covered with leaves on one side towards the mountains and that you see a sort of a sleeping place under the shelter composed of saplings to allow the rain to run clear of your person and a block of wood for a pillow and a wet blanket to keep you warm. Let us have a peep outside of the hut and here are met dirty blankets rolled round the shoulders of dirty niggers. Bundles of dirty socks enliven the scene. Tin plates and cooking pans, old boots and insect nets, wet clothes hanging at the fire. Also plants placed to dry on a sapling grating over the fire, bottles of insects, and a copy of the 'Vegetable Kingdom'.

Such was my camp on the mountain of Fernando Po. I bound a number of plants and I have sent you a sample according to [my] promise. You will see that the ferns principally belong to *Pteris, Asplenium, Aspidium, Hymenophyllum, Trichomanes, Blechnum, Polypallum* and *Lomamura* which cover the stems of the tree-ferns only one species and unfortunately could not find it in fruit several species of *Selaginella*. Amongst the flowering plants you will find Begoniaceae [and] Melastomaceae and several balsams or *Impatiens* etc. What I have sent will give you some idea of the mountain vegetation. I am not speaking of the lowlands. I am now at the Cameroons. As soon as possible I will be at the Victoria and the Cameroons Mountain. I will see what [vegetation is] there and let you know the result. It was my intention to write to your brother. I will leave it until I see the nature of the Cameroons vegetation that I might give him a comparative outline of the two places. The fever which I caught at Fernando Po has left a severe [bout] of dysentery which has threatened inflammation. If it should turn out as such it will be dangerous. My friends [*sic*] does not apprehend any danger and in a few days I will be all right with rest and care. I will collect all the palm seeds which I can find at the mountain. I am told that it is a country for palms. I will send you a share. I hear nothing more about the case which you was [*sic*] to send. I hope it will go to Old Calabar. It is the handiest place and there are plenty of good things to fill it with. I am so weak that I am not able to write much and I am sure that you will excuse me. You have always been kind in letting me know botanical news. I am sure you will not relax. Many thanks for the past and I hope to be in better spirits to returns [*sic*] the same in future. Has Seemann finished his flora on the South Sea Islands? I hope he has done me justice if not no matter.[6]

Milne was referring to Seemann's *Flora vitiensis*, within which Seemann (*see* pp. 312–319) paid tribute to Milne. The following letter was written in July 1865.

Multiple crises!

This drawing will give you an idea of this species of *Melastoma*. Fancy that you see from 50 to 80 lateral shoots all in blossom sparkling in the sunshine. It is a more brilliant pink but the want of paint has prevented me from giving that colour. It is the same as the seed which I sent last mail. When are you going to write? I am longing for a letter. I am sorry to say that I am under the necessity of leaving the Cameroon Mountain for three reasons. 1. It is the rainy season, the mountain rivers are flooded and the lowlands a lake. I cannot get up the mountain and plants are not in flower on this botanical field but I will return in September or October. 2. I must be sparing in my expenses it takes all to meet. 3. My health from so much exposure to sunshine and rain are [*sic*] ruined. I must go to Calabar where I can get medical advice and a month's rest. Calabar is the only station for medical advice. Upon the whole my system has got a fearful shake. My nerves are such that it is with a struggle that I can write my name or hold a brush. I am not able to write to your brother from the state of my health and I cannot say a great deal about Cameroons Mountain.[7]

The following extracts are from a letter written from Fernando Po in November 1865.

Burnt letter

I got your letter at Calabar on the first of this month and the watch which is in a fine going condition. I do not know how to thank you for all this kindness. I will try to pay it back with gratitude. But I must tell you that your letter came under a misfortune on board of the mail steamer. After glancing over the letter I laid it down upon the table and while looking over several other letters a young gentleman lifted your letter, divided it into two and lighted his *cigar* to my great mortification. The part which is left I see that you speak about £5 sent to the Consul of Fernando Po by Mr Lauch. Such an order has never reached the English Consulate. Perhaps it will be here on Monday night with the mail. And many thanks for your kindness in telling Mr Lauch to allow me a little more. It is kind, you are the only gentleman of consideration amongst my botanic friends.[8]

A glass of hot brandy

I am glad you are pleased with the *Melastoma*. I hope you got the box with the dried Fernando Po ferns. You must tell me when you write. Many thanks for the interest you always take regarding my health. I am glad to state that my health was never better. My reason for going to Old Calabar was for medical advice, a thing which I could not obtain at the Cameroons. Calabar is certainly not a healthy place and as for Fernando Po it is the worst place on the west coast. One Scotch firm within the last two years has lost nine young Scotsmen out of fifteen at this place, all with fever. Few whites can exist here and those that are here [are] never well, fever, fever day after day. Victoria, at the base of the great mountain, and the Gabon are the healthiest places on this part of the west coast. The further south one gets the better. Teetotalism is the best medicine which has been introduced. Month after month passes away without ever tasting of spirits or strong drinks of any kind. Dr [?Howsen] at Calabar ordered me to take a glass of hot brandy every night. I took it for a few weeks and now I have giving [sic] it up. It is true during the time I was taking the brandy I was never in better health and if I should be attacked with fevers again, of which there is no doubt, I will take a glass of hot brandy every night until I am better. Dr Mullings as well as Dr [?Howston] ordered me to take stimulants. Dr Mullings told me if I did not use a [word unclear] spirits I would not live. I will not use it as long as I can do without it. My constitution upon the whole is well adapted for such a climate as that of Western Africa; if it had not I would have [died].[8]

Milne died at Old Calabar the following year, 1866, after having succumbed to dysentery.[1, 2]

ASIA

J. ARNOLD (1818)

Joseph Arnold (1782–1818) was born in Suffolk, England. In 1808, he received an appointment as an assistant surgeon in the Royal Navy. This enabled him to travel and pursue his interests in natural history. In 1817, he was appointed to the staff of Sir Stamford Raffles, Governor of the East India Company's establishment in Sumatra.[1] Unfortunately, Raffles, in a letter dated 18 August 1818 to Sir Joseph Banks, was soon to report that Arnold had 'fell a sacrifice to his exertions on my first tour into the interior, and died of fever'.[2] In the same communication Raffles cited from part of a letter from Arnold to his friend, Dawson Turner, in which he related the discovery of the world's largest flower.[2]

Discovery of Rafflesia arnoldii

But here [on 19 May 1818 at Pulau Lebar on the Manna River, Sumatra] I rejoice to tell you I happened to meet with what I consider as the greatest prodigy of the vegetable world. I had ventured some way from the party, when one of the Malay servants came running to me with wonder in his eyes, and said, 'Come with me, Sir, come! a flower, very large, beautiful, wonderful!' I immediately went with the man about a hundred yards in the jungle, and he pointed to a flower growing close to the ground under the bushes, which was truly astonishing. My first impulse was to cut it up and carry it to the hut. I therefore seized the Malay's parang (a sort of instrument like a woodman's chopping-hook), and finding that it sprang from a small root which ran horizontally (about as large as two fingers, or a little more), I soon detached it and removed it to our hut. To tell you the truth, had I been alone, and had there been no witnesses, I should I think have been fearful of mentioning the dimensions of this flower, so much does it exceed every flower I have ever seen or heard of; but I had Sir Stamford and Lady Raffles with me, and a Mr Palsgrave, a respectable man resident at Manna, who, though equally astonished with myself, yet are able to testify as to the truth.

The whole flower was of a very thick substance, the petals and nectary being in but few places less than a quarter of an inch thick, and in some places three-quarters of an inch; the substance of it was very succulent. When I first saw it a swarm of flies were hovering over the mouth of the nectary, and apparently laying their eggs in the substance of it. It had precisely the smell of tainted beef. The calyx consisted of several roundish, dark-brown, concave leaves, which seemed to be indefinite in number, and were unequal in size. There were five petals attached to the nectary, which were thick, and covered with protuberances of a yellowish-white, varying in size, the interstices being a brick-red colour. The nectarium was cyathiform, becoming narrower towards the top. The centre of the nectarium gave rise to a large pistil, which I could hardly describe, at the top of which were about twenty processes, somewhat curved and sharp at the end, resembling a cow's horns; there were as many smaller very short processes. A little more than halfway down, a brown cord about the size of common whip-cord, but quite smooth, surrounded what perhaps is the germen, and a little below it was another cord somewhat moniliform.

Now for the dimensions, which are the most astonishing part of the flower. It measured a full yard across; the petals, which were subrotund, being 12 inches from the base to the apex, and it being about a foot from the insertion of the one petal to the opposite one; Sir Stamford, Lady Raffles and myself taking immediate measures to be accurate in this respect, by pinning four large sheets of paper together, and cutting them to the precise size of the flower. The nectarium in the opinion of all of us would hold 12 pints, and the weight of this prodigy we calculated to be 15 pounds.

I have said nothing about the stamina; in fact, I am not certain of the part I ought to call stamina. If the moniliform cord surrounding the base of the pistil were sessile anthers, it must be a polyandrous plant; but I am uncertain what the large germen contained; perhaps there might be concealed anthers within it.

It was not examined on the spot, as it was intended to preserve it in spirits and examine it at more leisure; but from the neglect of the persons to whom it was entrusted, the petals were destroyed by insects, the only part that retained its form being the pistil, which was put in spirits along with two large buds of the same flower, which I found attached to the same root: each of these is about as large as two fists.

There were no leaves or branches to this plant; so that it is probable that the stems bearing leaves issue forth at a different period of the year. The soil where this plant grew was very rich, and covered with the excrement of elephants.

A guide from the interior of the country said, that such flowers were rare, but that he had seen several, and that the natives called them 'Krubut'.[2]

Rafflesia, a south-east Asian genus, contains about thirteen species. All are parasites which grow on the trailing stems and roots of species belonging to the genus *Tetrastigma*. They do not produce leaves. The 'leaves' of the calyx referred to by Arnold are best interpreted as

bracts below the flower, while the 'petals' are perianth segments. Flowers are normally unisexual (Arnold's specimen proved to be male) and are pollinated by flies.[3] The flowers of the different species of *Rafflesia* vary greatly in size but in broad terms are otherwise very similar, there always being about five perianth segments surrounding a central opening. The smallest flowers are recorded for *R. manillana* (15 to 20 centimetres wide) and *R. rochussenii* (15 to 30 centimetres). Flowers in *R. arnoldii* are 55 to 100 centimetres wide and, although measurements of 100 centimetres have not been recorded, they are also very large in some other species; that is, *R. kerrii* (c. 70 centimetres), *R. keithii* (80 to 94 centimetres) and *R. schadenbergiana* (c. 80 centimetres).[4]

Arnold and Raffles are commonly accredited with the European discovery of the genus *Rafflesia*. However, unpublished manuscripts of the French surgeon-naturalist Louis Auguste Deschamps indicate that he collected plants of *Rafflesia*, but not of *R. arnoldii*, in Java sometime during 1794–1798.[4]

G. W. & A. W. WALKER *(1833)*

During his tenure as Governor of St Helena, General George Warren Walker (d. 1844) and his wife, Mrs A. W. Walker (d. 1844), had sent plants and seeds to two botanists — William Hooker in Glasgow and Robert Graham in Edinburgh. In 1830, Walker was sent to Ceylon (Sri Lanka) as Adjutant-General. Here,

> ... in unhurried journeys of inspection through all parts of the island, the palanquin bearers who carried him would command his interest by drawing attention to flowers seen by the way, and there the General collected ... Mrs Walker would travel less than her husband ... she did most of the correspondence regarding their plants, but he the business of despatching etc.[1]

One excursion was to Adam's Peak in 1833. Hooker published Mrs Walker's account of that trip, which commenced from Colombo on 24 January.

Something between a cradle and a coffin

30th. — Remained at Ratnapoora, preparing for our grand undertaking; this being the last European station on our route. An arm chair denuded of its legs, with Bamboos attached as shafts to carry it by, was prepared for Colonel Walker as an occasional help; though he proposed walking most of the way. Since we sent back our horses (which, by the way, we found we could have brought here at this dry season of the year, without difficulty) he has travelled in a Kandyan moonshull, something resembling a hammock, swung on a pole, in which way, the native great men used always to travel. They are now, however, adopting English customs, and to be seen on horseback; and, where the roads admit, in gigs and palankeen [that is, palanquin] carriages. The moonshull, however, has the advantage in very bad roads, as the coolies can carry it over anything. The position being recumbent, Colonel Walker found he could not so well look about him, and, therefore, preferred the chair, which, being elevated on the shoulders of the bearers, gave him a commanding view; though, I thought, neither a very secure nor comfortable position. My little palankeen, which I before described [as 'in shape something between a cradle and a coffin'], was very snug; but it had its defects, and inconveniences also: it was, however, very light and easily carried; being merely a strong frame of wood rattaned, as they do their bottoms.

31st. — In consequence of some delay in collecting our coolies, it was near one p.m. before we set off; the day excessively hot. Indeed, I think both Ruanwelle and Ratnapoora hotter than Colombo in the middle of the day; the heat there being tempered to our feelings by a cool breeze from the sea, although the range of the thermometer may be as high. As we were desirous of getting to Palabatula before dark, we had no time to lose. The atmosphere was particularly clear; and the outline of the mountains, which appeared quite close to us, almost harsh against the sky. Soon after leaving Ratnapoora we crossed the Cala-gunga, then so low that our people were hardly ankle deep in fording it. The road passes through a fertile and open country for about a mile and a half, when it becomes interspersed with jungle, so thick, on the banks of the river, as to conceal it from the traveller's view, though the sound of the rushing water is loudly heard ... Leaving the river to our left we again passed through open country with some cultivation. Three miles from Ratnapoora, came to the village of Matawelle, at the junction of a small stream, or *oyah*, with the Cala-gunga. The former we crossed, and halted for a few minutes to rest our coolies; and, while these are taking their rest, I may as well explain that, they are human beings, employed as porters and chairmen are at home, in carrying baggage or their fellow creatures. When employed in the last-mentioned manner, they are, on the continent of India, termed bearers, and consider themselves much superior to common coolies: here that distinction does not exist; so few people keep palankeens that there is no occupation for bearers as distinct from coolies. I have been induced to give this explanation in consequence of reading a note by the learned editor of one of the penny magazines, on an extract from some publication of India, I believe Captain Mundy's Sketches, in which he tells his readers, 'that coolies are small horses'. He would have been nearer the mark if he had called them 'black cattle' — but mine have rested long enough, and I must proceed on my journey.[2]

Those coolies!

Feb. 1st. — Breakfasted at eight; took a sketch, and set off at ten; our route the whole way was a precipitous ascent up the bed of a torrent at present quite dry. In many places, my position in my little palankeen became exceedingly awkward and uncomfortable, my feet being higher than my head. I tried to persuade the bearers to turn the vehicle, and carry me backward; but this they considered unlucky, and could not be prevailed on to do. My conveyance being very light and comparatively easily carried, I got far the start of Colonel Walker, and my people had a long rest, waiting till he came up. Not-withstanding the difficulties of the road, they seem to enjoy themselves much on this journey; talking, laughing, and singing, even during the most laborious ascents, where, I should have thought all their breath necessary for the exertion they had to go through in climbing the mountain, and carrying me. Every time they visit the holy shrine on the top of the Peak, I believe, they consider a step towards heaven; and to be well paid at the same time gives them considerable satisfaction. At an *ambulam* (or shed with rude benches round it, where the pilgrims may have a comfortable rest) about half way, we stopped for some time, and from thence walked for half a mile, botanising as we went, and finding at every step something quite new to us. We here began to recognise plants of the same genus with many which are common in the neighbourhood of Nervera Ellia, but of different species of *Impatiens*, two of them very curious, *Scutellaria*, the Rumboddè *Nilloo* (Acanthaceae) with the back of the leaf deep purple, but not in flower (the natives say it flowers but once in fifteen years), with many other genera and species of the same family. Near the *ambulam* there is a remarkable echo, which returns the sound almost immediately, very loud and distinct. I observed that the mountains here form a kind of amphitheatre; and that almost opposite to the precipice, on the brink of which we stood, there is a mass of rock, which I think must occasion the echo; the voice seeming to be reflected back from it, if I may use the expression. After walking till I was quite tired, I got into my palankeen again, and proceeded as before, with my heels higher than my head. In this day's journey we had but one short descent which brought us near the source of the Cala-gunga, the river we have crossed so often since we left Ratnapoora. I saw but one little patch of cultivation after we left Palabatula; which, I believe, is the highest inhabitable place in this part of the island. We soon began to mount again, and after passing over two or three places, where I really expected to be tilted out of the palankeen, I was safely deposited at Diabetma, twenty-five minutes after two p.m. The rest-house here is a large substantial building but wretchedly uncomfortable, being damp and dark, and black with dirt and smoke; it having been erected by government for the accommodation of the pilgrims who assemble here in great numbers; there being no huts or habitations of any kind after leaving Palabatula, excepting this rest-house. Our coolies seemed to consider themselves fully entitled to take up their abode under the same roof with us, and to prepare their food in the verandah, actually smoking us out of the house, although there are good out-houses and cook-rooms for the purpose. I never, anywhere else, saw them attempt such a thing before. Our servants were obliged to put out the fires they had kindled half a dozen times, before we could get rid of them.[2]

The temple

2nd. — The coolies declaring at Palabatula that they could not carry our camp bedsteads any further, from the increasing difficulties of the road, we were obliged to content ourselves with our mattresses laid on the benches we found in the room; rather a hard bed I thought. We were here glad to have recourse to our blankets, at night, the thermometer being 64° [Fahrenheit] when we went to bed, and 58° at six o'clock in the morning. Got up at seven, breakfasted and by half-past nine were again fairly under way. From Diabetma there is an immediate and steep descent; but we soon began to mount again, the road getting from very bad to a great deal worse, until it must have become quite impassible [*sic*], had not the smooth surface of the rock been cut horizontally and fashioned into steps, to the number of one hundred and twenty-seven. About half way up this stair there is a rude figure traced on the rock, said by natives to be the picture of the pious Rajé, who had the steps cut for the benefit of the pilgrims: the rock is called Darma Rajé Gal. Another descent brought us to the bed of the river Setagangula: here the pilgrims bathe, an act of purification before they approach the sacred mountain; the scenery and wood very fine. Got, on the banks of the river, a very curious species of *Impatiens*, growing to the size of a large shrub, a new *Pavetta* and a handsome yellow-flowered *Polygala* ... about mid-day a thick fog came on, which continues to envelop us now that we are safely arrived on the top of the Peak; which we reached at half-past two, having been five hours and a quarter from Diabetma, a distance of three and a half miles. I dare say we spent, at least, an hour and a half in botanising and amusing ourselves ... The circumference of the top of the Peak is about 180 feet, surrounded by a wall of masonry, about four feet high, in which there are, I believe, three openings. We entered that towards the south; on this platform, as it may be called, rises a mass of rock, about

OPPOSITE:
Impatiens walkeri,
a perennial species,
was first collected
by General Walker
and was named
after him by
William Hooker.
Illustration by
Walter Hood Fitch.
(Source and copy-
right: Royal
Botanic Gardens,
Kew)

W.Fitch, del. et lith.

Vincent Brooks, Imp

18 or 20 feet in height, on the summit of which the temple over the impression of Boodhoo's foot is erected. The temple is of wood, and is firmly fixed to the rock by numbers of strong iron chains. The holy foot-mark impressed in the rock, is about five feet in length and three in breadth, or thereabouts; Boodh, when one foot rested on the Sree Pada, and left its impression there, stepped across to Makoona, situated, the priest gravely and seriously assured me, in Siam [= Thailand]. There is a smaller temple, or shrine, placed lower down on the rock, where offerings are also made by the pilgrims, dedicated, I believe, to Samen; and also a kind of open belfry, in which two bells are suspended, and which our coolies, in turn, rung. Each stroke of the bell, we were told, commemorated a former visit; if so, some of them must have been from twenty to thirty times on the top of the Peak. I remarked, during our journey, that Sree Pada was always saluted by salaams, and sometimes prostrations, whenever it came in sight. We were accommodated for the night, in a hut, seven feet by five inside, in which we found two wooden benches; on them we placed our mattresses. One narrow leaf of our camp-table was placed against the wall, and between it and the bench we contrived to insert two chairs: these things our coolies brought up without difficulty, and we had a most comfortable dinner of cold meat and hot curry and rice prepared in the priest's hut before mentioned: never was such luxury known on the top of the Peak before.[2]

The party that ventured to the top of Adam's Peak consisted 'of forty persons; thirty coolies, four servants, an orderly soldier of the Ceylon Rifles, a native head-man, and a Boodhist [*sic*] priest, with a boy, his attendant'. However, not all were able to venture that far, some having to remain behind to look after luggage at Diabetma. The travellers and their entourage returned to Colombo on 9 February.[2]

In a subsequent letter to W. J. Hooker, Mrs Walker noted:

I was gratified to find that you considered my journal of our excursion to Adam's Peak worthy of a place in your *Companion to the Botanical Magazine* but I fear my writing must have been very indistinct as all the names of places are misspelt — besides several other errors of the press.[3]

(Note: The spellings that I have used throughout this chapter, for place names, are identical to those published by Hooker; for example, 'Ratnapoora' on page 51, instead of 'Ratnapura'.)

J. D. HOOKER (1847–1848)

In November 1847, following his voyage to the Antarctic (*see* pp. 297–304), Joseph Hooker left Portsmouth for north-east India and the Himalayas. He reached Calcutta in January the following year and prepared for an excursion with Mr Williams of the Geological Survey, who was shifting his camp to the sacred mountain of Parasnath, north-west of Calcutta. Hooker then proceeded to explore the Soane Valley.[1, 2]

Riding an elephant

After breakfast Mr Williams and myself started after the camp to Gyna, 12 miles distant; and I mounted an elephant, for the first time since you lifted me upon one at Wombell's show, a good twenty years ago. The docility of these animals is an old story, but it loses so much in the telling, that their gentleness, obedience, and sagacity seemed as strange to me as if I had never heard or read of these attributes. At the word of command my elephant knelt down, and I crawled or rather clomb [*sic*] up by his hind foot, or ear, and reached a broad pad, or in plain English, a mattress, lashed to his back, holding on by the ropes as he rose, and jogged off at an uncomfortable shuffling pace of four or five miles an hour, and (I took the trouble to count) 45 paces a minute. The swinging motion, under a hot sun, is very oppressive, but to be so high above the dust is an unspeakable comfort. The Mahout or driver sits cross-legged on the shoulder, and guides him by poking his great toes under either ear, enforcing obedience with an iron goad, with which he hammers the unhappy beast's head with quite as much force as you use to break a cocoa-nut, or drives it through his thick skin down to the quick. A most painful sight it is, to see the blood and yellow fat oozing out in the broiling sun from some dozen holes in his poor skull.

Our elephant was an excellent one, when he did not take obstinate fits, and so docile as to pick up pieces of stone if desired and with a jerk of his trunk throw them over his head for the rider to catch, thus saving the trouble of dismounting. This is geologising in true Oriental style, and no traveller's tale, I assure you.[2]

A *foul beast*

We proceeded to Chakuchee, the native carts breaking down in their passage over the projecting beds of flinty rocks, or as they hurried down the inclined planes which we cut through the precipitous banks of the streams. Near Chakuchee we passed an alligator [that is, a crocodile], just killed by two men, — a foul beast, about nine feet long, and of the Mager kind. More interesting than its natural history was the painful circumstance of its having just swallowed a child, that was playing in the water, while its mother was washing her domestic utensils in the river. The brute was hardly dead, much distended by its prey, and the mother standing beside it. A very touching group this was! the parent, with her hands clasped in agony, unable to withdraw her eyes from the cursed reptile, which still clung to life with that tenacity for which its tribe are so noted, and beside her the two athletæ leaning on their bloody bamboo staffs, with which they had all but dispatched the animal.

The *Butea frondosa* is in full flower here, and a gorgeous sight. In the mass its inflorescence resembles sheets of flame: individually the flowers are eminently beautiful, their bright orange-red petals contrasting brilliantly against the jet black velvety calyx ...

The poor woman who lost her child earns a scanty maintenance by making catechu. She inhabits a little cottage, and has no property but two Bhiles (oxen) to bring wood from the hills, and a very few household chattels; and how few these are is known only to persons who have seen the meagre furniture of Dangha hovels. Her husband cuts the trees [catechu] in the forests, and drags them to the hut; but he is now sick; and her only son, her future stay, was he whose end I have just described. Her daily food is rice, with beans from the beautiful blue-flowered *Dolichos*, trailing round the cottage; and she is in debt to the contractor, who has advanced her two rupees, to be worked off in three months, by the preparation of 240 lbs. of catechu. The present was her second husband, an old man; by him she never had any children, and in this respect alone did the poor creature think herself very unfortunate, for her poverty she did not feel. Rent to the Rajah, tax to the police, and rates to the Brahminee priest, are all paid from an acre of land, yielding so wretched a crop of barley, that it more resembled a fallow-field than a harvest-field. All day long she is boiling down the catechu wood, cut into chips, and pouring the decoction into large wooden troughs, where it is inspissated.

J. D. Hooker,
in middle age.
(Source and
copyright:
Royal Botanic
Gardens, Kew)

The Zillah is famous for the quantity of catechu its dry forests yield. The plant is a little thorny tree (a dire enemy of mine), erect, and spreading a rounded coma of well-remembered prickly branches. Its wood is yellow, with a dark brick-red heart: it is most productive in January and useless in June.[2]

The catechu referred to is *Acacia catechu*, the heartwood of which is used for tanning and dyeing (khaki cloth), and as a masticatory with the betel nut.[3]

Hunt for a tiger

There are many tigers on these hills; and as one was close by, and had killed several cattle, Mr Felle kindly offered us a chance of slaying him. Bullocks are tethered out, overnight, in the places likely to be visited by the brute: he kills one of them, and is from the spot tracked to his haunt, by natives, who visit the stations early in the morning, and report the whereabouts of his lair. The sportsman then goes to the attack mounted on an elephant, or having a roost fixed in a tree, on the trail of the tiger, and he employs some hundred natives to drive the animal past the lurking-place.

On the present occasion, the locale of the tiger was doubtful; but it was thought that by beating over several miles of country he might (or at any rate, some other game might) be driven past a certain spot. Thither, accordingly, the natives were sent, who built machans (stages) in the trees, high out of danger's reach; Mr Theobald and myself occupied one of these perches in a *Hardwickia* tree, and Mr Felle another, close by, both on the slope of a steep hill, surrounded by jungly valleys. We were also well thatched in with leafy boughs, to prevent the wary beast from espying the ambush, and had a whole stand of small arms ready for his reception.

When roosted aloft, and duly charged to keep profound silence, which I obeyed to the letter, by falling sound asleep, the word was passed to the beaters, who surrounded our post on the plain-side, extending some miles in line, and full two or three distant from us. They entered the jungle, beating tom-toms, singing and shouting as they ascended, and converging to our position. In the noonday solitude of these vast forests, our situation was romantic enough: there was not a breath of wind, an insect or bird stirring; and the wild cries of the men, and hollow sound of the drums broke upon the ear from a great distance, gradually swelling and falling, as the natives ascended the heights or crossed the valleys. After about an hour and a half, the beaters emerged from the jungle under our retreat; one by one, two by two, but preceded by no single living thing, either mouse, bird, deer, or bear, and much less a tiger. Mr Theobald caught a fever, from letting his sleeping head droop from out of the shade under a burning sun; and so ended our tiger hunt! The beaters received afterwards about a penny a-piece from the day's work; a rich guerdon for these poor wretches, whom necessity sometimes drives to feed on rats and offal.[2]

Hooker proceeded from the Soane Valley to Mirzapore, where he engaged a boat to carry him down the Ganges to Bhaugulpore.

Cruising the Ganges

My English friends would be amused to see me sometimes, when the boat has stuck in the middle of the Ganges, a not unusual occurrence if the wind blows hard and foul. The current, which runs three or four miles an hour, does not suffice to enable our floating cottage to be either tracked or pulled against such a wind. The banks are generously ten to 15 feet above the level of the river; on one side they are sloping and sandy, on the other, precipitous and formed of hard alluvium. Withered grass abounds on both banks, wheat, dhal (*Cajanus*) and gram [or chick pea] (*Cicer arietinum*), *Carthamus*, vetches and rice-fields (now cleared of their crops) are the staple products of the country. Bushes are few, except the universally prevalent *Argemone mexicana* and the *Calotropis*. Trees, also, are rare, and of stunted growth, [*Ficus*], the *Artocarpus* and some Leguminosae prevail most. I have seen but two kinds of palm, the toddy palm, and a *Phoenix*: the latter is characteristic of the driest locality. Then, for the animal creation, men and women and children abound, both on the banks, and plying up and down the Ganges. The sacred cow (of which the buffalo, called bhil, is used for draught) is common. Camels we occasionally observe, and more rarely the elephant; ponies, goats, and dogs muster strong. Porpoises and alligators [that is, crocodiles] infest the river, even above Benares. Flies and mosquitoes are terrible pests; and so is an odious insect, the flying bug, which infests my cabin at night, and insinuates itself between one's skin and clothes, diffusing a dreadful odour, which is increased by any attempt to touch or remove it. In the evening it is impossible to keep the insects out of the boat, and hinder their putting the light out; and of these the most intolerable is the above-mentioned flying-bug. Saucy crickets, too, swarm, and spring up at your face; whilst mosquitoes maintain a constant guerrilla warfare, that tries the patience no less than the nerves. Thick webs of the gossamer spider float across the river, during the heat of the day, really as coarse as fine thread, and being almost inhaled, they keep tickling the nose and lips.

The native boat which I now occupy is not unlike a floating haystack, or thatched cottage: its length is forty feet, and breadth fifteen, and it draws a foot and a half of water: the deck, on which a kind of house, neatly framed of matting, is erected, is but a little above the water's edge. My portion of this floating residence is lined with a kind of reed-work, formed of long culms [stems] of *Saccharum* [the sugar canes]. The crew and captain amount to six naked Hindoos [*sic*], one of whom steers by the huge rudder, sitting on a bamboo-stage astern; the others pull four oars in the very bows opposite my door, or track the boat along the river-bank. I have two servants, one, my factotum (Friday), alias Clamanze; and a mussulman, a table-attendant, who cooks and waits, is a handsome thin fellow, called Thirkal. In my room (for cabin I cannot bring myself to call it) is my Palkee, in which I sleep, and to which Clamanze has fitted mosquito curtains, a chair and table, at which I now write, and on it stands my compass and a huge pummalow, as big as a child's head, (most wretched eating). The pummalow is the immense vapid orange of the East and West Indies, whose English name I cannot remember. On one side are all my papers and plants, under arrangement to go home; on the other, my provisions, rice, sugar, curry-stuff, a preserved ham, and cheese (which two latter are my luxuries), etc. Around hang telescope, tin botanical box, dark lanthorn, barometer, and thermometer, etc. ...

I am fortunate in having to take this slow conveyance down, it costs me only about 10*l*. [10 pounds] altogether, whereas the steamer would have upwards of doubled that sum, and I should have seen nothing on the road nor been able to write and arrange, as I can here all day long. Most grievously I need the time, especially for my notes, journal, and correspondence. I have been annoyed by the want of a collector: the whole trouble of gathering, drying, etc., has fallen on my own shoulders, with that of Clamanze, who has always plenty to do for me, and who, in Mr Williams's camp, had to take his share of bullock-driving and transport of my goods. On the other hand the paucity of vegetation, burnt-up season, and absence of seeds or roots to collect, have allowed me to make a better illustrative collection of the botany of the countries passed through than I otherwise should have done. My specimens are well dried; this is not difficult with a little trouble: at this season three changings dry the majority, the difficulty being to prevent the drying too fast.[2]

Hooker disembarked at Bhaugulpore, from whence he proceeded inland to Darjeeling.

Gloomy forests and a sinister rest-house

Two thousand feet higher up, near Mahalderam (from whence the last view of the plains is gained), subalpine plants appear, — *Uvularia* or *Disporum*, *Berberis*, *Paris*, etc.; but here, night gathered round, and I had still ten miles to go to the nearest bungalow, that of Pacheem. The road, tolerably level, still led along the eastern slope of the Balasun valley, which was exceedingly steep, and so cut up by ravines, that it winds in and out of gullies, whose salient angles seem almost near enough to jump across. Night was ushered in by an impenetrably thick fog and Scotch mist, which made me hurry on apace. It soon, however, cleared off, with a transient thunder-storm, heightening the grandeur of the scene. The fog suddenly rose, and, looking aloft, the moon danced amongst the tree-tops. To the right the forest abruptly ascended; to the left, the black abyss of the valley, seen through the trunks, was really awful; occasionally a bright gleam of lightning shot across the sky, followed by a bellowing peal of thunder; and as the wind drove ragged masses of vapour down the valley, like smoke from a gun, I could not help likening the effect to that of a brave ship firing a salute ...

It was late before I arrived at Pacheem bungalow, the most sinister-looking rest-house I ever saw, stuck on a little cleared spur of the hill, surrounded by dark forests, and enveloped in mists and rain, hideous in architecture, being a miserable attempt to unite the Swiss cottage with the suburban Gothic; — it combined a maximum of discomfort with a minimum of good looks and good cheer. I was some time in finding the dirty house-keeper, in an outhouse hard by, and then in waking him. As he led me up the crazy verandah, and into a broad ghostly room, without glass in the windows, or fire, or any comfort, I felt strangely alive to the truth of my childhood's story-books, about the horrors of the Hartz forests, and of the benighted traveller's situation therein. Cold sluggish beetles hung to the damp walls, — and these I ruthlessly bottled. After due exertions and perseverance with the damp wood, a fire smoked lustily, and, by cajoling the gnome of a house-keeper, I procured the usual roast fowl and potatoes, with the accustomed sauce of a strong smoky and singed flavour.

Pacheem stands at an elevation of some 8,000 feet, and as I walked out on the following morning I met subalpine plants in abundance, but was too early in the season to get aught but the foliage of the generality: *Piddingtonia*, *Chrysosplenium*, *Viola* (of a different species from that of Kursiong), *Lobelia*, a small *Geranium*, *Fragaria*, little

Polygonum, five or six [species of *Rubus*], *Arum*, *Paris*, a delicate little *Isopyrum*, *Convallaria*, *Uvularia*, *Disporum*, *Carex*, creeping Urticeae, and succulent great ones too, *Arenaria* (or *Stellaria*), *Ainsliea*, *Rubia*, *Vaccinium*, and various gnaphaliums. Of small bushes, Corneae, Caprifoliaceae, and Araliaceae predominated, with *Symplocus* and *Limonia*, *Eurya*, bushy [species of *Rubus*], having simple or compound green or beautifully silky foliage, *Hypericum*, *Hydrangea*, *Berberis*, *Lonicera*, *Artemisia*, *Urtica*, *Adamia cyanea*, *Viburnum*, *Sambucus*, dwarf bamboo, etc.

The climbing plants were still *Panax* or *Aralia*, *Kadsura*, *Saurauja*, *Hydrangea*, *Vitis*, *Smilax*, *Ampelopsis*, *Polygonum*, and, most beautiful of all, *Stauntonia*, with pendulous racemes of lilac blossoms. Epiphytes were rarer, still I found *Coelogyne*, and several other genera of Orchideae, *Vaccinium*, and a most noble white *Rhododendron*, whose truly enormous and delicious lemon-scented blossoms strewed the ground.[2]

Hooker arrived at Darjeeling in April 1848 and continued to explore the Himalayan region.

An indescribable loathing

A loathsome tick infests the bushes at these elevations, both here [Tolongo] and at Darjeeling, and a more odious insect it has never been my misfortune to encounter; it is often as large as the little finger-nail, and manages to bury its proboscis and head, without causing more than very trifling pain. It can only be extracted by pure force, and that is sufficiently painful, its horny lancet being armed on both sides with reversed barbs. I have devised all manner of cunning tortures, chemical and mechanical, some of which, I am sure, must give the insect exquisite pain; but none will induce it to withdraw its hold; — the more you pull, '*the more it won't come*'. I can hardly summon courage to extract one from myself; not because of the suffering, but from an indescribable loathing of the creature, such as is called a 'scunnery' in Scotland, as some people have for snakes (in which I do not participate). Indeed, I am childish enough to make my servant keep a constant scrutiny on the exposed parts of my person, when tearing through the infested jungles, and always institute a thorough examination as soon as I get home. To leeches I am indifferent now, also *Papsas*, and other wholesome-looking blood-suckers; but in ticks, as in bugs, there is something revolting to me: — the very writing about them makes the flesh creep.[4]

OPPOSITE: *A view of Kangchenjunga from Singtam, Sikkim, based on a sepia drawing by Joseph Hooker and completed by the artist Walter Hood Fitch (1817–1892) for publication in Hooker's Himalayan Journals.* (*Source and copyright: Royal Botanic Gardens, Kew*)

Insatiable bloodsuckers

The weather continued very hot for the elevation (4,000 to 5,000 feet), the rain brought no coolness, and for the greater part of the three marches between Sintam [= Singtam] and Chakoong, we were either wading through deep mud, or climbing over rocks. Leeches swarmed in incredible profusion in the streams and damp grass, and among the bushes: they got into my hair, hung on my eyelids, and crawled up my legs and down my back. I repeatedly took upwards of a hundred from my legs, where the small ones used to collect in clusters on the instep: the sores which they produced were not healed for five months afterwards, and I retain the scars to the present day. Snuff and tobacco leaves are the best antidote, but when marching in the rain, it is impossible to apply this simple remedy to any advantage. The best plan I found to be rolling the leaves over the feet, inside the stockings, and powdering the legs with snuff.

Another pest is a small midge, or sand-fly, which causes intolerable itching and subsequent irritation, and is in this respect the most insufferable torment in Sikkim; the minutest rent in one's clothes is detected by the acute senses of this insatiable bloodsucker, which is itself so small as to be barely visible without a microscope. We daily arrived at our camping ground, streaming with blood, and mottled with the bites of peepsas, gnats, midges, and mosquitoes, besides being infested with ticks.

As the rains advanced, insects seemed to be called into existence in countless swarms; large and small moths, cockchafers, glow-worms, and cockroaches made my tent a Noah's ark by night, when the candle was burning; together with winged ants, May-flies, flying earwigs, and many beetles, while a very large species of *Tipula* (daddy-long-legs) swept its long legs across my face as I wrote my journal, or plotted off my map. After retiring to rest and putting out the light, they gradually departed, except a few which could not find the way out, and remained to disturb my slumbers.[5]

OPPOSITE:
Dendrobium
hookerianum,
an epiphytic orchid
discovered by
Hooker in 1848
and here illustrated
by Walter Hood
Fitch. (Source and
copyright:
Royal Botanic
Gardens, Kew)

Constant headaches

Chakoong is a remarkable spot in the bottom of the valley, at an angle of the Lachen-Lachoong, which here receives an effluent from Gnarem, a mountain 17,577 feet high, on the *Chola Range* to the east. There is no village, but some grass huts used by travellers,

which are built close to the river on a very broad flat, fringed with alder, hornbeam, and birch; the elevation is 4,400 feet, and many European genera not found about Darjeeling, and belonging to the temperate Himalaya, grow intermixed with tropical plants that are found further north. The birch, willow, alder, and walnut grow side by side with wild plantain, *Erythrina*, *Wallichia* palm, and gigantic bamboos: the *Cedrela toona*, figs, *Melastoma*, Scitamineae, balsams, *Pothos*, peppers, and gigantic climbing vines, grow mixed with brambles, speedwell, *Paris*, forgot-me-not, and nettles that sting like poisoned arrows. The wild English strawberry is common, but bears a tasteless fruit: its inferiority is, however, counterbalanced by the abundance of a grateful yellow raspberry. Parasitic orchids (*Dendrobium nobile*, and *densiflorum*, etc.), cover the trunks of oaks, while *Thalictrum* and *Geranium* grow under their shade. *Monotropa* and *Balanophora*, both parasites on the roots of trees (the one a native of north Europe and the other of a tropical climate), push their leafless stems and heads of flowers through the soil together; and lastly, tree-ferns grow associated with the *Pteris aquilina* (brake) and *Lycopodium clavatum* of our British moors; and amongst mosses the superb Himalayan *Lyellia crispa*, with the English *Fumaria hygrometrica* ...

It is a remarkable fact, that this hot, damp gorge is never malarious; this is attributable to the coolness of the river, and to the water on the flats not stagnating; for at Choongtam, a march further north, and 1,500 feet higher, fevers and ague prevail in summer on similar flats, but which have been cleared of jungle, and are therefore exposed to the sun.

I have had constant headache for several mornings on waking, which I did not fail to attribute to coming fever, or to the unhealthiness of the climate; till I accidentally found it to arise from the wormwood, upon a thick couch of the cut branches of which I was accustomed to sleep, and which in dry weather produced no such effects.[5]

By the time he returned to England in March 1851, Hooker had amassed a large collection of plants and recorded much information of interest to natural historians and ethnologists.

Works published by Hooker as a result of his time in India include *The Rhododendrons of Sikkim-Himalaya* and *Himalayan*

An illustration taken from Hooker's Himalayan Journals *of a living bridge in the Khasia Hills (Assam). The bridge was formed by linking the roots of* Ficus elastica *and other species. (Source and copyright: Royal Botanic Gardens, Kew)*

Journals — a popular account of his travels. He also co-authored *Flora indica*, a systematic account of the plants of India.

In 1855, he was appointed Assistant Director at Kew. His father had been Director since 1841 and Joseph succeeded Sir William to the position in 1865. Joseph retired from the Directorship in 1885 and died in 1911, aged 94.[1]

R. FORTUNE *(c. 1850–1855)*

Born in 1812 in Blackadder Town, Berwick, Robert Fortune was employed for a time as a gardener at the Royal Botanic Garden, Edinburgh. In the 1840s, he transferred to the gardens of the Royal Horticultural Society (RHS), Chiswick, and collected plants for the RHS in China during 1843–1846. He made further trips to China and Japan and, when employed by the East India Company, was responsible for the introduction of Chinese tea plants to India. Fortune was one of the first botanists to successfully exploit the use of the Wardian Case (*see* description in Appendices — pp. 329–334).

Fortune's family destroyed his notes and correspondence following his death in 1880 but he had published an account of his first expedition to China; that is, *Three Years Wanderings in the Northern Provinces of China*.[1] The following extracts are from articles published in *Gardener's Chronicle*.

The glories of the bamboo

The bamboo, as you are aware, is one of the most valuable trees in China, and is used for almost every purpose. Having from time to time noted down the uses to which I have seen it applied, my list seems so amusing that I send it to you for the readers of the *Chronicle*.

Bamboo is used in making soldiers' hats and shields, umbrellas, soles of shoes, scaffolding poles, measures, baskets, ropes, paper, pencil holders, brooms, sedan chairs, pipes, flower-stakes and trellis work in gardens, pillows are made of the shavings, a kind of rush cloak is made from the leaves for wet weather, and is called a To-e, or 'garment of leaves'. On the water it is used in making sails and covers for boats, for fishing-rods and fish baskets, fishing stakes and buoys; katamarans [*sic*] are rude boats, or rather floats, formed of a few logs of bamboo lashed firmly together, and launched upon the water. In agriculture the bamboo is used in making aqueducts for conveying water to the land; it forms part of the celebrated water

Corylopsis spicata, *a member of the family Hamamelidaceae, is a deciduous shrub growing to about 3 m tall. The pendulous inflorescences are about 6 cm long. Native to Japan, it is one of the many plants from the East introduced to Western gardens by Robert Fortune.*

wheel, as well as the plough, the harrow, and other implements of husbandry. Excellent water-pipes are made of it for conveying springs from the hills, to supply houses and temples in the valleys with pure water. Its roots are often cut into the most grotesque figures, and its stems finely carved into ornaments for the curious, or as incense burners for the gods. The Ningpo furniture — the most beautiful in China — is often inlaid with figures of people, houses, temples, and pagodas in bamboo, which form most correct and striking pictures of China and the Chinese. The young shoots are boiled and eaten, and sweetmeats are also made of them. A substance found in the joints called Tabasheer is used in medicine. In the manufacture of tea it forms the rolling tables, drying baskets and sieves; and last, though not least, the celebrated chop-sticks — the most important articles in domestic use — are made of it.

Gentle reader, however incredulous you may be, I must still carry you a step further, and tell you that I have not enumerated one-half of the uses to which the bamboo is applied in China. Indeed it would be nearly as difficult to say what it is *not* used for as what it is. It is in universal demand, in the houses and in the fields, on water and on land, in peace and in war. Through life the Chinaman is almost dependent upon it for his support, nor does it leave him until it carries him to his last resting-place on the hill side, and even then, in company with the cypress, juniper and pine, it waves over and marks his tomb.

At the time of the last war, when the Emperor of China, very considerately no doubt, wanted to conquer the English by withholding the usual supplies of tea and rhubarb, without which, he supposed, they could not continue to exist for any length of time, we might have returned the compliment, had it been possible for us to have destroyed all his bamboos. With all deference to the opinion of his celestial Majesty, the English *might* have survived the loss of tea and rhubarb, but we cannot conceive the Chinese existing as a nation, or indeed at all, without bamboo.[2]

In search of the golden larch

I have been acquainted with this interesting tree for several years in China, but only in gardens, and as a pot plant in a dwarfed state. The Chinese, by their favourite system of dwarfing, contrive to make it, when only a foot and a half or two feet high, have all the characters of an aged cedar of Lebanon. It is called by them the kin-le-sung, or golden pine, probably from the rich yellow appearance which the ripened leaves and cones assume in the autumn. Although I have often made inquiries after it, and endeavoured to get the natives to bring me some cones, or to take me to a place where such cones could be procured, I met with no success until last autumn. Then, however, I happened to visit a part of the country where I had not been before, and quite unexpectedly came upon some fine specimens of full grown trees covered with ripe cones. They were growing in the vicinity of a Buddhist monastery in the western part of the province of Chekiang, at an elevation of 1,000 or 1,500 feet above the level of the sea. Their stems, which measured fully five feet in circumference two feet from the ground, carried this size, with a slight diminution, to a height of 50 feet, that being the height of the lower branches. The total height I estimated about 120 or 130 feet. The stems were perfectly straight throughout, the branches symmetrical, slightly inclined to the horizontal form, and having the appearance of something between the cedar and larch. The long branchless stems were, no doubt, the result of their growing close together and thickly surrounded with other trees, for I have since seen a single specimen growing by itself on a mountain side at a much higher elevation, whose lower branches almost touched the ground.

I need scarcely say how pleased I was with the discovery I had made, or with what delight, with the permission and assistance of the good priests, I procured a large supply of those curious cones sent to England last winter. It was with great regret I read in this paper, and a letter from Mr Glendinning, that so few of these seeds had vegetated, and in order to increase the number by procuring another supply, I paid a visit this autumn to the place where I had been so successful last year, with what results I shall proceed to relate. Having arrived at the Monastery of Tsan-tsing — for that is the name of the place — I lost no time in visiting the spot of my last year's discovery. The trees were there as beautiful and symmetrical as ever, but after straining my eyes for half an hour I could not detect a single cone. I returned to the temple and mentioned my disappointment to the priests, and asked them whether it was possible to procure cones from any other part of the country. They told me of various places where there were trees, but whether these had seed upon them or not they could not say. They further consoled me with a piece of information, which, although I was most unwilling to believe it, I knew to be most likely too true, namely, that this tree rarely bore cones two years successively, that last year was its bearing year, that this one it was barren. A respectable looking man, who was on a visit to the temple, now came up to me and said that he knew a place where a large number of trees were growing, and that if I would visit the temple to which he belonged he would take me to this spot, and that there I would probably find what I wanted. I immediately took down the name of his residence, which he told me was Quan-ting, a place about 20 [?leagues] distant from the temple in which I was domiciled, and at a much higher elevation on the mountains. Having made an appointment for next day he took his leave of me with great politeness, and returned to his home.

Having procured a guide for Quan-ting, I set out early next day to visit my new acquaintance. Leaving the temple of Tsan-tsing, our way led up a steep pass, paved with granite stones. On each side of the road were forests of fine bamboos — the variety called by the Chinese 'maou', the finest I ever saw. The forests are very valuable, not only on account of the demand for the full-grown bamboos, but also for the young shoots, which are dug up and sold in the markets in the early part of the season. Here, too, were dense woods of *Cryptomeria*, *Cunninghamia lanceolata*, oaks, chestnuts, and such like representatives of a cold or temperate climate. The Chinese chestnut appears to differ slightly from the Spanish, but it is superior to that variety. A very pretty small one, about the size and form of the hazelnut, is much esteemed; both, I think, worth introduction to Europe. I have sent them both to India, and I am happy to hear that both are now doing well on the Himalayan mountains. Chestnuts have long been a desideratum in India; many fruitless attempts have been made to introduce them, but with Ward's cases we now work wonders.

Our road was long and rugged, and we were gradually attaining a higher elevation. We reached the temple of Quan-ting at last, and had no difficulty in finding our acquaintance of the preceding day, Mr Wang-a-nok, as he called himself. It now appeared he was a celebrated cook — the Soyer of the district — and had been engaged on this day to prepare a large dinner for a number of visitors who had come to worship at the temple. He told me he would be ready to accompany me as soon as the dinner was over, and invited me to be seated in the priest's room until that time. This little temple has no pretensions as regards size, and was in a most dilapidated condition. In one of the principal halls I observed a table spread and covered with many good things, which were an offering to Buddha, and before which the visitors, as they arrived, prostrated themselves. As the valley in which the temple is placed is fully 3,000 feet above the sea, I felt the air most piercingly cold, although it was only the middle of October, and hot enough in the plains in the day time. So cold was it that at last I was obliged to take refuge in the kitchen, where Mr Wang was busy with his preparations for the dinner, and where several fires were burning. This place had no chimney, so the smoke had to find its way out through the doors, windows, or broken roof, or, in fact, any way it could. My position here was, therefore, far from being an enviable one, although I got a little warmth from the fires. I was therefore glad when dinner was announced, as there was then some prospect of being able to get the services of Mr Wang. The priests and some of the visitors now came and invited me to dine with them, and, although I was unwilling, they almost dragged me to the table. In the dining-room, which was the same, by-the-by, in which they were worshipping on my arrival, I found four tables placed, at one of which I was to sit down, and was evidently considered the lion of the party. They pressed me to eat and to drink, and although I could not comply with their wishes to the fullest extent, I did the best I could to merit such kindness and politeness. But I shall not attempt a description of a Chinese dinner which, like the dinner itself, would be necessarily a long one, and will only say that, like all good things, it came to an end at last, and Mr Wang having finished his in the kitchen and taken a supply in his pockets, declared himself ready for my service.

Our road led us up to the head of the valley in which the temple stands and then it seemed as if all further passage was stopped by high mountain barriers. As we got nearer, however, I observed a path winding up round the mountain, and by this road we reached the top of a range of mountains fully 1,000 feet higher than any we had passed, or 4,000 feet above the sea. When we reached the top the view that met our eyes on all sides rewarded us richly for all the toil of the morning. I had seen nothing so grand as this since my journey across the Bohea mountains. On all sides, in whichever direction I looked, nothing was seen but mountains of various heights and forms, reminding one of the waves of a stormy sea. Far below us in various directions appeared richly cultivated and well wooded valleys; but they seemed so far off, and in some places the hills were so precipitous, that it made me giddy to look down. On the top where we were there was nothing but stunted brushwood, but, here and there, where the slopes were gentle, I observed a thatched hut and some spots of cultivation. At this height I met with some lycopods, gentians, and other plants not observed at a lower elevation. I also found a *Hydrangea* in a leafless state, which may turn out a new species, and which I hope to introduce to Europe. If it proves to be an ornamental species it will probably prove quite hardy in England.

We had left the highest point of the mountain ridge, and were gradually descending, when on rounding a point I observed at a distance a sloping hill covered with the beautiful object of our search — the *Abies kaempferi*. Many of the trees were young, and all had apparently been planted by man; at least so far as I could observe they had nothing of a natural forest character about them. One tree in particular seemed the queen of the forest, from its great size and beauty, and to that we bent our steps. It was standing all alone, measured eight feet in circumference, was fully 130 feet high, and its lower branches were nearly touching the ground. The lower branches had assumed a flat and horizontal form, and came out almost at right angles with the stem, but the upper part of the tree was of a conical shape, resembling more a larch than a cedar of Lebanon. But there were no cones even on this or any of the others, although the natives informed us they had been loaded with them on the previous year. I had therefore to content myself with digging up a few self-sown young plants which grew near it, and which I shall endeavour to introduce to England.

I now parted from my friend Mr Wang, who returned to his mountain home at Quan-ting, while I and my guide pursued our journey towards the temple at which I was staying by a different route from that by which we had come. The road led us through the same kind of scenery which I have endeavoured to describe — mountains; nothing but mountains, deep valleys, and granite and clay-slate rocks — now bleak and barren, and now richly covered with forests chiefly consisting of oaks and pines. We arrived at the monastery just as it was getting dark. My friends, the priests, were waiting at the entrance, and anxiously inquired what success had attended us during the day. I told them the trees at Quan-ting were just like their own — destitute of cones. 'Ah!' said they, for my consolation, 'next year there will be plenty'.[3]

Fortune incorrectly used the name *Abies kaempferi*. The golden larch searched for is *Pseudolarix amabilis* and is a gazetted rare species.[4]

J. MOTLEY (1855)

James Motley, perhaps born on the Isle of Man, was a civil engineer who in, or about, 1851 went to Labuan. In 1854, he was appointed Superintendent of the coal-mining operations of a private company in the territory of the Sultan of Bandjermasin, in south-east Borneo. Between 1851 and 1859, Motley gathered specimens of natural history in Malaysia, Sumatra, Java and Borneo. Many of his collections are housed at Kew.[1] The following extracts are from an account of a journey along the east coast of Sumatra.

The 'men of the mud'

When I last wrote to you I gave you an account of my first attempt to reach Sumatra, when I was obliged to return to Singapore for a larger boat. I started again on the 24th of January with a Bugis prahu, of about four tons burden, and six men besides my servant. I slept that night at a small settlement among the islands, which I have already described to you; and next day, about ten a.m., I got clear of the Archipelago and sailed down the coast of Sumatra: it is a mere line of low trees, and, as far as I could see, when the high water allowed us to approach it, of one species only, *Aegiceras majus* I believe, called in Malay 'api api'. The natives assured me that for miles along the coast no other plant is seen, except in the creeks, where there is a little mixture of fresh water. The shore is exceedingly flat, of mud so soft that it is hard to say where it ends and the water begins. Though the rise and fall of the tide is not more than six feet, the beach dries for some miles out, and we were aground at low water, where we could only see the trees like a dark line on the horizon; indeed about 150 miles to the southward the coast has literally never been seen from the sea, even by the surveyors who made the charts, from the impossibility of approaching it in a boat sufficiently near. Not a break nor a hillock could be seen, nor indeed does one exist on the whole line of coast for 50 miles inland. The country can hardly be said to be dry land, and the whole coast is notoriously unhealthy, and swarms with tigers and other wild beasts. At ten p.m. we anchored just on the equator, off Taryong Daloo, close to which the water is perhaps deeper, and there is probably a reef of coral, as the sea made a great noise all night.

25th. We had no wind this morning, but it being high water we pulled along close under the api api jungle. The number of birds here is astonishing: there were flocks of sandpipers and plovers, which must have consisted of hundreds of thousands of individuals, looking at a distance like large clouds, and completely whitening the jungle when they perched. Of herons I counted nine species; all around us were fishing innumerable terns, of two species; knee-deep in the water, close under the bushes, stood long rows of tall black and white ibises, looking like soldiers at drill, their heads laid back, their long flesh-coloured beaks resting on their white breasts; and every moment brilliant kingfishers glanced in and out among the trees.

About ten a.m. we came up to a tribe of a very singular race of Malays, the orang lant, or men-of-the-sea; though they might with greater propriety be called men of the mud. There are said to be nine tribes of them; they live entirely in their boats, never quitting the coast, but moving up and down over a certain district at the rate of a mile or two each day. The Malays of Singapore and the natives of Singu Rhio and the interior of Sumatra come here to trade with them, exchanging rice, cloth, sago, and salt, for dried fish and karang, a species of *Arca*, much used for food, and the shells of which are supposed to yield the purest and best lime for eating with the sirik and areca nut. They speak a little Malay, but have also a peculiar dialect of their own, which few of the Malays understand; and they are exceedingly averse to associating with other people, or marrying out of their own tribe. They differ a little in physiognomy from the Malays generally, the lower jaw being narrower, and the alae of the nose suddenly enlarged, as in the Papuans. A good many of the men had, for Malays, very strong black beards, and, though short, they are well formed; the calf of the leg is low down, large and decurrent; the shoulders high and broad, and the forearm muscular and well-developed. They are professedly Mahometans, but know very little about it, and retain many pagan customs, such as faith in augury, offering libations to spirits, etc., like the Dyaks of Borneo. Their language is said to resemble that of the Battas of the interior of Sumatra, a people I have not yet met with. This tribe was divided into two Kampongs, or villages as they call them, one of twenty, the other of about 50 boats of various sizes, and may have consisted of 300 to 400 persons. The smaller boats were laden with the fishing apparatus, to be hereafter described, and the larger formed their habitations. These boats are sheathed with thin planks or with the bark of the mangrove, to protect them from the Kapang,

or teredo [so-called 'ship-worm' but actually a boring mollusc], so
destructive in these seas; the longest were perhaps 40 feet long, and
of three or four tons burden. A sort of house, not high enough to
stand erect in, is constructed over the whole length of the boat, to
the ridge-pole of which are usually suspended two or three infants
swinging in small hammocks. The sides and roofs of these houses are
completely covered with fish, split open and drying in the sun, giving
out a horrible stench, and attracting a vast number of hawks, who
sailed round and round, swooping every now and then at the
tempting morsels, and succeeded occasionally in carrying a piece off,
in spite of the numerous naked urchins who kept guard with long
sticks. There were four species of these birds, the most numerous
being the red Brahminee kite of India: they were perfectly fearless,
sweeping past close to one's head; and it was interesting to watch
them devouring their prey on the wing, and really picking out the
pieces of meat with their beaks from between their clenched talons.
There were several Singapore prahus in company with these people,
waiting to buy fish. As we rowed past, an extremely filthy old
savage, who called himself Orang Kaya, or chief, came on board;
he told us that his office was hereditary, and that every man of his
family bore the same name, Pulek. He told me that his people
sometimes entered the rivers, but only far enough to get fresh water
to drink, which he said was very good. I felt somewhat interested
about this matter, as I began to suspect we should be some time in
reaching Indragiri, so I asked him to let me see it. He fetched a
cupful from his boat: it was muddy, nearly black, and not brackish,
but so actually salt that I could not touch it; yet he drank it with
great relish, and said it was better than the clear water we had
brought from Singapore: so much will habit do in modifying human
tastes. I exchanged with him some tobacco and an old pair of
trousers, to which he took a great fancy, for a bundle of dried fish
for the boatmen; and after a most barefaced attempt to steal my
short clay pipe (a high crime, for it was the only one I had with me),
he took his leave, and we pulled on. We soon got aground however,
about a mile from the trees, and were of course obliged to wait for
the tide. Shortly afterwards the whole tribe was in motion, following
us, and they moored themselves to poles stuck in the mud in a long
line, of which our boat was nearly the centre. They now began to
prepare their balat, or fishing weir; it was a sort of flexible paling,
made of strips of bamboo, an inch wide and four or five feet long,
fastened together by the twisted stems of a species of *Cissus* (this
material, like their boats, they get from the Malays). This paling is

doubled up and piled upon the small boats before mentioned, in lengths of 100 to 200 feet in each boat, and from these it is shot like a seine net, when the tide begins to ebb, in about six feet of water, and in a line parallel with the shore; as fast as one boat was exhausted another was brought up, and a fresh length joined on. A number of boys followed the boats, swimming, and with their feet striking the bamboos upright in the mud in a perfectly straight line, though it was impossible to see an inch into the muddy water. In a quarter of an hour they had laid down more than half a mile, besides a long piece at each end, at right angles to the main line, and moving up to the shore, enclosing altogether perhaps 50 or 60 acres of water. As soon as the water had ebbed far enough to allow the wakes of the larger fish to be seen as they swam about in the enclosure, the boys, taking advantage of the now unoccupied canoes, went paddling about after them with great agility, holding a long light spear, with the head of the paddle in the right hand, and seldom failing to transfix, even from a considerable distance, any unfortunate fish who ventured near enough to the surface to show his back free for a moment. When the water was about three feet deep, and the tops of the bamboos sufficiently above water effectually to confine the fish, the men began their work in good earnest. The fish, in their efforts to escape to deeper water, travelled along the inside of the enclosure, close to the bamboos, and the fishermen accordingly stationed themselves at intervals of about 12 or 14 yards, with a large bag-net open against the set of the tide; the water is so muddy that the fish cannot see this net before they strike it, when it is immediately raised, and the captive secured. The mud here is so excessively soft, that it is impossible to walk or even to stand upon it; and therefore every man, woman, and child is provided with a strange instrument of locomotion, without which life would be impossible for these people; it is called 'tongka', and is merely a piece of plank, about four feet long, and 18 inches wide, rounded and slightly turned up at each end. I was much puzzled at first to imagine what these planks could be, of which I saw so many in every boat; but when the tide went down the mystery was soon solved. Supported on the hands and one knee on the 'tongka', they paddled with the other foot in the mud, and skimmed over the surface with most wonderful rapidity, making the mud and water fly in all directions, and bespattering one another from head to foot with filth, which of course cannot be washed off again until the tide rises, a matter which distresses them but little. A brisk intercourse was now kept up from boat to boat by this means, and you can conceive nothing more absurd than the attitudes and action; it all looked natural enough as long as it was confined to the naked children, but to see grey-headed old men and women scuttling away among the sludge, and plastered with mud all over their grave wrinkled brown faces, was really most ridiculous: they looked so very little like human beings, that I felt almost surprised to hear them speak. From this mode of life the women are obliged to wear most grotesquely short drapery, not reaching their knees; and the upper part of their dress being in the usual Malay style, this too gives them a very odd appearance. The quantity of fish caught was very great, judging by the success of those near me; they were chiefly Scombridae and Pleuronectidae, but there were many other species. Two or three small sharks were taken; their flesh is highly valued. I saw several specimens of a ray, covered with blue spots and with a formidable spine near the base of his long filiform tail: the fish is much dreaded by the natives, and with good reason; it is exceedingly venomous. I have seen a European at Labuan suffer for twenty-four hours intense pain from a scarcely visible puncture in the ankle from one of these fish; the pain was accompanied by vomiting, shivering, spasms, and other symptoms of poisoning; it was followed by extensive ecchymossis up to the thigh, swelling and suppuration of the glands of the groin and axillae, and great general constitutional disturbance; and the wound was five months in healing, after forming several deep-seated abscesses and sloughing extensively. Several flat-tailed sea snakes of a dingy grey colour, called maroke, were within the weir; the natives say they are very poisonous, which I have reason to believe, but they refused to let me kill one, saying it would bring 'cheloka', or ill-luck, to their fishing; they were gently raised in the hand-net and put outside the enclosure. A small alligator [that is, a crocodile] was hotly chased, but he broke through the weir and escaped to the sea. Great numbers of fish were rejected, among them two species of *Syngnathus*, one very large, and all the Chaetodon tribe, some very curious and beautiful; but I had with me no means of preserving them. The natives believe them all to be poisonous; a vast number of shrimps, prawns, squillae, and other crustacea were also rejected, not, as the people said, because they were not good, but because they had plenty of fish without them. An ichthyologist who did not mind roughing it a little, and who would follow these people for a week, would reap a rich harvest indeed. I was told that the weir was the common property of the tribe, but that every man fished in it on his own account. When the mud was quite dry, or as nearly so as it could be, countless multitudes of small crabs, of five or six species, made their appearance, and were in constant motion, raking over the semi-liquid mud with their claws and feet, and every now and then raising themselves on four feet above the surface, and spreading their extended chelae in the air. I got two or three specimens of a little varnished black *Mitra*, crawling on the mud, but no other shells, except the *Arca* before mentioned. It rained heavily all the afternoon, and when during the night the tide rose and floated us, we had a strong head wind; so we were obliged to remain where we were until morning, only going out into deeper water.[2]

Mosquitoes

We entered the northern mouth of the Indragiri, now called Kwala Ioukko; this I knew very well from my chart, and supposed the steersman knew it also, as he came in without saying a word. It appears, however, that he had never been in this way before, and had not intended it, but had made a mistake; on discovering this, he wished to turn back and go up the main channel, which would have lost us one or two days, and it cost me some trouble to convince him that we could go where we were. The stream was at the mouth about a mile and a half wide, the banks fringed with nipa palm and padada (*Sonneratia acida*); the latter [a mangrove] always a sure sign that the water is nearly fresh, as on trial I found it to be. I could also distinguish, by its habit, the tall *Rhizophora* named tumino; but until it was dark in the evening we did not approach the shore near enough to see much of the vegetation. At six p.m. we made fast for the night to a tree at the mouth of a small creek; and a most unlucky locality we chose, for until about eight p.m. the mosquitoes drove us half mad: they are always troublesome enough, but those on the nipa swamps are always excessively venomous, every bite raising a large white weal. At nine p.m. came on a violent squall with torrents of rain; but we covered up the boat with Kajang or palm-leaf mats, and went to sleep, in hopes of weathering the storm comfortably: so we remained until past midnight; and when all (including, I am afraid, the watch) were asleep, a huge tree came down with the current, and, striking us with such a shock that I believed at first the boat must be utterly destroyed, tore us from our moorings, swept away all our shelter, and swept us down the stream with it. It was raining as it rains only in the tropics, blowing great guns, and thundering and lightening fearfully, so that we were all drenched in a moment. We were in a most dangerous position, for we were quite fast in the branches of the drift, and had it rolled over, the boat must have gone down; however, we got clear of it at last, after half an hour's hard work cutting away with choppers in the dark. The stream was now so strong in the middle of the river that our anchor would not hold; and as we did not know whether it was flood or ebb at this hour, we were obliged to try to light a torch to see the compass: in this we succeeded after several trials, and found we had been carried nearly out to sea again, so we got as quickly as we could to the bank, and made fast to the nipa-leaves until daylight.[2]

The nipa palm

On the 27th, at five a.m., it was still raining a little; but while the men were cooking their rice, I went ashore among the nipa [*Nypa fruticans*, or nipa palm], and got a few shells, — two species of *Neritina* and a *Cerithium* creeping on the mud, a pretty little pink *Anomia* on the stems of the nipa, and a *Bulimus* and a *Pholas*, the two latter apparently peculiar to the nipa; the latter forms its burrows in the soft pithy substance of thick bases of the growing leaves. It is far from pleasant to explore a nipa swamp: independently of the difficulty of getting along in the soft black mud, you are always half devoured by mosquitoes of the most venomous kind. Just as we started, a great blue heron perched on a stump near us; I put a rifle bullet through his neck, and he greatly improved our dinner, after several days of rice and salt-fish curry. Though neglected in these days in England, I have always found all the heron tribe excellent food. My servant took off all the meat from the breast and thighs, and, as he said, made beefsteaks of it; it was quite tender, and had in some degree the flavour of woodcock. We pulled and sailed all day up the river, passing the head of the delta about noon, and seeing until three p.m. hardly any vegetation except nipa and *Sonneratia acida*, with here and there a *Rhizophora*, or a tuft of the fern called peai (I believe, *Acrostichum inaequale*). The *Sonneratia* is a most beautiful tree, with very long slender pendulous branches; the flowers are handsome, the long stamens being of a rich dark pink, but they fall an hour or two after sunrise; the fruit is very conspicuous, with its great persistent star-shaped calyx; it is acid and slightly bitter, and is eaten by the natives as a condiment with their rice and salt fish. The creeping rhizomata of the nipa look very strange when exposed by the washing away of the mud: each internode is very short, but in order to give room for the attachment of the enormous base of the leaf, it is applied so

Drift fruit, 8–12 cm long, of the nipa or mangrove palm (Nypa fruticans) collected in northern Australia. This clump-forming species is wide-spread in parts of the Asian tropics, northern Australia and the western Pacific. It grows in brackish, tidal water and may form extensive stands in coastal lowlands. In some regions the fronds, commonly 5–7 m long, are traditionally used for thatching, the sugary sap is used in the manufacture of alcohol, and young seeds are eaten.

obliquely upon the last, that the whole resembles a number of discs laid in a row, and slightly overlapping each other; the upper side of these discs, a foot or 18 inches in diameter, retains the scars left by the disarticulation of the leaves, and the lower produces a tangled mess of simple fibres, about half an inch in diameter. The way in which these fibres runs into the mud has often forcibly reminded me of the carbonised traces of the fibres of Stigmariae in the underlay of the coals of Europe (here we have nothing of the sort). On the stems of the *Sonneratia* I saw a very handsome ivory-white foliaceous lichen, without fruit; there was a little pendulous *Appendicula*, with thick equitant leaves and minute axillary purple flowers; and another curious little plant of the orchid family, remarkable in having no leaves or stem — it consists merely of a few radiating fleshy fibres adhering to the tree; from the centre rise two or three spikes, bearing a few minute yellowish-green flowers. I have since seen it in abundance in Java, and especially in the island of Banku, where the trunks of *Pleurocarpus indicus*, planted about the town of Minto, were completely covered by it. A small fern, I think *Acrostichum nummulariaefolium*, creeps over the trees to the very extremities of the twigs. About three p.m. we arrived at a small island in the river, where the salt-water flood appears to cease almost at once. The nipa disappears as a social plant, a few scattered tufts only being seen; and some stunted patches of the moong, always a freshwater palm, begin to rise here and there above the jungle. The island takes its

name, Pulo Pullas, from the abundance of a beautiful little scarlet-fruited *Licuala*, so called. From this change in the vegetation, as well as from the presence of the island and a sand-bank, which reduced the depth to a fathom and a half, it is probable that at this point the freshwater stream and the flood tide exactly neutralise each other; and indeed above this, though the stream became less rapid, and its level rose on the flood-tide, we had no more current up the river. I saw today the first indication of elephants, or at least of some very large animal, coming to the river to drink. Our wooden anchor would not hold tonight in the soft mud, so we were obliged to make fast to a tree, though the men professed to be horribly afraid tigers would leap into the boat. We had another alarm tonight, for, being close to the bank, the rising tide jammed us under an overhanging tree; but the night was fine, and we soon got all clear, just as the old steersman saluted the dawn with a most dreary noise, by blowing into a bamboo which he called twong-twong.[2]

Monkeys and fireflies

28th. Off again at five a.m. The nipa has quite disappeared, and the padada is much less common, and not so well grown as lower down. Another social plant, the rangas of the [family] Anacardiaceae, seems to take its place; it is a bushy shrub or small tree, growing quite in the water; the leaves are of a bright clear green, when young very red, and it was now covered with fruit, about the size of an egg; the cotyledons very large and covered with a thick corky bark. Two other trees have received the same name of rangas: one is an enormous tree, growing also by the rivers, but quite in the interior; the other is also a large tree, of which I have seen neither fruit nor flower. It yields a red and dark brown veined wood, largely used for common furniture at Singapore. The bark of all three, and indeed of several other trees of the tribe, yields copiously a limpid juice, changing rapidly to a black varnish. The juice is exceedingly venomous, blistering the skin severely, and leaving foul little ulcers very difficult to heal. The trees are now beginning to be clothed with parasitical ferns; there are also a few small [Orchidaceae], chiefly *Dendrobium* and *Appendicula*, and abundance of the ubiquitous *Dendrobium crumenatum*. The current came down so strong about nine a.m., that we were obliged to anchor. I saw now the first alligators [that is, crocodiles]; one enormous fellow I fired at, and, I suppose, hit, for he threw his huge body quite out of the water with a tremendous splash. The natives say [a crocodile] never recovers from a wound, however small; he has nothing to scratch himself with, his feet being too short; and they say that the flies in the air, and the small fish in the water, never leave him a moment's peace: so that the wound becomes larger and larger. I have indeed seen [a crocodile] which I shot through the leg, taken two or three days afterwards, with almost the whole shoulder sloughed away, so that the story may be true. The quantity of monkeys seen here is wonderful. I only know the names of two, *Nasalis larvatus*, a horribly ugly animal, and *Hylobates concolor*, frequently trained by the Malays to gather fruit; but there are many other species: — the moniet; the sipai, a beautiful little black fellow with white stockings and long gloves; the lotong, a frightful animal, with a scowling face and grizzled black hair; the wa wa, or long-armed ape; orang hutan (this is the proper spelling: it is literally 'man of the woods'); the

ungku, which fills the whole country in the early morning with a
most frightful howling, the most unearthly noise I have ever heard.
We passed today many clear spaces covered with long grass, species
of *Anthistiria* and *Saccharum*; these are the favourite feeding
grounds of the elephants. The seed of the *Anthistiria* contains a good
deal of farina, and must be very nutritious. These places, I was told,
were formerly settlements, driven away by the tyranny of the Rajahs.
Met a prahu going to Singapore with gutta-percha; but all second-
rate quality. The Nakoda told me I should not reach the Rajah's
village for three days more. I took the opportunity of sending some
letters to Singapore. The fireflies tonight are most magnificent, the
whole jungle was lighted up by them: the light is not steady, but is
brighter at intervals of about two seconds; and I have often
remarked, that all the individuals on the same tree or branch are
subject to this augmentation of light at the same moment.[2]

Prior to World War II, Professor E. J. H. Corner used pig-tailed
monkeys (*Macaca nemenstrina*) to collect plant specimens from the
tops of forest trees in Malaya, the monkeys having being trained in
the Singapore Botanical Gardens. The monkeys were skilled enough
to collect epiphytes and cauliflorous flowers and fruit.[3]

Unpleasant fellows

29th. We pulled last night some distance in the dark. The jungle
has very much changed its appearance; it has a much more interior
look. Patches of grass come down here and there to the bank; the
trees are larger and more varied in appearance, and there are many
Scitamineae to be seen in the shade. There are also many rotans; one
species, in particular, is most elegant, it is called rotan tikus, 'mouse
rattan'; it has a glaucous pinnate leaf, with wedge-shaped premorse
leaflets and inflated thorny sheaths. At half-past six a.m. passed a
river on the left; it is named Chenaku. At this spot the river makes a
sudden turn to the north-east; its general direction has hitherto been
west. The calm clear beauty of this morning, as the sun rose, was
indescribable. We have now quite lost the rangas and padada; the
banks are chiefly fringed with *Paritium tiliaceum*, covered with its
magnificent yellow blossoms, which, however, are beautiful only in
the morning; a few hours' sun changes them to a dirty brick-red.
Mixed with this were a slender *Saccharum*, and two species of
Phyllanthus etc.; and all was matted together by a ternate-leaved
Cissus, with large black fruit like grapes, and a beautiful purple

Ipomoea. But the pride of all the vegetation here is the happily named *Lagerstroemia regina*: it is a magnificent tree, growing to a large size, and was now completely covered with lilac blossoms in spikes ten to 18 inches long, and in such abundance, that the woods were quite illuminated by it. Imagine *Lythrum salicaria* multiplied in size ten times, and grown to a large tree, it will give you some idea of this plant. Its wood is very valuable, being hard, tough, and almost indestructible; it is called here kamnuching, but elsewhere boongoor. We passed an enormous reed-bed; it seemed to be composed of two species of *Saccharum* and one *Arundo*; it was matted together by several Convolvulaceae and a cucurbitaceous plant like a *Luffa*. The long floating runners of the grasses, all fringed with trailing Confervae, shot far into the stream; and between the stems of the grass, in still places, where the current could not reach them, were little colonies of *Pistia stratiotes*, and a beautiful minute *Azolla*. Thousands of small black swallows, with chestnut-brown throats, were skimming about, or swinging in the wind, perched upon the feathery waving tops of the reeds; snow-white herons gravely stalking over the floating grass; and a flock of busy little finches clinging and searching about the dry panicles, made it a lively and beautiful scene. The river was a good deal swollen today, bringing down much drift; and the current was very strong, so that we made little progress.

About two o'clock reached the first settlement on the river, called Pulan Iumhaat. The clearings are not more than 200 to 300 yards wide, skirting the river for two or three miles; the stream is divided by an island, hardly above the now high water, but covered with padi, and the black species of *Coix*, called by the natives 'salli batu'; and here and there small patches of *Sorghum*; the whole interspersed with numerous anan-trees, *Saguerus saccharifer*. I stopped the boat near this place to get some curious pendulous birds' nests, of which there was a large colony on some low trees. The bird is a little finch or bunting; the nests are about two feet long, in shape like a Florence oil-flask; in the bottom is a hollow, as in an ordinary wine-bottle, across which is a little perch, on which the natives assure me the male bird roosts while the female sits on the eggs, which are deposited in hollows excavated in the upper part, which is at first built solid. The whole fabric is of fine grass, beautifully woven together, and is fastened very finely to the branch by a band of grass passing round it; it swings, however, quite freely in the wind. I got here some specimens of a curious black spiny *Neritina*, from the long floating runners of the reeds. We also got some unpleasant fellow-passengers, in the shape of a flight of large greenish-brown gad-flies, whose bite was very painful. A large Aroid leaf, probably a *Caladium*, was here very abundant and ornamental; I saw no flowers. About four o'clock stopped at a small house in a padi patch, at the mouth of a brook; the family consisted of an old man, two women, and several children, and certainly they were packed into the smallest possible room. There were two young men sitting in the house, whom, from their affectation of contempt, I knew at once to be Rajahs: they were, it appeared, the sons of a petty chief up the river, very oppressive and much disliked. There are many of these petty chiefs in the country, and they are a great curse to the people. They are not generally oppressed by their absolute rulers; their tribute is taken from them, it is true, in an irregular and irritating way, but they probably pay not half as large a proportion of taxes as we do in England; but every man who has a little royal blood in his veins, thinks he has also a right in some particular district also to collect the same tribute for his own use and benefit; and it not unfrequently happens, that the poor people, who dare not complain, pay two or three times over. The old man told us much of his grievances when his aristocratic visitors had taken leave. He then showed us his plantation: he had plenty of rice, ginger, turmeric, and remarkably large and fine capsicums; and he gave us some cucumbers, sugar-canes, and a kind of plantain called pissang nipa, from the closely packed fruit bearing a distant resemblance to that of the nipa: it was a good and sweet kind. They had here the largest domestic cats I have ever seen, of a dun colour, with light blue eyes, and very full in the cheeks, they all had the twisted tail of all the Malay cats.[2]

In 1859, the Dyaks were induced to rise against the ruling Sultan of Bandjermasin. Motley, his wife and three children, and other employees of the mining company were murdered during the uprising.[4]

Motley's name is commemorated in the generic name *Motleyia*, a monotypic genus of the Rubiaceae found in north-west Borneo, and in a number of specific epithets.

F. W. BURBIDGE *(1878)*

Son of a farmer, Frederick William Burbidge was born at Wymeswold, Leicestershire, England, in 1847. For a time Burbidge worked at the Horticultural Society's Garden at Chiswick, moving from there to Kew. At Kew he worked both in the garden and the herbarium. In 1877, having left Kew, he published a volume entitled *Cultivated Plants, their Propagation and Treatment*, and in the same year departed for Borneo and the Sulu Archipelago for a season of plant collecting.[1] Burbidge published an account of his trip in *The Gardens of the Sun*.[2] The following extracts from that work pertain to an ascent of Mt Kinabalu with nurseryman Peter Veitch, his employer.

Pitcher plants and rhododendrons

About seven o'clock next morning we started on our upward journey. It was hot work at first, but we could feel it perceptibly get cooler after the first 2,000 or 3,000 feet. At about 4,000 feet mosses are very plentiful, the finest species gathered being *Dawsonia superba*, which fringed the path, but nowhere in great plenty. A new white-flowered species of *Burmannia* was also gathered, and small-flowered orchids were seen. In one place a shower of small scarlet *Rhododendron* flowers covered the ground at our feet, the plant being epiphytal in the trees overhead. It was very misty, and the moss which covered every rotten stick, and the vegetation generally, was dripping with moisture, and every sapling we grasped in climbing upwards was the means of shaking a shower-bath on us from the trees above. At about 5,000 feet a dead and broken pitcher of *Nepenthes lowii* lying in the path led to the discovery of the plant itself scrambling among the mossy branches overhead, its singular flagon-shaped ascidia hanging from the point of every leaf. It is a vigorous-habited plant, with bright green leathery leaves, the petioles of which clasp the stem in a peculiar manner. The only plants we saw were epiphytal on mossy trunks and branches, and we searched for young plants diligently, but without success. All the pitchers hitherto seen are cauline ones, and as the plant has never yet been seen in a young state, it is an open question as to whether the radical

pitchers differ in shape or size, as is the case with most other species. As we ascended higher, epiphytal orchids, especially erias, dendrochilias, and coelogynes became more plentiful, and we came upon a large-flowered *Rhododendron*, bearing rich orange flowers two inches in diameter, and twenty flowers in a cluster! It grew on a dangerous declivity, and not one of our lazy men would venture to get it for us. Such a prize, however, was too lovely to forego, and after a wet scramble among the surrounding bushes, I secured it in good condition. Two or three other species were seen in flower, but none equal to it in its golden beauty. *Casuarina* trees became common, and higher up these were joined by two or three species of gleichenias, and a distinct form of *Dipteris*. *Phyllocladus* also appeared, and a glaucous-leaved *Dianella* (*D. javanica*). Here also were two of the most distinct of all rhododendrons, *R. ericifolium* and *R. stenophyllum*. On open spaces among rocks and sedges, the giant *Nepenthes rajah* began to appear, the plants being of all sizes, and in the most luxuriant health and beauty. The soil in which they grew was a stiff yellow loam, surfaced with sandstone-grit, and around the larger plants a good deal of rich humus and leaf debris had collected. The long red-pitchered *N. edwardsiana* was seen in

F. W. Burbidge. (Source: Gardeners' Chronicle 3rd series, vol. 6, 1889, p. 213. Reproduced with permission from the archives of the Royal Botanic Gardens, Melbourne)

two places. This plant, like *N. lowii*, is epiphytal in its perfect state, and is of a slender rambling habit. Highest of all in the great nepenthes zone came *N. villosa*, a beautiful plant, having rounded pitchers of the softest pink colour, with a crimson frilled orifice, similar to that of *N. edwardsiana*. All thoughts of fatigue and discomfort vanished as we gazed on these living wonders of the Bornean Andes! Here, on this cloud-girt mountain side, were vegetable treasures which Imperial Kew had longed for in vain. Discovered by Mr Low in 1851, dried specimens had been transmitted by him to Europe, and Dr (now Sir Joseph) Hooker had described and illustrated them in the *Transactions of the Linnaean Society*, but all attempts to introduce them alive into European gardens had failed. To see these plants in all their health and vigour was a sensation I shall never forget — one of those which we experience but rarely in a whole lifetime!

We reached the cave (altitude 9,000 feet) about three o'clock, wet and hungry, but far from unhappy. Our first care was to light a fire, which was not at all easy to do, since everything was dripping wet. We secured a bit of dry wood at last, however, and by whittling thin shavings from it with a knife, we managed to start a good fire, and some of the men were directed to cut fire-wood; but so paralysed were they by the wet and cold, that it was with the greatest difficulty that we could persuade them to do this. Poor old 'Musa' cut some wood and made a floor to the cave, after which some brushwood and leaves formed a substitute for a mattress. The next difficulty was to obtain water, since the men we had sent to search for it returned empty handed, having failed to find any. As a last resort I had to undertake this duty myself, and, descending the hillside, I found a tiny pool in a gully, from which I procured a little in our cook-pots. It was not near enough, however; and in wandering in search of more, I came upon a patch of the large *Nepenthes*, from the old pitchers of which I was able to augment my supply by carefully pouring off the rain water from a rather liberal under stratum of flies, ants, and other insect debris. Our guides slept under a rock a little further on and higher up the mountain side, and they found a stream from which good water was procured by our men in the morning and during our stay here.[2]

A cigar for comfort

It commenced to rain heavily at nightfall, and we found it very cold, although we kept a good fire burning nearly all night, one of the results being a draught towards an opening at the hinder part of the cave. The wet dripped from the roof all night, and the walls were also wet and slimy; indeed our quarters were neither extensive nor luxurious; still we made the best of them, and, after all, were rather sorry to leave them at last. We arose at daybreak to collect plants and roots, in the which we were tolerably successful; and before night we had secured all our collections in baskets and bundles ready for the men to carry down. It was very cool and misty in the morning, but about noon it became clearer, and it was hot indeed, the rocks and old trunks reeked in the sunshine. A slender-growing species of *Calamus* was very common in the low forest below the cave, and it supplied 'rattans' of excellent quality for tying up our plants. At least three showy species of *Coelogyne* grow on the rocks and mossy banks here, at 9,000 feet elevation; and a dainty little plant with reddish pseudo-bulbs in clusters, each bearing a single spathulate dark green leaf, is common. This last has erect spikes of pure white flowers and buds, reminding one of the lily-of-the-valley in cool, fresh purity, an effect partly due to its column being of a soft green tint, like a speck in the interior of the blossom. The coelogynes are very distinct and beautiful as seen here blooming among the coarse sedges and shrubs. One has white flowers with a blotch of gold on the lip, eight or ten of its waxy flowers being borne on an erect scape. Another has yellow sepals and petals, and a white lip corrugated with brown warts. Another, not so showy, has a nodding spike of white and brown flowers.

We ascended about 9,000 feet, and were delighted with the charming views obtainable during clear weather. The whole upper portion of the mountain along the south and south-eastern slopes is nearly devoid of vegetation, except where there are streams and rather sheltered gullies up which the stunted trees and a few other plants struggle up near to the summit. On the north-western side the rocks rise very precipitous; and here vegetation fails to gain foothold. Looking upwards in the early sunlight, we had clears views of the shelving granite slopes, on which are numerous shallow channels down which streams of water pour during misty and rainy weather. When we gained the top of the great spur the morning after our arrival at the cave, we were delighted at the immense panorama which lay at our feet as we looked back. Looking away south-west we beheld the coastline from the mouth of what our guides said was the Tampassuk River right down to Gaya Bay and Pulo Tiga, which was distinctly visible, the many-mouthed Menkabong River glistening like a silver net quite close to the coastline.

Looking south-east over a billowy sea of silvery clouds we saw a gigantic range of mountains, and from this the conical peak of Tilong rises through strata after strata of cloud, or stands out on a clear blue background of pure sky, according to the state of the atmosphere. This claims our interest as the beacon of a land unknown; and this magnificent peak, Tilong, is by repute as high, or even higher, than Kina Balu [sic] itself. Altogether we spent three days on the side of Kina Balu collecting plants, flowers, and seeds; and after a life on the plains and among the coast mountains — hills compared with this grisly giant — we found the climate most deliciously cool and invigorating. Rain generally commenced about 3 p.m., and continued until eight, the remainder of the night being clear, bright if moonlight, and cool — so cool, indeed, as to make a good camp fire and woollen shirts two or threefold and blankets very desirable. The mornings were generally misty, every leaf and branch dripping with the rain and heavy dews common here at night, especially during the wet season. About noon the sun was warm, and the temperature at 9,000 feet rises to 75° [Fahrenheit] if the day is fine and dry.

As I have elsewhere said, our Malay followers suffered much from what to them was bitter cold; indeed they seemed perfectly helpless, with scarcely energy to make a fire and cook their food. They have no notion of actively bestirring themselves in order to keep warm. Our food supply, too, — that is, the rice — ran short, and so the men were reduced to live on kaladi and sweet potatoes roasted in the embers and eaten with a little salt. Our Dusan guides also complained of the cold, and tried to hurry us in our descent; indeed at last they would wait no longer, and they slipped away, leaving us to reach their village alone as best we could. We were fully determined not to be defeated in our object, however, and keeping ahead of our own men we descended leisurely so as to gather plants by the way, until all had as much as they could possibly carry down. I carried my servant's load in order that he might carry a lot of rare specimens which I had secured for him in a handkerchief. The descent after the rain of the night before was difficult and dangerous, and we had a good many falls. Once I fell down a steep place a depth of about 20 feet, among shrubs and creepers, which saved me from serious injury. Mr Veitch and myself, my 'boy', and a solitary Labuan man, went on ahead of our main party, and just at nightfall discovered that we had lost our way. The right path lay across a clearing down which we turned instead of pushing across and striking the path beyond.

We floundered along in the gloaming down several dangerous steeps and across a rocky stream, in crossing which I stepped incautiously on a slippery water-worn boulder, and became thoroughly submerged in the water, which being from the heights above is icy cold, at least it seems so after one had been used to the heat of the tropics. This increased my discomfort, and poor Mr Veitch was but little better. Here we were at dark lost and benighted beside the rocky declivities of this mountain stream; but there was no help for it; and after vainly trying to strike a path, we gave up at the base of a large tree, and putting down our burdens, we resolved to pass the night here. To mend matters, it commenced to rain heavily about seven o'clock, and I am afraid we were not so happy as the mere possession of health and strength ought to have made us. We had no food except a couple of wet biscuits and about a half a glass of brandy in a flask. These we shared, and perhaps they were sweeter than the choicest viands would have tasted had we been in dress clothes and in comfortable quarters. Then Mr Veitch had a great find in his bag — a couple of cigars and a box of matches. Sitting in the smoking-room of a comfortable club, or in the billiard-room at home, one may smile at such a discovery; but, situated as we were, cold and wet, a cigar added much to our comfort.[2]

Burbidge's account of his time in Borneo and Sulu contained a chapter on tropical fruit, including a splendid description of the durian.

The regal durian, a universal favourite?

The regal durian (*Durio zibethinus*), like the finest of nectarines or melting pears, must be eaten fresh and just at one particular point of ripeness, and then it is, as many think, a fruit fit for a king. So highly is this vegetable-custard valued that as much as a dollar each is not infrequently paid for fine specimens of the first fruits of the durian crop brought into the Eastern markets. It is a universal favourite both with Malays and Chinese, but the opinions of Europeans vary as to the merits of this 'delectable epitome of all that is perfect in fruit food'. It is a paradox, 'the best of fruits with the worst of characters', and, as the Malays say, you may enjoy the durian, but you should never speak of it outside your own dwelling. Its odour — one scarcely feels justified in using the word 'perfume' — is so potent, so vague, but withal so insinuating, that it can scarcely be tolerated inside the house. Indeed Nature here seems to have gone a little aside to disgust us with a fruit which is perhaps of all others the most fascinating to the palate, when once one has 'broken the ice', as represented by the foul odour at first presented to that most critical of all organs of sense, the nose. As a matter of course, it is never brought to table in the usual way, and yet the chances are that whoever is lucky enough to taste a good fruit of it to begin with, soon develops into a surreptitious durian eater; just as a jungle tiger becomes a 'man-eater' after its first taste of human blood.

There is scarcely any limit to durian eating if you once begin it; it grows on one like opium smoking, or other acquired tastes; but on the other hand, the very suggestion of eating such an 'unchaste fruit' is to many as intolerable as the thoughts alone of supping off cheese and spring onions, washed down with 'stout and mild', followed by a whiff from a short 'dudeen' by way of dessert, and yet, while these incongruities are consumed at home with enjoyment, one must not be too hard on those abroad who relish the fragrant durian. About the middle or end of July durian fruit are very common in Singapore, and their spiny skins lie about the streets in all directions. As you pass along you become aware of a peculiar odour all around you — an odour like that of a putrid sewer when half suppressed by holding a perfumed handkerchief to the nose — a blending of a good deal that is nasty with a *soupcon* of something rather sweet and nice. On opening a fruit for yourself, however, you find that the perfume, like that of the musk plant, ceases to be evident after you have once had a fair whiff at it at close quarters. The flavour of the straw-coloured, custard-like pulp which surrounds the four or five rows of large chestnut-like seeds is perfectly unique: to taste it, as Wallace tells us, is 'a new sensation, worth a journey to the East to experience'; but much depends on a good fruit being obtained when perfectly, not over ripe. You then find the pulp sweet, rich, and satisfying; it is indeed a new sensation, but no two persons can agree as to the flavour — no two descriptions of it are alike. Its subtle action upon the palate — and perhaps this best explains the unceasing popularity it enjoys — is like music of a well-played violin on the ear, rich, soothing, sweet, piquant. The flavour of durian is satisfying, but it never cloys; the richness seems counteracted by a delicate acidity, the want of grape-like juiciness is supplied by the moist creamy softness of the pulp as it melts away ice-like on your tongue.

It is said that the best of whisky is that made by blending several good kinds together, and Nature seems to have blended four or five good flavours together when she made the durian. 'A *macedoine* of

Peint d'après nature par M.me Berthe Hoola van Nooten.à Batavia.

Chromolith par G. Severeyns Lith de l'Acad Roy de Belgique

DURIO ZIBETHINUS. L.

Emile Tarlier éditeur.à Bruxelles.

fruits', says a modern author, 'when well made and judiciously flavoured, is a delicious sweetmeat. The grape, the peach, the apricot, and the pine, meet in welcome harmony; the pear, the apple, and the cherry, and their friendly companionship, and all these opposing elements of flavour are blended with a soft and soothing syrup.' In a word, the durian is a natural *macedoine* — one of Dame Nature's 'made dishes' — and if it be possible for you to imagine the flavour of a combination of corn flour and rotten cheese, nectarines, crushed filberts, a dash of pineapple, a spoonful of old dry sherry, thick cream, apricot-pulp, and a *soupcon* of garlic, all reduced to the consistency of a rich custard, you have a glimmering idea of the durian, but, as before pointed out, the odour is almost unmentionable — perfectly indescribable, except it be as 'the fruit with the fragrant stink!'

The fruit itself is in size as large as a Cadiz melon, and the leathery skin is protected by sharp broad-based spines very similar to those of a horse chestnut. The name durian, in fact, is derived from these — the word *duri* in Malay meaning a 'spine' or 'thorn'. There are many varieties in the Bornean woods, some but little larger than horse chestnut fruits, and having only two seeds; others larger, but with stiff orange-red pulp, not at all nice to eat, however hungry you may be; and even the large kinds, with creamy pulp and many seeds, vary very much in flavour. The trees are monarchs of the forest, as a rule varying from 70 to 150 feet, or even more, in height, with tall straight boles and spreading tops, and the foliage is oblong-acuminate, dark green above, paler and covered with rufous stellate hairs or scales below. The fruits of the finer varieties fall when ripe, and accidents sometimes happen.

I saw a native who had the flesh torn from his shoulder by a blow from one of these armed fruits, and saw several narrow escapes, but personally I gave the trees a wide berth at fruiting time. Some varieties, especially the 'durianburong', or wild-bird durians, do not shed the fruits, which hang on the branches until the valves open, when the seeds fall to the ground, or are eaten by hornbills and other large fruit-eating birds and monkeys. I saw some magnificent specimens of durian trees in the Bornean forests north of the capital, and also in other Malayan islands, where the forests had been cleared for cultivation, and the trees left standing for the sake of their produce. Their clusters of large white flowers are produced about April, and form a great attraction to an enormous species of semi-diurnal bat, a kind which is said to be one of the greatest pests of Eastern fruit-groves.[2]

The Wallace referred to above was Alfred Russel Wallace (1823–1913), co-founder with Charles Darwin of the theory of evolution by natural selection. Burbidge's quote was from Wallace's book entitled *The Malay Archipelago*, which was an account of his travels and the natural history in that region of the world. It was during these travels that he formulated his ideas on evolution and also noted the divide within the archipelago between the Australasian and Asian faunal groups, this divide now commonly being known as 'Wallace's Line'.

In 1879, Burbidge was appointed Curator of the Trinity College Botanic Garden in Dublin, Ireland, a post he retained until his death in 1905.

H. O. FORBES *(1878–1883)*

Scotsman Henry Ogg Forbes (1851–1932), educated at Aberdeen and Edinburgh universities, worked in Portugal as a scientific collector from 1875 to 1877, and between 1878 and 1887 made important natural history collections, including many plants, in the Dutch East Indies and New Guinea.[1] The following extracts are from *A Naturalist's Wanderings in the Eastern Archipelago*.

Every man a naturalist

As soon as I was able to follow their discourse with ease, my daily talks with these men [at Genteng, Java] were a source of great pleasure to me. I soon found out that in regard to everything around them, they were marvellously observant and intelligent. Not one or two only, but every individual amongst them seemed equally stored with natural history information. There was not a single tree or plant or minute shrub, but they had a name for, and could tell the full history of; and not a note in the forest but they knew from what throat it proceeded. Every animal had a designation, not a mere meaningless designation, but a truly binomial appellation as fixed and distinctive as in our own system, differing only in the fact that theirs was in their own and not in a foreign language. Often enough this designation has so close a resemblance and sound to Latin, that it has been accepted by Western naturalists as if it had been so. One of the liveliest and most obtrusive of the squirrels in Java and Sumatra is a little red-furred creature called by the natives *tupai*, and to distinguish it from its more arboreal congeners they add, from its habit of frequenting branches near the ground, the word *tana* (for earth); and *Tupaia tana* is its accepted scientific term among European naturalists.

They have unconsciously classified the various allied groups into large comprehensive genera, in a way that shows an accuracy of observation that is astonishing from this dull-looking race. In this respect they excel far and away the rural population of our own country, among whom without exaggeration scarcely one man in a hundred is able to name one tree from another, or describe the colour of its flower or fruit, far less name a tree from a portion indiscriminately shown him.[2]

Ant plants in Java

The 14th of June [1879] is to me memorable as being the day on which for the first time I saw in its native habitat, and gathered there, that most singular of the vegetable productions of the Indian Archipelago, the *Myrmecodia tuberosa* and *Hydnophytum formicarum*. Their most striking characteristic will be indelibly marked in my remembrance by the sensations other than mental, by which their acquaintance was made.

In tearing down a galaxy of epiphytic orchids from an erythrina tree, I was totally overrun, during the short momentary contact of my hand with the bunch, with myriads of a minute species of ant (*Pheidole javana*), whose every bite was a sting of fire. Beating a precipitous retreat from the spot, I stripped with the haste of desperation, but, like pepper-dust over me, they were writhing and twisting their envenomed jaws in my skin, each little abdomen spitefully quivering with every thrust it made. Going back, when once I had rid myself of my tormentors, to secure the specimens I had gathered, I discovered in the centre of the bunch a singular plant I had never seen before, which I perceived to be the central attraction of the ants. It was called *Kitang-kurak* by my boy, who said it was the home of the ants. I was over-joyed with the revelation that a slice struck off by my knife, made an intricate honeycombed structure swarming with minute ants — a living formicarium.

In the space of a short search I found, generally high on the trees, abundance of specimens of both genera, which, not without several futile attempts and many imprecations and groanings on the part of my boys, were brought to the ground; and, at the ends of a pole over their shoulders, up which the infuriated dwellers would ascend to spread over their bare bodies to their frequent discomfiture, they were at last safely deposited in a spot in Mr Lash's garden, where I could examine them with comfort without disturbing their inhabitants.

The accompanying representation ... represents the general appearance of the epiphyte: a spine-covered bulb surmounted by a cylindrical axis bearing leaves and minute flowers, while the longitudinal section ... shows the complicated system of galleries — some of them papillated — inhabited by ants.[2]

Myrmecodia and *Hydnophytum* are just two of a number of genera of tuberous epiphytes of the family Rubiaceae which have a symbiotic relationship with ants. Ants, in return for a home, deter leaf-eaters — and all but the most zealous collectors — and through the debris they leave in the chambered tubers supply the plants with macronutrients.[3]

Destruction of the forests

As in Java the original forest [in Sumatra] is rapidly disappearing; each year sees immense tracts felled for rice-fields, more than is actually necessary, and also much wanton destruction by wilful fires. Trees of the rarest and finest timbers are hewed, half burned, and then left to rot; amid their prostrate trunks a couple of harvests are reaped, then the ground is deserted, and soon fills up with the fast-growing and worthless woods, or falls a prey to the ineradicable alang-alang grass. Our children's children will search in vain in their travels for the old forest trees of which they have read in the books of their grandfathers; and to make their acquaintance, they will have to content themselves with what they can glean from the treasured specimens in various herbaria, which will then be the only remains of the extinct vegetable races.

In every clearing, trees, from their gigantic size, have here and there escaped the axe, and been allowed to stand unmolested. One cannot resist a feeling of pity for the solitude of these towering monarchs, whose grandeur, concealed as they stood amid the multitude of their peers, can now be seen in all their stateliness. They look the very picture of strength and immobility; yet, though they have withstood, in the company of their fellows, the storm and sun of centuries, they survive their solitude but a very few seasons, getting feebler year by year, one great limb after another dying and dropping off, till all life ceases, when some lightning flash or sudden blast measures their noble stems on the ground.[2]

Fatal attack by a tiger

In resuming my journey towards the Kaba I had to give up my late delicious mode of travel, and change the river for the road. Reaching the village of Tandjong-Ning, I found that much tree-felling was going on in the forests pertaining to it; and, hoping to enrich my herbarium, I set up my camp for a while in its Balai, a structure that might have held an army. But the village was very unsavoury, as every sort of filth and refuse from the houses was allowed to drop through the floor to the ground below. I found that my fame had reached before me, and that not particularly favourably. For some time tigers had been prowling about in the district in great numbers, and, as the Dempo is called the 'Barracks of the Tigers', they had been scared from their natural home by a potent spell which I must have set up there when I ascended it. It was no use to deny the imputation — 'it was well known!'

Where the felling was going on in the forest, I obtained many fine specimens, and nowhere do I recollect to have seen such enormous trees. Thickly scattered about on the ground as they were, over an area of perhaps a mile square, I failed to realise the gigantic proportions of their prostrate trunks till I began to move about and travel along them. A human figure was lost among them. Standing by these trunks, my head often did not reach much more than to half the height of some of them, while their length of bare stem measured as much as forty or fifty yards before giving off a branch.

One afternoon, as I was returning from this forest with my men who had been felling trees, walking in line one behind the other as is their custom, a tiger suddenly slipped from the jungle bordering the road, and in a moment struck down a youth a few yards before me. I dared not fire for fear of striking the youth, but his father, who was walking just in front of him armed with a spear, dashed on it and gave it a right willing thrust, which, with the threatening group, made it quit its hold, when it sprang into the thick jungle. It was all the work of a moment; the stroke of its paw did not seem to be tremendous, but the claws of the brute had penetrated so deeply into the chest and shoulder of the youth that he survived scarcely a quarter of an hour after being carried into the village. Early next morning I was aroused by a great commotion, a loud screaming and scampering of feet, amid which I heard the word 'matjan' (tiger). Jumping up, I slid a cartridge into my Martini-Henry, and rushed out, to find every man brandishing a long spear in the one hand and a kriss in the other, all looking very scared. The tiger of the previous day had come after his unburied quarry, as they firmly believed and asserted against my doubts that he would, and had actually ventured into the middle of the village, and within thirty feet of my door which stood next to the house containing the dead body. The clamour had frightened it off into the impenetrable jungle which closely hedged round the village, whither I could follow it only a very short way.

As we re-entered the village the body of the youth was being brought out for burial amid terrible wailings of the women. It was sewed into a thick grass mat, on the top of which were spread flowers of the cocoa and pinang palms, and over which, as it was borne away, handfuls of yellowed rice were thrown. The villagers fell in behind the body, each man with a spear over his shoulder, their tips glittering in the sun like a regiment of bayonets, for fear of another sudden attack. The grave was made deeper than usual, and well protected on the top, as they affirmed that the tiger would certainly try to scrape up the body. The lamentations of the women, which were terrible to hear as the body was taken away, continued till the return of the people from the funeral, and then entirely ceased. It is difficult to learn whether these were really bitter mournings, or merely the following of their custom. The event, however, cast a visible gloom over the village, and I felt relieved when it returned to its more ordinary ways. For several nights after the funeral the father of the youth, sitting by himself alone in his house, chanted from sundown till daybreak what they call the *Tjerita bari*, or death dirge, a most plaintive lament; and to me it seemed the most saddening, woe-laden wail I had ever heard, rising and falling on the silent night like a wintry wind.

As expected, the tiger attempted to scrape up the body the night after its burial. Next night and for several others I watched the grave, but the tiger did not keep tryst with me; but when I was not there it never failed to come. I therefore assisted them to construct a snare to catch it on its first return. A fence was made at all such places as there was a possibility of approach to the grave, leaving on the cleared road a very conspicuous open gate, across which a thin cord was loosely drawn, connected with a green bamboo some thirty feet long bent by the strength of several men into a bow, at whose extremity a sharp spear was so arranged as to be shot athwart the entrance-gate, on the release of the bamboo by the tiger pressing with his breast on the twig-like cord in his way. Every night the trap was re-set for six days, without the tiger's appearance. The seventh it was left unset as apparently useless; next morning it was found that the tiger had been within the enclosure, and I saw it faithfully set in the evening. The following morning I was awakened by a great

chattering outside the Balai, and, starting up to learn the cause of
the uproar, I was informed that the trap had shot in the night, and
the spear had been broken off, but the tiger had not been found. I
was soon among the eager crowd, who had armed to beat the
woods. It was evident from the blood on the spear-shaft that it was
sorely wounded, and could not be far off. We had little need,
however, of gun or spear, for some thirty yards in the forest we
found the warm body of the feline. Transfixed from side to side, it
had cleared the high fence with one gigantic bound, and fallen dead
where it lay. As soon as it was known that the body had been found,
every man, woman and child hastened out of the village to see the
carcase of their enemy, every individual, save the youngest children,
bringing with him a knife or kriss. It was only with the very utmost
difficulty that I could, by standing on the body and uttering the
direst threats, prevent each of these blades from being thrust into the
skin, which I wished to preserve. With what savage delight and
revenge they did gloat over the carcase, and run their weapons into
its body when they could! What blood there was about was all used
up in dipping them in to insure bravery; and all passed their krisses
broadside over and over the body to absorb the potent emanation
from this personification of power and boldness. When the body
was being skinned the relatives of many of those who had perished
by tigers came and begged for a piece of the heart or brain, that they
might revenge themselves by eating it — especially one old woman
who had thus lost first her only son, and later had had her husband
carried off before her eyes.[2]

Drying specimens in Timor-laut (Yamdena)

The herbarium on which our present knowledge of the flora is based
is very small; my own would have been much larger but for an
unfortunate fire in the drying-house in which it was being prepared,
which consumed the greater portion of my botanical collection — a
heart-breaking episode which I give in my companion's [wife's]
words: —

> 'This afternoon, when quite alone, [Henry] and the hunters
> having gone to the opposite shore for the day, and Kobes to
> the well a mile off, while I was sitting in that miserable, restless
> condition which succeeds a fever attack, a longing seized me
> to look out of the door, for I had for many days been unable
> to leave my sleeping apartment. Fortunate impulse! Kobes had
> piled half a dozen great logs on the fire of the drying-house

(an erection like our dwelling, and all the Tenimber tenements, of bamboo and atap thatch, now, at the close of the dry season, very inflammable) and left them to the whims of a strong breeze, which, at the moment I looked, had just fanned the fire into fierce flames. I sped into the village for help, but met the Postholder with his men running towards me, attracted by the rushing noise of the flames. Without a moment's delay some of them cut great palm branches to interpose between the burning house and the overhanging eaves of our dwelling, others tore apart the framework, scattered the bundles of plants, and beat the flames with green branches, while the Tenimber natives poured on water which they carried in gourds and bamboos from the sea close by. With what breathless anxiety I watched the effect of each gust of wind, for the thatch of our house — in which were stored tins of petroleum and of spirits of wine, and a quantity of gun-powder — was already scorched. Had it caught, nothing could have saved the whole village, nor us from the vengeance of the people. At last the flames were got under [control], and I had time to realise that the few charred and sodden bundles before me was [*sic*] all that remained of more than 500 of the first gathered specimens of the flora of Tenimber collected at such risk and pains. I could not bear to stand on the shore, as usual, to welcome the home-coming boat, but long ere it touched [shore], the ruined drying-house had told them the disheartening news of the disaster that had happened.'[2]

G. FORREST *(1905, c. 1931)*

Born at Falkirk, Scotland, in 1873, George Forrest was schooled in Kilmarnock Academy and from there went to work for a chemist. In the pursuit of a career as an apothecary, he roamed the Scottish hillsides collecting plants. After the receipt of a small legacy, he travelled to Australia and South Africa before returning to Scotland in 1902. For a time he secured work at the herbarium of the Royal Botanic Garden, Edinburgh, but he soon had the opportunity to travel and collect plants in China, his various trips sponsored by individuals or syndicates.[1,2] The following incident occurred in 1905, not 1895 — as stated in the article. Lamaism is a form of Buddhism found in central Asia, the priests or monks being called lamas and their places of residence and worship lamaseries.

Hunted by the lamas

Few realise the great hardships and dangers which have to be faced in order to secure new plants for cultivation in Europe. In the warmer regions there is danger from miasma, fever, animals and snakes. Not infrequently too, the collector has to seek his specimens among savage or semi-civilised peoples, who, in most instances, strongly resent his intrusion into their midst; thus seldom a year passes without toll being exacted in one way or another.

I will describe an incident I experienced whilst plant-collecting in Western China. In the NW corner of the Chinese province of Yunnan, where China, India and Tibet meet, and by the banks of the great Mekong River, at an elevation of 5,000 feet, was the French Catholic mission station of Tzekou. It is a country of mighty rivers; there, in a single degree of longitude, are four of the mightiest in the world, the Yangtze or River of Golden Sand, the Mekong, the Salwin and the Irrawaddy; and of vast mountain ranges which tower up between the parallel rivers to far above the limit of eternal snow, which, at that latitude (28° N) is about 17,000 feet. The narrow valleys, broken by cross ridges and great spurs, are cut off from each other by difficult and dangerous passes, closed for half the year by snow. The great rivers, which flow through funnel-like gorges, are quite unnavigable; the upper Mekong can only be crossed by bridges consisting of a single rope composed of split bamboos, across which passengers are slung, trussed up with leather thongs like chickens ready for the spit. Numerous tribes, nearly all of Tibetan origin, have settled and built their huts among the valleys and ridges. The diversity of customs, languages and religions in this little-known corner of the world is truly remarkable; like the slopes of the Caucasus, it might be called the country of the hundred nations. Here and there in the folds of the mountains the lamas of the yellow sect have established huge *gombas*, or lamaseries, and, by a combination of force and fraud, have become the real masters of the country; they terrorise the poverty stricken and superstitious peasantry, and pay little or no regard to the nominal sovereignty of the Celestial mandarins.

In the summer of 1895 [*sic*], I found myself collecting in these mountains, my headquarters being with the hospitable and venerable chief of the Tzekou mission, Père Dubernard. He first settled at Tzekou when Napoleon III was at the height of his power, and he had never left the country since. The region was unsettled, the Lama world around had been disturbed by the British invasion of Lhassa in 1904, and still more rudely shocked by the attempt of the Chinese to establish themselves at Batang, a small town on the great road from Szechuan to Lhassa. These circumstances led to a rebellion of the Batang lamas, and the murder, with all his followers, of a high Chinese official at Batang in March of that year. At the same time, the French missionaries stationed there, with all their converts, were killed, and the mission stations destroyed.

The trouble was not long in spreading south to Atuntze, a small Chinese-Tibetan trading station, situated on a terrace high above the left or east bank of the Mekong, and only two and a half days' journey from Tzekou, which nestled under the cliffs close to the right bank of the Mekong, in latitude 28° N. Chinese officials and troops were sent to Atuntze in April to restore order, but it is needless to add they only made confusion worse confounded, and in a few days they were completely hemmed in. Rumours and counter-rumours poured into the mission at Tzekou day by day, adding to the difficulty of our situation, and the terror of the native Christians. It soon became clear that the lamas meant business and were determined to pay off old scores of jealousy against the missionaries, who had endeavoured for so many years, not without success, to deliver the people from the moral and material chains of Lamaism.

Even our friends among the Tibetans fell away from us or proved false. The mission house was indefensible, and, if defensible, we had no one to defend it save two aged French priests and myself. Therefore, when on the evening of July 19 the news came that the towns of Atuntze had fallen, that the Chinese troops had been wiped out almost to a man, and that the lamaseries were all up and concentrating their forces to attack Tzekou, immediate flight became necessary.

The rising moon that night saw us making our way back by a narrow and dangerous track along the right bank of the Mekong, the two Fathers on their mules and myself and the little band of native Christians on foot; on our left roared the Mekong in furious flood, on our right rose the great Mekong-Salwin dividing range. We hoped to reach the village of Yetche, 30 miles to the south on the left bank of the river, where there was a friendly chief and some Chinese troops; but, unfortunately, as in the dark we passed the lamaserie of Patong, owing to a noise made by some of our party, we were detected, and a shrill signal whistle was sent across the river to warn the countryside of our escape. Early next morning, at the next village, we were told that the enemy, by executing a forced march, had crossed the river to the south, and had raised the people therein, thus cutting off our retreat. The local headman, a drunken and treacherous rascal, found many excuses to delay our flight, and thus we lost more valuable time. Eventually we got away from him, and proceeding early in the afternoon we reached a height to the south of the village. From this point we had a clear and extensive view looking to the north, and saw a great column of smoke rising in the still morning air over the site of Tzekou. Then the last hope of escape left us and we knew the enemy was hot on our track. Descending from the height into the next cross valley, I was for pushing on as long as we had the strength left to do so, hoping that we might be able to break through to the south before the enemy had time to form a complete cordon around us. However, after the sight of the destruction of their home, the last vestige of spirit seemed to leave my two companions; they became utterly despondent and began to make preparations for the worst, insisting on making a stop by the side of the stream in the valley for the double purpose of holding a meeting with our followers, and taking some food.

So dangerous was the situation that, whilst my companions were engaged at their devotions, I left them and ascended a small auxiliary spur to reconnoitre. To the north I had a clear view of the crest of the ridge we had descended, and had not long to wait ere my expectations were realised. Suddenly there appeared a large number of armed men running at full speed in Indian file along the path we had just traversed. I gave the alarm at once and immediately all was confusion, our followers scattering in all directions. Père Bourdonnec became completely panic stricken, made his way across the stream, by a fallen tree, and, despite my attempts to stop him, rushed blindly through the dense forest which clothed the southern face of the valley. However, escape in that direction I was sure would be impossible, as our delay had given the enemy time to mature their plans and close in on us; the Père had not covered 200 yards ere he was riddled with poisoned arrows and fell, the Tibetans immediately rushing up and finishing him off with their huge double-handed swords. Our little band, numbering about 80, were picked off one by one, or captured, only 14 escaping. Ten women, wives and daughters of some of the followers, committed suicide by throwing themselves into the stream, to escape the slavery and worse, which they knew awaited them if captured. Of my own 17 collectors and servants only one escaped.

The valley in which we were surrounded was a rift in the hills some four miles long by one and a half broad, closed to the east by the Mekong, and to the west by the dividing range, while to the north and south were high ridges occupied by the enemy, and thickly clothed with pine and mixed forests. When I saw all was lost I fled east down a breakneck path, in places formed along the faces of beetling cliffs by rude brackets of wood and slippery logs. On I went down towards the main river, only to find myself, at one of the sharpest turns, suddenly confronted by a band of hostile and well-armed Tibetans, who had been stationed there to block the passage. They were distant about 100 yards, and sighting me at once gave chase. For a fraction of time I hesitated; being armed with a Winchester repeating rifle, 12 shots, a heavy revolver and two belts of cartridges, I could easily have made a stand, but I feared being unable to clear a passage before those whom I knew to be behind me arrived on the scene. Therefore I turned back, and after a desperate run, succeeded in covering my tracks by leaping off the path whenever I rounded the corner. I fell into dense jungle, through which I rolled down a steep slope for a distance of 200 feet before stopping, tearing my clothes to ribbons, and bruising myself most horribly in the process. I then got behind a convenient boulder and made every preparation for a stand should they succeed in discovering my ruse, which I never doubted but they would. Fortunately, however, they did not find me, and, presuming I had continued my course up the valley, rushed past my hiding place. There I lay till night fell, when I attempted to escape south but, after toiling up 3,000 feet of rock, and through forest and jungle, I found a cordon of lamas, with watch-fire and Tibetan mastiffs, which precluded all hopes of escape in that direction, and, as daylight approached, I had to return to my hiding place by the stream. The following eight days and nights were hopeless repetitions of the first; the days were spent in hiding in the most convenient spot I could find at dawn, the nights in trying to elude the watchfulness of my enemies and get away south. For that time, a period of nine days, all the food I had consisted of two dozen ears of wheat and a handful of parched peas, which I providentially found where they had been dropped by a fugitive or some of the lamas. During some of these days I was kept continually on the move, tracked and hunted like a wild beast by the lamas and their Tibetan adherents, who thirsted for my blood. On the second day I was forced to discard my boots to avoid leaving distinctive trails, burying them in the bed of the stream; another day I had to wade waist deep for a full mile upstream to evade a party who were close on my heels; once a few of them came on me suddenly and I was shot at, two of the poisoned arrows passing through my hat; another time my hiding place was discovered by a Tibetan woman, one of many who had been sent out to track me down. Once as I lay asleep under a log in the bed of a stream, exhausted by my night's fruitless journey up the mountain side, I was awakened by the sound of voices, and a party of 30 lamas in full war paint crossed the stream a few yards above me. Armed as I was I could have shot down most of them, but, though enraged as I was at the time, I held myself in check, as I knew that to fire but one shot would be to bring a hornet's nest about me. My only chance was to keep still.

At the end of eight days I had ceased to care whether I lived or died — my feet swollen out of all shape, my hands and face torn with thorns, and my whole person caked with mire. I was nearly dead through hunger and fatigue, and on the evening of the eighth day and morning of the ninth was quite delirious for a time. Then I knew the end was near, and determined to make one more bid for life. In the valley there happened to be two small villages of four to six huts each, peopled by Lissoos, a sub-tribe of Tibetans, and I decided on holding up one of these, to force the inhabitants to give me food. This plan I carried out on the evening of the ninth day. Fortunately, instead of opposing me, the people proved friendly. The one and only food of these people consists of parched barley, or wheat coarsely ground; it is called 'tsaniba'. This they offered me, and having but little self-control, after such a long starve, I partook it ravenously, in fact to such an extent that I almost died of the effects. As it was, to add to my trials, I brought on inflammation of the stomach, from which I suffered for many months. The headman of the village proved one of the best friends I ever had, and at once commenced making arrangements to smuggle me out of the country. After four days spent in restful hiding, we descended the valley until we reached its junction with that of the Mekong. Here we were met by the headman of a village situated there, and he informed us that though the majority of the rebels had returned north, there were still many powerful bands scouring the countryside in search of me; in fact, one had spent the previous night in his village. He suggested we should go into hiding until after sunset, when he would send out some of the native hunters to escort us to a farmhouse a few miles distant, where we could spend the night in peace; then, on the following day, with guides he would send to me, I was to ascend west to almost the summit of the dividing range, and striking south we should skirt the troubled region and thus reach safety. This plan we eventually carried out, but the misery of all is entirely beyond my powers of description. It was the middle of the rainy or summer season, and I soon found myself in the thick of the worst downpour Yunnan had known for a generation. Up and up we climbed, struggling through cane-brakes, cutting our way through miles of rhododendrons, tramping over alps literally clothed with primulas, gentians, saxifrages, lilies etc., for these unknown hillsides are a veritable botanist's paradise, till we reached the snow-fields on the backbone of the range, at an elevation of from 17,000 to 18,000 feet. We had no covering at night; no food but a few mouthfuls of parched barley, and the rain and sleet fell in such deluges that to light a fire was impossible. On reaching the summit we turned south, travelling in that direction for six days, over glaciers, snow and ice, and tip-tilted, jagged, limestone strata, which tore my feet to ribbons. On reaching this point, we hoped we had got beyond the danger zone, and commenced our descent eastwards towards the Mekong. Down, down we went, over sharp, jagged rocks and through bamboo brakes, until we reached the inhabited zone at about 9,000 feet, and here, to put the finishing touch to my misery, I seriously hurt one of my feet. Round most of the villages, the inhabitants are in the habit of placing

on the paths around their maize fields what they name 'panji'.
These are sharpened and fire-hardened pieces of bamboo of
12 to 18 inches in length; they are buried in the ground fully
three-quarters of the full length, the sharpened end being upwards,
and covered loosely with soil or leaves. In approaching one of the
villages by an exceptionally muddy path, I unfortunately stepped on
one of these 'panji'. Had I been in a normal condition of health, I
might possibly have had strength enough to have thrown myself
back in time, but I was so weakened by the experiences I had passed
through and by the exposure, that I simply fell forward on it; the
spike, fully an inch in breadth, passing between the bones of my foot
and protruding a couple of inches from the upper surface. I suffered
excruciating agony for many days, and it was months before the
wound healed completely.

Finally, we arrived on the right bank of the Mekong opposite the
large village of Yetche. The chief of this village was a friend of mine.
My troubles then were almost over. This excellent man came across
the river, at great risk to himself, bringing clean cotton cloths for me,
beside a large quantity of food, such as pork, eggs, chicken and
cakes, and at last I got what I required even more than those, a
change of clothing, a good wash and a night's rest.

As bands of lamas were still prowling about near Yetche,
disguised as a Tibetan and accompanied by my faithful guides and
others, I continued my course down the right bank of the river, till
four days later, I arrived opposite the little Chinese-Tibetan township
of Hsias Wei Hsi, where Chinese troops were stationed. After much
delay, everyone, even there, being panic-stricken, I managed to get
some of the people to come down and assist me over the single rope
crossing the river at that point, and on reaching the town found
another missionary (Père Monbeig) who had also escaped from a
station in the west. He and the Chinese officials welcomed me as one
returned from the dead, and a few days later, he and I, accompanied
by an armed escort of 200 Chinese soldiers, commenced our journey
south to the nearest city — Talifu — which we reached in safety in
the course of 19 days.

Later, I received from the military mandarin, named Li, a detailed
account of the death of my two companions. As I mentioned, I saw
Père Bourdonnec shot down; later the body was disembowelled,
beheaded and quartered.

Père Dubernard escaped for two days, but was eventually run to earth in a cave farther up the valley. His captors broke both arms above and below the elbow, tied his hands behind his back, and in this condition forced him to walk back to the blackened site of Tzekou. There they fastened him to a post and subjected him to the most brutal mutilation; amongst the least of his injuries being the extraction of his tongue and eyes and the cutting off of his ears and nose. In this horrible condition he remained alive for the space of three days, in the course of which his torturers cut a joint off his fingers and toes each day. When on the point of death, he was treated in the same manner as Père Bourdonnec, the portions of the bodies being distributed amongst the various lamaseries in the region, whilst the two heads were stuck on spears over the lamaserie of the town of Atuntze.

I was reported dead for almost three weeks, but, fortunately, though there seemed no reason to doubt the authenticity of the information, the news was withheld from England for a time by the Consuls and the authorities at the Foreign Office, on the chance that I might have escaped; thus my family mourned my loss for only a week.

Although escaping with my life, I lost everything I possessed, all my camp equipment, ammunition and guns, cameras, stores; in fact, my all with the exception of the rags I stood in, my rifle, revolver and two belts of cartridges.

OPPOSITE:
Rhododendron
sulfureum, *found in
western Yunnan and
upper Burma, was
introduced into
cultivation in Britain
by Forrest in 1910
and in subsequent
years. The water-
colour was by
Lilian Snelling
(1879–1972).
(Source and copy-
right: Royal Botanic
Gardens, Kew)*

What was much more serious, I lost nearly all the results of a whole season's work, a collection of most valuable plants numbering fully 2,000 species, seeds of 80 species, and 100 photographic negatives. It is difficult to estimate the value of such a loss; coming from an entirely unexplored area, probably one of the richest in the world, there was undoubtedly a very large percentage of new species. I had sent scraps of specimens home in my letters, and about a dozen of those, or one-third of the number, proved to be new species.[3]

In late 1930, Forrest travelled to China to commence his seventh collecting trip in that country. His harvest was large.

An abundance of seed

Of seed, such an abundance, that I scarce know where to commence, nearly everything I wished for and that means a lot. Primulas in profusion, seed of some of them as much as 3–5 lbs., same of

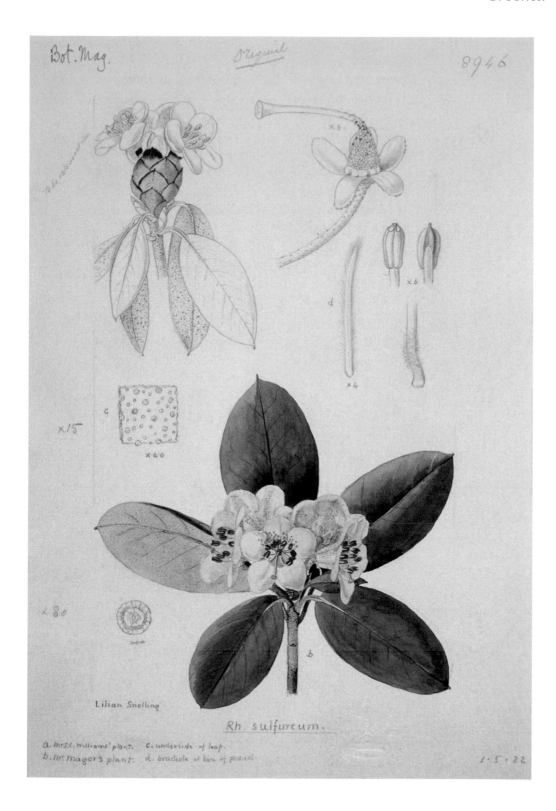

Bot. Mag.   Original   8946

Lilian Snelling

Rh. sulfureum.

a. Mr J.C. Williams' plant.   c. underside of leaf.
b. Mr Magor's plant.   d. bracteole at base of pedicel.

1·5·22

Meconopsis, Nomocharis, Lilium, as well as bulbs of the latter. When all are dealt with and packed I expect to have nearly, if not more than two mule loads of good clean seed, representing some 400–500 species, and a mule load means 130–150 lbs. That is something like 300 lbs of seed ... [4]

In early January 1932, word was received in Britain that Forrest, out for the day with his gun, and about four miles from the Consulate of Tengyueh, had at one stage called for help to his colleagues. Members of his party found him unconscious. He never revived.[1,2]

Forrest contributed a myriad of species to British gardens, including fifty species of *Primula*. His collections also included 260 species of *Rhododendron* that were new to science.[5]

AUSTRALIA &
NEW ZEALAND

R. W. LAWRENCE *(1833)*

Robert William Lawrence (1807–1833), born in England, emigrated to Van Diemen's Land (Tasmania) and became overseer of his father's estate of Formosa, near Cressy. Lawrence had an interest in natural history and corresponded with, and sent specimens to, British botanist William Hooker. The following is extracted from an account of a visit to the western mountains.[1]

'Rugged and romantic' country

January 15, 1833 ... None of the gentlemen who had engaged to accompany me on my expedition to the lakes and along the western range of mountains, having arrived, with the exception of Mr Curson, we started with three men at about six o'clock A.M., carrying with us a week's stock of flour, tea and sugar, etc. But we had scarcely walked six miles before we discovered that we had forgotten our shot, the sending of a man back for which detained us nearly three hours. During the time we were obliged to wait, the mountain tops became enveloped in clouds, and there was every appearance of approaching bad weather. At length we had a pretty heavy fall of rain, accompanied by a squall, and by the time the man had returned with the shot, all was clear again and promised favourably. On his return we proceeded onwards, and reached about half-way up the 'Flat-topped mountain', where we halted for the night. Our tent was of the most portable description, consisting of two strong sheets, sewed together and stretched over such a frame as we could most conveniently construct, from sticks of the *Prostanthera lasiantha* and other shrubs. Nothing remarkable had occurred in the course of this day.

The base of this mountain, to one-third of its entire height, is composed of white sandstone (free-stone) of excellent quality for building; so that, though the prospect be far distant, we may hope, that at some future time, substantial stone dwellings will take the place of the miserable wooden fabrics that now form the town of Formosa. I had not much time to ramble here, though desirous of

The bark of the trunk of the Tasmanian snow gum, Eucalyptus coccifera. *The bark is commonly grey but in summer and autumn the old bark is shed to reveal yellow and pinkish new bark, a feature highlighted here by a splash of water.*

collecting some of the minerals that usually accompany this kind of rock, as my principal objective was to attain great elevations and collect specimens of the plants peculiar to them. In the evening we kindled a very large fire, that our friends at home might observe the height to which we had ascended.

January 16 ... The rill from which we obtained water yielded some mosses, one of which I at first hoped would prove to be the rare *Dawsonia polytrichoides*, but on closer examination it turned out to be a species of the allied genus *Polytrichum*, and also an aquatic moss of peculiar aspect, which was unfortunately destitute of fructification. After collecting these, we continued our ascent, the way becoming more precipitous as we advanced. In the course of the day we arrived at the summit of the 'Flat-topped mountain', climbing over places which I felt very uncomfortable at looking down upon, but which my lighter and more active companion scaled with the apparent ease of a kangaroo. During the morning we passed the usual mountain plants, and gathering specimens of all such as were either in fruit or flower; among these were *Drymophila cyanocarpa*, several species of *Pultenaea*, *Lomatia polymorpha*, and individuals of the genera *Leucopogon*, *Hakea*, *Orites*, etc.

Mr Curson took two men to hunt, while I remained at a spot where we had fixed to encamp: after two hours, however, they returned empty-handed, while I had collected in the vicinity of the tent two species of *Richea*, a *Eucalyptus*, and several other plants. The country here presents a rugged and romantic appearance, consisting of small wet flats or plains, over which are scattered projecting columns of basalt, and hemispherical masses of a kind of moss, resembling beautiful green velvet cushions, interspersed with fragments of rock, that bring to mind the appearance of ruined castles. After our tent was erected, we despatched two men again to hunt, but a severe snowstorm coming on, they returned unsuccessful. It was so cold that the men's kangaroo-skin caps and pouches were quite stiffened, and snow fell all night.

January 17 ... The ground was covered to the depth of several inches with snow, but the sun, on its rising, gave promise of a fine day. After looking round and admiring for a short time the extensive panoramic scene beneath us, Mr Curson and I started with two men to hunt. The circumstances of the dogs having lamed themselves in ascending the mountain, and the ground being very stony, again caused us disappointment. We saw many kangaroos, both of the forest and brush kind, and observed excrements of the 'Hyena' (*Didelphis* or *Thylacinus cyanocephalus*); but very few traces of quadrupeds, except these now named ... This morning's collection of specimens and seeds was satisfactory; a *Richea*, a new and small *Pultenaea*, a trailing *Exocarpus* and a creeping aphyllous shrub being amongst the most remarkable. After resting a short time in the tent, we packed up and proceeded due south towards the lakes, the mountains running east and west ...[1]

The last known individual of *Thylacinus cyanocephalus*, the Tasmanian tiger (or wolf), died in captivity in 1936.

January 18 ... Two of the men went out to hunt at day-break, one of whom returned to breakfast, the other had lost himself. After waiting for him for several hours, we fired some shots, which had the effect of leading him to us, though without any game. We spent some time in arranging our specimens of plants, and then proceeded towards the lakes, the first and smallest of which we reached in about two hours. Here I found a *Veronia*, which I had never seen before, with deeply divided leaves. While walking through some underwood, a kangaroo started before us, which I succeeded in shooting. The next, or middle lake, was soon in sight. Here we heard the noise of dogs, which was attributed to a party of blacks

*Windswept vegetation in alpine Tasmania, which would have been a familiar sight to Lawrence and Gunn. This photograph highlights cushion plants, a habit formed by various species (*Abrotanella forsterioides, Donatia novaezelandiae, Dracophyllum minimum, Pterygopappus lawrencei*). In the background the grey-green shrubs with red-brown inflorescences are* Richea scoparia, *a member of the family Epacridaceae and one of the most conspicuous and widespread montane plants in Tasmania.*

hunting. While walking along a plain leading to Lake Arthur, we discovered a herd of what we thought wild cattle, but, on shooting one of them, we found it to be branded with the letters J. J., and soon after we were surprised at seeing a flock of sheep. We arrived at the largest lake, called Lake Arthur, and in the evening shot one of the numerous ducks, which frequent it.

January 19 ... This morning we took about 14 lbs of meat from the bullock we had killed; but while sitting down to breakfast upon the spoil, three men arrived, who turned out to be the overseer and stock-keepers belonging to a Mr Jones of Jericho, the proprietor of the cattle and sheep we had seen, and who had settled in this neighbourhood only a week before. We were glad of the opportunity to explain what we had done, and found the overseer so civil that he even invited us to his hut. Here I saw *Bellendena montana* in flower, and an *Epacris* new to me. We remained near the lake all day, gathering several rare plants, and one in particular, belonging to the [family] Compositae, which I had never before seen.[2]

Lawrence and his companions returned to Formosa on 22 January. William Hooker was soon to record that in that same year, not only Lawrence, 'at the early age of twenty-six, but his wife, were both, in the short space of a fortnight, suddenly removed from all sublunary enjoyments'.[2] Lawrence's wife, after giving birth to their daughter, 'was in a few days seized with a fever which terminated fatally within a month — fatally to Lawrence's happiness and peace'.[3] On 18 October, his birthday and first anniversary of his marriage, Lawrence was found dead in his bed, publicly said to have 'been carried off in a fit of apoplexy'.[3]

Lawrence left an important botanical legacy. In his short time he collected many plants which proved new to science, including several named for him, for example, the plum pine (*Podocarpus lawrencei*) and a cushion-plant (*Pterygopappus lawrencei*). He is also commemorated in the name of the malvaceous genus, *Lawrencia*. Arguably of greater importance than his collections was his introduction of Ronald Campbell Gunn to the study of botany. [4, 5] During the 1830s and 1840s, Gunn made numerous collections for William Hooker at Glasgow (and subsequently Kew) and his son Joseph (*see* pp. 57–69 and pp. 297–304), collecting 'indefatigably over a great portion of Tasmania' and transmitting specimens 'to England in perfect preservation, and ... accompanied with notes that display remarkable powers of observation, and a facility for seizing important characters in the physiognomy of plants, such as few experienced botanists possess'.[6]

J. DRUMMOND *(1839–1853)*

Brother of Thomas (*see* pp. 217–228), James Drummond was born in the Scottish county of Angus, seemingly in late 1786 or January 1787.[1,2] For some years he was curator of the botanical garden of the Royal Cork Institution, Ireland. In 1829, after the Institution had closed down the garden, he and his family emigrated to the fledgling Swan River Colony (Western Australia). For some time he managed the botanical garden, but following withdrawal of funding he eventually settled at Hawthornden farm in the Toodyay Valley. Encouraged by William Hooker, he was to spend many years collecting plants for botanists at Kew and other institutions.[1,2] The following extracts are from letters and manuscripts forwarded to W. J. Hooker from 1839 until the early 1850s.

Making fire

One of the most striking plants to a stranger is our common blackboy, a fine arborescent species of *Xanthorrhoea*, growing from ten to 15 feet high, with a trunk about a foot in diameter, and a flower-stalk almost as high as the plant itself; the common kind is sometimes repeatedly branched in a dichotomous manner, all the branches of equal thickness. The spot where the town of Fremantle now stands was originally a grove of this *Xanthorrhoea*, called here blackboys, but which now get scarce in the neighbourhood of the settlements from the numbers used as firewood. The genus is of very slow growth, the largest specimens must be several hundred years old; these furnish the natives with a favourite article of food in the larvae of a large brown species of *Cerambyx*, and also afford a good substitute for lucifer-matches. When the indigenous tribes happen to be without fire in the bush, they select an old but sound flower-stalk of *Xanthorrhoea*, with the dry flowers and seed-vessels remaining: of these they make a small heap on the ground; then break off about a foot or 18 inches of the upper part of the flower-stalk, and split the remaining part in the middle, placing one half with the split side up, over the little heap of withered flowers; this done, they apply the

small end of the broken off part to the middle of the split portion holding it upright between the palms of their hands and rolling it backwards and forwards with rapidity. Thus a small hollow is soon formed in the split stalk like the half of a bullet-caster, when they make a small orifice on one side for the fire to escape into the dried flowers, where it spreads as in tinder, the whole process not occupying three minutes even in wet weather. In very wet weather, they are, however, sometimes obliged to substitute the pounded leaves of the blackboy, which are always found dry under large plants, instead of the old flowers.[3]

James Drummond.
(Courtesy of Robert
Gadsdon)

In the 1830s and early 1840s, there was concern in the Swan River Colony with unexplained stock losses. Drummond was involved in the investigation to find the cause.

Gastrolobium calycinum *(Fabaceae), York Road poison, one of a group of poisonous peas of south-west Western Australia, referred to in the text and collected by James Drummond.*

Poisonous plants

We have at length discovered the plant which has destroyed many of our sheep, goats and cattle ... It is not the *Lobelia*, (as I had surmised) but a leguminous plant growing about two and a half or three feet high, with glaucous lanceolate leaves, about two inches long, ending in a sharp point, and each furnished with two minute, prickle-like stipules; the flowers are orange-colour, and produced, several together, on a sort of raceme which grows from the axils of the upper leaves. The leaves are frequently three in a whorl; the flowers when expanded, are about half an inch in diameter; they are succeeded by hairy seed-vessels, about the size of a large pea, which are spotted with brown, and permanently crowned by the style.

There has been much difference of opinion among the settlers, as to the cause of the death of so many of our flocks and herds. Dr Harris, who has had much experience in sheep and cattle, was of an opinion that the animals died of a dangerous inflammatory disease

... but his son, Mr Joseph Harris, thought with me that the animals died of poison. He had lost about 50 sheep on his farm, on the William River, a few days before I visited him, and the exact spot where the sheep had been feeding, when they were thus affected, was known. I found that there were but a few plants of which the sheep ate on these occasions, which could possibly cause their death, and these I determined to put to the test of experiment. The *Lobelia* I had tried a few days before ... it appeared to have no bad effects on a sheep to which it was given ... this leguminous plant ... we determined to put ... to the test ... for there is nothing in the taste or smell of the plant that in the least indicates its poisonous properties. A few handfuls of the young tender shoots were pounded in a mortar, and water added, and the juice squeezed out. We had about a middle-sized tea-cupful of the mixture, of which about three parts out of four were water. It was put into a bottle, and given to a he-goat, a fine healthy animal. About eight o'clock at night the animal ate about an ounce of the plant of his own accord, after he swallowed the juice. At five o'clock in the following morning, he continued to chew his cud, but appeared languid, when we gave him about half as much more of the same mixture. Soon after he got the second dose, he began to call out, as goats always do when suffering from this poison: at ten o'clock he died. We opened him an hour after death, and found the heart and lungs gorged with dark-coloured blood ... I had observed this plant at Black-Adder Creek where accidents have happened, and on the Toodyay road; and I have, since we discovered its dangerous properties, found it on the York road, where so many of our animals have been lost.[4]

Further studies concluded that a number of native peas (all now placed in *Gastrolobium*) were the cause of the stock losses. The toxin was monofluoroacetic acid, the salt of which is today marketed as the poison '1080'. Marsupials native to the area where these plants occur display a much higher resistance to the poison than domesticated livestock.[5] Experiments on native fauna have shown that populations of a species in western Australia where these plants are found have a higher tolerance of fluoroacetate than eastern Australian populations of the same animal species, this presumably being a result of selection in western populations for an increased capacity to detoxify fluoroacetate.[6] The high resistance of native Western Australian fauna means that in that State it is possible to lay '1080' baits to kill introduced foxes, a major predator of native animals.

Seed collecting and luminescent fungi

I have received the books you were so kind to send me, by the *Henry*, all safe. They will be of great use to me. I am going on collecting specimens to send home by the ship that takes home the wool. She will sail from this place about Christmas next. I have made an agreement with Messrs Low & Co., of the Clapton Nursery, to send them bulbs and seeds of our Swan River plants, to the value of £100 per annum. The time for collecting seeds of most of our plants is very short, and I shall have plenty to do to supply their order, together with collecting specimens. You observe, in your letter of July 30th 1840 that the fungi of this country are worth picking up. They are very numerous and many of them very curious. We have species belonging to most of the European genera [and] in several instances I think the same species which grow in England are found. But there are several genera here which I think are not known in England. One genus of which I have met with two species never appear over the surface of the ground unless accidentally thrown up. One species which grows in siliceous sand is an exact globe covered when dry with a hard crust like dark coloured sand paper. The fungus dries up and occupies a very small space in the inside of the globes. They are sometimes sent home as curiosities from this country, but few know what they are. I once met with a pear-shaped smaller species evidently of the same genus growing in clay ground. We have one genus which grows up like *Lycoperdon* but it bursts and five or six red coloured wrinkled bodies shaped like lobster's claws growing in a circle with their points turned inwards show themselves. They give out a sort of grey coloured powder which is probably the seed. Another genus grows up like *Lycoperdon* and when it bursts it exhibits a regular network formed into hexagonal meshes about half an inch across. These meshes are smeared with a foetid gelly [*sic*], and a quantity of the same substance is found on the bottom between the valves. But the fungi I wish particularly to give you some account of in this letter are two [species] of *Agaricus* of the division which has the stem at one side of the pileus, which are parasitical on the stumps of trees. There is nothing very remarkable in their appearance but they give out a very curious light in the night time, which I have not met with described in books. The first species in which I observed this property was about two inches across. It was growing in clusters on the stump of a *Banksia* tree near the jetty at Perth, W. Australia. The stump at the time was surrounded with water. I happened to be passing [on] a dark night and was surprised to see what I thought a light in such a place. On examination I found it proceeded from a species of fungus. It is six or seven years since I observed this plant ... this fungus when laid on a newspaper gave out a sort of a phosphorescent light by which we could read the words round it on the newspaper. It continued to give out this light for several nights gradually diminishing as the plant dried up. I met with no more of these light producing fungi until a few weeks ago. I was out collecting plants, on an ironstone hill in the Toodyay district, when I was struck with the beauty of a large fungus of the same division of agarics but measuring 16 inches across and about a foot from the root to the extremity of the pileus, and weighing about [five pounds]. It was very smooth [and] of a yellowish-brown above, the gills of a dirty white. It gradually got thinner towards the outer edge of the pileus, which was waved and sinuated. I carried home this species, on account of its beauty, for to make a full collection of Swan River fungi it would require an entire season, and it would require a person who could make drawings or models of them. It was hung up inside of the chimney of our sitting-room to dry. I happened to have to pass through it in the night time, when I observed the fungus giving out a remarkable light of the sort described above. The light given out by the fungus [was] of a whiter colour than any light I have ever seen. It continued to give it out for four or five nights but gradually diminishing in quantity as the plant dried up. We showed the plant to the natives when giving out light, that is in the dark when the light of the fire was dull and the candles out. They called it a *chinga*, their name for a spirit, and they were much afraid of it. I certainly think it is an extraordinary will-o'the-wisp.[7]

The following is part of an account of Drummond's fourth major collecting trip, this one a journey in 1846–1847 to the Stirling Ranges and Cape Riche. During that journey he collected specimens of the spectacular *Hakea victoria*.

Banksia cones and *Hakea victoria*

I determined to have another view from the top of Mongerup. I hid our supply of flour and pork as well as I could in case of a visit from the natives. I had now to bring water from the native well. Starting at 5 o'clock I reached the highest summit of the hill by 11 o'clock. I ascended by the north-east angle, and at about the height of 2,000 feet I found, first making its appearance, a splendid

Banksia, with leaves more than 9 inches long, and about five wide, irregularly jagged and sinuated like an English oak. To this splendid plant I have given the specific name of *hookeri*. From the remains of the flowers they appear to have been scarlet. I had scarcely time to make myself acquainted with this fine *Banksia*, when I found another exceedingly interesting and beautiful plant, a species of *Genetyllus* [that is, *Genetyllis*, a synonym of *Darwinia*], growing to the size and having a considerable resemblance in habit and foliage to *Beaufortia decussata*, but having the inflorescence inclosed by beautiful bracts, white, variegated with crimson veins. These bracts are as elegantly formed as the petals of the finest tulip, and they are almost as large, hanging in a bell-shaped form from the ends of the slender branches. I thought I could never gather enough of this charming plant and I procured abundance of perfect seeds. As one is obliged to use the hands as well, and almost as often, as their feet, in ascending or descending these very steep hills, I had gone very lightly equipped. I was therefore obliged to make use of my shirt and neck-handkerchief, making the shirt into a bag, to bring down a supply of *Banksia* cones. Securing the load so as not to impede the use of my hands, I reached our sleeping place at 3 o'clock, much fatigued with my load, but highly gratified, having this day found at least two plants which will continue to be admired while a taste for the beauties of nature remains to the human race ...

West Mount Barren was distant about 4 miles. Just before I reached this sleeping place, and afterwards in greater abundance between it and Mount Barren, I found a most extraordinary plant, a species of *Hakea*, growing 12 or 14 feet high. The true leaves of the plant are 7 or 8 inches long, and about 2 in breadth, variously jagged and sinuated as in *Hakea undulata*, but by far the most conspicuous part of the foliage of this superb plant are its bracts. These make their appearance with the flower-buds and when the plant is 3 or 4 years old they are borne in regular whirls, each circle or whirl being from 7 to 9 inches in height, each formed of 5 rows which have each 5 bracts; the lowest bracts of the whirl are the broadest, they vary from 4 to 5 inches, the whole breadth across, in full-grown, middle-sized specimens, being about 10 inches and they regularly decrease in size to the upper-most bracts, which are only about 4 inches across from outside to outside, each whirl is a year's growth of the plant after it bears the first flowers. The variegation of these bracts is so extraordinary that I almost fear to attempt a description. The first year they are yellowish-white in all the centre

of the bracts, and the same colour appears in the veins and in the teeth which grow on the margin. The second year, what was white the first year has changed to a rich golden-yellow. The third year what was yellow the second changes to a rich orange, and the fourth year the colour of the centre of the same bracts, their veins and marginal teeth, are turned to a blood-red. The green, which has a remarkably light and luminous appearance the first year, varies annually to deeper and darker shades; and the fourth year when the centre of the bracts has acquired a blood-red colour, the green of the same series is of the richest hue, the whirls below change to darker and duller shades, until they ultimately fade into the dull and withered leaves of other climes. The flowers I have not seen. The stem and buds of the upper series, which are the only ones unopened, [are] white and velvety; the other series contains seed-vessels, mostly with perfect seeds. To this, the most splendid vegetable production which I have ever seen, in a wild or cultivated

Hakea victoria *(Proteaceae) growing at East Mount Barren, Western Australia.*

131

state, I have given the name of our gracious Queen, *Hakea victoria*. It will soon be in cultivation in every garden of note in Europe, and in many other countries ... I thought it incumbent on me to send *Hakea victoria* in some form to my subscribers, and in this plant pressure is altogether out of the question, as the bracts break before they will bend in any direction. I tied up 16 of the bract-bearing tops in two bundles, tying them together with the creeping shoots of the black creeper, *Kennedya nigricans*, and slung them one at each side of my old grey poney [*sic*], Cabbine. The load, although not a very heavy [one], was a most awkward one to get through the bushes, and he never since I got him carried anything so unwillingly. One specimen 14 feet high I carried in my hand all the way to Cape Riche; but not withstanding all the care I took, the brilliant colours in the bracts of this extraordinary plant were much faded before I could get them to K.G.S. [King George Sound].[8]

Having returned from the latter journey in March, Drummond commenced a further trip to the south in the spring. He was forced to turn back due to a bout of ophthalmia.

Ophthalmia

In the last letter I wrote you I stated my intention of travelling to the south intending if possible to go as far east as Lucky Bay. I intended to cross the country to Cape Riche more to the east, so far as to give me a new field, but I had only got about 100 miles from home when I was laid up with a severe attack of inflammation in my eyes. For a fortnight I was quite blind, obliged to live day and night with a wet towel over my head and face. This severe attack of ophthalmia put a stop to my botanising for this season. I was obliged to make my way home the best way I could, travelling mostly by night, my eyes being unable to bear the light.[9]

In 1850–1851, Drummond made his sixth, and final, major collecting trip, this time north to Champion Bay. His substantial collection included specimens of *Verticordia*, or feather-flowers.

Discovery of *Verticordia grandis*

The splendid genus *Verticordia* produces several fine new species; the large scarlet *Verticordia* which I call *V. grandis* first appears on the sand plains to the east of the Hill River. But it is seen in the greatest perfection on the sand plain to the north of the spring called by

Mr Brown, the 'diamond of the desert'. It grows to be five to six feet high, with glaucous, round, and rather fleshy leaves about half an inch in diameter. The flowers appear in their greatest beauty on the second or third year after the plants have been burned down. The bush is then two to three feet high and one mass of scarlet flowers. I found another *Verticordia* with similarly shaped but thinner leaves

Thelymitra antennifera, *or lemon orchid, is widespread in southern Australia and was first described by English botanist John Lindley from specimens gathered by Drummond.*

and a much more slender habit, sparingly scattered over the great sand plain between the Murchison and the Hutt [rivers]. Its flowers are lilac, and each seems marked with five blood red spots, the appearance [being] produced by the undivided part of the calyx, which is of a very dark red colour, being seen through the almost transparent corolla. When well grown and not injured by neighbouring plants, everyone of its numerous, slender branches are loaded with flowers, and in this state it may well contest the prize of beauty even with *V. grandis* herself. Another new lilac-flowered *Verticordia* with glaucous, heart-shaped, indented leaves, with several unbranched stems from the same root, which terminate in small corymbs, grows sparingly about nine miles to the north of the Hill River, also near the base of Mount Lesseur, and I have seen specimens which were collected by Mr Edward Whitfield near his residence on the Moore River. This is one of the rarest species of this beautiful genus. Another remarkable new red and yellow *Verticordia* growing to the height of five or six feet, with corymbs of variegated red and yellow flowers, grows abundantly on the sand plains to the north of the Hutt River. Another beautiful yellow species growing to twice the height of *V. grandiflora*, with larger flowers and longer leaves, is found on the sand plains near Smith's River. I have several other supposed new species of *Verticordia*, which require further examination.[10]

Grevillea eriostachya, *an open weeping shrub growing to c. 2 m tall, is widespread in sandplain communities in eremaean regions of Western Australia and parts of Central Australia. The flowers are laden with nectar and are traditionally a much-sought-after food by Aboriginal people. It was named by John Lindley from specimens forwarded by both Drummond and Captain James Mangles (1786–1867), another early collector in the Swan River Colony.*

Botanist Dr William Harvey visited the Swan River Colony and in his memoirs referred to Drummond's discovery of *Verticordia grandis.*

> On the 19th [April 1854] Mr Drummond ... arrived, having come upwards of forty miles to have a chat with me, and to ask me to visit him in the country ... He is a venerable looking man, with snow-white hair and long beard, square-built frame and ruddy features, and an intelligent eye, that lights up with enthusiasm when on his favourite subject. His habit for years has been to traverse the country in the collecting season, with his three ponies and one or two natives, and to live for months together in the bush, shifting his quarters as he exhausts each neighbourhood. He had many things to tell me about the local vegetation, and particularly of several new and curious genera which he had recently discovered in a newly-opened country three hundred miles to the northward. He gives a

most glowing account of its vegetable riches, reports two new genera of Proteaceae, besides innumerable beautiful species of the same order, and a superb *Verticordia*, with brilliant crimson flowers, as large as half-a-crown (the usual size of the flowers of the old species being a threepenny piece), and the shrubs perfect sheets of bloom, so beautiful that the wagoner who drove him used to stop and turn his bullocks out of the road, to avoid trampling down this plant. Mr Drummond gathered so much of it the first day he saw it, that after putting into papers as many specimens as he required, he made fairly his bed of the remainder. Unconsciously he had plucked such a quantity and stuffed his bags ...[11]

After a short illness James Drummond died in 1863. Numerous plant species were first described from specimens gathered by Drummond and more than 100 bear his name.[2]

W. COLENSO *(1845)*

Born in Penzance, Cornwall, William Colenso (1811–1899) was a missionary attached to the Church Missionary Society in the North Island of New Zealand. He collected plants for Kew and many New Zealand species bear his name. Colenso was not only interested in natural history, but also in ethnology and the Maori language.[1,2] In May 1878, when addressing the Hawke's Bay Philosophical Society, Colenso reminisced about his 1845 trip to the Ruahine Range, in the North Island. An embellished account was subsequently published, extracts from which are given below.

Where their bones lay bleaching

During the summer I saw pretty nearly all the Maoris of the immediate neighbourhood [Hawke's Bay], dwelling between Tangoio and Patangata, who were then numerous; and I also wished to see, or to know something more of, those dwelling in the inland Patea country, beyond the Ruahine mountain range, of whom I had formerly heard. Of them, however, I could learn but little, save that they were believed to be there, isolated completely from the outer world, and that no way, or track was open, or known, by which they could be reached, except the long roundabout one by way of Taupo Lake; which, it was further said, would be of itself a two to three weeks' journey. For a long time I could not hear of a guide, or of any one who really knew anything of the mountain passes, which, evidently had never been visited from this (the Eastern) side. At last I found a middle-aged Maori named Mawhatu, who, when very young, had been taken away prisoner into the interior from Hawke's Bay by a fighting party, and who had subsequently escaped from slavery. Mawhatu had therefore gone twice (in going and returning) through the mountain forests; but, as several years had elapsed since, and the journey was difficult, for some time he was very unwilling to go. The resident natives, too, especially the principal chiefs, Te Hapuku, Tareha, Puhara, Te Moananui, and others, were greatly against my going thither, believing I should never return; representing the mountain passes as being frightful,

William Colenso. (Source: As shown opposite p. 52 in The Mystery of the Moa, by T. L. Buick, published in 1931 by Avery, New Plymouth. Reproduced with permission from the archives of the Royal Botanic Gardens, Melbourne)

where several Maoris had from time to time been lost through attempting the journey; particularly a *taua* (an armed party), which had left Taupo to invade Hawke's Bay, south, a few years ago, and were all lost to a man in the dreadful passes on the snowy summits, where their bones now lay bleaching! And, also, though many years before, — a famed ancestor of theirs, named Te Rangitauira, who, in peacefully travelling from Patea to Hawke's Bay (and yet not by the summits) had also miserably perished with his people in a snowstorm. However, by dint of perseverance, I succeeded in getting Mawhatu, my *quasi* guide, and some other stout young natives to accompany me; and we were to start soon after the snow should be completely gone, — by which time I should also have finished building my chimney, a matter of very great importance to me. The snow was late that summer before it wholly disappeared; it was still there glistening white in the mornings' sunbeams up to the middle of January, 1845 …

Having made all my little preparations, and got my travelling party of six baggage-bearers together on Monday, the 3rd February, the next morning at eight a.m. we started from Waitangi, — and after a long and wearisome journey by Okokoro (near the present Pakipaki) and the Taheke (on the E side of Poukawa Lake), we gained the islet in the Lake Rotoatara by eight p.m., all hands being pretty well knocked up; the whole country being so rough and wet, and the slippery Maori foot-track through the dense scrub so very narrow! (from their turning-in their feet, and, being without shoes, never deviating from it,) that it often caused me to slip, and to stumble right and left.

I noticed but few interesting plants this day ... After a restless night, the next morning I found myself too unwell to rise early, but as I wished to get over the range before Sunday (so as to spend that day quietly somewhere at Patea), we started afresh at 11 o'clock, and travelling slowly on in a westerly direction halted at sunset on the banks of the river Mangaonuku, in Te Ruataniwha plain.

Thursday morning was ushered in by heavy rain! which, to my great regret, continued to pour throughout the whole day. My situation here was very uncomfortable, for my old tattered summer tent (as we were not near any forest and not carrying poles) had been but slightly pitched, supposing when we halted that we were only here for a few hours, and intending to leave early in the morning, — but there was nothing better. To add to one's misery was the oft repeated statements of my natives, — that the rivers would be flooded and so prove impassable after this downpour! — they were already getting disheartened.

A night of heavy rain was followed by a dirty-looking lowering morning, but as we hoped the rain was over [and] we started at nine a.m., making directly across the great plain, through the long dripping grass, every now and then stumbling across some wild pigs, which here were both numerous and large, and in some instances were quite prepared to stand and shew [*sic*] fight! which they invariably did whenever we came suddenly upon them without their seeing us, or we, indeed, them. On reaching the river Waipaoa, — which we did not far from the present village of Tikokino, — (there were no natives residing in these parts then) we travelled up its stony bed, wading across it with difficulty several times, as it was nearly three feet deep and rapid withal. At three p.m. we reached the junction of this river with the river Maakaroro, and proceeded up the stony bed of the latter until six p.m., when, it being nearly dark where we were, we halted for the night in the bed of the river.

I was gratified in finding several new and interesting plants on the banks of this river. Here the drooping *Carmichaelia odorata* (which I had first detected in 1843, inland from Te Wairoa,) grew plentifully on the immediate banks of the stream, filling the air with its fragrance; — here, also, especially on low banks subject to winter floods, was the pretty *Euphrasia cuneata*, nestling in graceful little clumps among the larger shrubs and trees; this plant presents a really elegant appearance in its native homes, but I fear it will prove impatient of culture in the open garden; I often tried it and failed; — on the shaded cliffy sides of the river two or three species of the peculiar orchidaceous genus *Corysanthes* (*C. triloba, C. rivularis* and *C. macrantha*) [now included in *Corybas*] were more plentiful than I had ever seen them, and of large size, shewing [*sic*] that this was their true habitat; provokingly however, they were mostly found in the cliffs over deep water, in the angles and bendings of the stream, where they were snugly ensconced in their mossy beds, and could not readily be got at; — while here and there among the cliffs, wherever a rill of water was found trickling down its stony and mossy bed, the elegant white *Oxalis* (fitly named by Allan Cunningham its discoverer, *cataractae*) was to be found ... Further on, in the thickets on the river's banks, I noticed that pretty and neat species of myrtle, *Myrtus pedunculata*, bearing a profusion of small edible fruit, its hard stony seeds however, are a great drawback to its use; growing with it was the very handsome southern species (or variety, according to Dr Hooker,) of *Hoheria*, (*H. populnea* var. *lanceolata*) [= *H. sexstylosa* Col.] which when fully in blossom is a most lovely flowering tree; here, also, it was that I discovered another species of *Carmichaelia* (*C. flagelliformis*), a tall shrub of peculiar growth, with long pendent thong-like branches, bearing only a few flowers ...

Early the next morning we resumed our journey, as before keeping in the bed of the river, and every now and then wading its cold stream from side to side, so as to escape the prostrate trees, and drift wood, and boulders, and to have a little easier walking. Several times, both yesterday and today, we were so dissatisfied with our course, from being continually wet and very cold from the icy water, and without the rays of the sun in the deep narrow bed of the river, — and also from the little progress we were making in spite of all our continued efforts, — that we tried to force our way through the thickets and 'Bush' growing on the river's banks, but found that we could not get on that way, so had to take to the cold river again. At three p.m. we arrived at what appeared to be the immediate base of the upper mountain which rose steep before us; here two rivers met, each nearly of the same size, and coming from opposite directions; we tried both for a short distance but found their beds so narrow and steep, and partly choked with dead trees and shrubs, and masses of stone, that we gave up all thoughts of going any further in that way, and so prepared with a good heart to climb the face of the narrow tongue of land which lay between the two streams. It was easy to see, here, that our guide Mawhatu was at a loss; evidently he had been in the main river below before, but where to turn off from, or to leave it, he knew not. About an hour before we had arrived at the fork, we had on a sudden a fine clear view of the summit towering high above us, yet, apparently, not very distant; it seemed a round-topped hill, and is called, by the old Maoris, Te Atua-o-mahuru. This had been often pointed out to me when at Waitangi (it being one of the conspicuous peaks of the range,) as the head over which our course lay; it had now, however, a slight coating of snow on it, no doubt from the late rains. There it stood alone, uprearing its proud crest in solemn grandeur! —

'Soaring snow-clad through its native sky,
In the wild pomp of mountain majesty.'

But the sight of that snow there on the ridge before us did not increase our comfortable feelings and thoughts.

As we were now leaving the river and entering into the dense mountain forest, I travelled with my pocket compass in my hand, having taken bearings occasionally during the day in the river, where also, we had, at times, seen for a few moments the sun peering down through the trees. It was of no use now (as it then seemed to us in our happy ignorance) to think of drawing-back, although had we known clearly what was before us we should certainly have done so, — therefore we persevered and kept on steadily in as straight a course as we could until six p.m., when, it being nearly dark, we halted in the forest, not knowing where we were; but believing we had not much further to go to gain the wished-for summit. I immediately sent two of my companions to seek for water, which we had greatly needed for the last three hours, and fortunately they found some in a declivity in the side of the spur not very far off. This spring, I afterwards learned, is called Te Wai-o-kongenge — fit name! (That is, The spring, or water of weariness, — or, of being quite worn out!)

Our journey this day was a very fatiguing and disagreeable one all the way we had come, for it lay in the river's bed, either in the water or along its stony and rocky banks, which gradually contracted. In some places the sides of the river were perpendicular, and in others impending, and from 100 to 250 feet high, with fine forest of *Fagus* on the top; the trees of which were continually falling down along with the earth into the river beneath. Here and there an immense mass of earth had slipped quietly down the upright cliffs bringing the large trees with it, standing as they originally grew; these had been arrested in their descent when about halfway down, and there they stood in the side of the cliff fair and flourishing; in two or three spots during the day I noticed a double slip or subsidence of this nature, in which there were two tiers of living trees so standing in the side of the cliff; adding not a little of a novel and picturesque nature to the scene. I had fully intended in passing-on to take on my return a sketch of this unique landscape, but (as it will be seen) pressing circumstances prevented me ...

It was now Saturday night, and, our slender supper and prayers over, we sat for a while in the deepening gloom of the forest to talk, or, rather, to ruminate moodily over our position ... Our supply of food was running short, and there was nothing eatable in those forests. We, however, supposed and hoped we had not much farther to go ere we should reach the summit; and then to descend to the native villages on the western side, of which we had heard and where we looked for food and welcome, would not take us long. One of my party was distantly related through his mother with the Patea tribe, although he had not seen any of them for many years, if at all! And so, after some talk, we arranged, that he (Paora) and my *quasi* guide, Mawhatu, should rise at break of day and start away without any load over the mountain tops for Patea; and, if possible, get some of those natives residing there to come to see us, bringing a supply of provisions with them. We had also heard that the mountain passes if still under snow would prove impassable to my baggage-bearers.

Without doubt we all slept soundly that night, being helped thereto by the constant serenading of the weka (*Ocydromus australis*) and the owl (*Athene novae-zealandiae*)! No other sound was heard, for there was no wind, not even the plaintive sough of the night-airs ...[3]

Invasion of the blue-bottle flies

We, who were to remain there, did not wake and get up till ten a.m., and when we did we found ourselves completely invaded! A large blue-bottle fly inhabits that zone of forest in countless numbers, and is most audacious and teasing. Our blankets and woollen clothing had been attacked and were literally filled with its eggs; the hair of the natives' heads had also similarly suffered. We were not long in doing all we could to save ourselves, our provisions, and our clothing from this new foe, which I, in all my travelling, had not before met with. Had it not been for these blue-bottles we should have passed a most tranquil day of rest! everything there was so delightfully cool and still, fit emblem of the Sabbath ... We left the tent, etc. and retreated some distance into the dry woods, and there sat on the soft thick moss, where we held Divine Service, — in all likelihood the first Christian service on that mountain ... We spent the day quietly, sometimes reading together (in the New Testament, our only vernacular book), sometimes thinking on and talking of our two absent companions; no one caring to move about. The water too, of our little spring, taken a little further up, was delightfully cool and good tasted, — indeed delicious. My poor companions, however, had suffered much from their long walk with naked feet over these horrid stones and so much wading! and having but little to eat, and tobacco not yet being in fashion among them, they preferred sleeping to talking ... Towards evening my friends were all on the *qui vive*, expecting every moment to hear the absent ones returning; but, after many false alarms, and no small display of superstitious fears on their part, dark night again enshrouded us, and they went to sleep ...[3]

Keeping in the track

The next morning we were awake and up very early, — to escape our foes, which commenced their persecution with the sun, and to receive our absent friends, and, it might be, visitors; for no Maori likes to be taken unawares. Our scanty meal and prayers ended, we agreed to go on towards the summit, thinking it was near, and hoping soon to meet those whom we were anxiously expecting. Leaving our tent and all baggage there, and taking our axe with us, (my natives each only wearing a shirt,) we started. Hour after hour, however, passed in arduous toil before we gained the top; the primeval forest being so filled with decaying trees and prostrate limbs and tangled shrubs and herbage, that we could scarcely get through it. We had some difficulty also in finding and keeping in the track of our two companions who had preceded us; this, in an untrodden forest is curious, and deserves mention; — the guide, or foremost one, (if he is right in his course) every now and then half breaks through the top or conspicuous side branch of a shrub or small tree, and allows it to hang down; this operation, called *pawhatiwhati*, is of great use to those behind, and to strangers and stragglers, who, of course, look out for it, taking care not to do the same. And these marked trees so remain and are of service for several years, as I have often proved. Care, however, must be taken not to confound those broken or bent purposely by man, with those broken accidentally by big falling branches of the higher trees, or bent down by the weight of the snow in the winter. Certain thick stemmed and tough shrubs, in particular those having large leaves, are well fitted for the purpose, and are always selected, if at hand; — as various species of *Panax*, and of *Coprosma*; — for the half broken and reverted branch dries gradually and so retains its leaves on it, which, after a little experience, is easily caught by the sharp eye of the Maori. At times (in after years) when puzzled as to our course in the forests, I have both known of, and joined in, a consultation over the broken branch of a shrub; — whether it was done purposely by man, or accidentally through natural causes; and times have been with me and my party when even life depended on it! In the event of branches wrongly broken, and so having to retrace one's steps and alter one's course, — first, the hanging branches are plucked away, and, secondly, a handful of tops of leafy branches, or big ferns, is placed on the moss athwart that erring path or opening, which serves to warn those who come after; this also remains in tact for years.

There is yet another means of forming and finding a track through those mountain forests, particularly of those high up where *Fagus solanderi* is the common or only tree. For in those subalpine woods the trees sometimes grow widely apart, and there the ground is densely carpeted with an erect closely-growing perennial moss, resembling in texture a Turkey carpet. Some of those untrodden undisturbed spots have appeared to me so enchantingly beautiful, especially when extra adorned with the lovely compact *Hymenophyllum* ferns, that I have thought it a desecration to tread on or to disturb them. This moss if trodden on by a travelling party never afterwards rises to its former pristine state; not that it dies, or that the eye of man can detect the difference, — the difference is detected only by the *touch*, by the practised *foot* of the woodsman. I was some years in learning before I succeeded in mastering it, but I eventually did so; but then I wore boots. Here, in this case, the only enemy is the wild pig; but, fortunately, he does not generally keep so high up on the mountains.[3]

Neither man nor beast

In our ascent we passed over two of the worst of the 'passes', and they were bad indeed! frightfully so. One in particular, as if an avalanche of half the mountain's side had suddenly slipped down into the distant gulph below, leaving a ragged razor-back edge of loose loamy sandy soil at a very acute angle. On this, which extended for 300 yards, connecting two peaks, nothing grew, as the sand and earth was continually rolling down. The old Hawke's Bay natives had informed me, that the bones of a *taua* ... composed of some 12–20 men lay bleaching at the bottom; the *taua* having attempted the pass when snow lay on it, through which they were carried off their legs down to the bottom and miserably perished! Some of my companions, whose hearts beat high on arriving at the famed spot where the deadly enemies of their tribe had been lost, declared, on gazing down, that they could see some of their white bones below jutting up! which tale they told with great relish and with many embellishments on their return. The stream which ran bounding through the narrow valley beneath was so far distant, that, though we could see its waters sparkling in the sun, we could not hear it. This pass was never attempted in the winter season, nor yet immediately after heavy rains or the melting of the snow, nor in windy weather. Here, on the open western summits, we lingered until 3 p.m., (the natives with me not knowing what course to take, and all fearing to go astray, — for, after gaining the high tableland to the W of the pass, we found it open, flat, and intersected with shallow snow-runs, and low bushes, and boulders, so that one might easily have proceeded in almost any direction) and though we kept up a good constant look-out, — the Maoris with their keen eyes, and I with my telescope, — we failed to discover any signs of natives approaching, or of any human habitation or cultivation, or fire or smoke, in all that enormous tract of open country of several score miles in extent, that lay like a desolate wilderness panorama before us!

We had, however, no doubt as to our two absent companions having passed on; here were their footsteps, plain enough on the pass; one, evidently, having had a rather ugly slide downwards, before he recovered himself. We, being thus doubly warned, kept nearer to the ridge; but the earth was much firmer today at noon, than it was to them yesterday morning. Being warned, however, by the declining sun, we, unwillingly and with heavy hearts, and hungry and thirsty to boot, returned to our cheerless encampment, regaining it in silence by six p.m. Soon after, however, we heard voices! and our two absent companions bounded into our midst. We welcomed them heartily, but they sat down and burst into tears, crying bitterly yet quietly, in which we all more or less joined, as we knew the action was symbolic of bad tidings; and it was some time before the two newly-arrived ones could speak, they were so dreadfully exhausted. Having drunk a little water and recovered themselves, they soon told their sad tale. They had had nothing to eat since they had left us, save a few small cabbage-tree tops, they had found yesterday growing among the fern lands lower down the mountain, which they had broken off and eaten raw. They had travelled all day yesterday from early dawn till dark, when they lay down wearied among the fern, without even the common solace of the pipe; arising again this morning by daylight to renew their tramp. In the whole of the country through which they had travelled (and they must have travelled many miles), they could not find a living being, — neither man nor beast. They had, indeed, gained an outlying eastern village of Patea, called Te Awarua, situated on the upper Rangitikei River, but it was without inhabitant, and without cultivations or stored food ... Poor fellows! it was painful to look at them; they were sadly worn and torn, both in body and mind, and in clothing, too, with their long journey over such a desolate and rugged country, and with their great exertions, and want of food. We soon got them a small supply out of our little rapidly lessening store; and, after they were refreshed, we considered our situation, and determined *una voce*, that as we had but little food left (a mere handful of rice), and the nearest village was at Te Rotoatara Lake, we would retrace our steps without delay, and hasten thither early tomorrow.[3]

A profusion of Flora's stores

I have told the story of our troubles, I will also give that of our joys, — or, rather, (speaking correctly), of *mine*, — for I was quite sure that my companions shared it not with me, — quite the contrary; — so I had it all to myself.

On quitting our encampment this morning and ascending through the forest, the first novelty I discovered was a handsome fern, a species of *Alsophila* (*A. colensoi*) — a genus new to New Zealand, though plentiful in Australia ... But when at last we emerged from the forest, and the tangled shrubbery on its outskirts, on to the open dell-like land just before we gained the summit, the lovely appearance of so many and varied beautiful and novel wild plants and flowers richly repaid *me* the toil of the journey and the ascent, — for never before did I behold at one time in New Zealand such a profusion of Flora's stores! in one word, I was overwhelmed with astonishment, and stood looking with all my eyes, greedily devouring and drinking-in the enchanting scene before me. I had often seen what I had considered pleasing botanical displays in many New Zealand forests and open valleys, particularly at the Kerikeri waterfall (Bay of Islands, — before it was rudely disturbed before civilisation!) — and in a sweet well-remembered glen near the E. Cape, — again at Lake Waikare, — and on the mountains of Huiarau and of Ruatahuna, far away in the interior, — but all were nothing when compared with this, — either for variety or quantity or novelty of flowers, — all, too, in sight at a single glance! Splendid celmisias and ranunculuses in countless number, intermixed with elegant whalenbergias and beautiful veronicas, ourisias and euphrasias, gentians and dracophyllums, astelias and calthas, gnaphaliums and gaultherias, and many others. Here were plants of the well-known genera of the bluebells, and buttercups, gowans and daisies, eyebrights and speedwells of one's native land, closely intermixed with the gentians of the European Alps, and the rarer southern and little known novelties, — *Drapetes, Ourisia, Cyathodes, Abrotanella,* and *Raoulia* ... It was observable, also, that while all those plants already named with many others were small-sized dwarf plants, pretty nearly of a uniform height, only rising a few inches above the soil, and growing together as thickly as they could stow, — more indeed, in this respect, like short turfy grasses, or mosses, — there were also among them several new species of the common New Zealand genera, — the known species of which in other parts were mostly to be found as tall shrubs and small trees, — but here the new species were only of a very low rambling prostrate habit, resembling large trailing mosses, almost hidden among the low herbaceous plants already mentioned; those new plants comprised *Myrsine nummularia, Pittosporum rigidum, Podocarpus nivalis, Coriaria angustissima, Dracophyllum recurvum*, and several elegant alpine species of *Veronica* ...

But how was I to carry off specimens of those precious prizes? and had I time to gather them? These mental questions completely staggered me for I realised my position well. We had left our encampment early that morning, as I have already said, thinking the crest of the mountain range was not far off, and, consequently, taking *nothing* with us; so we were all empty-handed and no 'New Zealand flax' (*Phormium*) grew there. However, as I had no time to lose, I first pulled off my jacket, or small travelling coat, and made a bag of that, and then (driven by necessity!) I added thereto my shirt, and by tying the neck, etc. got an excellent bag; while some specimens I also stowed into the crown of my hat. I worked diligently all the time I was there, — and, though I did all that I possibly could, I felt sure I left not a little untouched. Fortunately the day was an exceedingly fine one, calm and warm, so that I did not suffer from want of clothing. That night I was wholly occupied with my darling specimens, putting them up, as well as I could, in a very rough kind of way, among my spare clothing, bedding, and books; only getting about two hours sleep towards morning.[3]

A circle of fixed bayonets

Of the peculiar and novel plants which grew on that mountain the large new species of *Aciphylla* (*A. colensoi*) was the one which we were all the most likely to remember, — not only for a few weeks but for all time! It gave us an immense deal of unpleasantness, trouble and pain, — often wounding us to the drawing of blood. I suppose, that each of the party — speaking quite within probability, — received at least 50 stab wounds from that one plant, —which my native companions (without boots or trowsers [sic]) justly termed, *infernal*! I will attempt to describe it from memory (although it is more than 25 years since I last saw it in its mountain home). Imagine a living circle of five feet diameter (the size of the full grown plant), with all its many harsh spiny ray-like leaves radiating alike outwardly from its carrot-shaped root, forming almost a plane of living elastic spears, composed of sharp and stiff points, or flat spikes, each several inches long, these make up the leaf, and many of them are set on each long leaf-stalk of nearly two feet in length; from the centre rises the strong flowering stem, an erect orange-coloured spike or stalk five to six feet high, containing many hundreds of small flowers, gummy (or having a varnished appearance) and strong-scented. The general appearance of these plants, at times, reminded me of a lot of large shallow umbrellas opened and fixed upside down on the ground. Of course there were hundreds of smaller plants, also forming circles, of all sizes, from three inches diameter upwards; while some still younger ones were just pushing their needle-like points (not in a circle but drawn together) through the mossy soil. These plants rarely ever intermixed their spear-shaped leaves to any great extent; they seemed as if they just touched each other with their living circle of points, and when we should put our feet as warily as possible on some tolerably clear spot between them, we were often caught on all sides as if in a man-trap, and not infrequently roared pretty loudly from the pain, while our vain attempts to extricate ourselves often increased it. More than once each of us was so seriously caught as not to be able to move without assistance. On one occasion in particular we all (save *one* — the sufferer!) had a hearty laugh over an adventure with one of these plants: — one of our party had been pricked, or stabbed, rather severely by an *Aciphylla*, insomuch that the blood spurted out; at the sight of this he got enraged, and obtaining the long-handled axe, which another was carrying, he hastened toward the plant, vowing he would cut it up by the roots! the spear-like leaves, however, spreading-out all round like a circle of fixed bayonets, — being longer (including their big leaf stalk) than the helve of the axe and very elastic, quite kept him from doing any harm to the plant, which seemed to mock his impotent rage; so, after gaining a few more pricks for his labour, he was obliged, doubly vexed though he was at our looking on and laughing, to give up the unequal combat![3]

As a footnote, Colenso recorded that the latter 'story was too good to be lost, especially to a fighting race like the Maori, and the joke was long kept up at the expense of the poor fellow!'

F. W. L. LEICHHARDT *(1844–1845)*

Friedrich Wilhelm Ludwig Leichhardt (1813–?1848) was born in Trebatsch, Prussia. At the time of his arrival in Australia, in 1842, Leichhardt was one of the most highly qualified scientists to have ventured to that continent.[1] Near the end of September 1844, Leichhardt, with a party consisting of nine other men, seventeen horses and sixteen oxen, left the Darling Downs region of Queensland to travel overland to Port Essington, an isolated outpost on the Cobourg Peninsula, approximately 200 kilometres north-east of today's city of Darwin, in the Northern Territory. This expedition was very much orientated towards scientific discovery and Leichhardt provided a very readable account of the party's ultimately successful attempt to reach Port Essington.[2]

Thanks to his botanical training, Leichhardt was in a good position to identify edible native plants and thus avoid scurvy. He was also one of the first to record the use of plants by Aborigines; for example, in northern Queensland he noted the use of *Nymphaea*, or water lilies.

Water lilies

May 15. — We returned to our camp. The natives had visited my companions, and behaved very amicably towards them, making them not only presents of spears and wommalas, but supplying them with seed-vessels of *Nymphaea*, and its mealy roasted stems and tubers, which they were in the habit of pounding into a substance much resembling mashed potatoes.[2]

June 21. — A shower of rain fell, but cleared up at midnight. We travelled nine miles north-west to lat. 16° 9' 41", over a country very much like that of the two preceding stages, and past several fine lagoons, richly adorned by the large showy flowers of a white *Nymphaea*, the seed-vessels of which some families of natives were busily gathering: after having blossomed on the surface of the water, the seed-vessel grows larger and heavier, and sinks slowly to the bottom; where it rots until its seeds become free, and are either eaten

Ludwig Leichhardt, c. 1850. (Reproduced with permission from the National Library of Australia, Canberra)

by fishes and waterfowl, or form new plants. The natives had consequently to dive for the ripe seed-vessels; and we observed them constantly disappearing and reappearing on the surface of the water. They did not see us until we were close to them, when they hurried out of the water, snatched up some weapons and ran off, leaving their harvest of *Nymphaea* seeds behind. Brown had visited another lagoon, where he had seen an old man and two gins; the former endeavoured to frighten him by setting the grass on fire, but, when he saw that Brown still approached, he retired into the forest. We took a net full of seeds, and I left them a large piece of iron as payment. On returning to the camp, we boiled the seeds, after removing the capsule; but as some of the numerous partitions had remained, the water was rendered slightly bitter. This experiment having failed, the boiled seeds were then fried with a little fat, which rendered them very palatable and remarkably satisfying. The best way of cooking them was that adopted by the natives, who roast the whole seed-vessel.[2]

Nymphaea macrosperma, *undoubtedly one of the species Leichhardt saw being eaten by Aboriginal people.*
It occurs in northern Australia and New Guinea and has sweetly scented flowers with petals up to c. 5 cm long.

The seeds, stems and tubers of various species of *Nymphaea* are widely eaten by Aboriginal people throughout northern Australia.

Death of Gilbert

Leichhardt's party included John Gilbert, primarily remembered as a major collector of birds for John Gould, but also a collector of plants. Gilbert lost his life when the camp, by a lagoon on current Dunbar station, near the Nassau River,[3] was attacked by natives.

> *June 28.* — ... At the end of our stage, we came to a chain of shallow lagoons, which were slightly connected by a hollow. Many of them were dry; and fearing that, if we proceeded much further, we should find no water, I encamped on one of them, containing a shallow pool; it was surrounded by a narrow belt of small tea trees, with stiff broad lanceolate leaves. As the water occupied only the lower part of this basin, I deposited our luggage in the upper part.

Mr Roper and Mr Calvert made their tent within the belt of trees, with its opening towards the packs; whilst Mr Gilbert and Murphy constructed theirs amongst the little trees, with its entrance from the camp. Mr Phillips's was, as usual, far from the others, and at the opposite side of the water. Our fire place was made outside of the trees, on the banks. Brown had shot six *Leptotarsis eytoni* (whistling ducks), and four teals, which gave us a good dinner; during which, the principal topic of conversation was our probable distance from the sea coast, as it was here that we first found broken sea shells, of the genus *Cytherea*. After dinner, Messrs Roper and Calvert retired to their tent, and Mr Gilbert, John, and Brown, were platting [*sic*] palm leaves to make a hat, and I stood musing near their fire place, looking at their work, and occasionally joining in their conversation. Mr Gilbert was congratulating himself upon having succeeded in learning to plat [*sic*]; and, when he had nearly completed a yard, he retired with John to their tent. This was about 7 o'clock; and I stretched myself upon the ground as usual, at a little distance from the fire, and fell into a dose, from which I was suddenly roused by a loud noise, and a call for help from Calvert and Roper. Natives had suddenly attacked us. They had doubtless watched our movements during the afternoon, and marked the position of the different tents; and, as soon as it was dark, sneaked upon us, and threw a shower of spears at the tents of Calvert, Roper, and Gilbert, and a few at that of Phillips, and also one or two towards the fire. Charley and Brown called for caps, which I hastened to find, and, as soon as they were provided, they discharged their guns into the crowd of the natives, who instantly fled, leaving Roper and Calvert pierced with several spears, and severely beaten by their waddies. Several of these spears were barbed, and could not be extracted without difficulty. I had to force one through the arm of Roper, to break off the barb; and to cut another out of the groin of Mr Calvert. John Murphy had succeeded in getting out of the tent, and concealing himself behind a tree, whence he fired at the natives, and severely wounded one of them, before Brown had discharged his gun. Not seeing Mr Gilbert, I asked for him, when Charley told me that our unfortunate companion was no more! He had come out of his tent with his gun, shot, and powder, and handed them to him, when he instantly dropped down dead. Upon receiving this afflicting intelligence, I hastened to the spot, and found Charley's account too true. He was lying on the ground at a little distance from our fire, and, upon examining him, I soon found, to my sorrow, that every sign of life had disappeared. The body was, however, still warm, and I opened the veins of both arms, as well as the temporal artery, but in vain; the stream of life had stopped, and he was numbered with the dead.[2]

The expedition continued, with the wounded eventually recovering, and Leichhardt recording accounts of their culinary delights and clothing problems.

Emus for the pot

July 24. — ... Shortly after this morning, we saw a brood of thirteen emus, on the plain which we were about to cross. John, Charley, and the dog pursued them, and killed the old one; which, however, severely wounded poor Spring in the neck. When we came up to them with the train, the twelve young ones had returned in search of their mother; upon which Brown gave chase with Spring, and killed two. This was the greatest sport we ever had on our journey. Upon making our camp, we cut part of their meat into slices, and dried it on green hide ropes; the bones, heads, and necks were stewed: formerly, we threw the heads, gizzards, and feet away, but necessity had taught us economy; and, upon trial, the feet of young emus was [*sic*] found to be as good and tender as cow-heel. I collected some salt on the dry salt ponds, and added it to our stew; but my companions scarcely cared for it, and almost preferred the soup without it. The addition, however, rendered the soup far more savoury, at least to my palate.[2]

Cycads and Pandanus

Sept. 16. — ... We passed through tea-tree forest, and a succession of *Cycas* groves, and came out into plains, and to the heads of sandy creeks with tea-tree shrubs and *Salicornia*. We were just turning to the westward, expecting to find a large salt-water river before us, when we heard Charley's gun, the signal of his having found water. He soon after joined us, and guided us on a footpath, three miles south-west, to a large well, near a much frequented camping place of the natives, under the banks of a magnificent salt-water river. Its banks were covered with a close forest of *Cycas* palms. The well was formed by the natives, who had raised a wall of clay, by which they caught the fresh water which sparingly oozed out of a layer of clay very little above the mark of high water.

We unloaded our bullocks: but having watered our horses, we found that the supply of the well was not even sufficient for them, and

Cycas arnhemica *in* Eucalyptus miniata/E. tetrodonta *forest in central Arnhem Land, Northern Territory. Large tracts of land in northern Australia are covered by this eucalypt community and would have been traversed by both Leichhardt's party and Mueller and other members of the North Australian Expedition (see pp. 161–166).*

that it was filling very slowly. The poor bullocks had, therefore, to wait until the water could again collect. We had fairly to defend it against our horses, which eagerly pressed towards the water, or stood anxiously waiting at the steep slopes, like cats and dogs round a dog's meat cart …

The river or creek at which we encamped, and which I called 'Cycas Creek', at two miles lower down, entered a still larger river … Charley saw a shoal of porpoises in it when he went down the river to fetch the horses. Wishing to ascertain how far the salt water extended, and whether any fresh water lagoons were near us, I took Charley, and followed a foot-path of the natives which led up Cycas Creek, and passed a succession of *Cycas* groves …

As we passed the *Cycas* groves, some of the dry fruit was found and tasted by several of my companions, upon whom it acted like a strong emetic, resembling in this particular the fruit of

Pandanus spiralis,
*a tree growing
to c. 8 m tall.
Photographed at
Cape Hotham,
Northern Territory.*

Zamia spiralis R. Br. of New South Wales. The natives, at this season, seemed to live principally on the seeds of *Pandanus spiralis* R. Br. and *Cycas*, but both evidently required much preparation to destroy their deleterious properties. At the deserted camp of the natives, which I visited yesterday, I saw half of the *Pandanus* covered up in hot ashes, large vessels (koolimans) filled with water in which roasted seed-vessels were soaking; seed-vessels which had been soaked, were roasting on the coals, and large quantities of them broken on stones, and deprived of their seeds. This seems to shew [*sic*] that, in preparing the fruit, when ripe, for use, it is first baked in hot ashes, then soaked in water to obtain the sweet substance contained between its fibres, after which it is put on the coals and roasted to render it brittle when it is broken to obtain the kernels.

I also observed that seeds of *Cycas* were cut into very thin slices, about the size of a shilling, and these were spread out carefully on the ground to dry, after which, (as I saw in another camp a few days later) it seemed that the dry slices are put for several days in water, and, after a good soaking, are closely tied up in tea-tree bark to undergo a peculiar process of fermentation.[2]

Leichhardt was correct in recording that cycad seeds must be appropriately prepared to remove poisonous compounds but the seeds of *Pandanus spiralis* (or screw palms) are not poisonous. These latter plants, extremely common in swampy conditions, are an important species in traditional Aboriginal society. Seeds, parts of the fruit, and the bases of young leaves are eaten, leaves are a source of fibre, stems may be used to construct rafts and didgeridoos and to carry fire, and the roots are sometimes used as a source of dye. Furthermore, young leaf bases, stem apices and prop roots are sometimes used as medicine.

Threadbare clothing

Sept. 17. — I stopped at Cycas Creek, to allow our old bullock to recover, as it was easier for us to drive him than to carry his meat, heavily laden as our other bullocks were.

The emu meat became so tainted that it affected our bowels, and I had consequently to reserve it for the dog. As the nutritious qualities of our meat decreased, I had increased the daily allowance from five pounds to seven; allowing two pounds and a half for breakfast, the same quantity for luncheon, and two pounds for dinner. Mr Roper has slowly recovered, but sufficiently to mount his horse without assistance.

We were sadly distressed for want of clothing. The few shirts which we had taken with us, became so worn and threadbare, that the slightest tension would tear them. To find materials for mending the body, we had to cut off the sleeves, and, when these were used, pieces were taken from the lower part of the shirt to mend the upper. Our trowsers [*sic*] became equally patched: and the want of soap prevented us from washing them clean. We had, however, saved our shoes so well, by wearing moccasins while travelling along the eastern coast, that everyone was well provided, particularly after the death of Mr Gilbert, whose stock of clothes I divided among my companions.[2]

In his journal Leichhardt recorded that at the commencement of the expedition every member of his party had, at his request, provided themselves with three shirts, two pairs of trousers and two pairs of shoes. Some members also had waterproof ponchos made of calico impregnated with oil. At the time of this request he had expected that their journey would take no more than seven months. When the above was recorded, they had been travelling for nearly a year.

No transport, no specimens

Throughout this journey Leichhardt had used horses for riding, and both horses and bullocks as pack-animals. At least one horse was eaten after breaking a leg, and bullocks were also treated as mobile larders. On breaking down, they were slaughtered and their meat dried. Unforeseen losses of bullocks and horses were, however, detrimental to the scientific achievements of the expedition. Food supplies had to take priority over natural history collections.

Oct. 6. — One of the bullocks had become so weak that he was unable to carry his load; it was, therefore, put on one of our spare horses, which were still in excellent condition. I steered for one of the detached mountains at the northern end of the range, and travelled about twelve miles north-west, before we came to its foot. We had, however, to leave our bullock on the way, as the difficult nature of the country and diarrhoea together had completely exhausted him.

Oct. 7. — John and Charley went back to fetch the bullock, and, in the mean time, I occupied myself in examining our packs, in order to dispense with such things as were least necessary; for, with an additional weight of 130 pounds of dried meat and hide, our pack-bullocks were overloaded, and it was now imperative upon me to travel as lightly as possible. Thus I parted with my paper for drying plants, with my specimens of wood, with a small collection of rocks, made by Mr Gilbert, and with all the duplicates of our zoological specimens. Necessity alone, which compelled me to take this step, reconciled me to the loss.

Oct. 21. — After waiting a very long time for our horses, Charley came and brought the dismal tidings that three of the most vigorous of them were drowned, at the junction of the creek with the river. Although the banks of the Roper were steep and muddy, the large creek we had passed was scarcely two miles distant, and offered an easy approach to the water on a rocky bed. It remained, therefore, inexplicable to us how the accident could have happened.

This disastrous event staggered me, and for a moment I turned almost giddy; but there was no help. Unable to increase the load of my bullocks, I was obliged to leave that part of my botanical collection which had been carried by one of the horses. The fruit of many a day's work was consigned to the fire; and tears were in my eyes when I saw one of the most interesting results of my expedition vanish into smoke. Mr Gilbert's small collection of plants, which I had carefully retained hitherto, shared the same fate. But they were of less value, as they were mostly in a bad state of preservation, from being too much crowded. My collection had the great advantage of being almost complete in blossoms, fruit, and seed, which I was enabled to ensure in consequence of the long duration of our expedition, and of the comparative uniformity of the Australian Flora.

Oct. 26. — We enjoyed most gratefully our two wallabies, which were stewed, and to which I had added some green hide to render the broth more substantial. This hide was almost five months old, and had served as a case to my botanical collection, which, unfortunately, I had been compelled to leave behind. It required, however, a little longer stewing than a fresh hide, and was rather tasteless.[2]

The last statement suggests that no specimens were retained after the Roper incident, contradicting that of 21 October which indicated that only those on one horse were disposed of. Leichhardt recorded elsewhere that the greatest number of them, between 4,000 and 5,000 specimens, had been thrown away at the Roper and only 'interesting remnants' retained.[4] The remnants were also nearly lost, as the following extract shows.

A *thorough soaking!*

Nov. 4. — ... Our bullocks had become so foot-sore, and were so oppressed by the excessive heat, that it was with the greatest difficulty we could prevent them from rushing into the water with their loads. One of them — that which carried the remainder of my botanical collection — watched his opportunity, and plunged into a deep pond, where he was quietly swimming about and enjoying himself, whilst I was almost crying with vexation at seeing all my plants thoroughly soaked.[2]

After a journey lasting over fourteen months, the party arrived at Port Essington on 17 December 1845.

In 1848, Ludwig Leichhardt, in command of a small party of men, began an east–west traverse of Australia. After leaving the Darling Downs, the expedition was never heard of again, its fate a matter of conjecture. Unfortunately, it is for this ill-fated attempt that Leichhardt is probably most remembered. His abilities as a scientist, explorer and bushman have at times been severely criticised but perhaps with little justification.[5, 6]

F. J. H. MUELLER *(1855–1856)*

Ferdinand J. H. Mueller (later Baron von Mueller), born in Germany in 1825, emigrated to Australia in 1847 and secured the post of Government Botanist of Victoria in 1853. With broad interests in his adopted country, he supported exploratory expeditions (for example, those of Giles, *see* pp. 167–180) and also undertook expeditions of his own. During 1855–1856 he was Botanist on the North Australian Expedition (1855–1856) led by A. C. Gregory, to which the following extract relates.[1, 2, 3]

Daily routine of life in the field

During the latter period of our journey [from Victoria River to the Gulf of Carpentaria], the plants increased to such a number for the collection, that I was unable to describe from fresh specimens at all; but during the earlier part of this section of the expedition, I found, particularly on Sundays, time for writing detailed descriptions of the more interesting plants, which, as regards the gay colours of *Hibiscus*, the tender flowers of *Stylidium* or *Mitrasacme*, or the easily forgotten habitual characters of [*Eucalyptus* species], was, I think, of some importance. Up to this time I have finished upwards of 500 botanical descriptions. I regret to add that many of the specimens, after being carried for such a distance by our pack-horses, have suffered materially, above all by breakage, and when the rainy season set in at our approach to the East coast I lost many specimens or damaged them in drying, a process which after our long daily stages was in the humid evening air not easily accomplished, particularly as we could not load our poor pack-animals in such a climate with large heavy tents at the outset from the Victoria River. Moreover we hoped to obtain new supplies at the Albert River, so that I was unable to take more than half a ream of light paper for securing specimens. In consequence of our not meeting the schooner at the Gulf I was during the latter part of our expedition seriously impeded in my operations for want of material to dry my plants. Still I am glad to state that I lost no species entirely, and it is due to Mr Gregory's wise arrangements that I succeeded in bringing my collections safely home.

Ferdinand Mueller. (Source: As shown on p. 134 of Curtis's Botanical Magazine dedications 1827–1927: portraits and biographical notes *by E. Nelmes & W. Cuthbertson, published in 1931 by the Royal Horticultural Society, London. Reproduced with permission from the archives of the Royal Botanic Gardens, Melbourne)*

Impossible as it was to remain far behind of the party on account of the hostilities of the natives, which attacked us twice — I have not secured so many kinds of seeds as I might have wished, particularly during the latter part of the exploration, one bagful being unfortunately lost on a very rainy day, when we broke through some dense mountain scrub; — but when I say, Sir William, that I never lost a single minute in repose or useless occupation, I trust with tranquillity of my mind, that you will be content with the small quantity I have to offer. My time indeed was so much occupied, that I could not even write my journal at daylight, but I devoted part of my two hours' nightly watch on the bivouac-fire for the purpose.

Perhaps it may be interesting to you to picture the daily routine of our life in the field. We were roused precisely at four o'clock a.m. by the last sentry on watch, finished our simple breakfast in ¼ of an hour, went at once out in search of our horses, and managed

Top:
Red sand dunes of Central Australia, in full bloom in August 1988, showing shrubs of Acacia *(yellow-flowered) and* Aluta maisonneuvii *(purple-flowered). In the background is a young tree of* Allocasuarina decaisneana, *the desert oak. Both it and A.* maisonneuvii *were described by Mueller.*

Bottom:
Senecio gregorii, *a member of the daisy family, growing in the bed of Ellery Creek, Central Australia.
It is named after A. C. Gregory who, after leading the North Australian Expedition, collected the plant in 1858 during an unsuccessful search for Ludwig Leichhardt (see pp. 150–160).*

generally to have them caught, driven in, saddled, and packed, a little past sunrise. We travelled hardly ever less than eight hours, often ten, at the rate of about three miles an hour; but when grass or water was not conveniently found sometimes considerably longer. Unloading, going through our little domestic duties, repair of cloaths [sic] and saddlery, attendance to our noble animals, without which we should have been helpless beings in the wilderness, pitching our calico sheets, and refreshing ourselves by a hasty meal would occupy us for better than an hour; the rest of the day, about two hours at the average, was allotted to the

TOP:
Aluta maisonneuvii
(syn. Thryptomene
maisonneuvii*),*
a shrub belonging to
the Myrtaceae and
growing to about
1.5 m tall, was
described by
Mueller from a
specimen attributed
to explorer John
McDouall Stuart,
who successfully led
an exploring party
across Australia
during 1861–1862.

CENTRE:
Rulingia loxophylla,
named and described
by Mueller from
specimens he
collected during the
North Australian
Expedition.

BOTTOM:
The spiny-fruited
Tribulus forrestii,
a member of the
Zygophyllaceae
and one of a
number of species
collected by explorer
John Forrest and
sent to Mueller
for naming.
Photographed
near Carnarvon,
Western Australia.

TOP:
Rananculus
anemoneus, *a
perennial herb
confined to alpine
and subalpine tracts
of the Kosciuszko
region of New South
Wales and collected
and named by
Mueller. Flowers are
commonly 4–6 cm in
diameter.*

BOTTOM:
Leucochrysum
albicans *subsp.*
alpinum *in exposed
alpine herbfield in
Mt Kosciuszko
National Park.
This perennial herb,
an everlasting daisy,
was first described
by Mueller as
Helichrysum
incanum var.*
alpinum *from a
collection he
gathered in the
Australian Alps.*

special duties of our respective departments. I would employ myself in examining the plants around our camp, in attending to the specimens and seeds snatched up on the way or writing botanical notes. At night we stretched ourselves on our blankets, and generally in full cloaths [sic], to be ready for defence at a second's notice, the gun alongside us, the revolver under our head.

During our journey around the southern part of the Carpentaria Gulf, the season was so dry that even that precious providential gift of nature, the purslane, was parched and bitter. Our rations were small, the salt pork melted by the heat to ¼ of its original weight, which of course remained the standard; it became rancid and most indigestible. Game was scarcely to be had. But when we proceeded to the eastern part of the continent, rain-showers had refreshed the vegetation, and we enjoyed not only the *Portulaca* again, which was valuable above anything of the kind in being gathered without loss of time and being in its fresh state at once ready for use, but we relished also occasionally the boiled *Chenopodium erosum*, which is hardly inferior to spinage [sic], although we could badly afford the time for collecting it.[4]

Mueller remained Government Botanist until his death in 1896 and for many years was also the Director of the Royal Botanic Gardens, Melbourne. He was a prolific writer and named about 2,000 species of plants.[2]

W. E. P. GILES (1872–1874)

Born in Bristol, England, in 1835, W. Ernest P. Giles was a major explorer of the deserts of central Australia and, when conditions permitted, he, and sometimes his associates, gathered botanical specimens for Ferdinand Mueller (*see* pp. 161–166).[1] During August–September 1872 Giles was exploring to the west and south of Alice Springs.

A new palm

Saturday, 31st August. — Last night was clear and cold; the stars, those sentinels of the sky, appearing intensely bright, and to the explorer they must ever be the objects of admiration and love, as to them he is indebted for his guidance through the untrodden wilderness he is traversing. The thermometer went down to 24° [Fahrenheit] by daylight, but upon the appearance of the sun, the temperature rose rapidly. Several hundreds of pelicans in a large flock made their appearance upon the waterhole near the camp this morning; but no sooner they discovered us than they made off, before a shot could be fired at them; they came from the north-westward, and indeed all the aquatic birds, which I have seen upon the wing, come and go in that direction. Though there are plenty of small fish in the river, yet I do not think they are large enough for mobs of pelicans to exist upon; these birds therefore must have come from some larger waters, I should suppose, up in the tropics; the largest fish I have seen in the Finke was not bigger than a sardine. I am in hopes we shall get through this glen today, for however picturesque and wild the scenery, it is very difficult and bad travelling for the horses, and consequently more trouble to get them along. We made but a late start this morning; there was no other road than to continue following the windings of the creek through this mountain-bound glen, in the same manner as yesterday. After travelling some miles, I observed several natives in the glen, ahead of us. Immediately upon their discovering us, they raised a great outcry, made several fires, and raised great volumes of smoke, probably as signals to their friends in the first instance, and to intimidate us in the second,

which latter effect did not take place. They then considered it their interest to be off themselves, and they ran away further up the glen; I saw also another lot of some 20 or 30 scudding away over the rocks and hills to our right; they left all their valuables in the camp, which we saw as we passed. One gentleman most vehemently apostrophised us from the summit of a rocky hill, and most probably ordered us away out of his country. We paid, as may be supposed, but little attention to his yells; as his words to us were only wind, we passed on, leaving him and his camp as mere incidents in a day's march. Soon after leaving this native camp we had the gratification to discover a magnificent specimen of the fan-palm, growing in the channel of the watercourse, with the drift of floods washed against its stem; its dome-shaped frondage contrasting strangely with the paler green foliage of the eucalyptus-trees, which surrounded it.

It was a perfectly new botanical feature to me, nor did I expect ever to have met it in this latitude. I had certainly been on the look-out for such an object, as I had noticed portions of palm-leaves and branches in the flood-drifts against the butts of trees in the glen. This fine specimen was 60 feet high in the barrel. I obtained a quantity of its leaves for my kind and generous friend, the Baron von Mueller, which I brought with me. After passing the palms we continued our march amongst the defiles of this mountain glen, which appears to have no termination, for neither signs of a break nor anything but a continuation of this range could be observed from any of the hills I ascended. It was late in the afternoon, when we left the palm-groves, and in two miles further we encamped; the distance travelled by us since starting was considerably over 20 miles, but I only made good 12 in a straight line from last camp.

Sunday, 1st September. — Last night was bright and cool, but the thermometer did not descend lower than 34°. This being Sunday I made it a day of rest, at least for the horses. I was myself compelled to make an excursion into the hills, to endeavour to discover when and where this apparently interminable glen would cease; for with all its grandeur, picturesqueness and variety of scenery it was such a difficult road for the horses, and so stony, that I was getting heartily tired of it ...

Monday, 2nd September. — ... We started early and proceeded up the glen, still following its mazy windings. In less than two miles we passed the junction of the northern tributary, noticed by me yesterday, and continued on over rocks, under precipices, crossing and recrossing the creek, turning and winding to all points of the compass. One bend perhaps ran west for half a mile, the next turn was perhaps south and so on, so that nearly three miles had to be travelled to make one good. Today we passed again several clumps of the beautiful palm, growing mostly in the bed of the creek, where they helped considerably to enliven the scenery. I collected also today and during the other days, since we have been in this glen, a number of most beautiful flowers, which grow in profusion in this otherwise desolate glen. I was literally surrounded by fair flowers of many changing a hue. Why Nature should scatter such floral gems in such a stony sterile region is difficult to understand, but such a variety of lovely flowers of every colour and perfume I have never met with previously. They alone would have induced me to name this Glen of

The Central Australian cabbage palm, Livistona mariae *subsp.* mariae, *discovered by Giles. The subsp.* mariae *is endemic to an area of about 60 sq. km in the bed of the Finke River and its tributaries. This photograph was taken in Palm Valley, Northern Territory.*

Flora, but, having found in it also so many of the stately palm-trees, I have called it the Glen of Palms. While we were travelling, a few slight showers fell upon us, giving us warning that heavier falls might be expected. I was most anxious to reach the mouth of the glen if possible by night, so heartily tired was I of such a continuously serpentine track. I therefore kept pushing on. We encountered several natives today, but they invariably fled into the fastnesses of their mountain-homes. They raised great volumes of smoke however, and their vociferations only ceased when we got out of earshot. The pattering of the raindrops became heavier; yet I kept on, hoping at every turn to see an opening, which would form the end, or rather the beginning of this glen, but night and rain descended upon us, and I was compelled to camp another night in this valley. I found a small sloping sandy and firm piece of ground a little off from the creek, having some bloodwood trees (peculiar species of eucalypt) growing upon it, and above the reach of any flood-mark. One can never be too careful in selecting a site for a camp on a water-course, for in one night a flood might come and wash everything to destruction. I was very fortunate in finding so favourable a spot, as there was sufficient ground for the horses to feed upon, and some good feed upon it also. By the time we had our tents erected and everything snug the rain fell in earnest; but we were warm and comfortable, and fell asleep in peace and tranquillity, thanking Providence we were much better off than many of our fellow creatures in the midst of civilisation.[2]

Mueller subsequently described and named the palm, *Livistona mariae*.

Most abominable insect of its kind

Wednesday, 18th September. — In the course of the night some drops of rain fell; it was cloudy and close, and the thermometer at daylight stood at 61° [Fahrenheit]. I sent Robinson away back to our old camp upon the little plain, feeling pretty sure that as the missing horse had returned there once he would do so again; and as he had had plenty of time to get through the scrub I thought it probable Robinson would have only to ride there to get him. There was a hot wind blowing today from the NW. The sand was flying about in all directions, and it was a most uncomfortable and disagreeable day; the thermometer indicated 96° in the shade, and I was only too glad when night approached, as the wind seemed inclined to lull. [Robinson] returned in the evening, having been successful in finding the horse at the old feeding ground, and I took special care to find a pair of hobbles for him for this night at all events. The atmosphere was heavy and loaded, and it seemed probable, that a fall of rain would occur, as the heat experienced by us for the past few days was quite unseasonable; the flies also were most insufferably pertinacious, not that they were so numerous, but I never met even amongst their congeners upon the Darling anything like such persistence, and I therefore consider the tropic fly of Australia the most abominable insect of its kind.[2]

A large ring of Triodia photographed south of the Hamersley Ranges, Western Australia.

The scourge of Triodia

Monday, 23rd September. — The night was again cool and clear, and the thermometer stood at 30°. A heavy dew fell, but no frost appeared. The horses wandered a bit in the night, and it was late in the day when we got away from the camp. I proceeded along the foot of the ranges, which here ran nearly WNW. Close to their foot the country is full of stones, but open and thickly covered with enormous branches of *Triodia*, which by this time the horses dread like a pestilence; I have encountered this scourge for more than 200 miles. All round the coronets of most of the horses, in consequence of being so continually punctured with the spines of this vegetable, it has caused a swelling or tough enlargement of the flesh and skin, giving them the appearance of having ring-bones, many of them having the flesh quite raw and bleeding; they are also very tender-footed, from traversing so much stony ground as we have had to pass over. Bordering upon the open *Triodia* ground, to the south of us, is the scrub, composed chiefly of mulga, though there are various other shrubs and bushes growing amongst it; it is so thick, that we cannot see one-third of the horses at once; they of course continually endeavour to make for it, to avoid the stones and *Triodia*, for generally speaking, the pungent grass and mulga appear antagonistic plants; the ground however is usually soft in the scrubs, and on that account the horses also seek it. I have occasionally allowed them to travel in the scrub out of kindness to them, until some dire mishap forces us out again; for the scrubs are mostly so dense, that the horses are compelled to crush through it, tearing the coverings off their loads, and occasionally — indeed frequently — forcing sticks in between their backs or sides and their saddles; then we hear a frantic crashing through the scrub, and the sound of the pounding of horse-hoofs being the first notice we receive, that some frightful calamity has occurred; then, as soon as we can get through it ourselves, and round up the horses, we find one missing, whose tracks have to be found; then portions of the load are picked up here and there, and perhaps in the course of an hour the horse is again found and repacked, and we push on again. Sometimes it is varied by there being two horses that have disencumbered themselves instead of one; when those accidents occur we push out again immediately for the open though stony ground, for there at least we can see what is going on. These scrubs are really dreadful, and one's skin and clothes get torn and ripped in all directions. After these mishaps, one of which occurred upon this day's travels, I continued on and travelled ten miles, to the foot of a hill I had been steering for.[2]

The genus *Triodia* (including *Plectrachne*) contains a little over sixty species and is a member of the Poaceae or grass family. It is widespread within Australia, being the dominant component of the arid hummock grassland communities that cover about a third of the continent. Some species form extremely large hummocks or rings, the largest being up to six metres wide, and some — as experienced by Giles's horses — have pungent, flesh-penetrating leaves.[3] Species of *Triodia* are commonly known as 'spinifex', for example by Warburton (*see* p. viii), an unfortunate appellation as this is also the generic name (that is, *Spinifex*) of a coastal grass.

In 1873, Giles, with a party of four men — himself, William Henry Tietkens, Alfred Gibson and James Andrews, and twenty-four horses, left the Overland Telegraph Line at Ross's Waterhole and headed for Western Australia via the Musgrave Ranges, Mt Olga, and Tomkinson Ranges. As with all explorers, Giles and his colleagues made use of local fare whenever they could. During the early part of this expedition he recorded the gathering and consumption of eggs of the lowan, a mound-building bird more commonly known as the mallee fowl (*Leipoa ocellata*).

Luxuries in the wilderness

Today we came upon three lowans' or native pheasants' nests. These birds which somewhat resemble guinea-fowl in appearance, build extraordinarily large nests of sand, in which they deposit small sticks and leaves; here the female lays about a dozen eggs, the decomposition of the vegetable matter providing the warmth necessary to hatch them. These nests are found only in thick scrubs. I have known them five to six feet high, of a circular conical shape, and a hundred feet round at the base. The first, though of enormous size, produced only two eggs; the second, four, and the third, six. We thanked Providence for supplying us with such luxuries in such a wilderness. There are much easier feats to perform than the carrying of lowans' eggs, and for the benefit of any readers who don't know what those eggs are like, I may mention that they are larger than a goose egg, and of a more delicious flavour than any other egg in the world. Their shell is beautifully pink tinted, and so terribly fragile that, if a person is not careful in lifting them, the fingers will crunch through the tinted shell in an instant. Therefore, carrying a dozen of such eggs is no easy matter. I took upon myself the responsibility of bringing our prize safe into camp, and I accomplished the task by packing them in grass, tied up in a handkerchief, and slung round my neck; a fine fardel hanging on my chest, immediately under my chin. A photograph of a person with such an appendage would scarcely lead to recognition. We used some of the eggs in our tea as a substitute for milk. A few of the eggs proved to possess some slight germs of vitality, the preliminary process being the formation of eyes. But explorers in the field are not such particular mortals as to stand upon such trifles; indeed, parboiled, youthful, lowans' eyes are considered quite a delicacy in the camp.[4]

During this same expedition, on 20 April 1874, Giles, accompanied by Gibson, left their base camp on the edge of the Rawlinson Range with the intention of exploring the country 100 miles to the west.

Only a pint or so left

Wednesday, 22nd April. — ... we turned the horses out, having come twenty miles. I found one of our large water-bags had leaked, and we had not as much water as I had anticipated. Gibson here preferred to keep the big cob to ride, instead of Badger, so after giving Badger and Darkie a few pints of water each, Gibson drove them back on the tracks [with the expectation that they would return to the base camp] ... We gave our two remaining riding horses all the water contained in the two large water-bags, except a quart or two for ourselves, which gave them a pretty fair drink, though not a tenth part of what they would have swallowed — they fed a little while we remained here. The day was quite too hot for traversing such a country; the thermometer, while we were here, standing at 96°, though we had not yet reached the hottest time of the day. We hung the two kegs with water (five gallons each) up in a tree with the pack-saddles, water-bags (now empty), and other gear. The supply in the kegs was, of course, intended to water the horses and ourselves on our return. Starting again, we made another twenty miles by night, the country still covered with small stones and thickly clothed with *Triodia*; there were thin patches of low scrub at odd intervals ... It was late by the time we encamped, and the horses were much in want of water, especially the big cob, who kept coming up to the camp all night, and tried to get at our water-bags, pannikins, etc. The extraordinary instinct of a horse, when in agony of thirst, in getting hold of any utensil, that ever had water in, is surprising and most annoying. We had one small water-bag hung in a tree, and I did not think of it, when my mare came up straight to it, and took it in her teeth, forcing out the cork and sending the water up (which we were both dying to drink) in a beautiful jet, which, descending to the earth, was irrevocably lost. We had now only a pint or so left.[2]

The following day, within thirty miles of the supply of kegged water, Gibson and Giles parted company. Giles had instructed Gibson to take the, by then, one remaining horse and return on their outward tracks, via the kegs of water, to their base camp and direct Tietkens to bring relief.

Appalling news

Friday, 24th April (till 1st May). — ... As soon as it was light this morning, I was again upon the horse-tracks, and reached the kegs about the middle of the day. Gibson had been here, watered the mare and gone on; he had left me about two and a-half gallons of water in one keg; and it may be imagined how glad I was, to get a drink; I could have drank [*sic*] the whole quantity in an hour, but I was compelled to economy, for I could not tell how many days would elapse, before assistance would come; it could not well be less than five days — it might be more. After quenching my thirst a little, I felt ravenously hungry, and on searching among the bags all the food I could find was eleven sticks of smoked horse-flesh, averaging about one and a-half ounces each. I was rather staggered to find, that I had little more than a pound weight of meat, to last me till assistance came. However I was compelled to eat some at once, and proceeded to devour two sticks raw, as I had no water to boil them in. After this I sat in the shade, to reflect on the precariousness of my position. I was 60 miles from water, and eighty from food; my messenger could not well return before six days, and I began to think it highly probable, I should be dead of hunger if not thirst before anybody could possibly arrive. I looked at the keg, it was an awkward thing to carry empty; there was nothing else to carry water in, as Gibson had taken all the bags. The keg when empty with its straps and rings weighed 15 lbs., and now it had 20 lbs. of water in it, I could not carry it without a blanket for a pad for my shoulder (I had left my blanket here when going out), so that with my revolver and cartridge pouch, and other things on my belt, I staggered under a weight of about 50 lbs., when I put the keg on my back; I had 14 matches only, Gibson had all the others. After I had thoroughly digested all points of my situation, I concluded, that if I did not help myself, Providence wouldn't help me either. So I started away with the keg on my back, bent double with it, and could only travel so slowly, that I thought it scarcely worth while travelling at all; I got so thirsty at every step I took, I longed to drink every drop of water I had in the keg, but I restrained myself. The thermometer did not rise quite so high today as yesterday, it going up only to 90° in the shade. I only got three miles away from the kegs, and to do that I travelled most of it in the moonlight, after the sun went down. The next few days I shall pass over with the remark, that as long as water lasted in the keg I carried it, and averaged about five miles a day. To people, who cannot comprehend this country, it may seem absurd, that a man could not travel faster than that. All I can say is, there may be men who would do so; but most men in the position I was in, would simply have died of both hunger and thirst, for by the second day my horse meat was all gone. I had to remain in what shade I could find during the day, and I travelled by moonlight at night. At 15 miles from the kegs the two loose horses we had turned away from there, had left the main line of tracks, which of course ran east and west; these two horses left them at a slight incline, going on about ESE. Gibson, I was grieved to see, had gone in the loose horses' tracks; but I felt sure he would and they also would return to the main-line, and I therefore could not investigate any further in my present position; so after following them about a mile I turned again to the main line of tracks, anxiously looking at every step to see, if Gibson's horse-tracks returned into them. They never did ...

On the 26th I almost gave up the thought of walking any further; for the exertion in this dreadful country, where the *Triodia* was almost as high as myself, and as thick as it could grow, was quite overpowering, and being now almost starved I felt quite light-headed, and after sitting down on several occasions, when I got up again my head would swim round, so that I fell down many times, and was often oblivious for more than a quarter of an hour ... On the 29th I had emptied my keg, and was still over 20 miles from the Circus; but in this *April's ivory moonlight* I plodded on desolate, yet all undaunted, and reached the Circus-water just at dawn of day. Oh, how I drank; oh, how hungry I was; and I thanked Providence that I had so far at least relieved myself from that howling wilderness, for I was now once more upon the Rawlinson-Range, though still twenty miles from home. There was no sign of any tracks of anyone having been here since I left it; the water all but gone. I wondered what had become of Gibson; he had certainly never come here, and how could he reach the Fort [McKellar] without coming here — that was the question; but I was in such a miserable state of mind and body, that I ceased to add any more vexatious speculations as to what had delayed him. I remained here continually drinking and drinking, until 10 a.m. The ground was now of course all small stones, my feet were very sore, and I could only go at a snail's pace over them. So weak had I become, that by late at night I had only accomplished 11 miles, and lay down about five miles from the Gorge of Tarns, again choking for water. Most of these days the thermometer has stood at 92° in the shade. I omitted to mention, that just after I left the Circus I picked up a small dying wallaby, whose mother had thrown it from her pouch. It weighed about two ounces, and was scarcely furnished yet with fur. The instant I saw it, like an eagle I pounced upon it and ate it raw, dying as it was, fur, skin and all. The delicious taste of the creature I shall never forget. I only wished I had its mother and its father, to serve in the same way. On the 1st of May, at one o'clock in the morning, I was walking again, and reached the Gorge of Tarns long before daylight, and could now indulge in as much water as I desired, but it was exhaustion I suffered from. My reader may imagine with what intense feelings of relief I stepped into Fort McKellar at daylight and awoke Mr Tietkens, who stared at me, as though I had been one, newly risen from the dead. I asked him, if he had seen Gibson, and to give me some food. I was appalled to hear that Gibson had never reached the camp ...[2]

Gibson perished in the desert which now bears his name. The remaining members of the party safely returned to civilisation.

The following year Giles, for much of the time approximately following the 30th parallel, successfully crossed from Pt Augusta to Perth. The success of that expedition was largely due to the use of 'ships of the desert', camels being capable of travelling ten to twelve days without a drink but horses requiring water at least once every twelve hours.[5] However, camels sometimes still suffered.

Poisoned camels

On the 16th [June 1875, a few miles NE of Lake Gairdner] ... I was riding in advance along the old track, when old Jimmy came running up behind my camel in a most excited state, and said, 'Hi, master, me find 'im, big one watta, plenty watta, mucka (not) pickaninny (little); this way, watta go this way,' pointing to a place on our left. I waited until the caravan appeared through the scrub, then old Jimmy led us to the spot he had found. There was a small area of bare rock, but it was too flat to hold any quantity of water, though some of the fluid was shining on it; there was only enough for two or three camels, but I decided to camp there nevertheless. What water there was, some of the camels licked up in no time, and went off to feed. They seemed particularly partial to a low pale-green-foliaged tree with fringe-like leaves, something like fennel or asparagus. I have often gathered specimens of this in former journeys, generally in the most desert places. The botanical name of this tree is *Gyrostemon ramulosus*. After hobbling out the camels, and sitting down to dinner, we became aware of the absence of Mr Jess Young, and I was rather anxious as to what had become of him, as a new arrival from England adrift in these scrubs would be very liable to lose himself. However, I had not much to fear for Mr Young, as, having been a sailor, and carrying a compass, he might be able to recover us. Immediately after our meal I was going after him, but before it was finished he came, without his camel, and said he could not get her on, so had tied her up to a tree and walked back, he having gone a long way on my old tracks. I sent Tommy and another riding-camel with him, and in a couple of hours they returned with Mr Young's animal.

Fruiting branch of Gyrostemon ramulosus. *This small tree is the plant suspected by Giles of poisoning his camel. The species is dioecious; that is, individual plants have either male flowers or female flowers. It is one of a number of species that was first described after being collected during the 1800–1804 French scientific expedition to Australia under the command of Captain Nicolas Baudin.*

The following morning, the 17th, much to my distress, one of our young bull camels was found to be poisoned, and could not move. We made him sick with hot butter and gave him a strong clyster. Both operations produced the same substance, namely, a quantity of the chewed and digested *Gyrostemon*; indeed, the animal apparently had nothing else in his inside. He was a trifle better by night, but the following morning, my best bull, Mustara, that had brought me through this region before, was poisoned, and couldn't move. I was now very sorry I had camped at this horrid place. We dosed Mustara with butter as an emetic, and he also threw up nothing but the chewed *Gyrostemon*; the clyster produced the same. It was evident that this plant has a very poisonous effect on the camels, and I was afraid some of them would die. I was compelled to remain here another day. The first camel poisoned had got a little better, and I hoped the others would escape; but as they all seemed to relish the poisonous plant so much until they felt the effects, and as there were great quantities of it growing on the sandhills, I was in great anxiety during the whole day. On the 19th I was glad to find no fresh cases, though the two camels that had suffered were very weak and afflicted with spasmodic staggerings. We got them away, though they were scarcely able to carry their loads, which we lightened as much as possible; anything was better than remaining here, as others might get affected.[4]

In 1876, again with camels, Giles also successfully led an expedition from the west coast, via the Gibson Desert, to the central Overland Telegraph Line.

In the annals of Australian botanical history Giles's collections were important. During his first (1872) and second (1873–1874) exploring expeditions he collected no fewer than 253 species of plant, at least forty of which were named and described by Mueller.

Giles died at Coolgardie, Western Australia, in 1897.[1]

D. SULLIVAN *(1882)*

Daniel Sullivan, born in 1836, was for many years the headmaster of the State school at Moyston, a small township situated a few kilometres west of the Grampians in western Victoria.[1] In 1882, in an introduction to a check-list of the plants of the Grampians, Sullivan recorded how he came to collect specimens.

The monotonous routine of village life

To vary the monotonous routine of village life, I commenced, about nine years since, to collect mosses and ferns as an agreeable recreation after the harassing work of my school was over for the day or week, as the case might be; and, having consulted Baron von Mueller with regard to the scientific names of such plants, that kind and eminent botanist advised me to make a complete collection ... of plants of every description occurring in my neighbourhood, all of which he kindly promised to name for me ...

The vegetation of the Grampians and adjoining mountains is not, generally speaking, luxuriant, but it is varied and beautiful, each range, and even the peaks and gullies of the same range, having special objects of interest exclusively confined to their own narrow limits, and vainly sought for elsewhere. In no part of Victoria does the incomparable *Epacris impressa* form so prominent and beautiful a feature in the landscape as about these mountains, where, for many miles in extent, it stretches out before the admiring gaze of the beholder in all the possible shades of rose, pink, and white, which, contrasted with the tall grass-trees (*Xanthorrhoea australis*) and the glossy foliage of the young stringy-bark tree, leaves on the memory an impression not readily effaced.[2]

In a subsequent paper, Sullivan referred to an unusual encounter when collecting a native pea.

Bushranger or escaped lunatic?

A curious incident occurred to me on the heath-ground near Mount Abrupt, while gathering specimens of this plant: — four strapping

Daniel Sullivan. (Source: Portrait collection, Royal Botanic Gardens, Melbourne, from the original at Moyston State School. Reproduced with the permission of the archives of the Royal Botanic Gardens, Melbourne, and of the Headmaster, Moyston State School)

fellows rode up within about 20 yards of where I stood. A warm debate ensued as to my object in wandering about in so lonely a place. One, who appeared to be the leader, was of the opinion that I was a surveyor; another, that none but an artist would take so much notice of surrounding objects; the third maintained that I was connected with the Kelly gang, and that before many days there would be some bank robberies in the neighbourhood. The expression of this notion was, I confess a great relief to me for I was just beginning to think that the veritable Kelly party stood before me.

The grass-tree, Xanthorrhoea australis, *flowering in November 1988 amongst stringy-bark (*Eucalyptus baxteri*) after a fire in the Grampians, the plant-hunting ground of Daniel Sullivan.*

The fourth suggested that I was an escaped lunatic from the Ararat Asylum, and considered it their duty to take me to Dunkeld to be forwarded thence to my old quarters. The opinion of the leader at last prevailed, and so I was permitted to enjoy my rambles in peace.[3]

Sullivan was one of many amateur botanists to make a significant contribution to the study of Australia's plants. By 1882, he had gathered 1,600 species of Victorian plants. He died in 1895.[1]

W. B. SPENCER *(1894)*

The use of animals in exploration and the hardships they, not just the explorers, encountered has been mentioned in both the Introduction and elsewhere in this book. As also mentioned, the camel was a great boon to the exploration of arid regions of Australia. However, Walter Baldwin Spencer (also known as Professor Baldwin Spencer) (1860–1929) made it quite clear that they are not always the best of animals to work with. This extract is from Spencer's narrative which formed part of a four-volume report of the Horn Scientific Expedition to central Australia in 1894.[1]

At the time of writing this narrative, Spencer was Professor of Biology at The University of Melbourne. Although he occasionally gathered herbarium specimens, the study of botany was not his major interest. During the Horn Scientific Expedition he was primarily responsible for zoology and photography and it is for his later anthropological studies in central and northern Australia that he is most remembered.[2, 3] However, the experiences related below were also applicable to Professor Ralph Tate (1840–1901), who was responsible for botanical aspects of the expedition, and indeed to all members of the party.

Qualities of filthiness, viciousness, and crass stupidity

In judging of the results of the expedition it is only fair to remember that some two thousand miles had to be traversed slowly, for the most part on camel-back, and that out of a total of one hundred and twenty-five days spent in the field, less than twenty were available for actually 'spelling' in camp; that is, whilst during each of more than one hundred days an odd hour or two were available for collecting, the time during which we were really free to make anything like a searching investigation was of necessity very limited indeed.

In such a district as central Australia it is not always possible to stop just when and where you want to; waterholes during the dry season — that is, the winter months — are few and far between, and certain stages have to be made to reach them. In the scrub-covered country, it must also be remembered that travelling is often slow and tedious and from a collector's point of view a camel is the most unsatisfactory of beasts.

Perched high up between heaven and earth, you may often see, say, a lizard or an insect which you are anxious to secure, but long before you can persuade your camel to sit down the animal is far away and safely hidden. The chances are, too, that you return from a fruitless search to find that your camel, which above all things dislikes to be left behind its companions, has trotted away. Anyone who has attempted the task knows well the difficulty of persuading the beast to sit down when it does not want to do so, and will sympathise with the feelings of an unexpert [*sic*] rider who attempts to safely mount a camel which is anxious to be up and off after its fellows.

A camel has a peculiar way of its own of getting up, which is bad enough when done slowly; but when it is in a hurry, then you have to be very careful not to get an ugly bump or fall. The moment you are in your seat behind the hump, or perhaps before you are there, he rises with a jerk half way up on his hinder legs, throwing you forwards; before you have time to recover your balance up go the front legs half way, then it rises completely on its hind legs and finally on its front legs — a fourfold movement of a most disagreeable nature. To make it sit down, the magic word 'h_sht' must be repeated until it kneels down on its front legs; then it swings backward half way down on its hind legs, then completely down on its front legs, and, lastly, completely down on its hind legs.

Then, too, the movement of the beast when it walks or trots has a peculiar churning effect on specimens, and as it is not always possible to safely stow them away when on the march, many a one is bruised and spoilt. In walking it does not move its feet like a horse — two diagonally opposite ones at a time — but the two near or the two off feet are lifted simultaneously.

In arid country, such as we for the most part traversed, the camel certainly has great advantages; but it must be confessed that you first mount your beast without any expectation of pleasure, that you derive none whatever from your association with him, and that you part company without any regret on either side.

The bull camels will fight furiously for the possession of the cows, biting each other fiercely with their powerful canine teeth. The victor, if it does not entirely disable the vanquished one, will chase the latter away at headlong speed, utterly regardless of anything in its way; and if the flight takes place at night, as it once did with us, and the flight of the vanquished one happens to be directed through the camp, then the consequences may be very serious, as two infuriated camels running 'amuck' require to be given a wide berth.

A bull camel has a remarkable habit of in some curious way forcing the air in behind the uvula and forming a bladder, which begins to come out at one side of the mouth. The beast makes a loud bubbling sound, the bladder in the meantime growing larger and larger until it is as big as its head. Then the bubbling ceases, and the bladder is gradually withdrawn.

The neck is so long that when you perhaps imagine yourself well out of harm's way, you are startled to hear a sudden snap and find that the beast has made a savage bite at you. If angry, they will try and get you down upon the ground and endeavour to pound you with the hard callosity on their chest. Altogether, it is best to be on your guard when dealing with camels; there is no getting fond of them, and of all beasts of burden they combine in the highest degree the qualities of filthiness, viciousness, and crass stupidity.

The ordinary baggage differs, as it has been said, from the riding camel as much as a thoroughbred does from a cart horse; and of all the methods of travelling, the back-breaking swing of a rough camel is the most monotonous. A good riding camel will travel as fast as ten or twelve miles an hour, and keep this up for many hours during the day, but the ordinary loading ones will not cover more ground than between two and three miles an hour. They always travel in single file, and it is most difficult to get two to walk side by side, so that conversation whilst on the march is conducted under difficulties.

However, their powers of endurance, despite their vicious disposition, render them invaluable in dry countries such as the interior of Australia. They will feed on thorny desert plants which nothing else will eat, and can, when trained, go for days together without drinking — the longest record in Australia being, I believe, the 24 days' waterless march on the recent Elder Expedition. Such abstinence as this must, however, cause considerable suffering to the animals …

We had altogether some twenty-five camels and two horses, each member of the scientific staff having his own riding camel, the remainder being loaded with various weights according to their carrying capacity, the heaviest load weighing between seven and eight hundred pounds.

Perhaps the most curious part of the whole caravan was a buggy drawn by a pair of camels. This was only taken over the first two hundred and fifty miles of our journey, when we were travelling along the track by the telegraph line as far north as Crown Point, where we were not sorry to leave it behind. Out in the bush it would have been impossible for it to have travelled, and even along the rough track, where travelling was comparatively easy, it was not exactly an unmixed blessing when rough-creek beds had to be crossed. In the illustration [not included here] the camels are represented as sitting down in the position in which they have just been harnessed; when standing up they naturally looked very ungainly and far too big in comparison to the size of the buggy. Though in some parts of Australia, such as the West, camels are now regularly used for this purpose, they seem to be much more fitted for carrying burdens than to serve as draught-animals.

All the camels used were the singe-humped ones, and the saddles are so made that they are kept in place by the hump itself, partly by girths. A loading camel will carry a big box on either side and another package on the top. Everything, of course, is fastened on while the camel is sitting down, the beast frequently expressing its disgust and annoyance at the process by growling and gnashing its teeth. Unless securely fastened on, the slow but steady churning movement, which is much like a combined pitching and tossing and rolling, will soon put the packages out of place.

For the first day or two, until the weights are fairly adjusted, the loads are continually shifting and stoppages are frequent. Each camel has a hole bored through one side of its nose, and into this a wooden peg is fixed, shaped something like a little dumb-bell; to this a string is tied, and so in a baggage train a string passes from the nose of one animal to the tail of the one next in front, for of course they walk in single file.

So long as the travelling is easy this is right enough, but in difficult country, as when, for example, a creek with steep sides has to be crossed, it is not easy to avoid a break-away. The front one of the camels coming first to a steep descent and carrying a heavy load is very apt to go down with a sudden run, which probably means that the hinder one stands still and the nose-string is broken. The nose-peg itself is not infrequently pulled out and has to be replaced or, if the string by good fortune simply comes untied (the knot is always a loose one) from the tail of the front animal, the hinder ones will stand still, sniffing the air in a stupid, idiotic kind of way, until they are led up to the front one and the damage repaired. In difficult country this often takes place, and so travelling is slow work, and the distance traversed may not average more than two or, at most, three miles an hour during the day.

Going down a steep bank a camel will often slip down on its haunches, and going up one will climb on its knees. Often there is serious difficulty in getting them to cross a creek holding water. Mr A. W. Howitt told me an ingenious plan adopted by himself when he was out in charge of one of the parties despatched to search for the remnant of the ill-fated Burke and Wills Expedition. He had come to a creek full of water, and the camels steadily refused to go into it. At last a happy idea struck him; he had one of the beasts brought up and made to sit down broadside on to the creek. He and his men ranged themselves on the land side of the animal, which was then made to get up, but whilst in the act, and at a given signal when the beast was off its balance, a united push sent it sprawling into the water, across which it then made its way.

Whilst on the march our daily programme was much the same. Usually just before sunrise we were up and dressed. Very shortly after sunrise we had breakfast. Our camp cook, Laycock, was an old hand at the work, his experience dating back to the building of the overland telegraph line; and thanks to him, so long as we remained in the main camp we lived in comparative luxury. Breakfast — always hot and most welcome — was eaten when usually the temperature was not much above freezing point. The black boys and the Afghans brought the camels into camp, and along with them the odour of their undigested feed.

Whilst the loading of the baggage-camels took place, each of us saddled and packed our own beast. A riding saddle is so made — they are wonderfully crude and heavy structures — that you can pack your personal belongings in front of the lump, while behind is a seat for yourself in such a position that the animal can, when it desires to do so, whisk its filthy tail on your back.

The reins of a riding camel consist of two strings, one passing round each side of the neck and attached in front to the single wooden peg inserted in one side of the nose. Owing to the fact that a hard pull is liable to at once bring out the peg, this gives the rider the minimum of control over a beast so naturally stupid as the camel. More than once, when I had stayed behind the rest to endeavour to secure some particular beast or to take a photograph, my camel started off at a quick trot to catch up the train. All that I could do was to hold on to my camera and luggage and hope that the train was not far ahead; the camel was sure to reach it safely, but there was every chance of the camera and myself being left behind. I may say that I had christened my camel the 'Baron', after my distinguished friend and counsellor, the Baron von Mueller [*see* pp. 161–166], whose name is a household word with us in Victoria, in the hope that, as the bearer of such a name, he would behave himself accordingly, but I was disappointed in him.

Once mounted, we travelled slowly on at a walking pace for perhaps ten or twelve miles, with plenty of time to observe the nature of the country, but with no or little opportunity to collect. Then came a halt in the heat of the mid-day for lunch, when collecting was made difficult by reason of the flies which settled on your face. After the halt, another march of the same length brought us at dusk to our camping place for the night. The camel train was brought into camp forming a semicircle; each camel was unloaded, and then, after being hobbled, was set free for the night to find what feed it could. The camp fire was lighted, notes were written up, specimens labelled and packed away, and then we lay down and slept in the open under the perfect clearness of the desert sky. As a general rule the nights were very cold, not infrequently the thermometer registering several degrees below freezing point; but the air was so dry that the cold was comparatively little felt, even when our water-bags were frozen solid.[1]

F. J. GILLEN (1894)

Born in South Australia, Francis James Gillen (1855–1912) was for many years associated with the Overland Telegraph Line that ran between Adelaide and Darwin, and in 1892 was appointed the post and telegraph stationmaster at Alice Springs. From an early age he had interests in natural history and anthropology and in 1894, when the Horn Scientific Expedition visited Alice Springs,[1] his interests were further stimulated. Sometimes he was assisted in collecting specimens by Aboriginal people and undoubtedly the harnessing of their skills was usually beneficial. This was not always the case, as the following extract from a letter of Gillen's to Professor Baldwin Spencer (*see* pp. 184–189) shows.

Horsefeed!

The niggers captured two rats, both males, since I last wrote but unfortunately both got away. The portly Dolly very nearly walked on a snake at my kitchen door a few days ago, her yell quickly brought me on the scene and his snakeship is now snugly stewing in your collecting box — a fine specimen of a rare species which I have never seen out of these ranges. I have also added a few lizards to the collection. Several niggers are out now furnished with collecting boxes. It is with us a season of 'after rain' & I feel that for the Credit of the Country I must send you something. I am also trying to raise a rare weed or two for the old savage. Sorry the Simpson Gap helic[h]rysum was not new — we are getting a very nice collection of plants together but I am afraid nothing new. My wind is not good enough for climbing the high ranges. I have no taste for such violent exercise even if my wind were right, I am however anxious to get a good collection from the Mt Gillen Range & with that purpose in view I sent one of my Boys out the other day and instructed him to fill a bag with all sorts of different flowering plants and pretty grasses. He did so & upon returning emptied the contents of the bag into the horse yard where one of my thoroughbreds happened to be kept for the night. An hour or two afterwards he grinningly informed me, 'Me bin Giveum Grass longa Nanto.' The atmosphere was blue with profanity for half an hour afterwards ... [2]

Although he collected biological specimens, it is for his anthropological work that Gillen is most remembered. Having first met Spencer during the Horn Scientific Expedition, the two subsequently collaborated in ground-breaking, anthropological work.[1] The 'old savage' he referred to in this extract was Professor Ralph Tate, who was responsible for botanical aspects of the expedition.

M. KOCH (1899–1925)

Born in Berlin, Max Koch (1854–1925) emigrated to Australia in 1878. He initially worked on wheat farms and then on Mt Lyndhurst sheep station in South Australia and when time allowed, he gathered plants and seed for sale to Australian and overseas botanic gardens and herbaria. The following letter is apparently his first to Kew Gardens.[1, 2]

Offer of plants

In order to raise funds for a tour of scientific exploration on my own [account] into the central part of the Australian continent, where I propose to make extensive collections of the flora and fauna, insecta and reptilia, I send sets of dried plants of the district I live in to botanic museums. I therefore am so free in offering dried indigenous plants of the Mt Lyndhurst District (at the northern portion of the Flinders Range) at £1 per 100 specimens and seeds or fruits at 6d per packet. The botanic names are well authenticated, remarks as to the uses of plants are made and aboriginal names as far as known are recorded on each ticket. I should be pleased to receive an order, having no doubt that a long and continued intercourse will be the result, if once a connection is established.[3]

Koch's offer was accepted. In 1904, he moved to Western Australia, working for a time on the Rabbit Proof Fence before commencing work in the saw-milling industry. His interest in botany, and plant-collecting, was maintained. The following extracts are from letters Koch wrote to Kew in 1924.

Old acquaintances

I have been collecting herbarium material and carpological specimens and ripe seed at Merredin last season and I stayed at that place from beginning of September 1923 to beginning of last month. While passing through Perth I saw Mr O. H. Sargent the honorary Botanist to the W. A. Museum with a view of verifying some of the names I had attached to the plants, partly from memory, backed up by Bentham's descriptions in the *Flora australiensis*, which you had sent me a year or two ago. I found Merredin, which is situated on the 'Goldfields Line' from Perth to Coolgardie and Kalgoorlie, about 170 miles from Perth, a most ideal spot for my purpose and I collected there over 300 species in flower or fruit and registered altogether nearly 400 species growing in a small circumference of the town. As this was the first time since I started to take interest in the flora of Australia that I was enabled to devote my whole time to it — I had lost my job on the State Saw Mills on account of old age — I derived much enjoyment from my excursions in the bush where every step I took brought me in touch either with an old acquaintance or with a hitherto unknown friend, whom to know better I diligently searched in the *Flora australiensis* at my leisure with more or less success. Of course there are quite a number of plants which have been discovered since the *Flora australiensis* was issued. It is my practice to name the plants in the first place as near as I can and then send specimens to the Government Botanists of Victoria and New South Wales for verification, comparison with types, identification, or, if found to be new, for description and naming. Thus the plants I send to my subscribers across the ocean will bear names of nearly as correct as our Australian knowledge of them will permit. Regarding the carpological specimens I took the care to correctly watch them, and I remained in the Merredin district practically to the end of the season to get seeds thoroughly matured; indeed with a number of species easily dehiscent I waited too long and hence missed the seeds altogether.[4]

A compliment to Kew

About four months ago I had got a collection of plants and also carpological specimens ready to send away when I fell very seriously ill which circumstance nearly landed me in the grave. However I made a recovery and the first act will be to despatch the long delayed material to you (which constitutes the remainder of the specimens taken last year in Merredin). Having been so very close to my end I take this opportunity of letting you know how much I have appreciated my connection with your Department. You were one of the very first botanical institutions who took specimens from me and for that reason the material in your hands from me either from South Australia or Western Australia is the most complete in comparison with the other one time quite numerous places which had plants from me. I need not mention what great encouragement

The wreath plant, Lechenaultia macrantha, *a member of the Goodeniaceae, is an uncommon species found in heathlands of south-west Australia. It was described by German botanist Kurt Krause from a specimen gathered by Koch in September 1905. The hollow pollen cup (indusium) that terminates the style is the defining characteristic of this family.*

your Department has given me in my botanical studies and what great moral and financial support it has afforded me during the long period from 1897 [?1899] up to date. The little success I may have achieved in more correctly defining some species or by the bringing under notice of quite a number of new species must in a great measure be attributable to the support from your Department. Although this collection I will shortly send you will be the very last I will be able to put together, you will have the distinction of having had the very first and the very last of my efforts in distributing plants and seeds of our Australian flora.[5]

Before his death in the following year (1925), Koch found time to document his botanical activities and was justifiably pleased with his achievements.

No idle moments

Taking into consideration that all this work has been achieved after doing seven night shifts per week (from 1908 to 1915 and 1916 to 1919) of 12 hours' duration and that several hours per day had to be given to household duties [such] as making a vegetable garden, looking after a fowl run, building and improving the house etc., the performance is probably hard to beat. It was however a labour of love and the incentive of increasing my income and thus enabling me to keep my at that time large family in more comfortable circumstances made me turn every minute to the best use. I certainly had no idle moments![6]

Through Koch's efforts about forty new species became known to the scientific community.[1, 2, 6]

W. A. MICHELL *(1903)*

Mr W. A. Michell was an engineer involved in mining operations in north-west Australia. This letter was sent in 1903 to his cousin, W. N. Winn, who forwarded Michell's plant collections, of which there were seemingly very few, to Kew.[1, 2, 3]

Some of them have prickles!

Yours of July 7th came to hand by the last mail, for which I thank you much. Since then I have pressed a few flowers and am sending them by this mail. Don't be alarmed at the label on the cardboard box (Gelignite) for it isn't an anarchist's trick. If, however, the flowers have absorbed one half of the language which I found necessary for pressing them, then be careful, for they will be quite liable to explode with violence, and wreck the whole city. Some of them have prickles as you will soon feel, and altogether, I don't know when I've been so disgusted with a job before. At the results I mean. The bally things wouldn't lie flat until I got a case of Gelignite on top, and when I next looked at them, they seemed more like ghosts than themselves. However, such as they are I'm sending them. I only wish they were better. Collecting minerals is child's play to collecting and pressing flowers, and I'm afraid I shall never have enough patience to press flowers decently. If any of these dried and squeezed specimens should prove of interest to you, I shall be happy to send some more or to keep an eye open for anything else you may be interested in, in the way of flowers. The hot season is now commencing and blooms are dying away giving place to seed pods. As soon as these latter are ripe I will send you some.[1]

EUROPE

P. E. BOISSIER (*1837*)

Born into a wealthy family, Swiss botanist and traveller P. Edmond Boissier (1810–1885) never needed to work but, with early botanical interests kindled by renowned botanist Augustin de Candolle, was one of the major taxonomic botanists of the nineteenth century. His publications include the *Voyage Botanique dans le Midi de l'Espagne* and the pioneering *Flora orientalis*, the latter covering a vast area from Greece to the borders of central Asia and India. Boissier described 103 genera and 3,602 species himself and a further twenty-eight genera and 2,388 species with others.[1, 2] The following extracts pertain to a journey he made in Spain during 1837.

The public promenade of Malaga

Malaga, like Valence, still shows its Arabic origin in the labyrinths of narrow crooked streets, lanes without any thorough-fare, and numerous odd turnings which puzzle the stranger, and render long practice necessary to enable him to find his way about the city; but here the general aspect is brighter and clearer, the pavement better laid, and the houses freshly painted, and almost all of them equipped with balconies. In the Merchant's Quarter the style of the shops is perfectly oriental. They are long and narrow, and separated from the street by the bench or counter, which a customer never passes, but across which the goods are shown and sold to him.

The public promenade or Alameda, is planted with *Melia azedarach* (Pride of India), *Gleditsia* and oleanders. There are also several shrubs of the beautiful *Mimosa farnesiana*, called *Carambuco* by the Andalusian women, who adorn their lovely black tresses with its bunches of yellow and highly-scented flowers. Hither, in the evening, come all the population of Malaga, to enjoy the refreshing sea-breeze, and to meet their acquaintances. The *aguadores* may be seen in all directions, lauding their iced-water and *Azucarillos*, large lumps of porous sugar, which are dipped in the cold liquid, and eaten before they melt. There the pretty *Malagueñas* appear to the greatest advantage, and prove their right to that character for beauty

which is assigned to them pre-eminently among the fair ones of
Spain. It were [*sic*] no easy task to describe their light and graceful
carriage, and the pleasing contrast presented between their dark
uniform costume, and the sparkling animated countenances of its
wearers. I cannot but think that such an unobtrusive style of dress is
far more simple, dignified, and becoming, than the bright colours
and variegated materials in which our northern ladies take so much
delight.[3]

Trouble at the custom-house

The first few days after my arrival were taken up by a troublesome,
though not very important piece of business, to which I shall allude
for the benefit of those botanists who may hereafter visit Spain. I
had brought with me from France a stock of plant-paper, of a
quality which is not procurable, and is even prohibited, in this
country. It would have been an easy matter enough to smuggle it
into Malaga; and I might have been warned to do so, by all the
plague this paper had already caused me at Valence. But I was so
foolishly honest as to exhibit it at the custom-house, feeling sure that
the letters I was carrying to all the chief authorities in the city must
needs remove every difficulty. I however found that I was in the
hands of a host of officials, who had no greater delight than to
annoy a stranger, headed by an old rogue of an *Administrador*, who,
anticipating but little profit on the occasion, was pleased to entrench
himself in high formality and unimpeachable character! Applications,
backed by the *Gefe Politico*, attestations and representations, were
alike ineffectual. After scrawling and signing sheet after sheet of
stamped paper, I had no resource but to leave the unlucky subject of
litigation in their hands, and finally received it five months after,
exactly when I was leaving Spain; thanks to my petition having been
transmitted to Madrid. Very fortunately, I found that the common
Spanish paper might be made to serve my purpose, though it is so
small that every sheet [was] required to be opened out before I could
lay my specimen upon it.[3]

A perfect earthly paradise

The time had now arrived for me to quit Malaga and make an
excursion on the sea-shore and mountains in the Province of Ronda.
The season was peculiarly fitted for this tour, and it was my
intention to devote a month to it, previous to visiting the high lands
and lofty mountain chains of Grenada, where vegetation is much

backwarder. For this object I purchased a strong mule, which should carry my plant-paper and the small quantity of luggage necessary for myself, such an animal being indispensable for a journey of the kind. It was thus only I should be enabled to stop where I liked upon the road and to penetrate into districts never visited by the carriers. I engaged the services of a man from the environs of Velez, whose name was Antonio, a thorough specimen of the Andalusian peasant; he was always lively and talkative, singing his ballads as he went in excellent spirits, except when I compelled him to go with me upon the mountains, which he held in most devout detestation.

We set off from Malaga at 11 in the forenoon, clad, like the people of the country, with a peaked *sombrero* on our heads, cartridge-box at the girdle and musket on the shoulder. This garb, which is always worn by travellers, whether townsfolk or peasantry, is remarkably convenient, allowing people to go about without exciting any curiosity; while the sight of a coat and beaver hat never fails to raise a commotion in every village, and sets the dogs barking, and inasmuch as it is considered to mark the wearer as an Englishman, it affords an unfavourable badge for attracting the attention of plunderers. After quitting the city, we traversed a monotonous part of the Vega lying between the sea on the right hand and a line of sandy hills on the left. The fields presented not the slightest shadow, and the deficiency of water causes perfect sterility in the dry years. The waters of the Guadaljora might be brought hither with little difficulty or expense. I noticed *Galium glomeratum*, *Cichorium divaricatum*, *Scolymus maculatus* and *S. hispanicus*. The road was enlivened by numerous parties of peasants on their way to the city, coming from the large villages of Coin, Alhaurin and Churriana and Torremolinos, where all the bread used in Malaga is made, because of the excellent quality of their water. We soon fell in with the Guadalhorce or Rio de Malaga, a large stream which rises near Antequera and is brought over the ruins of an aqueduct and bridge of Roman construction. Most of the arches having fallen, the pillars chiefly remain, their massive shafts entwined with shrubs and climbing plants. These long ruins, which may be seen in many places in the fields, have a striking appearance and remind the traveller of the Campagna of Rome.

We had now reached a height, equal to that of the eastern extremity of the Sierra de Mijas, by which all day long, our view of the sea had been shut out, and we passed at a small distance the

country residence called *Retiro*, which the Malagueños vaunt too
much to strangers, but where they find what is certainly very rare in
their neighbourhood, shade and running streams. The country
through which we now travelled was delightful and fertile; either
farms girdled with orange groves, or forests of olive trees, among
which the gentle breeze allayed the heat of noon and from whence
the eye might catch distant prospects through the trembling leaves.
This lovely valley did not continue long with us, and leaving it we
ascended an uncultivated and vast plain which slopes southward
from the Sierra. All this open space was dotted with species of
Cistus, thorny shrubs, and here and there, a few clusters of stunted
evergreen oaks. About midway, we came to a hut made of leaves,
where four peasants from Alhaurin mounted guard; many
plundering attacks, which lately occurred in this neighbourhood,
having given rise to this precaution, and indeed it had been difficult
for robbers to select a spot more favourable for their purposes, for
they might everywhere lay ambushes among these wild thickets and
escape pursuit by fleeing to the mountains. Though vegetation was
somewhat monotonous, I still gathered some interesting plants, as
Cleonia lusitanica, *Stachys italica*, *Thapsia villosa*, *Dianthus
serrulatus* and the elegant *Linum suffruticosum*, which grew
abundantly among the bushes, its corollas being successively pink,
white, and yellow. After walking for about five Spanish leagues, we
descended by an easy slope to Alhaurin, a perfect earthly paradise,
full of mulberry and orange trees, and watered with numberless
brooks. So fertile is the land by nature, that splendid harvests are
ripened beneath the shade of these trees; and a naturalist need to
have visited southern Spain, ere he can form an idea of the
productive power of its soil, when blessed with a moderate degree of
moisture. All was full of freshness and life here, while the heat of the
sun had already scorched up the environs of Malaga. The hedges of
brambles and of *Coriaria myrtifolia* were adorned, as in other parts
of temperate Europe, with many delicate species of plants, as
Fumaria capreolata, *Campanula erinus*, *Geranium robertianum* and
G. lucidum, *Veronica cymbalaria*, *Fedia cornucopiae*, *Centranthus
calcitrapa* and *Arenaria spathulata*. The village which lies
embosomed in this ocean of lovely verdure does not disparage from
the aspect of the country; for it is large and clean, many of the
inhabitants of Malaga possessing villas in it, where they shun, during
the height of summer, the scorching heat of the coast; in addition to
several English families, who, coming originally only to spend the
winter, have become so much attached to the place, as to settle

finally in it. The public-house, or *Posada*, where I stopped, was
however, in disagreeable contrast with the rest of the village, being
filthy, inconvenient and infested with bugs; while to complete my
annoyance, a party of gypsies here called *Gitanos*, had taken up
their abode in it, and being the roughest and rudest people on earth,
they spent the whole night in bawling, shouting and quarrelling.[3]

The delights of discovery

My friend Hoenselaer had strongly urged me to climb the Sierra de
Mijas, where he promised me a rich harvest, spite of its apparent
sterility. To reach this mountain, I retraced a part of the Malaga
road, and quitting it to the left hand, soon reached a beautiful
nascimiento, whose abundant stream turned several mills. The
argillaceous soil around the spring was decked with those delicate
[species of *Helianthemum*], of which the blossoms only expand
at the earliest morning hour and drop away as soon as the sun is
fairly risen; these were *H. niloticum*, *H. intermedium*, *H. salicifolium*
and *H. aegyptiacum*, growing along with *Micropus supinus*,
M. bombacynus and *Evax pygmaea*. On arriving at the foot of
the wall of rock, mentioned above, I was delighted to find a vast
number of lovely plants that I have never seen before, flourishing
beautifully in this moist spot, with a north exposure. There were
Herniaria polygonoides, the fragile and delicate *Linaria villosa*, its
leaves covered with a gummy and fragrant exudation, and then came
Saxifraga globulifera and *Campanula velutina*, gracing the angular
and rough fractures of the stones with tufts of white and blue
blossoms. Wherever the rock formed hollows and caverns, might be
seen enormous tufts of *Fumaria corymbosa*, a plant which seems to
shun the outward air and of which the peduncles may be observed
lengthening and stretching in every direction after the flowers are
past, seeking to deposit its seeds in the fissures. I also gathered there
Ephedra altissima and, Queen of all, *Anthyllis podocephala*, a lovely
shrub with silky leaves, and crowned with clusters of golden yellow
flowers. The distance I had yet to go in the day forbade my doing
more than take a superficial glance at these treasures, which the
proximity of the village would allow me to revisit the following day,
so I regretfully forsook these rocks and pursued my way among
slopes, covered with species of *Cistus*, rosemary and Kermes oaks.
We continued ascending by a ravine, called *La Cañada del Infierno*;
it was now dry and the bottom was covered with a fine sand, among
which grew abundance of *Alyssum serpyllifolium*, *A. atlanticum*,

and *Mercurialis tomentosa*; this sand is found, here and there, all over the mountain being formed by the decomposition of the white calcareous crystal of which the mountain itself consists. I gathered in succession several species peculiar to the mountainous region, viz. *Macrochloa arenarria*, a gigantic kind of grass, which bears, on a stalk five or six feet long, a large golden spike, *Armeria alloides*, with white blossoms, *Senecio arachnoideus* and *S. minutus*, *Echium albicans*, a magnificent plant, whose aspect recalls the individuals of the same genus which are peculiar to the Canary Islands, and *Reseda undata*, called by the shepherds, in allusion to its long straight round flower-spike, 'Hopo de Horra' or fox's tail.

During this excursion I enjoyed, to the full, the delights of discovery; a pleasure which was keenly renewed and varied during every successive excursion in Andalusia, and which cannot be felt in Central Europe, where every inch of ground has been trodden and re-trodden by experienced botanists. Here and there, some flocks of goats and sheep were wearily seeking their scanty food amid this thorny vegetation, where hardly a trace of the gramineous tribe is to be seen. The owners drive these poor animals to the mountain from Alhaurin, Mijas, and other surrounding villages, whither they return in the evening, and it is incomprehensible how the slender portion of vegetation that can thus be collected should afford them sufficient strength to accomplish this long daily journey.[3]

The Sierra de Mijas and Spanish hostelries

The Sierra de Mijas, at whose western extremity I was posted, runs from West to East as far as Torremolinos, one league distant from Malaga. Its summits are rounded and the sides furrowed by numerous ravines, consequent on its sandy formation. Towards the south the slope is more rapid than on the north, and between it and the sea lies a country regularly intersected with undulating hills and little valleys through which passes the road, usually travelled, from Malaga to Gibraltar, past the Castle of Fuengirola. I found the high parts of the mountains covered with shrubs, many of them similar to those of the plains, the elevation not being sufficient to produce, in this latitude, a total change of vegetation. *Ulex australis* prevailed, mingled with rosemary, *Juniperus oxycedrus*, *Cistus incanus*, *C. salvifolius*, *C. monspeliensis* and *C. atriplicifolius*. A *Helianthemum*, with white flowers and downy foliage, formed elegant little bushes; and, combined with most of the plants which I have already enumerated, as belonging to the subalpine region, I noticed *Borkhausia albida*, *Valeriana tuberosa*, *Carex gynobasis*, *Erysimum canescens*, *Orchis anthropophora*, and *Asphodelus fistulosus*. In the clefts of rock which terminate the mountain on the south side, I gathered the beautiful *Linaria tristis*, with flowers of a blackish-purple hue, *Calendula suffruticosa*, *Saxifraga globulifera* and an umbelliferous plant, which grows upon Mount Atlas, *Bunium glaberrimum*; it was not in flower, but I recognised it by the peculiar form of its leaves.

The approach of evening could alone induce me to tear myself away from this rich harvest; I descended to the Cross of Mendoza and thence to Alhaurin by a rapid slope which leads straight to the *nascimiento*, and along which, in spite of its aridity, I gathered several rare species, as *Matthiola varia*, *Brassica humilis*, a new kind of *Herniaria*, a curious velvety-leaved variety of *Ranunculus gramineus* and a lovely *Iris*, near *I. xiphium*, its purple blossoms spotted with yellow. The Cross of Mendoza is a shoulder of the mountain where stand several ancient and rudely carved wooden crosses; it is a much venerated place of pilgrimage in the country and my *posadera* (landlady) assured me that she had often walked thither (*los pies descalzos*) barefoot, to obtain the exemption of her son from the conscription. Her devotion had succeeded, 'Blessed be the Holy Virgin', said she, 'my son is now married and an honest man like his father'. This was equivocal praise, for rarely have I met with a greater rogue than the landlord of that inn. Every body knows that the hostelries in Spain contain no provision for the traveller's use, and if a new comer ventures to ask what he can have to eat, the constant reply is *Caballero, lo que Vmd. trae*, 'Sir, whatever you may please to have brought with you'. It is, therefore, necessary to purchase for one's self in the village here and there, what is wanted. In some of the more civilised places, the host undertakes this office, laying a profit upon every article; and at the moment of departure a long bill is handed in, where every item is specified, down to the oil and salt which have been used in preparing the food, and the traveller is amazed to find that he has quite as much to pay for these wretched provisions as in the best *Fondas* of the city.[3]

J. H. BALFOUR *(1844)*

John Hutton Balfour (1808–1884), born in Edinburgh, for some time practised medicine. However, botanical studies gradually drew him from his patients and in the early 1840s, when elected to the Glasgow University Chair of Botany, he gave up his medical practice. In 1845, he returned to Edinburgh as Professor of Medicine and Botany, and Keeper of the Royal Botanic Garden, and continued to work in the sphere of these offices until his retirement in 1879.[1] The following is extracted from an account of a botanical excursion across the peninsula of Kintyre and the island of Islay in August 1844.[2]

Grouse-hunting on Kintyre

A party, consisting of Mr Babington, author of the *Manual of British Botany*, Dr Parnell, author of the work of *British Grasses*, Mr John Miller, jun, Mr John Alexander, Mr R. Holden, Mr Risk, Mr Craig, and myself, left Glasgow by the St Kirian steamboat, at 11 a.m. on Saturday, 10th August, 1844. There was a large party on board, returning from the Highland Society's Cattle Show. The day was remarkably fine, and we had an excellent view of the beautiful scenery on the shores of the Firth of Clyde. This in some measures compensated for the slow progress of our boat, which did not reach Campbelton [*sic*] till near nine p.m.

Campbelton [*sic*] is prettily situated on an inlet of the sea, the opening of the bay being protected by an island, which, however, becomes a peninsula at low water. The island is composed of a porphyritic rock, which is sometimes used for making ornaments of various kinds. The climate is mild, and many of the more delicate plants stand the winter well. On visiting one of the gardens in the vicinity, under the guidance of Mr Stewart, chamberlain to his Grace the Duke of Argyll, we found myrtles, hydrangeas, and other tender plants, thriving in the open air, and we observed a fine *Fuchsia* hedge, which was in full flower, and contributed in no small degree to ornament the garden.

John Hutton
Balfour. (Source:
As shown on
p. 174 of Curtis's
Botanical Magazine
dedications
1827–1927:
portraits and
biographical notes
by E. Nelmes &
W. Cuthbertson,
published in 1931
by the Royal
Horticultural
Society, London.
Reproduced with
permission from
the archives of the
Royal Botanic
Gardens,
Melbourne)

On the 12th of August we left Campbelton [*sic*] early, and
proceeded by the shore towards Kildalloig, and thence by the rocky
and sandy shores of the Mull as far as Ballishear. The cliffs are not so
precipitous as those on the Galloway coast, and did not produce many
rare plants. The most interesting plants were found on the shore.
Some of the party who went inland were by no means successful in
their botanising, but this may probably be attributed in some measure
to their having spent a portion of their time with Mr Stewart, enjoying
the pleasure of grouse-shooting. The result of their sport was found to
be no means unacceptable at the end of the day's work.

Among the plants met with, I may notice *Epilobium angustifolium*,
which grew in great profusion and beauty, *Hypericum androsaemum*,
a common plant in all our western counties, *Hieracium umbellatum*,
Convolvulus soldanella and *C. sepium*, *Atriplex laciniata*, *A. rosea*
and *A. angustifolia*, *Sinapis monensis*, *Helosciadium nodiflorum* both
in a large erect and in a small creeping form, *Cotyledon umbilicus*,
Vicia sylvatica, *Lolium temulentum*, and *Epilobium virgatum* ...[2]

On the island of Islay

August 17th. — The morning was very showery and unpromising, and, in place of visiting Portnahaven as had been proposed, we proceeded along the shore to Bowmore, and thence round Laggan Point as far as the mouth of the River Laggan, along the banks of which we botanised as far as the bridge. The piscatorial members of the party considered the day peculiarly favourable for enjoying the luxury of a nibble; but their success was not so great as they anticipated, and, as usual, this was attributed to some fault on the part of the river and the fish. One of the party expatiated in glowing terms on the mode in which he hooked a salmon, described his excitement on the occasion, and all the emotions which arise in the bosom of one whose fly, for the first time in its existence, has been honoured by the grasp of so noble a visitor. But unfortunately this splendid animal preferred living in its native river, even with the appendage of a hook and a broken line, to the pleasure of contributing to the repast of a hungry botanical party. Some sea-trout, river-trout, and parr were taken, but even Parnell's prepared minnow, or *minnow-persuader*, as it was called, though wielded most dextrously by the Doctor himself, failed to procure a large supply, and we looked in vain for the salmon which he had promised for dinner.

August 22nd. — Leaving Port Ellen at seven a.m. we went along the shore to Ardinsteil, where we breakfasted with Mr Stein. On our way we picked *Galeopsis versicolor* and *Convolvulus sepium*. After breakfast we directed our course towards Loch Knock and Knock Hill, where Mr Campbell has a summer residence called Ardimersay Cottage. Here there is a considerable extent of thriving plantations, and we spent some hours in the examination of them. The chief plants which rewarded our exertions were *Circaea intermedia, Carex laevigata, Hymenophyllum wilsonii, Polypodium phegopteris, Cardamine sylvatica* and *Prunus cerasus.* On rocks in the neighbour-hood were seen *Milium effusum, Tanacetum vulgare,* and *Inula helenium,* evidently an escape from an old garden. Near the cottage there is an old fort now in ruins, called Dun-naomh-aig, and pronounced Dunavaig, remarkable as being the last held by the MacDonalds. It was taken by the Campbells, who it is said resorted to the method of cutting the water pipes which were conveyed under the sea in the bay, and thus causing a surrender. The rock of the fort seems to be impregnable on all sides but that next the land. In the vicinity of the cottage a place is shown which is said to be the grave of the Princess Isla.

Epilobium angustifolium, *a species that not only grows in profusion on the peninsula of Kintyre but also throughout much of the temperate regions of the northern hemisphere. This photograph was taken in north-west Canada.*

After partaking a refreshment, kindly supplied by the housekeeper at the cottage, we walked partly by the shore and partly inland, as far as Kildaton, where porphyritic rocks present themselves. Here a fine old church is seen in ruins. It had two windows on the east end, and two at each side, with two doors. Two stone crosses differing slightly in character are seen, one in the churchyard surrounding the chapel, and the other at a little distance from it. Some curious old gravestones occur. Nettles and *Anthriscus sylvestris* now grow in profusion within the precincts of the chapel, and the procumbent variety of the common juniper on its walls. The various species of nettle seem to follow the footsteps of man,

and delight to grow in places where nitrate of lime is produced:
> 'At the wall's base the fiery nettle springs,
> With fruit globose, and fierce with poisoned stings.'

In boggy places, in the vicinity of the old chapel, we found *Helosciadium nodiflorum*, *Hypericum elodes*, *Carex remota* and *C. filiformis*. This part of the island is separated from the district near Islay House by a lofty range of hills, some of them attaining an elevation of 1,500 or 2,000 feet, and composed chiefly of quartz rock. We ascended one of them called Ben Vigors or Ben Bhiggars, and found it by no means productive. The principal plants collected were *Gnaphalium dioicum*, *Lycopodium selago*, *Arctostaphylos uva-ursi*, *Carex rigida*, *Armeria maritima* var. *alpina* and *Juniperus communis* var. *nana*. The occurrence of *Arctostaphylos* would probably indicate an elevation of at least 2,000 feet, corresponding with the subalpine region of Mr Watson. On reaching the summit of the hill we were involved in mist and rain, and the guide who had accompanied us lost his way, and after wandering for an hour or two landed us in the valley whence we had ascended. Fortunately he knew the direction which our place of destination bore to the valley, and accordingly we followed our compass and crossed the hills in a very thick mist, amidst the fears and doubts of our guide as to the correctness of our procedure. Our anxiety as to the result of our exploration made us forget all the discomfort of a thorough drenching, and one of the party who had been complaining sadly of fatigue now walked on most manfully. After reaching the summit of the range of hills, (probably the summit of Gloan Leor), we descended, not without doubts as to the result. At this time a slight clearance took place in the mist, and we descried some green patches of verdure which seemed to indicate a limestone district. We knew that this was the geological nature of the district which we wished to reach, and our hopes of extrication from our difficulties brightened considerably. We now proceeded on our descent with increased vigour and alacrity, and reached Allaladh, when some oat cakes and milk from one of the cottagers were most thankfully received, and ere long we had the pleasure of finding ourselves at Cattadale, where a conveyance was waiting to convey us to Ealabus. This adventure shows, in a certain degree, the importance of knowing the geology of a district, and the kind of vegetation which is connected with particular rocks.[2]

The above quotation used by Balfour was from Letter 18 of *The Borough* by George Crabbe (1754–1832).[3] The nettle concerned was *Urtica pilulifera*, believed to have been introduced to Britain by the

Romans. The Mr Watson referred to was Hewett Cottrell Watson (1804–1881), the 'father of British topographical botany'.[4]

Excursion on Arran

The following is Balfour's account of an excursion he made to the Island of Arran in 1869.

One of our trips seems specially worthy of record, on account of the adventures which marked it. On the morning of Friday, 17th September, a party of eight, consisting of myself, Messrs Robert, James, and Alexander Finlay, Isaac B. Balfour, J. H. Balfour, jun., Miss Balfour, and Miss Finlay, proceeded by the early boat to Invercloy, with the view of visiting Glen Sannox and returning by Glen Rosa. The day was not promising, and rain came on very heavily. In spite of this we proceeded along the shore towards Corrie, gathering abundance of good ferns and other plants, chiefly with the view of supplying the Edinburgh Botanic Garden. Long before reaching Corrie we were thoroughly drenched, and we surprised my friend the Reverend Lewis Irving, who was residing in a cottage within a couple of miles of Corrie, by presenting ourselves in a wretched plight at his cottage door. The weather was so bad that we had resolved to return, and after getting under the shelter of some of the sandstone rocks, and finishing our lunch at the early hour of 9 a.m., we were about to sound a retreat, when a slight symptom of clearance appeared in the south, and the rain abated. On then we went to Corrie, and as the sun's rays enlightened our path for a time, our spirits revived. At Corrie we got the benefit of a kitchen fire to dry part of our habiliments, and after replenishing our stock of viands, we started for Glen Sannox. At the foot of the glen we examined an old churchyard, enclosed within good walls, with an iron gate, but no church near. Our attention was specially called to the profuse flowering of some fine fuchsias. The following are the trees and shrubs growing in the churchyard: — *Thuja chinensis, T. occidentalis, Juniperus communis, J. sabina, Cupressus sempervirens, Taxus baccata, Quercus robur, Betula alba, Hedera helix, Buxus sempervirens, Laurus nobilis, Fraxinus excelsior, Cotoneaster microphylla, Ilex aquifolium, Arbutus unedo, Fuchsia* with a stem 22 inches in circumference, *Prunus lusitanica,* and *P. spinosa.*

Passing the old locality of the Baryta Quarry, we entered Glen Sannox, and had a long and toilsome walk among the heather. The

Pink drifts of Armeria maritima, the thrift, a common coastal plant that was undoubtedly familiar to Balfour.

day became dull, and thick mist covered the tops of the mountains, but we persevered. In place of ascending by the usual route for the summit of Goatfell, we visited a corry [or corrie, cirque] on the right hand under Caistael Abhail, where we gathered some alpine plants, such as *Saxifraga stellaris*, *Alchemilla alpina*, *Thalictrum alpinum*, and *Lycopodium selago*.

The ascent was a difficult one, and on our reaching the top we congratulated ourselves on the prospect of at once descending into Glen Rosa. The mist prevented us from seeing the top of Goatfell. Without much consideration, we descended by a rocky declivity into a valley through which a fine stream ran, with beautiful waterfalls of a most picturesque character — the rocks being precipitous, and the ravines very deep. *Asplenium viride* was seen in several places. The day had kept fair for some time, although the mist was coming lower on the hills and the ground was very wet. After proceeding for a mile or so on our route, it was obvious that we had gone into the wrong glen, and we saw before us a long stretch of a valley as desolate as possibly could be, with a large stream running through it. The banks of the stream were very marshy. In some places a pole more than six feet long could scarcely reach the bottom, and caution was required lest we should be immersed in a quagmire.

We now suspected that we had got into the Iorsa Valley, and we were subsequently confirmed in this opinion when we came upon the Lake of Iorsa. The weather now assumed a very threatening aspect. Rain descended in torrents without intermission, and we were all thoroughly drenched. The bad plight in which we now were; the uncertainty as to the extent of the journey still to be accomplished; and the approach of darkness, all tended to cause considerable alarm, especially in my own mind, as the conductor of the party — two of whom were young ladies, and two young boys of about 12 or 14. They all, however, kept up their spirits well, and I tried to conceal my anxiety and alarm for fear of dispiriting them ...

The risk, humanly speaking, was no doubt great. The walk had already extended to between 20 and 30 miles over very rough and mountainous ground, and the prospect before us was anything but satisfactory. The failure of strength on the part of any one among us would have been a very serious matter.

We had husbanded some of our provisions. I had taken with me some whisky from the inn at Corrie, in case of need. The scanty supply of viands and this stimulant now stood in good part to us. I thought at the time of St Paul, who, after tossing about in the deep for 14 days, without seeing sun or stars, and when no small tempest lay on his part, said, 'I pray you take some meat, for this is for your health'. So it was that with grateful acknowledgement of God's kindness we discussed the provisions within our reach, and it may be truly said that 'we were all of good cheer', although we could not tell when we might get another meal. The ladies were wonderfully courageous, and encountered all the difficulties of the way with astonishing equanimity, or, I should rather say, with wonderful buoyancy. They helped in no small degree to stimulate our efforts and our perseverance.

The weary valley seemed never to show any termination, and not a house or human being was to be seen. On turning a part of the valley we saw in the distance a little opening in the sky, and we sent a scout up the hill in order to ascertain if the sea could be observed in the distance. The ascertaining of this would, we hoped, help us to determine our position. He came down with the pleasing intelligence that he obviously saw a bay stretching out some miles off. This announcement added new vigour to our efforts. The sudden appearance of a small herd of red deer helped also to give us some excitement, and we watched their movements with interest. The waters from the hills and all round came down in torrents, and in some places it was very difficult to cross them. In the course of two hours the rain had swollen them to an enormous extent.

As the evening was closing in, we thought we could discern something like a house in the distance, but there was no light to assist in its detection. The very hope of this being a human habitation cheered us; but ere long we were brought to a halt. A stream which came down on our right hand, i.e. on the north side of our path, and which was afterwards found to proceed from Beinn Bharrain, was so deep and impetuous as to forbid our progress. Isaac Balfour tried to pass, but failed. We saw no alternative but to follow the stream down to its junction with the Iorsa, which, although swollen, was not rushing in such a tumultuous manner as its tributary. One of the more adventurous of the party (Mr Robert Finlay) ventured into the river and found that he could stem the current, and that the depth was about three and one-half or four feet. By good management we all got across in a condition not easily described, and anything but comfortable.

Our road was still very rough, and, moreover, darkness had set in, as it was now eight p.m. We groped our way, and kept well together in case of accident. At length we found a stile over which we passed, and came to a wooden bridge which spanned the Iorsa near its embouchure. Crossing this we met a young man, the first person we had seen from the time we left Glen Sannox.

This was a most providential occurrence. He was looking for the return of a brother, and while doing so, he came in contact with us. We could not help seeing God's hand in this event. It was an answer to prayer ... I have often thought amidst all my wanderings over mountains, and valleys, and plains, travelling by sea and land in quest of plants, with large parties, how grateful I should be that there has not occurred any untoward event, involving serious consequences to life or health.[5]

NORTH AMERICA

T. DRUMMOND *(1825–1827)*

Brother of James (*see* pp. 124–136), Scottish born Thomas Drummond (1793–1835) worked for some time at the nursery of Doo Hillock, Forfar,[1] and while there published a work on the mosses of Scotland. In 1825, together with naturalist Dr John Richardson, he sailed from Liverpool as a member of Captain John Franklin's expedition to explore the Arctic coast of Canada. For a long period of time Drummond was with neither Franklin nor Richardson, leaving the main expedition, and subsequently rejoining it there, at Cumberland House on the Saskatchewan River. In the intervening period he travelled to the Columbia River and the Rocky Mountains.[2,3]

Travel conditions

The distance between the junction of the South Branch River with the Saskatchewan, and the Rocky Mountains House, may be estimated at from 700 to 800 miles. At Edmonton House, the brigade for the Columbia left the Saskatchewan, making a portage of 100 miles to the Red-Deer River, which falls into the Athabaca Lake; and as I still adhered to my resolution of accompanying it, I found it necessary to reduce my luggage into as small a compass as possible, and therefore left my specimens under the charge of the gentlemen at Edmonton House, only carrying with me a small stock of linen and a bale of paper.

The second day, after leaving Edmonton House, brought us to the commencement of the woody country, which continues all the way to the Rocky Mountains. The trees consist of *Populus balsamifera* and *P. trepida*; the white spruce fir and the birch, with *Pinus banksiana* occasionally in the drier situations, and then, more rarely, the balsam poplar. These are the only trees which occur north of this latitude, though in some localities, and in deep swamps, the *Pinus nigra* and *P. microcarpa* may occasionally be seen. Almost the only plants which we remarked as peculiar to this district, were a species of *Delphinium*, allied to *D. elatum*, and a curious aquatic, resembling in habit the *Hydrocharis morsus-ranae*, of which I gathered no specimens at the time, for it was out of flower, and I never saw it again.

We crossed the Portage in six days, without meeting with any serious accident. The horse, however, which carried my bale of paper, unluckily fell down in crossing Papina River, by which the plants were thoroughly soaked; and as the speed with which the brigade proceeded precluded all hopes of getting them dried by the way, I found myself unwillingly compelled to carry them on in a damp state, until we reached Fort Assinaboyne, a small establishment belonging to the [Hudson's Bay] Company upon Red-Deer River, where we spent two or three days preparing the canoes and cargo for our ascent of the river to the mountains. The Red-Deer River, on which this Fort is situated, is probably one of the most southern streams which empties its waters into the frozen Ocean. The whole distance from Fort Assinaboyne to the Rocky Mountains, following the general course of the river, which runs in a nearly due west direction, may be estimated at about 200 miles. The country is thickly wooded with the same species of trees as were mentioned before; the *Pinus banksiana* and *Populus balsamifera*, however, becoming more frequent.

It was now ascertained that the canoes were so heavily laden, that it would be necessary for some of the party to go by land, and I gladly agreed to be one of these, in order to have the opportunity of seeing the country, and judging of its probable productions. We quitted the Fort accordingly, on the 1st or 2nd of October, and started in high spirits for a journey on horseback. A heavy fall of snow, however, which took place on the 4th, put a final period to collecting for this season; it also rendered our progress through these trackless woods very unpleasant, our horses becoming soon jaded, when the only alternative was to walk, and drive them before us. To add to these misfortunes, the poor animals were continually sinking in the swamps, from which we found it no easy task to extricate them. The Red-Deer River is very rapid, so that its rise must be considerable, though not discernible when travelling through the woods which skirt it. The general appearance of the country is flat, intersected with lakes and swamps, and occasionally broken undulating ground. The weather during this part of our journey, proved very unfavourable; snow and a thick fog prevented

Thomas Drummond. (Source and copyright: Royal Botanic Gardens, Kew)

my making much observation on the vegetation, which, however, appeared to bear the same character until we approached the mountains. It also forbade my getting any view whatever of the Rocky Mountains, until we actually reached them. We arrived at Jasper's House on the eleventh day, having travelled a distance of 200 miles since we quitted Assinaboyne Fort, under disadvantageous circumstances; but all the party were in good health, and we were joined by the canoes on the day following.[3]

Fresh mutton

At the junction of the Assinaboyne with the Red-Deer River, I was first gratified with a sight of the Rocky Mountains sheep. At this season their flesh is excellent, superior, in my opinion, to the best English mutton. After they have been once disturbed, they become so shy and vigilant, that it is difficult to approach them, taking refuge in the inaccessible precipices, but coming down to the grassy hills to feed, where the hunters frequently surprise them.[3]

Indian customs

Our route now lay along the Assinaboyne River, and we proceeded slowly, encamping at every 15 or 20 miles, and often remaining two or three days in the same spot, for the sake of hunting. The following is the circumstance which hindered our reaching the Smoking River. The hunter whom I had engaged was accompanied by his brother-in-law, an Iroquois Indian, whose wife was taken in labour. According to the custom of these tribes, the women quitted the tent in which she had lodged, until she should be delivered, and owing to the extreme severity of the weather, the ground being covered with snow, and the mercury indicating 38 degrees [Fahrenheit] below zero, both the mother and her infant perished. The despondency which this event excited in the minds of the survivors, was so deep, that ten or fifteen days elapsed before they could be induced to quit the spot.[3]

Lonely existence

At this time, January 10th, the snow was about two feet deep, and it gradually increased till the 27th of March, its greatest depth being from five to six feet. Our horses began to suffer considerably from the unusual severity of the winter: the hunters lost the whole of the young ones of the preceding year, and one which I had received from the Company died also. The animals of all kinds were becoming more and more scarce, so that my hunter resolved upon leaving this spot, and accordingly removed 80 or 100 miles farther down the river, but I preferred remaining where I was, though my situation became very lonely, being deprived of books or any source of amusement. When the weather permitted, I generally took a walk, to habituate myself to the use of snow shoes, but I added very little to my collection. The hunter returned about the beginning of March ...[3]

Grisly bear

On the 9th [April, at Jasper House] I had the pleasure of meeting Mr McMillan, who brought me, from Edmonton House, my tent, another supply of paper, and a little tea and sugar, by which my situation was rendered comparatively comfortable. The winter, he assured me, had been remarkably severe, and vegetation was a full month later than usual. The ducks and geese now began to return, so that my time was fully occupied till the 6th of May, when the brigade arrived, having crossed the Rocky Mountains from the Columbia River. They found me encamped near a small lake, about half-way between Jasper's House and the commencement of the Portage, living upon white fish, which, though small, are of an excellent quality, and which I did not observe in any other lake among the Rocky Mountains. I agreed to accompany the brigade as far as Jasper's House, and accordingly set out with them on horseback. Having crossed the Assinaboyne River, the party halted to breakfast, and I went on before them for a few miles, to procure specimens of a *Jungermannia* [a liverwort], which I had previously observed in a small rivulet on our track. On this occasion I had a narrow escape from the jaws of a grisly bear; for, while passing through a small open glade, intent upon discovering the moss of which I was in search, I was surprised by hearing a sudden rush and then a harsh growl, just behind me; and on looking round, I beheld a large bear approaching towards me, and two young ones making off in a contrary direction as fast as possible. My astonishment was great, for I had not calculated upon seeing these animals so early in the season, and this was the first I had met with. She halted within two or three yards of me, growling and rearing herself on her hind feet, then suddenly wheeled about, and went off in the direction the young ones had taken, probably to ascertain whether they were safe. During this momentary absence, I drew from my gun the small shot with which I had been firing at ducks during the morning, and which, I was well aware, would avail me nothing against so large and powerful a creature, and replaced it with ball. The bear, meanwhile, had advanced and retreated two or three times, apparently more furious than ever; halting at each interval within a shorter and shorter distance of me, always raising herself on her hind legs, and growling a horrible defiance, and at length approaching to within the length of my gun from me. Now was my time to fire: but judge of my alarm and mortification, when I found that my gun would not go off! The morning had been wet, and the damp had communicated to the powder. My only resource was to plant myself firm and stationary, in the hope of disabling the bear by a blow on her head with the butt end of my gun, when she should throw herself on me to seize me. She had gone and returned ten or a dozen times, her rage apparently increasing with her additional confidence, and I momentarily expected to find myself in her grip, when the dogs belonging to the brigade made their appearance, but on beholding the bear they fled with all possible speed. The horsemen were just behind, but such was the surprise and alarm of the whole party, that though there were several hunters and at least half-a-dozen guns among them, the bear made her escape unhurt, passing one of the horsemen, (whose gun, like mine, missed fire) and apparently intimidated by the number of the party. For the future, I took care to keep my gun in better order, but I found, by future experience, that the best mode of getting rid of the bears when attacked by them, was to rattle my vasculum, or specimen box, when they immediately decamp. This is the animal described by Lewis and Clark in their *Travels on the Missouri*, and so much dreaded by the Indians. My adventure with the bear did not, however, prevent my accomplishing the collecting of the *Jungermannia*.[3]

The vasculum, commonly a box constructed of sheet metal and with a hinged lid and a shoulder strap, in which collectors kept specimens prior to pressing, is now rarely used. Plastic bags are more convenient. Many modern collectors also use lightweight day-presses, placing specimens in the press as soon as they are gathered.

Cold feet

Having accomplished our preparations, I embarked my stock of specimens, and, with Mr McDonald and his family, began to descend the river. The winter had set in with all its rigour; the cold became severe, the river had subsided greatly, and being choked with snow, and full of rapids and shallows, we found great difficulty in proceeding, being often obliged to quit the boat and lift her over the stones. We, however, continued to drift along with the stream for a few days; but our boat was so large and heavy that she frequently struck against the shallows, and we were almost worn out with fatigue, with our being continually obliged to jump into the half frozen water to endeavour to force her along. Mr McDonald's legs were much cut and bruised with the floating ice, and I, who kept on my stockings to avoid this misfortune, suffered on the other hand with frost, which rendered my wet clothes a most painful encumbrance. The ice and snow now became so intense and heavy, that though we had calculated on reaching Fort Assinaboyne before the river became wholly impassable, we found ourselves unable to proceed, and stuck fast on the seventh day, when not more than halfway on our voyage. As Mr McDonald's family were incapable of travelling, he agreed to encamp and remain with the luggage, while a clerk belonging to the Company and myself prosecuted our journey on foot to Fort Assinaboyne, whence we were to send horses to his assistance. We had calculated on reaching this place in three days, but it was the fifth evening before we arrived, having, however, met with no other hindrance than the unavoidable hardships of such a journey.[3]

High tea

In the beginning of February, I received the agreeable intelligence from Dr Richardson of the complete success of his undertaking, and that he expected to be at Carlton House in February, where he desired me to join him as soon as convenient. Accordingly, I quitted Edmonton House in the middle of March, taking with me a single specimen of every plant gathered among the Rocky Mountains; also a train of dogs, and a half-bred and Indian guide. Owing to some misunderstanding between the Hudson's Bay Company and the Indians of the plains, it was considered unsafe to pursue the usual track between the Posts, which very much lengthened our route and caused us considerable inconvenience. We proceeded for a few days along the river, and then struck into the wooded country north of the Saskatchewan, to avoid encountering the hostile tribes. We shortly began to feel symptoms of snow blindness, which considerably retarded our progress, and although we had a sufficient supply of provisions for this journey in usual cases, we still found our stores considerably diminishing. The blindness became worse, and although we fired at several animals, we did not succeed in killing any. To add to our distresses, we now discovered that we had gone too far into the woods, by which the distance that we had to traverse was much increased. Our dogs became excessively fatigued, so that we were under the necessity of cutting up our sledge and carrying the luggage ourselves. The provisions were wholly spent, and I was compelled to destroy a fine specimen of the jumping deer ... although it was the only one we had been able to procure, and I had carried it all the way from the Columbia River, where I had killed it. As I had not been very particular in divesting this skin of the flesh, it proved the more valuable on that account. Our ignorance of the actual distance which lay between us and the Fort, prevented the Indians from desponding, for we expected to reach it every succeeding night; but we grew weak with exhaustion, and proceeded, therefore, but the more and more slowly. Within about a day's journey of the Fort, the half-bred Indian recognised the spot where we were, and we had the good fortune to kill a skunk, an animal which I have omitted to mention in my former list, and which afforded us a comfortable meal. This creature, when hunted, discharges an intolerably foetid liquid upon its pursuers, and few dogs will afterwards attempt to destroy it. The one which we killed on the evening before we reached the Fort, proved tolerable eating, although it had a strong flavour of this obnoxious liquid.[3]

The foul-smelling liquid of the skunk is emitted from the anus and may travel from three to four metres. According to one reference, the anal glands should be removed before the animal is cooked; the same author stated that in flavour the flesh of the skunk is similar to that of sucking pig.[4]

Before concluding the account of his sojourn, Drummond described his typical camping arrangements. This was followed by an account of a near-mishap in Hudson Bay, in which botanist David Douglas (*see* pp. 229–237) was also involved, just prior to the return to Britain.

Camping facilities

The snow-shoe travelling, and the mode of encamping during winter has been so frequently described, that it is quite unnecessary for me to detail them here. One of the principal inducements for fixing upon any particular situation is when it affords dry wood in abundance. The snow is then cleared away with the assistance of the snow-shoes, and trees of a large size having been felled, they are divided into lengths fit for carrying. You may then, after lighting a fire collect a parcel of pine branches, the white spruce and balsam if procurable, are the best, with which a space is covered sufficient for a bed, and proceed to prepare supper. Pemmican [dried meat] is the best and most convenient food to be carried upon a journey. Without a pound of this and a little tea, no one should think of travelling in these desert wilds; it affords an excellent meal, and the hunter may afterwards prepare for rest by rolling round him the blanket which he always takes with him. If the fire be occasionally renewed, the weather seldom causes much inconvenience. To a person accustomed to all the luxuries a civilised country can afford, this mode of life appears hard and uninviting, but the change takes place gradually, and is therefore but little felt. It seems strange, too, to live entirely on animal food, without any vegetable or salt, but it procures no inconvenience, as I can attest from an experience of about eighteen months, when I enjoyed a state of perfect health.[3]

Storm in Hudson Bay

On the 1st of September, we encountered a dreadful storm in Hudson's [*sic*] Bay, from which we escaped as if by miracle. We had gone to visit the ship, which lay at five or six miles distance from the Fort; the party consisting of Captain Black, Lieutenant Kendall, Mr David Douglas, the Doctor belonging to the establishment, and myself, with eight men. On leaving the vessel to return to the Fort in the evening, the wind blew rather freshly, but little danger was apprehended; it suddenly, however, increased to a hurricane, and we were compelled to return if possible to the ship, but after several vain attempts, we found this to be impracticable. We, therefore, threw out an anchor until a boat should be sent to our assistance from the ship. This was immediately done, the boat being furnished with a tow line, and just as it had neared to within 20 or 30 yards of us, our anchor gave way, and we were driven off, at the mercy of the winds and waves. Our masts were almost immediately carried overboard, and after a dreadfully severe, but ineffectual attempt to approach the vessel by dint of rowing, we were compelled to give over, and to submit to being carried out to sea. By this time the water had become very rough, and our little bark was tossed about like an egg-shell, which caused all the men to get sick, and utterly incapacitated them from making the smallest effort to save themselves and us. We continued baling out the water with our hats, as much as we could. Lieutenant Kendall exerted himself to the utmost, and he succeeded in setting up a temporary mast, which enabled Captain Black to keep the head of the boat to windward,

Oenothera drummondii, *a native of North America and named after Thomas Drummond, is now a weed in south-west Western Australia, the stamping ground of Thomas's brother, James (see pp. 124–136).*

and we continued to drive before the wind farther and farther out to sea. The night was dark in the extreme, with tremendous thunder and rain, the billows rolling mountains high, and breaking continually over us, which, added to the severe cold, caused us great suffering. Mr Douglas became dreadfully ill, and the rest were in so benumbed a state, that it was hardly possible to make the necessary exertion to keep the boat from sinking, which could only be done by relieving her constantly from the water as fast as she filled. I shall never forget the sound of the waves as they approached us: sometimes, by the skill of our steersman, we partly avoided them, but much oftener did they dash over us with tremendous fury, and had two of these billows followed in quick succession, our instant destruction would have been inevitable, but by constant baling we kept the boat afloat. The storm continued without abating during the night, and at break of day we found ourselves rapidly drifting towards a lee shore. This we avoided by tacking, and we still continued to drive to sea. Towards the middle of the next day, the hurricane began to diminish a little in violence, but the sea was still dreadfully agitated, and it was not till the middle of the following night that our oars could be of the smallest service to us. At this time we were entirely out of sight of land, without compass to guide our course; the sun, too, was not visible. As the storm diminished, the men recovered from their sickness, and the oars were again plied, and with some success, as it afterwards appeared that we had gone a distance of 60 or 70 miles in the Bay. With the aid of the tide and our oars we retraced our way back, and never shall I forget the joy that beamed on every countenance when the masts of the ship were visible.[3]

Drummond arrived back in London in October 1827. He subsequently became Curator of the Belfast Botanic Garden (1828–1831). However, he soon left that position to become a botanical collector. Financial support was provided by the Edinburgh and Glasgow botanic gardens, and by private subscribers, the last of whom paid two pounds per 100 specimens. Drummond returned to North America in April 1831,[5] and William Hooker received specimens and letters from him for several more years, the last letter having been written in Florida on 9 February 1835.[6] That same year, Hooker reported that Drummond had perished in Cuba.

Drummond was the collector of many plants that were new to science and was responsible for the introduction of a large number into

Pub. by S. Curtis. Glazenwood Essex. Oct.ʳ 1. 1835.

cultivation in Europe. The commonly cultivated *Phlox drummondii* is one of a number of plants which bear his name. When naming it, Hooker recorded that the plant

> ... bids fair to be a great ornament to the gardens of our country. Hence, and as it is an undescribed species, I am desirous that it should bear the name and serve as a *frequent* memento of its unfortunate discoverer ... He has, indeed, accomplished enough, by his zeal and his researches, to secure himself a lasting name throughout the botanical world: yet it is impossible not deeply to regret the loss, both as concerns our favourite science and his friends.[7]

D. DOUGLAS *(1825–1831)*

Born in Scone, Scotland, David Douglas (1799–1834) was attached at an early age to the local garden of the Earl of Mansfield. In 1818, he moved to another garden at Valleyfield, near Culross, and had access to the owner's botanical library. From there he gained admission to the botanic garden in Glasgow and gained the respect of the Curator, Stewart Murray, and the then Professor of Botany at Glasgow University, William Hooker. He was soon recommended to Joseph Sabine, Honorary Secretary of the Horticultural Society, as a botanical collector. Douglas was subsequently despatched to the United States, returning in the autumn of 1823 with a good collection of fruit trees. In July 1824, he left to explore the botanical riches, and collect other objects of natural history, of America's north-west. He landed at the mouth of the Columbia River in 1825.[1, 2, 3, 4] Food shortages, physical hardships and, at times, uneasy relationships with the Indians are recorded in his journal.

Shooting prowess

I killed one of these birds flying, last July [1825], during an excursion of 12 days, which I had made principally for the sake of obtaining roots or seeds of the *Cyperus* ... The bird, a fine large male, was perched on a stump close to the village of Cockqua, one of the principal chiefs of the Chenook [= Chinook] nation. This tribe was at war with the Clatsops and some other Indians ... and many were the feats of strength and dexterity which they performed, in order to show their superior powers, among which were hitting a mark with a bow and arrows, and a gun. One individual passed the arrows through a small hoop of grass, six inches in diameter, thrown up into the air by another person, and then with his rifle struck a mark 110 yards distant, exclaiming that none of King George's Chiefs could do the like, any more than chaunt [*sic*] the death-song, and dance war-dances with him. On this bravado, deeming it a good opportunity to show myself a fair marksman, the poor silver-headed eagle was made to pay for it. I lifted my gun, which was charged with swan-shot, walked to within 45 yards of the bird, and throwing a stone to raise him, brought him down when flying. This had the desired effect; many of the natives, who never think of the possibility of shooting an object in motion, laid their hands on their mouths in token of fear, a common gesture with them. The fellow, however, still showing himself inclined to maintain his superiority, gave me a shot at his hat, which he threw up himself, when my shot carried away all the crown, leaving nothing but the brim. My fame was hereupon sounded through the whole country, and a high value attached to my gun. Ever since, I have found it of the utmost importance to bring down a bird flying when I go near any of their lodges, at the same time taking care to make it appear as a little matter, not done on purpose to be observed. With regard to the hat in question, I may mention that it was woven of the roots of *Helonias tenax*, which the Indians of the Columbia call 'Quip-Quip', and on my observing the tissue with attention, Cockqua promised that his little girl, 12 years of age, should make me three or four after the European shape, giving me at the same time his own hat, and a large collection of baskets, cups, and pouches of the same material, for which I paid in tobacco, knives, nails, and gun-flints. The roots of *Cyperus* and *Thuja* are also used for the same purpose.[5]

Lichen cakes and currants

Thursday the 11th [May 1826]. At seven this morning we gained the summit of the last range of hills which lie between the Columbia and Spokan Rivers, and beheld one of the most sublime views that could possibly be, of rugged mountains, deep valleys, and mountain-rills. At noon reached the old Establishment, where Mr Finlay received me most kindly, regretting at the same time that he had not a morsel of food to offer me, he and his family having been subsisting for several, at least six, weeks on the roots of *Phalangium quamash* (*Scilla esculenta*, Bot. Mag. t. 2774), called by the natives all over the country, 'Camass', on those of *Lewisia rediviva*, (Bot. Misc. t. 70), and on a black lichen (*L. jubatus*), which grows on the Pines. The mode of preparing the latter is as follows: — after clearing it thoroughly from the dead twigs and pieces of bark to which it adheres, it is immersed in water, and steeped till it becomes perfectly soft; when it is placed between two layers of ignited stones, with the precaution of protecting it with grass and dead leaves, lest it should burn. The process of cooking takes a night, and before the lichen cools, it is made into a cake, much in the way as the *Phalangium quamash*; when it is

considered fit for use. A cake of this kind, with a bason [*sic*] of water, was all that Mr Finlay had to offer me. Great, therefore, was my pleasure in being able to requite his hospitality by giving him a share of the provision with which Mr Dease's liberality had supplied me, and which, though far from luxurious fare, was yet the best that he and his family had tasted for a long time. I had also some game in my saddle bags, which I had killed by the way, and of which I gave him half. The principal object of my visit to Mr Finlay was to get my gun repaired, and as he was the only person who could do it, within a distance of 800 miles, and this article being a matter of, perhaps, vital importance to me, I hastened to inform him of my request ...

Two days were devoted to botanising in this neighbourhood, where I found three fine species of *Ribes* in flower: the *R. aureum*, which bears, as Mr Finlay informs me, a very large and excellent yellow berry ...; a white-blossomed, apparently new species, whose snowy and fragrant long spikes of flowers are enough to recommend it for culture in England, even without considering its abundant produce of well-flavoured and black currants, which resemble those of our country, except in being rather more acid; and another kind, with a green flower, that is succeeded by a small black gooseberry. Of all these, and many other plants, I engaged Mr Finlay to collect specimens and seeds for me; as well as of an interesting kind of *Allium*, which grows about 40 miles distant, and of which the roots, that I saw, were as large as a nut, and particularly mild and well tasted.[5]

A stolen knife and letters from home

I embarked at ten a.m. on Monday, the 10th [July 1826]; and, the river being at its height, proceeded for two or three hours at the rate of 12 miles an hour, when the great swell obliged us to put on shore. And as the same cause rendered it impossible to fish for salmon, a horse was killed, on whose flesh, with a draught of water, I made my supper. After a cheerless night, during which the mosquitoes were excessively troublesome, I proceeded about 50 miles the next day, when I breakfasted on similar fare. While doing this, an Indian, who stood by my side, managed to steal my knife, which had been further secured by a string tied to my jacket; and as it was the only one I possessed, for all purposes, I offered a reward of tobacco to get it returned. This bribe being ineffectual, I commenced a search for its recovery, and found it concealed under the belt of one of the knaves. When detected, he claimed to be paid the recompense; but as I did not conceive him entitled to this, as he had not given it at first (nor given it at all indeed), I paid him certainly, and so handsomely, with my fists, that I will engage he does not forget the 'Man of Grass' in a hurry. Having halted at night below the Great Falls of the Columbia, I saw smoke rising behind some rocks, and, thinking it might be Indians fishing, walked thither in quest of salmon. Instead of their savage countenances I found, however, to my great delight, that it was the camp of the brigade from the sea. I cannot describe the feeling which seizes me, when, after travelling some weeks together with Indians, I meet a person whom I have known before; or if even they are strangers, yet the countenance of a Christian is at such times most delightful. In the present instance I had the additional happiness of finding myself in the society of those who had ever treated me with cordiality, and who now seemed to vie with one another in acts of kindness towards me. Observing my dejected and travel-worn plight, one fetched me some water to wash with, another handed me a clean shirt, and a third busied himself in making ready something more palatable than carrion, for my supper; while my old friends, Messrs McDonald and Wark, handed me those best of cordials, my letters from England! Two of these, from Mr Sabine and my brother, were peculiarly gratifying. Those persons who have never been, like me, in such a remote corner of the globe, may perhaps think I should be ashamed to own my weakness on the present occasion; but long as I had been kept in ignorance of everything respecting my dearest friends, my anxiety was not allayed by *one* perusal of my letters, and no less than four times during the night did I rise from my mat to read and re-read them, till, ere morning dawned, I had them, I am sure, all by heart.[5]

Hostile Indians, and a new pine

[Oct. 1826] Weather dull, cold, and cloudy. When my friends in England are made acquainted with my travels, I fear they will think that I have told them nothing but my miseries. This may be very true; but I now know, as they may do also, if they choose to come here on such an expedition, that the objects of which I am in quest cannot be obtained without labour, anxiety of mind, and no small risk of personal safety, of which latter statement my this day's adventures are an instance. I quitted my camp early in the morning, to survey the neighbouring country, leaving my guide to take charge of the horses until my return in the evening, when I found that he had done as I wished, and in the interval dried some wet paper which I had desired him to put in order. About an hour's walk from my camp, I met an Indian, who on perceiving me, instantly strung his bow, placed on his left arm a sleeve of racoon skin, and stood on the defensive. Being quite satisfied that this conduct was prompted by fear, and not by hostile intentions, the poor fellow having probably never seen such a being as myself before, I laid my gun at my feet, on the ground, and waved my hand for him to come to me, which he did slowly and with great caution. I then made him place his bow and quiver of arrows beside my gun, and striking a light, gave him a smoke out of my own pipe, and a present of a few beads. With my pencil I made a rough sketch of the cone and pine tree which I wanted to obtain, and drew his attention to it, when he instantly pointed with his hand to the hills 15 or 20 miles distant towards the South; and when I expressed my intention of going thither, cheerfully set about accompanying me. At midday I reached my long-wished-for pines, and lost no time in examining them, and endeavouring to collect specimens and seeds. New and strange things seldom fail to make strong impressions, and are therefore frequently over-rated; so that lest I should never see my friends in England to inform them verbally of this most beautiful and immensely grand tree, I shall here state the dimensions of the largest I could find among several that had been blown down by the wind. At three feet from the ground its circumference is 57 feet nine inches; at one hundred and thirty-four feet, 17 feet five inches; the extreme length 245 feet. The trunks are uncommonly straight, and the bark remarkably smooth, for such large timber, of a whitish or light-brown colour, and yielding a great quantity of bright amber gum. The tallest stems are generally unbranched for two-thirds of the height of the tree; the branches rather pendulous, with cones hanging from their points like sugar-loaves in a grocer's shop. These cones are, however, only seen on the loftiest trees, and the putting myself in possession of three of these (all I could obtain) nearly brought my life to a close. As it was impossible either to climb the tree or hew it down, I endeavoured to knock off the cones by firing at them with ball, when the report of my gun brought eight Indians, all of them painted with red earth, armed with bows, arrows, bone-tipped spears, and flint-knives. They appeared anything but friendly. I endeavoured to explain to them what I wanted, and they seemed satisfied, and sat down to smoke, but presently I perceived one of them string his bow, and another sharpen his flint-knife with a pair of wooden pincers, and suspend it on the wrist of the right hand. Further testimony of their intentions was unnecessary. To save myself by flight was impossible, so, without hesitation, I stepped back about five paces, cocked my gun, drew one of the pistols out of my belt, and holding it in my left hand and the gun in my right, showed myself determined to fight for my life. As much as possible I endeavoured to preserve my coolness, and thus we stood looking at one another without making any movement or uttering a word for perhaps ten minutes, when one, at last, who seemed the leader, gave a sign that they wished for some tobacco: this I signified that they should have, if they fetched me a quantity of cones. They went off immediately in search of them, and no sooner were they out of sight, than I picked up my three cones and some twigs of the trees, and made the quickest possible retreat, hurrying back to my camp, which I reached before dusk. The Indian who last undertook to be my guide to the trees, I sent off before gaining my encampment, lest he should betray me. How irksome in the darkness of night to one under my present circumstances! I cannot speak a word to my guide, nor have I a book to divert my thoughts, which are continually occupied with the dread lest the hostile Indians should trace me hither, and make an attack; I now write lying, on the grass, with my gun cocked beside me, and penning these lines by the light of my 'Columbian candle', namely an ignited piece of rosiny wood. — To return to the tree which nearly cost me so dear. The wood is remarkably fine-grained and heavy; the leaves short and bright-green, inserted, five together, in a very short sheath; of my three cones one measures fourteen inches and a half, and the two others are respectively half an inch and an inch shorter, all full of fine seed. A little before this time of year the Indians gather the cones and roast them on the embers, then quarter them and shake out the seeds, which are afterwards thoroughly dried and pounded into a sort of flour, or also eaten whole.[5]

Douglas had discovered the sugar pine, which he named *Pinus lambertiana*.

In March 1827, Douglas left Fort Vancouver and, travelling via Hudson Bay (*see* pp. 225–226), returned briefly to England. In 1829–1830, he returned to the Columbia River region and visited California, continuing to collect plants, many unknown to science, and introduce them into cultivation in Britain.

The rapidity of spring

My whole collection of this year [1831] in California may amount to 500 species, a little more or less. This is prodigiously small I am aware — but when I inform you that the season for botanising is not more than three months your surprise will cease. Such is the rapidity of spring that plants like on the table lands of Mexico and platforms of the Andes in Chile bloom only for one day. The intense heats set in about June when every bit of herbage is dried to a cinder. The facility of travelling is not great wherein much time is lost as is the case as a matter of course in all new countries. It would require at least three years to do anything like good in California and the expense to me is not the least of the drawbacks. At present I can do nothing more and will content myself with particularising the present collection. Of new genera I am certain of 19 or 20 at least and I hope you will find many more. Most of them are highly curious. Of species there may be about 340 new.[6]

Beaver. In the seventeenth century, European demand for fur was so great that the Hudson's Bay Company was chartered in 1670 to hunt beavers and other animals in North America. The fur business was still booming when Douglas arrived to collect plants and his success was in part due to the fact that he had been allowed to stay at the Company's trading posts, ride its horses, paddle its canoes and make use of its guides. The beaver was also a good source of food for Indians and trappers, and the liver and fatty tissue of the animal's tail were particularly relished.

Douglas discovered numerous plants — cryptogams as well as vascular plants,[7] and was responsible for introducing many species into cultivation in Britain; for example, he discovered, and/or introduced to horticulture, eighteen species of *Penstemon*.[4] Other horticultural introductions included the Californian fuchsia (*Ribes speciosum*), Californian poppy (*Eschscholzia californica*) and the silk-tassel bush (*Garrya elliptica*).

He is probably most widely remembered in the common name of the important timber tree, the Douglas fir (*Pseudotsuga menzeisii*), which was named and described from specimens collected by Archibald Menzies but was introduced to cultivation by Douglas.

Douglas's final expedition was to the Sandwich Islands (Hawaiian Islands). It was there that he met his death in 1834, seemingly the result of falling into a covered pit that had been excavated for the purpose of trapping wild cattle. After falling in Douglas was gored by a bullock trapped in the pit. The entire episode was recorded by missionaries, who raised the possibility of foul play. Following an autopsy, authorities saw no reason to pursue the matter further.[1, 3]

A. GRAY *(1841)*

Asa Gray was born in New York in 1810 and subsequently became one of the most eminent nineteenth-century botanists. Prior to his 1842 appointment as the Fisher Professor of Natural History at Harvard University, Cambridge, he had published a textbook, *Elements of Botany* and, with John Torrey, the *Flora of North America*. These works were followed with further text books, floras and other major taxonomic accounts, including an account of the plants collected by Augustus Fendler in New Mexico, *A Manual of the Botany of the Northern United States*, and an account of the botany of the United States Exploring Expedition under the command of Charles Wilkes.[1]

A comparatively minor botanical account by Gray was of an excursion in 1841 to the mountains of North Carolina; this account included notes on the botany of the higher Allegheny Mountains.[2] Gray was accompanied by John Carey and J. Constable and the account commenced with a summation of the work of previous botanists in the region, including André Michaux (1746–1802) and his son François (1770–1885), and the Reverend Mr A. Curtis who provided Gray with an itinerary. Travelling from New York, Gray was initially struck by the extent of the weed flora.

Vile foreign weeds

As the Ashe County had not been visited by Mr Curtis, nor, so far as we are aware, by any other collector, and being from its situation the most accessible to a traveller from the north, we determined to devote to its examination the principal part of the time allotted to our own excursion.

Intending to reach this remote region by way of the Valley of Virginia, we left New York on the evening of the 23rd of June, and travelling by railroad, arrived at Winchester, a distance of 300 miles, before sunset of the following day. At Harper's Ferry, where the Potomac, joined by the Shenandoah, forces its way through the

*Asa Gray.
(Source:* Journal
of Botany 26:
*opposite p. 161
(1888). Reproduced
with permission
from the archives
of the Royal
Botanic Gardens,
Melbourne)*

Blue Ridge, in the midst of some of the most picturesque scenery in
the United States, we merely stopped to dine, and were therefore
disappointed in our hope of collecting *Sedum telephioides*,
S. pulchellum, *Paronychia dichotoma*, and *Draba ramosissima*;
all of which grow here upon the rocks. We observed the first in
passing, but it was not yet in flower. On the rocky banks of the
Potomac, below Harper's Ferry, we saw, for the first time, the
common locust tree (*Robinia pseudoacacia*) decidedly indigenous.
It probably extends to the southern countries of Pennsylvania, and,

from this point southward, is everywhere abundant; but we did not meet with it east of the Blue Ridge. From Winchester, the shire-town of Frederick County, we proceeded by stage-coach, directly up the Valley of Virginia, as that portion of the State is called which lies between the unbroken Blue Ridge, and the most easterly ranges of the Alleghenies ... Our first day's ride was to Harrisonburg, in Rockingham County, a distance of 69 miles from Winchester. From the moment we entered the valley, we observed such immense quantities of *Echium vulgare*, that we were no longer surprised at the doubt expressed by [the botanist] Pursh, whether it were really an introduced plant. This 'vile foreign weed', as Darlington, agriculturally speaking, terms this showy plant, is occasionally seen along the road-sides of the northern States; but here, for the distance of more than a hundred miles, it has taken complete possession, even of many cultivated fields, especially where the limestone approaches the surface, presenting a broad expanse of brilliant blue. It is surprising that the farmers should allow a biennial like this so completely to overrun their land. Another plant, much more extensively introduced here than in the north, (where it scarcely deserves the name of a naturalised species,) is *Bupleurum rotundifolium*, which in the course of the day we met with abundantly. The *Marrubium vulgare* is equally prevalent; and *Euphorbia lathyris* must also be added to the list of naturalised plants. The little *Verbena angustifolia* is also a common weed. We collected but a single indigenous plant of any interest ...[2]

In perfect helplessness

On Tuesday, the 29th of June, we crossed the New River, arrived at Wytheville, or Wythe Court-house towards evening; and at Marion, or Smythe Court-house, on the middle fork of the Holston, early in the morning ... At Marion, we determined to leave the valley road, and to cross the mountains into Ashe County, North Carolina; the morning was taken up in seeking a conveyance for this purpose. With considerable difficulty, we at length procured a carry-all, (a light covered wagon, with springs, drawn by one horse), capable of carrying our luggage and a single person besides the driver, a simple shoemaker, who had never before undertaken so formidable a journey, and who, accordingly, proved entirely wanting in the skill and tact necessary for conducting so frail a vehicle over such difficult mountain-tracks, for *roads* they can scarcely be called. He had first to ascend the steep ridge, interposed between the Middle and the South Forks of the Holston, called Brushy Mountain; during the ascent of which, we commenced botanising in earnest. The first interesting plant we met with, was *Saxifraga erosa* [described by the botanist] Pursh, but only with ripe fruit, and even with the seeds for the most part fallen from the capsules ... During this ascent, we collected *Galium latifolium* Michx. just coming into flower; and we subsequently found this species so widely diffused throughout the mountains of North Carolina, that we were much surprised at its remaining so little known since the time of Michaux. On a moist rocky bank by the road-side, we gathered some specimens of a *Scutellaria* ... Towards the summit of this ridge we first noticed the *Magnolia fraseri* which resembles the umbrella-tree (*Magnolia umbrella*), in the disposition of its leaves at the extremity of the branches. This, as well as *M. acuminata* (the only other species of *Magnolia* that we observed), is occasionally termed cucumber-tree; but the people of the country almost uniformly called the former wahoo, a name which, in the lower part of the southern States, is applied to *Ulmus alata*, or often to all the elms indifferently. The bitter and somewhat aromatic infusion of the green cones of both these magnolias in whiskey or apple-brandy, is very extensively employed as a preventive against intermittent fevers; a use which, as the younger Michaux remarks, would doubtless be less frequent, if, with the same medical properties, the aqueous infusion were substituted.

Nearly at the top of this mountain we overtook our awkward driver awaiting our arrival in perfect helplessness, having contrived to break his carriage upon a heap of stones, and to overthrow his horse into the boughs of a prostrate tree. So much delay was caused in extricating the poor animal, and in temporary repairs to the wagon, that we had barely time to descend the mountain on the opposite side, and to seek lodgings for the night in the secluded valley of the South Fork of the Holston ...

The next day (July 1st), we crossed the Iron Mountains (the great chain which divides the States of North Carolina and Tennessee, and which here forms the north-western boundary of Grayson County, Virginia), by Fox-Creek Gap, and traversing the numerous tributaries of the North Fork of New River, which abundantly water this sequestered region, we slept a few miles beyond the boundary of North Carolina, after a journey of nearly thirty miles. It must not be imagined that we found hotels or taverns for our accommodation, as, except at Ashe Court-House, we saw no place of public entertainment, from the time we left the Valley of Virginia, until we finally crossed the Blue Ridge, and quitted the mountain region. Yet we suffered little inconvenience on this account, as we were cordially received at the farm-houses along the road, and entertained, according to the means and ability of the owners, who seldom hesitated either to make a moderate charge, or to accept a proper compensation for their hospitality, which we therefore did not scruple to solicit from time to time ...[2]

Objects of curiosity

On the 2nd of July we continued our journey (11 miles) to Jefferson or Ashe Court-House, a hamlet of 20 or 30 houses, and the only village in the county. Intending to make this place our head-quarters while we remained in the region, we had the good fortune to find excellent accommodation at the house of Colonel Bower, who evinced every disposition to further our inquiries, and afforded us very important assistance. We may remark, indeed, that during our residence amongst the mountains, we were uniformly received with courtesy by the inhabitants, who, for the most part, wanted the general intelligence of our obliging host at Jefferson, and could scarcely be made to comprehend the object of our visit, or why we should come from a distance of seven hundred miles to toil over the mountains in quest of their common and disregarded herbs. Objects of curiosity as we were to these good folks, their endless queries had no air of impertinence, and they entertained us to the best of their ability, never attempting to make unreasonable charges. A very fastidious palate might occasionally be at a loss, but good corn-bread and milk are everywhere abundant, the latter from preference being used quite sour, or even curdled. Sweet milk appears to be very much disliked, being thought less wholesome, and more likely to produce the milk sickness, which is prevalent in some very circumscribed districts; so that our dislike of sour, and fondness for fresh milk, were regarded by this simple people as among our very many oddities. Nearly every farmer has a small dairy-house built over a cold brook or spring, by which the milk and butter are kept cool and sweet in the warmest weather.[2]

Heavily timbered with chestnut

We botanised for several days upon the mountains in the immediate neighbourhood of Jefferson, especially the Negro Mountain, which rises abruptly on one side of the village; the Phoenix Mountain, a sharp ridge on the other side; and the Bluff, a few miles distant in a westerly direction ... The mountain sides, though steep or precipitous, are covered with a rich and deep vegetable mould, and are heavily timbered, chiefly with chestnut, white oak, the tulip-tree, the cucumber-tree, and sometimes the sugar maple. Their vegetation presents so little diversity, that it is for the most part unnecessary to distinguish particular localities. Besides many of the plants already mentioned, and a very considerable number of northern species which we have not room to enumerate, we collected, or observed on the mountain-sides, *Clematis viorna*, in great abundance; *Tradescantia virginica*; *Iris cristata* in fruit; *Hedyotis* (*Amphiotis*) *purpurea*, which scarcely deserves the name, since the flowers are commonly almost white; *Phlox paniculata?*; *Aristolochia sipho*, without flowers or fruit; *Ribes cynosbati*, *R. rotundifolium* Michx. and *R. prostratum*; *Allium cernuum* and *A. tricoccum*; *Galax aphylla*; *Ligusticum actaeifolium*, the strong-scented roots of which are eagerly sought for and eaten by boys and hogs; the ginseng, here called sang, (the roots of which are largely collected, and sold to the country merchants, when fresh, for about twelve cents per pound, or, when dried, for triple that price); *Menziesia globularis*, mostly in fruit; and the showy *Azalea calendulacea*, which was also out of flower, except in deep shade ...[2]

In Gray's time, the majestic American chestnut, *Castanea dentata*, was common in the deciduous forests of the eastern part of the United States, sometimes contributing to more than 40 per cent of the overstorey trees in mature forests.[3] It is therefore not surprising that in the above extract he merely recorded its presence on the mountainsides. However, by the middle of the twentieth century the species had been all but eliminated from the landscape. From an estimated one thousand million trees its numbers plummeted to just 180 in all of North America in 1963.[4] This rapid decline was the result of chestnut blight. The blight is caused by an Asian fungal parasite, *Cryphonectria parasitica* (syn. *Endothia parasitica*), which entered America in nursery stock in the early 1900s. It kills by destroying the cambium layer and effectively ring-barking the trees.

Beds of balsam twigs and moss

On the 7th of July, we started for the high mountains farther south; having hired a cumbrous and unsightly, but convenient, tilted wagon, with a pair of horses and a driver, (who rode one of the beasts according to the usual custom of this region), for the conveyance of our luggage, and which afforded us, at intervals, the luxury of reposing on straw, at the bottom, while we were dragged along at the rate of two or three miles an hour.

Our first day's journey, extending to about twenty-four miles, was somewhat tedious, for we found no new plants of any interest. We saw, however, a variety of *Lonicera parviflora*? with larger leaves and flowers than ordinary, the latter dull-purplish; probably it is the *Caprifolium bracteosum* var. *floribus violaceo-purpureis* of Michaux. The following morning we reached the Watauga River (a tributary of the Holston), and leaving our driver to follow up the banks of the stream to the termination of the road at the foot of the Grandfather, we ascended an adjacent mountain, called Hanging-rock, and reached our quarters for the night by a different route. The fine and near view of the rugged Grandfather amply rewarded the toil of ascending this beetling cliff, where we also obtained the *Geum* (*Sieversia*) *radiatum*, probably the most showy species of the genus. Its brilliant golden flowers evince a disposition to become double, even in the wild state, and we often found as many as eight or nine petals. This tendency would doubtless be fully developed by cultivation. Around the base of these mountains we saw *Blephilia nepetoides*, and another labiate plant not yet in flower, which we took for *Pycnanthemum montanum* Michaux.

The next day (July 9th) we ascended the Grandfather, the highest as well as the most rugged and savage mountain we had yet attempted, although by no means the most elevated in North Carolina, as has generally been supposed. It is a sharp and craggy ridge, lying within Ashe and Burke counties, very near the north-east corner of Yancey, and cutting across the chain to which it belongs (the Blue Ridge), nearly at right angles ...

I should have remarked, that so much time was occupied in the ascent of this mountain, as nearly to prevent us from herborising around the summit for that day; since we had to descend some

distance to the nearest spring of water, and to prepare our
encampment for the night. The branches of the balsam afforded
excellent materials for the construction of our lodge; the smaller
twigs, with large mats of moss stripped from the rocks, furnished
our bed, and the dead trees supplied us with fuel for cooking our
supper, and for feeding the large fire which we were obliged to keep
up during the night. We returned to the top next morning, and
devoted several hours to its examination, but the threatening state of
the weather hindered us from visiting the adjacent ridges, or the
southern and eastern faces of the mountain, and we were
constrained to descend, towards evening, to the humble dwelling of
our guide, which we hardly reached before the impending storm
commenced.[2]

The most beautiful of all mountains

Our next excursion was to the Roan Mountain, a portion of that
elevated range which forms the boundary between North Carolina
and Tennessee, distant about 30 miles south-west from our quarters
at the foot of the Grandfather, by the directest path; but at least
60 by the nearest carriage road. We travelled, for the most part,
on foot, loading the horses with our portfolios, papers, and some
necessary luggage, crossed the Hanging-Rock Mountain to Elk
Creek, and thence over a steep ridge to Cranberry Forge, on the
sources of Doe River, where we passed the night. On our way, we
cut down a service-tree (as the *Amelanchier canadensis* is here
called), and feasted upon its ripe fruit, which throughout this region
is highly and, indeed, justly prized, being sweet, with a very
agreeable flavour; while, in the northern States, so far as our
experience goes, this fruit, even if it may be said to be edible, is not
worth taking. As services are here greedily sought after, and
generally procured by cutting down the trees, the latter are becoming
scarce in the vicinity of the 'plantations', as the mountain settlements
are universally called ...

We climbed the north flank of the Roan, through the heavily
timbered woods and rank herbage with which it is covered; but
found nothing new to us, except *Streptopus lanuginosus* in fruit,
and among the groves of *Rhododendron maximum* towards the top
we also collected *Diphysicum foliosum*, a moss which we had not
before seen in a living state. In more open moist places near the

summit, we found the *Hedyotis* (*Houstonia*) *serpyllifolia*, still beautifully in bloom, and the *Geum geniculatum*, which we have already noticed. It was just sunset when we reached the bald and grassy summit of this noble mountain, and after enjoying for a moment the magnificent view it affords, had barely time to prepare our encampment between two dense clumps of *Rhododendron catawbiense*, to collect fuel, and make ready our supper. The night was so fine, that our slight shelter of balsam boughs proved amply sufficient; the thermometer, at this elevation of about 6,000 feet above the level of the sea, being 64° Fahr. at midnight, and 60° at sunrise. The temperature of a spring, immediately under the brow of the mountain below our encampment, we found to be 47° Fahr. The Roan Mountain is well characterised by Prof. Mitchell [in the *American Journal of Science and Arts*, Jan. 1839], as the easiest of access, and the most beautiful of all the high mountains of that region.

> 'With the exception of a body of (granitic) rocks, looking like the ruins of an old castle, near its south-western extremity, the top may be described as a vast meadow, (about nine miles in length, with some interruptions, and with a maximum elevation of 6,038 feet) without a tree to obstruct the prospect; where a person may gallop his horse for a mile or two, with Carolina at his feet on one side, and Tennessee on the other, and a green ocean of mountains, raised into tremendous billows, immediately around him. It is the pasture ground for the young horses of the whole country, during the summer. We found the strawberry here in the greatest abundance, and of the finest quality, in regard to both size and flavour, on the 30th of July.'

At sunrise we had fine weather, and a most extensive view of the surrounding country; in one direction we could count from eight to 12 successive ranges of mountains, and nearly all the higher peaks of this whole region were distinctly visible. Soon, however, a dense fog enveloped us, and continued for several hours, during which we traversed the south-western summit, and made a list of the plants we saw ... We made a hasty visit to the other principal summit, where we found nothing that we had not already collected, expecting *Arenaria glabra* Michx., and descended partly by way of the contiguous Yellow Mountain.[2]

A reputed antidote to snakebite

Retracing our steps, we returned next day to the foot of the Grandfather Mountain, and reached our quarters at Jefferson the second day after. We had frequently been told of an antidote to the bite of the rattlesnake and copperhead, (reptiles not unfrequent throughout this region,) which is thought to possess wonderful efficacy, called Turman's Snake-root, after an 'Indian Doctor', who first employed it; the plant was brought to us by a man who was ready to attest its virtues from his personal knowledge, and proved to be *Silene stellata*! Its use was suggested by the markings of the root beneath the bark, in which these people find a fancied resemblance to the skin of the rattlesnake. Nearly all of the reputed antidotes are equally inert, such herbs as *Impatiens pallida*, etc. being sometimes employed; so that we are led to conclude that the bite of these reptiles is seldom fatal, or even very dangerous, in these cooler portions of the country.[2]

Gray died in Cambridge in 1888. During his long career he produced more than 700 publications. His private herbarium collection was also the foundation of the Harvard University Herbarium, with Gray donating more than 200,000 specimens and 2,200 books when it opened in 1864.[5]

C. GEYER *(1843–1844)*

Carl ('Charles') Andreas Geyer was born in Dresden, Germany, in 1809. After working in Dresden's botanic garden and other horticultural establishments, Geyer left Germany in 1834 for North America to satisfy a desire to explore new countries. His first major journey was in 1835 when he went to the plains of the Missouri. In 1836 and the following years, he was part of a surveying team operating between the Missouri and Mississippi rivers. In 1841, he was involved in an expedition in Iowa; in 1842, he travelled in upper Illinois; and in 1843 and 1844 — in the upper Missouri, the Rocky Mountains and in the Oregon Territory.[1,2] During these travels he collected copiously and in 1845, he arrived in England 'with a very valuable and beautifully preserved collection of plants'.[2] He subsequently wrote a very long article about his 'botanical journey' during 1843 and 1844. Within it Geyer recorded that he, as with other scientific travellers such as David Douglas (*see* pp. 229–237), had received assistance from the Hudson's Bay Company, and had also benefited greatly by assistance from various missionaries, both Catholic and Protestant. Much of his text is confined to describing the botanical characteristics and sometimes geological features of the country passed through, but occasionally he touched on other subjects, including notes on Indian tribes and their food sources, the behaviour of rattlesnakes and prairie dogs, and the delights, or otherwise, of travel.

Choicest plants, prairie dogs and bison

The Platte or Nebraska River is shallow and rapid with an average breadth of a mile, and presents within this region most picturesque scenery from the innumerable small verdant islands which appear as if sailing in its rapid stream. Most of these islands have at least one tree in their centre, and some of them small groves, either of poplar, elm or *Negundo* [maple], their luxuriant branches bending in the wind. Along the banks scarcely a tree is to be seen, except at the mouths of rivers and junctions of rivulets. The thickets of *Salix longifolia*, *Amorpha frutescens* and *Rosa parvifolia*, when all in bloom, afford a pleasant contrast to the adjoining trackless drifting sandy ranges of the valley, formed by local currents of wind from the hills. These sandy tracts are the abode of *Stipa avenacea*, *S. juncea*, *Agrostis cryptandra*, and the pretty *Eriocoma*; sometimes on firmer sand, the *Crypsis squarrosa* twines over the surface. Only *Stipa avenacea* grows densely; scattered amongst it I found the pretty *Machaeranthera*, like *Centuary* [*Centaurea*], with us, amongst corn. These different species of *Stipa* formed the favourite food of our horses, but only before their panicle was developed; as soon as the spikelets came out, the animals would not touch this genus, but fed on the *Eriocoma*. Scattered amongst these sand-grasses generally were groups of *Cleome integrifolia*, *Asclepias speciosa*, *Argemone grandiflora*, *Calymenia multiflora*, and *Chrysopsis villosa*. The more fertile parts of the valley still present *Pentstemon* [= *Penstemon*] *grandiflorum*, and *Batschia gmelini*, with *Lathyrus palustris*, *Sisyrinchium anceps*, *Pentstemon pubescens*, *Potentilla anserina*, *Zigadenus*, *Aster*, and *Solidago*, in moist places ...

But it is to the gravelly plains and ridges that the attention of the botanist is chiefly attracted; especially the wide extending ridges, which, wherever they appear, give shelter to the rarest and choicest plants of the surrounding country. These ridges prevail along the whole eastern slope of the Rocky Mountains; alternating with almost every geological formation; and may be traced across the Missouri, about the mouth of Platte River eastward, in an irregular interrupted line to Lake Michigan, and southward likewise to the Ozark Mountains of Missouri; perhaps, also through Arkansas to Texas.

The plants of these ridges bear a resemblance to the subalpine flora, with somewhat of the robustness of those species which inhabit the plains below. There are no grasses with creeping roots, except the simple *Panicum muehlenbergii*, in this region, and on the upper Missouri; but several beautiful [grasses] grow only here, amongst which are *Aristida pallens* and *Agrostis brevifolia*. *Atheropogon oligostachyon* and *Sesleria dactyloides* are abundant. The most conspicuous plants are *Mammillaria simplex*, *Bartonia ornata*, *Lupinus pusillus*, *Sida coccinea*, *Gaura coccinea*, *Pentstemon albidum* and *P. grandiflorum*, *Astragalus hypoglottis*, *A. assurgens* and *A. caryocarpus*, *Echinacea angustifolia*, *Lygodesmia juncea*, *Psoralea esculenta*, *P. canescens* and *Glycyrrhiza*, *Evolvulus argenteus*, *Polygala alba*, *Oenothera serrulata*,

Diplopappus pinnatifidus Hooker, *Calymenia angustifolia, C. hirsuta* and *C. decumbens, Aster sericeus, Solidago nemoralis, Schrankia uncinata, Erysimum asperum, Linum multicaule* ...

Several of the above named plants may be seen also in the plains, which, however, are characterised by others more robust, amongst which *Helianthus atrorubens* and *Echinacea purpurea* are conspicuous, *Heliopsis scabra, Columnaria pinnata, Rudbeckia columnaris,* with yellow and deep fuscous-purple rays. *Allionia nyctaginea* grows in stony places. On sunny slopes I observed *Petalostemon candidum* and *P. violaceum, Coreopsis delphinifolia,* [species of *Psoralea*], *Astragalus,* [species of *Phaca*], *Koeleria, Panicum muehlenbergii* and *Polypogon glomeratus.*

Small sandy denuded places are occupied by the beautiful *Petalostemon villosum* and *Oenothera albicaulis,* and also by *Crypsis, Cleome integrifolia, Opuntia missourica* and *Artemisia caudata.*

In these plains occur flats, or slightly depressed and somewhat circular places, sometimes one mile in circumference, covered with a delicate carpet of the pretty [grass] *Sesleria dactyloides.* Within them the Prairie Marmot (*Arctomys ludovicianus* Say) burrows; so that the spots are often called prairie-dog villages by Anglo-American travellers. These creatures live together in great numbers, and feed, at least generally, on this little grass. Their habitations probably communicate, though each pair seems to have but one entrance, around which a heap of naked earth forms a little elevation, from which the inmates survey the village. A small species of owl lives peaceably with the marmot; it is a restless little bird, apparently on good terms with the marmots, but ever on the alert, for fear of the rattlesnakes; which, strange to say, inhabits the same quarters, but is probably an intruder. This owl seems to have as good a sight in the noon-day sun as its European kindred have at night; for I have remarked it moving about all day, passing and repassing from one burrow to another. When I visited these habitations at sunrise, I never failed to see alternately marmots, owls, or rattlesnakes peeping out of the apertures. In a plain at Shienne River, on the upper Missouri, I found one large village deserted by marmots, and tenanted solely by rattlesnakes; the latter having probably overpowered and destroyed the legitimate occupants, or driven them out.

On the earth-heaps of these burrows, I saw *Solanum triflorum*, and never elsewhere, it grows prostrate in patches; *Oenothera pinnatifida*, *Sida coccinea* and *Lupinus pusillus* are here also together.

The scarlet colour, with which tracts of thousands of acres may be seen glowing during the months of May or June, is occasioned by the *Sida coccinea*; the white, by *Oenothera pinnatifida* and *O. coronopifolia*; blue and purple by several species of *Pentstemon* [= *Penstemon*], and yellow by the dense masses of *Helianthus tubaeformis* and *H. petiolaris*.

Before closing the description of this region, I must mention the great inconveniences to which the traveller is exposed in it; foremost come the incessant rains during the months of May and June, which fall so heavy [*sic*], that the water runs an inch deep upon the ground, accompanied too with violent winds. Next are the mosquitoes during calm nights, and swarms of blood-thirsty horse-flies by day, plaguing alike man and beast incessantly. Not less annoying are the night watches, necessary here to guard the animals from the marauding Pawnees, especially after a hard journey and in bad weather. However, after weary day and sleepless night are past, when once the morning sun makes its appearance, all troubles are over and almost forgotten. Every one is engaged in breaking up camp, talking about the most probable adventures of the coming day; some prepare to hunt the buffalo or bison, some the antelope, and others to go in search of strayed horses etc. Perhaps a bellowing band of bisons rushes across the river, or a troop of wild horses appear prancing in the morning sun, and dashing over the plains, or a capering antelope is seen on the brow of the hills, or something else to add excitement to the scene. Quickly the whole cavalcade has mounted again, and proceeds onward through that inhospitable and dangerous wilderness.[2]

Feasting on ants and grasshoppers

In the *Artemisia* bushes (wild-sage-plains of the Anglo-American travellers) lives a beautiful gallinaceous bird, the so-called 'sage-cock' (*Tetrao urophasianus*); as grey as the *Artemisia* itself, and the flesh of it as bitter too. It assembles in little flocks, seldom more then eight or twelve together, and lives, at least, generally, on the *Artemisia* leaves. The desert region about the Great Salt Lake is the Sierra de los Grallos of the New Mexicans, or Grasshopper Desert; containing great part of the country of the Shoshonies, Bannak and Eutaw Indians, tribes ever on the move and in the saddle, amongst whom are some of the best horsemen in the world, especially the famous Shoshonies or Snake Indians and the Eutaws. The Bannaks, a related tribe to the Shoshonies, however, have almost nothing of the skilful horsemanship of their cousins; but live the most wretched life of any Indians in the West. They are generally designated 'Root-diggers' and are very well described by Captain Bonneville. Oftentimes, when they can get neither game nor roots to live on, they eat grasshoppers; a species of *Gryllus*, very large and fat, of every shade of brown and black, wherewith these deserts abound. For this purpose they are caught in large quantities, boiled alive without ceremony and eaten like craw-fish. It is said that the soup of them is very sweet and a favourite drink; even gentlemen of the Hon. Hudson's Bay Company, who have been compelled to live on it, spoke to the same effect. In case of scarcity of such grasshoppers, the Bannaks make soup of a large species of ants [*sic*], which abounds towards the uppermost waters of the Arkansas River, and further south in the Sierra de los Mimbras, upper California and Texas. Few quadrupeds exist in the wide deserts; antelopes may have been abundant once, now they are very few in number and so shy that they never come within rifle-shot. A middle-sized species of hare, white with a black tail, dwells in the neighbourhood of the Oases, but is very rare. Small birds are scarcely seen.

It is hardly necessary to say anything about the difficulties the traveller has to endure traversing these wide deserts. Want of water and of game, and the hot noon-day sun, are rather trying; but still not worth while mentioning, for the ever-bright sky and the cool nights make ample amends for them. The atmosphere is pure and exhilarating, so that if there is no want of food in the camp, I am sure every traveller will be disposed to number those days among the best of the long journey, not forgetting the wild blazing camp-fires of *Artemisia* bushes.[2]

The stench of countless numbers of rattlesnakes

When I went [to collect] this *Bartonia*, I had a most singular adventure with rattlesnakes. I resolved to camp for the coming Sunday on a narrow enclosed prairie, between the sandy woods, the mountain, and the Spokan River, close to a rapid. After dismounting I went to the river to drink, and found, on a small gravelly plain at the water's edge, some granite boulders lying scattered about, the whole spun over by [the fern] *Marsilea*. Engaged in examining it, I was attacked by a large rattlesnake, which I despatched instantly, and thought no more of the circumstance, especially as some Indians came passing by, from whom I purchased an excellent dried salmon. As I had not had much to eat for the past week, I prepared a good supper of salmon, which I roasted on sticks by the fire. Meanwhile, I went to hobble my animals, and being alone, was engaged till dark. While taking my supper, I heard a noise; a mule, which I had tied up for the night, became exceedingly uneasy; but I did not leave my meal. After having done, I took up my tin cup to go to drink at the river, the moon shining bright. The noise seemed close to me, resembling the sound produced by dragging sticks over hard ground at a distance. As soon as I had traversed the small grassy prairie and stood at the bank, but three or four feet above the gravelly, stony water's edge, I, to my astonishment, beheld countless numbers of rattlesnakes, dashing and whirling on the gravelly space below. The moon shone clear, and I could distinctly see that they were crawling under and above each other, especially near the rounded granite boulders, which lay here and there. Around these they kept rattling, incessantly, the greater number beating their rattles against the stones. The noise was increased by the rustling of their scaly bodies on the gravel. The stench on the spot was very disgusting. Struck by fear, I retreated to my camp-fire, wrapped myself in my blanket, and watched, fearing these guests should take it in their heads to come to my fire, and find me asleep. The noise continued till near ten o'clock, when it gradually but quickly subsided, and I went to sleep. As soon as daylight appeared, I got up, saddled my mule, and looked for my horses, in order to leave that unpleasant camp, but the horses were astray in the mountains, and I returned after a fruitless ride of nearly three hours, being compelled to remain. I now began to examine the spot by the water's edge, and found it deserted, just as quiet as on the afternoon before. The rattlesnake I had killed was lying there only. Not satisfied with that examination, I got a pole, and commenced lifting the large flat stones, thinking the creatures must be under them, but after all my searching, I could not see a single one. That no snake got bitten by another during the exciting dance, seemed to me very evident and remarkable, for it would have, by the length of the rendezvous, remained on the spot dead.

To tell marvellous tales of snakes and hunting-stories has been so common in America, that every one must be careful to relate a true adventure, lest he excites suspicion at the mere mentioning of what he is going to say, that it will be a hoax ...

A few days after, I had the pleasure of seeing Chief-factor Macdonald at Fort Colville, to whom I was resolved, at all risks, to relate my snake-adventure ... When I mentioned the fact to him ... [he said] that he had had occasion to witness the very same thing at his camp, about Priest's Rapids, on the Columbia, about a day before me. I saw it on the evening of the 22nd of July, 1844.

Often had I heard of such assemblages of rattlesnakes, on the Upper Missouri, for example; but I always doubted the truth of it, till that evening. Possibly these reptiles congregate, before moving to their winter-quarters, under ground; but that would have been rather early, for I saw rattlesnakes above ground, fully six weeks afterwards. The rocky banks of the rivers of Oregon are full of these reptiles.[2]

Included within his publication — as an extensive footnote to the main narrative — was a long description by Geyer of the difficulties of winter travel.

An unplanned swim

I set out from the Skitsoe village in the beginning of December 1843, to go to Fort Colville on the Columbia River, a distance of about 180 or 200 miles on the winter road. Not finding an opportunity to go in company, and finding also the prices the Indians demanded to guide me too high for my limited means, I, at last, came to the resolution to go alone, though utterly ignorant of the route and the country generally. Having exchanged a fine fat horse I commenced my journey under the auspices of a snowstorm, which increased, the higher I ascended the wooded plateau. The third day in the morning, every vestige of a path had disappeared, the storm continued, and the depth of the snow made it impossible for me to proceed further onward, the more so as I had lost the path entirely, being in the midst of a lightly wooded plateau. To return was now the only alternative left for me, but to find my way back another difficulty. I now dismounted again and struck a camp, hoping that by waiting a day or so the snow storm might abate, that I might be enabled to see a little at a distance. I built myself a shelter of spruce branches, lit a fire, gathered wood for the long night, and

finally worked two to three hours very hard to free a space of
ground from snow to make grazing easier for my horse, who,
moreover did not like the stormy climate and seemed impatient to
return to the valley, which compelled me to 'hobble' him; that is,
to tie his forefeet together with a leather strap. Two of the dullest
days of my life did I spend in this wretched camp, on a bed of spruce
branches, watching the fire and my horse, but the storm continued
with unabating fury, the snow now averaging three feet in depth.
On the morning of the third day, I resolved to return at any risk,
striking an easterly direction by my compass. I took my horse by
the reins, and with the hatchet in my right, I commenced marking
the trees as I passed onward through the deep snow, avoiding defiles,
till late in the afternoon, when I found myself at the verge of a
sudden slope towards a narrow valley below, in which I recognised
black spots indicating a rivulet; descending with some difficulty,
I was much pleased to find a path a little above the valley, which I
followed, and brought me to the crossing place of Coeur-d'Aleine
River in the afternoon of next day. The snowing now changed to rain
in the valley, which at last fell heavily, so I hastened to get myself
across the river. No canoe being on this side, I had no alternative
but to swim for one; to do that I had to break the thin ice with
my hatchet on my way, which had filled the open space since my
late passage. Cold soon drove me back to the banks to light a fire,
which I did by discharging one of my pistols into a heap of fine dry
cedar or *Thuja* bass, which an Indian had hidden under a piece of
an old canoe. At last, after several swimmings and landings, I made
the whole distance and brought over a fine canoe; one of those frail
things mentioned above, made of cedar or *Thuja* bark and basket
willows. First, I brought over my saddle and saddle-bags, returning
again I took my horse on the line, and warming myself through,
stepped in the canoe to swim my horse across, when he suddenly
turned back frightened, upset me with my frail canoe. Now I had to
swim once more, but this time with my clothes on; however, I soon
managed to push myself on the other shore with the canoe, which
got broke [*sic*] against the ice by this operation. I now had to take
my saddle and saddle-bags on my back, and travel five to six miles
in rain and storm along the banks of the river, while my horse was
trotting and neighing triumphantly on the other side, with head and
tail upright. Patiently I marched on through meadows and morass,
and arrived just at about dark, at the village. Rushing to the fire in
one of the Indian lodges, I was laughed at heartily, for every one
could easily guess what had befallen me. At last, an Indian woman

having amused herself a long time, by my vain efforts, to free myself of my buckskin shirt, gave me a helping hand. The sensation of wet buckskin on the skin, can only be compared with that of taking a frog in the hand.

... the foregoing account I could have omitted, was it not connected with the one following. To give it so that the reader may get at least some idea, I have thought proper to give every detail of the winter-excursion. Perhaps he may get impatient, on account of the length; but I am sure he will not envy me.[2]

Something in favour of smoking tobacco

One would think that this would have been sufficient to make me stay where I was, and at my return I thought so myself; but, after three days had elapsed I heard that some Indians were going to drive a number of horses to a certain good pasture, the road they had to go was partly the same as to Fort Colville. I concluded to join them, as they promised to bring me on the right track. Not in the least did I dream that this adventure would outdo the former; but, prepared for a journey of four days, [I] crossed the river where I found the Indian who had caught my horse, where I saddled him, to join my party. They, however, had lost some horses in the woods, for which they were searching; towards evening they came, but as it was too late now, we had to camp at the crossing for the night; hobbling our horses we lit a fire, and resolved to start as early as possible next day. A stormy night set in again, accompanied by pelting rain, which lasted for three days. On the third day towards noon, our roads parted. I got my information from the Indians how to travel on, but I found that these Indians have not that aptness to describe a route, so as to understand it at once, which I so often admired with the Indians of the Plains. I understood what he marked on the ground; to follow it strictly, I copied it on a piece of paper. Accordingly, I had to take the second trail on the right, after following the path I was in for a short distance. This I did. Soon I found that I was ascending again a wooded plateau; this made me distrustful of my road, so I instantly returned, examining the way again; finding however that I was perfectly right, I resolved to travel on as fast as possible. The fifth day I was again on a crested high plateau, snowy, stormy weather again set in, but this time accompanied by a piercing wind; however, I kept my road steadily, it was one that led to a distant Gamass [camass or quamash] prairie or root-ground of the Indians, frequented therefore by numbers of pack-horses, who had, in passing with their loads, snatched the bark from the pine trunks, which marks helped me to find the path again when I lost the track. Soon I became uneasy again as to the right way; knowing that my course lay northward, I found by my compass that I had pursued a south-easterly direction for the last three days; so that instead of wide plains and rivers, I had met only small valley prairies with rivulets. I now returned again, convinced that I must be wrong. This was the eighth day since I started from the village, with provisions for four days only; consisting of dry buffaloe [*sic*] meat and Gamass bulbs; these I had to manage now well, so that a third part of a breakfast was now my ration for the whole day. I had no rifle with me to kill game, nor did I meet any, except a moose-deer, which by its lazy amble kept my tired horse soon out of shooting distance, both with rifle and pistol. The snowing had now ceased; but the ground was covered two feet deep, and the labour I had every evening to free a piece of grassy ground for my horse, was very tiresome. In the evening, when I struck camp, I had first to gather wood for a fire for the long night, which lasted from four o'clock in the afternoon to eight in the morning. Above three hours passed in labour, the other long part I passed in sleeping, smoking, stirring the fire, looking for my horse and so on. When hunger pinched me, I smoked tobacco; to allay thirst, I kept several snow balls near the fire in front of my bed, the latter consisted of spruce branches, which I licked when they were thawing. Here I cannot omit to say at least something in favour of smoking tobacco; and in no other way, I think, can smoking be excused as anything like being useful or necessary. The most pinching hunger and that peculiar faint feverish sensation accompanying it, is at once removed, as well as the sharp appetite, by smoking tobacco. The luxury of a pipe of tobacco, in such cases, cannot be conceived by any smoker, if he has not experienced it. The excitement is naturally soon over, and increases the more the stomach is tortured by fasting. A frequent repetition is therefore necessary. True, that a certain debility of the stomach must be the consequence; but this cannot outweigh an expediency so great, when life is in the other scale. But little progress did I make in my return, owing to the snow and the feebleness of mine as well as of my horse. On the third day towards camping time, I noticed by the marks on the pine trunks, that a path forked off to the right. Striking my camp at the place, I walked a distance and convinced myself that it bore a north-westerly course. Next morning I followed it, and found, to my great satisfaction, that I descended considerably. Already at noon, the snow began to disappear, my path became plainer, and at last brought me to a narrow rocky defile, when after another descent I observed a wide plain stretched before me, with but little snow and plenty of fine grass. The afternoon was beautiful, and my horse trotted on briskly along a woody seam of basaltic rocks. About sunset, I observed four horses grazing in the plains, which made me believe that I must be near an Indian village. Believing that some of the people might come and see after these horses, which they commonly do every two days, I resolved to camp on the spots; and to be easily recognised I put fire to a dry pine, covered with resin which burnt the whole night like a torch. A bright beautiful night ensued, which I enjoyed, feeling some hope of being now near the end of my trying excursion. The sun rose beautifully above the snow towering mountains next morning, when my horse came to my campfire voluntarily, having had an excellent grazing night. The four other horses also were only a short distance off. Mounting and proceeding onward I met several paths forking off from the main, and while I checked my horse, not knowing which one to take, my eyes caught at the distance an object which turned out after a minute or two, to be an Indian on a white horse, galloping over the plains towards the smoke column of my burning pine tree. At once I put the heels to my horse and dashed up to him. A short parley in words and signs ensued, of where we came from and where we were about to go. I understood from him that I was on the direction both to Fort Colville and the Spokan Mission station. He was an old, coarse and wild-looking fellow, but agreed, and was willing at once to bring me to the crossing place of Spokan River, for which he asked seven balls and powder, a high price in that country for a two hours' ride. The passage through the river was rather difficult, the crossing place being immediately below a high waterfall. After I had paid off my guide, and smoked a pipe with him, he turned very civil, and accompanied me a short distance further, showing me the road afterwards to the nearest Indian village. For the additional trouble, he again asked to be paid by some flints and a piece of tobacco, which I did. He returned to fetch his horses. Trotting along a series of trap rocks, covered with scanty pines and tracts of sandy woods for three or four hours, I found myself at once on the brink of a precipice, overlooking a small river in a narrow valley below, and discerned an Indian village on an elevated bank opposite. To my right, I recognised Spokan River in a rather broad valley. Both rivers joined a short distance below, and enclose a point of land of classic reputation in Oregon; namely, the place where the trading company led by the great pioneer Wilson P. Hunt, of St Louis, built their first trading post, which was the first that was surprised by the British North West Traders. Nothing remains now but a little elevation of the place where the chimney stood.

Seeing so many paths I made directly for the village, which looked pretty neat; the lodges were constructed of thick poles, covered with new rush mats in the shape of our house-roofs. A great number of men, women, and children surrounded me as soon as I had dismounted in the village, but contrary to what I was used to, the tone in which I was spoken to, by two or three saucy-looking young men, especially by a half-blooded ferocious youngster, did not please me at all. When I asked for the road to Colville, he said he did not know, demanding in the same harsh voice sundry things, especially tobacco with every possible ill grace. At my refusal he changed his language to a still more offending manner which brought me a little in harness; the more so as the rest not possessing the same boldness, joined in a kind of sneer peculiar to the Indian only. I leaned on the neck of my horse, holding the reins in my hand, keeping myself quiet, when the former insolent fellow undertook to examine my saddle-bags, not daring, however, to take them down; while the others felt the mane of my horse, whose fat condition seemed to excite their appetite for horse-flesh, which these Indians are very fond of. This was too much for me; I lifted up the bear-skin that covered my pistol-holsters, took out the pistols, and placed them in my belt. This manoeuvre succeeded, and brought them at once to better grace. They imagined me to be, in their own saying, 'a poor fellow without a gun.' The insolent half-breed lost more of his tact than the others; he stepped back amazed, crying out 'Stem!' (what!) pleading some ignorance to hide his fear. For this, I took out a pistol, levelling it at him with a doubtful laughing mien, imitating suddenly the sound of the report of a gun with my full voice. At this he shrunk visibly; he was now laughed at by some boys. Without looking at any one I swung myself into the saddle to be off. Three or four came forth now to show me the road, for which I gave them a little tobacco.

I was glad to find myself alone again. The afternoon was beautiful, and I enjoyed the picturesque scenery along Spokan River, the path leading right above along the high banks of the same. At sunset I struck camp under a gigantic *Abies balsamea* [a fir tree] near the river.[2]

In a footnote, Geyer recorded that this same tree had been initialled "D.Dgls.", which he assumed to be those of David Douglas (*see* pp. 229–237), who had visited the area one summer.

I made a shelter of a blanket, and stretched on my bear skin, I mused over the changes of the day, and over past times, for it was Christmas Eve. While I was so sitting and smoking a pipe, another Indian came up on a white horse; riding up to my fire he bent himself over his horse's neck, looking at my saddle, at myself, and the fire, for several minutes — this with an air of nonchalance which all North American Indians possess — at last I motioned him to dismount, which he did. He was a half naked youngster with a dejected countenance, who soon let me know his ill-luck, that he had lost every thing, gambling with the Sayelpies at Fort Colville. He also told me, that to go to the Mission establishment I had to cross a high snowy mountain. He stirred the fire, and fetched more wood for the night, watered the horses, so that I offered him a smoke, which he greedily accepted. After it I got out the small remains of the provisions, which I shared with him. Again we had a smoke, during which I made him the proposition, to guide me to the Mission next morning, which he promised. The pay was a saddle-blanket. Early in the morning of Christmas day, I followed the Indian over the mountain, the top of which was wrapped in a snow storm; towards noon we began to descend, and soon arrived in the valley Tshimakain. Soon I shook hands with Messrs. Eells and Walker, and accepted the permission joyfully to make myself at home in their residence ... I state here, that I shall remember their kindness throughout the whole of my life. The sudden exchanges from hunger and cold in the wilderness, for the comforts of civilised life were not without a reaction on my health; but in three days the revolution was over, and I could enjoy the luxury again of sleeping under a roof, of which I had not had an opportunity for eight long months in succession.[2]

In 1845, following his stay in England, Geyer returned to Dresden after an absence of nearly 12 years, but looking 'at least 20 years older'.[1] He died in November 1853, nine days short of his forty-fourth birthday.

CENTRAL AMERICA
&
SOUTH AMERICA

G. U. SKINNER *(1837–1841)*

George Ure Skinner was born in 1804 in Scotland. He commenced his working life as a bank clerk but later turned to general business. In 1831, he travelled to Guatemala where he was in partnership with a Mr Klée, and during his stay there found time to indulge in a childhood interest, natural history. Initially he was more interested in collecting insects and birds than plants and Skinner is accredited with making the first collections of about twenty species of bird. However, encouraged by British orchidologist James Bateman (1811–1897), he subsequently devoted himself more to the collection of plants and was responsible for the introduction of many species of orchid into cultivation in England.[1] The following extracts are from letters sent from Guatemala to William Hooker in 1837.

Orchids, cacti and 'poisoned' water

… cholera was raging in Gualair and Zacapa when I arrived at Ysabal … Thus was I obliged to forgo my proposed two days dedication to rest and the collecting of curious cacti for His Grace of Bedford in Zacapa and obliged to make a route … by the River Polschic, which runs through that most interesting of all countries, the Vera Paz. I suffered severely from mosquitoes but reached Guatemala attended by two Indians bowing under a load of orchids all new to me, and a hundred thousand thanks my dear Sir for your press. It was called into action, and the moment the roads are again open you will receive my collections. The plants are all thriving and flowering about me, and I am delighted at it as my dried specimens suffered much from being sometimes two days without my getting them exposed — many mouldered on my hands, but had you seen the privations I was put to, travelling through a country only inhabited by Indians whose language I could not understand and the difficulty of getting an interpreter for only one in a thousand speak Spanish, yet if a botanist could be found, who will climb the rocks with me I will dedicate six months some day only to scour the riches of this splendid floral region.

LÆLIA SUPERBIENS.

In cactus the only new ones I saw were some fantastic fellows hanging from the summit of trees bearing flowers as large as my hat, in many instances — but my means would not admit of my getting them. Fire ants prevent almost anyone mounting a tree — and the prickles of the cactus — but I have all around me here splendid things of the same description but I fear known to you all. Odd as it may appear I could not see a single 'turkshead' — the road was too rich for them, the arid sandy plains is where they abound — Zacapa and Guastatoya — there are millions. Could I go out of the gates of the city I should have had a few ready now, but we are all shut up here. I wrote to Mr Chatfield our Consul at San Salvador requesting him to notice in his rides about that city and if he had any to send me some by an Indian. This gentleman had a narrow escape the other day. He is in the habit of taking a ride every afternoon in this neighbourhood of the city and a report has been current that foreigners wish to get possession of the country (arising from the inroads of the Belize people) and to effect their object they had poisoned all the rivers etc.!! A number of Indians having watched Chatfield in a detached place, fell upon him and carried him prisoner to a village called 'Suyotango'. They then menaced him with knives and threatened his life, to discover the evil attending all their village. He asked them for water, the poison water, and drank an enormous quantity, this presence of mind saved his life for they then released him. The President wishes to punish these Indians but Chatfield interfered and has behaved nobly with them.[2]

Cinnamon, cloves and essences of rose and myrrh

Dreadfully have we suffered and are suffering from the cholera here — and all my plans have been completely upset, it is impossible for me to comply with my promise, for the cacti for the Duke of Bedford if the *Acteon* is here before December, but if it pleases God to spare me I shall make it a sacred obligation on my return to England next spring. I send you now two splendid Quesals [= Quetzals] or *Troganus splendens* (Gould) — one of which you will please pass over to Mr James Davidson ...

I have many plants already collected for you, and have to regret that it will be some months before I can send you, about 40 specimens which I have of ferns besides many general specimens — in cassias, verbenas, asclepiads ...

OPPOSITE: *Schomburgkia superbiens* (*syn.* Laelia superbiens), *an orchid collected by Skinner in Guatemala. This is taken from the original lithograph by Miss S. A. Drake; it was published in* The Orchidaceae of Mexico and Guatemala, *by James Bateman. (Source and copyright: Royal Botanic Gardens, Kew)*

With my favourite the Orchidaceae I have a most splendid collection here. One of the finest things you can conceive flowered about a week ago while I was in Instapa and my partner by my orders dried one flower stem with 6 flowers of this size and preserved in spirits another 6 from the sister bulb. The lip has the most curious figure and is as white as snow, the sepals and petals maculated and of colours yellow, purple, white and rose so beautifully displayed as to beggar description — the odour is described to me by all my friends here as cinnamon, cloves and essences of rose and myrrh. I regret I did not smell it but my duty called me to Istapa where I was enjoying no such delights, my occupation being the cure of cholera subjects — every person nearly being more or less sick. The dried specimen is for you, the 'spirited fellow' for Mr Bateman — along with the plant — which I brought from the [?] — it is a *Stanhopea* — for the figure of the labellum see other side [there is a sketch on the back of the paper].[3]

The following extracts come from letters written in 1838 and 1841.

Specimens overboard

I am at a loss what to say to you, such have been circumstances that all my endeavours have been rendered futile to send you dried specimens ... [Three ?months] collections were lost on board the vessel, when I was shipwrecked ... [the specimens all being badly exposed to the water] ... but you shall have them as they are. Then again for the Duke of Bedford what can you say for me in that quarter, about a dozen specimens I picked up in Guayaquil, a rascally boy threw overboard in Costa Rica while cleaning the decks — and I, 70 miles distant in the interior — but Mr Cope H.M. Consul while in Guayaquil told me that Lord Edward Russel was there during his absence and he could hardly have avoided picking up what I did, they were so striking ... The *Sulphur* was to touch there and as a gardener from Kew was on board I requested Mr Cope to show him what struck me as new ...[4]

Pleasant dreams

As luck would have it your letters of November 17th and of December 7th reached me together [on the] 25th ... two days after I had cleared my house of all my collections of Orchidaceae. But feeling most anxious to prove to you that I should do all in my power to make up a small collection for Mr Wailes I started off for my various habitats on the shores of the Pacific and only returned late last night — but I never made a finer collection, and on my way ... had a most extraordinary dream. Believe me, it is a fact — I saw distinctly for two consecutive nights in my sleep — the [orchid] of which I accompany you a rough sketch and so strongly was it forced on me the second night, that I returned to where I fancied its habitat might be — and although at a place where I never had been before, and which cost me all my clothes and shoes — being literally torn in shreds by climbing over precipices and rocks and spending two days in the woods, I found the plant and in bloom. It is quite a romance but positively perfectly true and your letters have been the means of my making this discovery and Mr Wailes who sanctions the cause. You will all laugh at my story, but I cannot credit myself, therefore must submit to be laughed at. However the plant is no joke. I found some with bulbs 36 inches long and as thick as my wrist — perfectly solid. I brought five Indians loaded and have them now in my garden here. I enclose you a flower or two, to show you what it is — and I fancy it is positively new — to everybody — for I cannot get rid of my dreams.

I have for Mr Wailes at least 50 species ... he must not be surprised that I have drawn on him for £20 today for I have travelled about 280 miles to collect them and my Indians have cost me 64 dollars. The rest I will require to forward them down to the coast. I have written [to] Mr Wailes to say I will send him particulars with the list of the plants which I will get away next week to Belize.

I am sorry to see the loss of the *Hebe* near Bologne. She carried three packages from me, a lot of dried specimens for you and some preserved in spirits, with drawings of [? *Lob.*] *macrantha* and *Laelia superbiens* — all addressed to Mr Bateman — and I much fear all Hartweg's collections were on board too, of his dried specimens, oaks and 21 packages of Orchidaceae.

There was a plant which I have known for many years, but only four have I seen which I pointed out to Mr Hartweg and which he tried hard as I often had done to get at, — but these four plants are situated in a marsh near Amatitlan completely surrounded by hot water, so hot as to [be] impossible to reach them at ordinary times. However yesterday on my return I made the attempt by forming a bridge of rushes over the marsh and after some difficulty succeeded in reaching the plant. I found its roots completely immersed in hot mud with a thick coat of sulphur on the top and surrounded with rushes and sedges. The stems are from seven to 14 feet high and the leaves come out from the stem almost at equal distances about an inch to two inches apart, and almost opposite — varying however a little alternately — it is a most curious plant for from the fructification being like some species of ... *Scolopendrium* (I know not if I am right in so calling them — but I mean those I have sent you before of this form whose thecae [are] innumerable on the back of the leaf — see the examples here sent you enclosed; one with the thecae and the other without. I found only two stems in the immense bundle with thecae — so extraordinary has this plant struck me that I cannot resist now sending it [to] you — with my attempts at a sketch. The veins in the leaf of this fern are the most beautiful I ever beheld in nature. I have large dried specimens for you but you may judge from the enclosed specimens for the present ...[5]

The fern referred to in the above letter was probably a species of *Acrostichum*, perhaps *A. aureum*. The Mr Hartweg referred to was German botanist Carl Theodor Hartweg (1812–1871), who collected in North America, Central America and South America for the Horticultural Society of London during the years 1836–1843 and 1845–1847.[6]

Skinner did not settle permanently in Guatemala but maintained business interests there for many years. When in his sixties, to wind-up his business affairs in Guatemala, Skinner made his thirty-ninth voyage across the Atlantic. On his outward journey, during a stop in Panama, he contracted yellow-fever and died on 9 January 1867.[1] One of many species to carry Skinner's name is the orchid *Cattleya skinneri*, the national flower of Costa Rica.

F. W. HOSTMANN *(1838–1843)*

In 1838, F. W. Hostmann, a German by birth but a long-time resident in the Dutch colony of Surinam, approached William Hooker, then Professor of Botany at Glasgow University, suggesting that he would forgo his 'vocation as medical man' if adequate funds were forthcoming to support his wish to become a full-time collector of botanical specimens (seemingly herbarium specimens only).[1] In 1840, he forwarded an account of his early activities to Hooker.

Into a pathless wilderness

Confident that the offer I advanced respecting the collection of Surinam plants would be found reasonable ... I had embarked into it, before I received your answer [in a letter dated 6 August 1839] on the subject ... I resolved in the month of December last year finally to quit the practice of my profession for the sake of botany. Having never before extended my excursions beyond the boundaries of cultivated land of this colony I had, in the first instance, to ascertain the required means of penetrating into a more interesting interior and consequently directed my course towards the south most limits ...

Allow me Sir William to direct your attention upon the circumstances that I purposely commenced this experimental excursion at the setting in of the rainy season, a season, it would seem by perusing the annals of Natural History, is not sufficiently profited of by botanical collectors in a similar country like Surinam; I allude for instance to Mr G. Gardner, when travelling in Brazil, [and] to Dr Schomburgk, not long ago botanising in British Guiana; both of these complain of having been prevented from botanising by heavy showers of rain, and while I give them full credit as far as regards the inconvenience of an intemperate rainy season, in a country which is either thinly or not at all inhabited, and, more-over destitute of roads, I just would observe, that, should these difficulties opposed to the collection and drying of plants during this season prove to be insurmountable, the botanists of Europe would have to disperse with the greater part of the plants of Guyana, it being a well known fact, that not only the greater number of plants, but also the more interesting ones in this country are flowering during the wet season, while in the dry season vegetation, in some places disappears, and in general may be considered to be in a lingering state, till it is revived by rain ...

You kindly recommended heavy pressure in drying plants, an expedient which hardly can be applied upon the smaller herbaceous plants, while the more succulent ones, and particularly all trees, shrubs, Orchidaceae, Aroideae and such-like, would much sooner corrupt than dry, and at events turn black and lose their leaves. It is to be considered for granted that artificial heat only can remediate an inconvenience, which otherwise puts the impossibility of drying plants of whatever description, in this country out of question. Difficult as it is unquestionably to dry plants in a tropical forest, in what ever way it might be undertaken, it hardly will be found less troublesome to prevent dried plants from attracting moisture, which however is indispensable. I think that I can remediate both these difficulties.

That he, who ventures into a pathless wilderness, has to contend with innumerable privations and dangers is to be considered as a matter of course, and in this respect I believe, Surinam suffers no comparison with any country in the world hitherto visited by travellers in search of plants. In the Brazil for instance, travelling is facilitated by roads [which], indifferent as they may be, are practicable still for mules, so that from the south of this vast country to its northern extremity it cannot be said that locomotivety meets with any material obstruction, the less as the manner, in which this country is inhabited, favours the traveller to provide himself with the necessary means of subsistence. Here, travelling by land, he has to force himself a passage with the assistance of an axe or cutlass, or guided by the course of a river, which without exception, can only be navigated with small canoes and considerable dangers, he can, in both cases only provide himself with the most necessary means of subsistence, and this for no length of time, depending for the rest on the chance of his gun, which if they should fail, or he did not understand and often be reduced to occasionally to feed on such abject game as an alligator or monkey, would actually expose him to starvation ...

My first excursion lasted only a fortnight ... I shall not venture to give you a description of the general appearance of the vegetation I met with; to do this in a superficial way can avail to nothing particularly not to a man who keeps such a lofty station among botanists, as this is the case with you, and who consequently can conjecture by analogy, what may be expected in a country like this. That Orchidaceae are perhaps more numerous than anywhere else, one might be led to suppose, by meeting with them at every step; in the lower land they chiefly cling to trees and many seem to be entirely covered with them; in more elevated situations they [are] also to be met with at the ground; a few are growing in the water, and these, by their rare occurrence, I do not believe to be common; others, and very grand ones too, will thrive in savannahs, sterile in such a degree, that I cannot conceive on what they feed. If this splendid family is unrivalled as far as regards of colour, delightfulness of scent and singularity of form, it is left far behind the Leguminosae respecting the number; while our barren plains which otherwise fatigue the eye, are humbly adorned with a great variety of the most minute ones of them, others — and these are numerous, range with the largest trees of the forest, a rank which is disputed them by still others of the same family that are ascending and finally mastering their lofty relations.

Palms are very numerous; there are amongst them [some] that climb and disappear between the brushwood, and while several of this distinguished family contend in the shade of shrubs not exceeding six feet, others are towering above the highest trees, making their magnificent crowns in the clouds; very strange it appeared to me that many of them seem to be limited to a very small tract of land, appearing no where else. There is a variety of ferns, both arborescent and small ones to an extreme; for instance, I met with one of the latter which full grown did not exceed half an inch. I noticed but few aquatic plants.[2]

Hostmann subsequently gave notice of his intention to reside amongst the Bush Negroes of Anka.

Bush Negroes of Anka

You must have noticed that the greatest impediments towards exploring the remote parts of Surinam, reside in the difficulties of travelling and transport. The southern frontiers of this colony, formed by the large River Marowina ... the upper part of which separates Surinam from Cayenne: — and here it is, that about 100 years ago, distant 60 German miles from the mouth of the river, a horde of unfranchised Negro slaves, has settled on the mountainous banks of this end of the still larger river Lava which joins the former. These Maroons, Bush Negroes, (as they are called) have been recognised by the Dutch Government of former times, roam in savage independence on the extensive wilds, bordered by the Rio Negro ... The political position of these Bush Negroes, and several other hordes occupying the upper part of the Surinam and Saramacca rivers induced the colonial Government to maintain a Resident among them. This post is, in one respect, of prodigious importance; still the remoteness of the place, the interrupted communication, the difficulty of providing the first and most urgent means of subsistence. And perhaps more than all this, the being compelled to dwell with a horde of savage and untimely-freed Negroes, or be utterly content with solitary confinement, destitute of any medical aid, if required, all these circumstances, added to the smallness of the salary attached to the office, has caused it till lately to be held by people of the very lowest classes, ranking in civilisation rather below or at a level with those savages toward whom they had to represent a respectable Government. For these reasons, all who during 80 years, have chosen this employment, holding it as a forlorn post, the very last refuge of an honest name, have either died prematurely (partly through despair and by their own choice) or returned with bodily constitution broken and health for ever impaired. It is to be expected that even uncivilised man, of lower extraction, holding this situation, should either die in despair or survive the deepest degradation to which man can sink (for to associate with the Negroes in question supposes no less than to be a Brute). To live secluded from anything like human society, remote from all civilisation, to dwell in the middle of endless and more ferocious men, reduced to converse exclusively with flowers and animals, this I should think, is not the business of the [?] would presuppose the man, who can submit to such an existence without injuring his reputation, to profess an ample share of resignation, refinement, and an uncommon taste for Natural History.

I must leave it to guess whether I could claim to be ranked in the second [that is, latter] category; but sure enough it is, that to the astonishment of the population of Surinam, I accepted the office of Post-holder Resident among the Bush Negroes of Anka.[3]

Highly edited versions of the above letters were published by Hooker. He noted in his introduction that he had received excellent collections, representing 500 plant species, from Hostmann. In a further letter Hostmann gave an account of his trip to the district of Anka.

Preparations

I was at full liberty to postpone my departure [for Anka] to a more favourable season; but as experience is only to be derived from fair trials I preferred to depart from Paramaribo [on] the 20th of March 1840 in the heaviest of a rainy season, which the eldest inhabitants cannot recall ever to have witnessed so excessive. I was accompanied by a gentleman who could become useful on account of his acquaintance with the Bush Negroes and in whom I had excited some taste for natural history; besides that I carried with me an assistant, and a few trusty black servants all used to collect[ing] and prepar[ing] objects of natural history. Having dispatched the greater part of my baggage by sea, and with a schooner, to the mouth of the Marowina, I embarked in a canoe of 40 feet length by six feet in breadth, covered with a moveable tent of oiled canvas. The better to form an idea of the different articles I had to carry with me into the bush it is necessary to know that the communications between Anka (the name of the residence) and Paramaribo requires [*sic*] two months, and that I had resolved completely to settle at this place, directing my excursions from there as deep into the interior, including the French Guyana, as I might find it possible, being guided in these excursions by Bush Negroes and Indians, employing the former in transplanting the collected objects and expecting interesting particulars from the latter as far as regards properties of vegetables. Our canoe was manned with six Negroes ...[4]

A snake tale

Travellers bound on a similar errand frequently have one or the other story to tell, so as to season narrative which otherwise — as in this case here — would be insipid. I have nothing of this kind to furnish, if you except the meeting of one of those horrible snakes which is known here under the trivial [name of] jarrakooka and which, having been roused out of his dark abode, nearly killed one of our men; for there is no interval between wounding and killing. The mere aspect of this animal is frightful and more than calculated to impart the careless wanderer with what he has to apprehend from it: a flat cordate head, fixed to a very narrow neck, large projecting, glittering eyes, with still larger cavities below them, the body inflated, ending in a thorn, the whole monster covered with carinated scales, horny to the touch — it is impossible to behold this animal without feeling sick. Nothing can be compared with the poison communicated by two long fangs in the upper jaws, if it is not the swiftness with which this poison decomposes the soundest body; excruciating pain succeeds the wounding, and while blood issues from all the apertures of the body, the muscular parts upwards the wounded place are destroyed instantaneously by gangrene; these symptoms are succeeded by sudden death, which is announced by immediate putrefaction, but though the offensive exhalations never fail to attract a number of vultures [even] the most voracious of them, *Cathartes aura*, rejects the corpse. This snake, generally six feet in length is of a dirty yellowish colour with black rhomboidal spots and is known by the name of *Trigonocephalus rhombeatus*.[4]

The snake described by Hostmann is the bushmaster, now known as *Lachesis muta*. The morphological description of the snake is accurate but that of the bite symptoms somewhat exaggerated.[5]

Vampire bats

Once more we stopped with a horde of Indians, arriving the 7th of April at the frontier post Armina ... There is nothing interesting at the post Armina if you except hundred thousands of bats, which are hanging under the roofs of the thatched houses; their whistling interrupts the monotonous silence of the day and increases in proportion that the sun declines, when with the last glance of it they all at once alight, starting in a black cloud toward the east ... This bat, a very small one is it, which sucks the blood from all warm-blooded animals and in preference that of men, and making the experiment on myself, I must confess that the way in which this is done is sufficiently interesting. Led by instinct they choose a remote part of the body where there is less chance to be caught. I offered them my feet uncovered, and soon had the pleasure to see one occupied with each of my great toes. I hardly could feel when, under continual vibrations, which the animal made with the wings [the] wound was inflicted; a few minutes afterwards they both seemed to have their competent portion and dropped at the ground; to my great astonishment I found the wound pretty considerable and of a triangular form ...[4]

This is not an exercise to be repeated! Vampire bats can transmit diseases such as rabies, and open wounds from which they lap blood can become infected by bacteria or parasitic insect larvae.

Roast monkey

The leader of the party, the honest Captain Arabi, with great politeness and as a mark of particular distinction which I owed to my diplomatic character offered to me a portion of a roasted monkey and not [to] remain behind the Savage in civility, I suppressed the aversion I felt in eating of an animal so much alike our species, but was obliged to avow that in reality it has a fine flavour and was at all events palatable. Mountain cabbage and the leaves of *Lobelia surinamensis* were used in place of greens, and the palm beverage I mentioned above, with the fruits of another palm constituted the dessert.[4]

Shooting the rapids

The 9th a very fine morning, we departed. We saw a pretty mountain in front, the sight of which awoke in me all the reminiscences of a happier past, and lost in reveries regarding my native home I had insensibly arrived at a place which forced me to pay more attention to the present and gave rise to serious apprehensiveness for the future. Whimsically the Bush Negroes called this place 'Gunshot', a place of which the name will not be effaced easy [*sic*] from my memory. The river being forced into a smaller bed, the shore mountainous, there is formed a narrow defile, and while large fragments of rocks obstruct the passage the constrained mass of water, foaming, bursts forth with redoubled fury. My mind has been used to strong impressions in such a degree that I want themselves [as] a stimulant; but it seemed to me quite impossible to ascend this fall and an attempt to do it could only be regarded as an act of the most daring temerity; however there was no other passage and while there could be no speaking of remaining here or returning there was left no other choice than to prepare the means which the occasion could furnish, to pass the cataract. All canoes previously fastened, our men went into the bush to look out for natural cordage, yielded by several lianes of an uncommon strength. With the assistance of these and the combined force of all the Negroes each canoe was dragged along the shore, and the strength of 40 men was hardly sufficient to overpower the descending stream and save them from being engulfed; they succeeded and now came down to our assistance. I could have left the boat and stepped on shore, but a stranger to the sensation of fear, if you accept the fear to be taken for a coward, I preferred to remain in it with 12 men who with long poles had to prevent the boat from sliding into the main current, where no human power could have saved us: our lives depended on this manoeuvre and on the solidity of the ropes with which the boat was dragged by the Negroes on shore; already we had arrived above the cascades, when the steersman, Captain Arabi, with all the strength of voice he could command of, ordered the Negroes on shore to secure the ropes and not suffer them to slip. It is characteristic amongst these people, and may be considered the effect of an excess of liberty, that nobody amongst them understands to command, and that consequently nobody obeys — regardless of the order given by what they called their Captain. Want only they had slipped already the lines fastened to our boat before the [men] sitting in it had had time to throw away the poles and taken up their paddles, to guide the boat along the shore, and taken by the current, our boat was swinging into the river. There was no time for deliberation and with Falconer one might have reflected:

'No season this for council or delay,
Too soon the eventful moments haste away.'

There depended a man's life on every moment, and the loss of a few would have joined us infallibly in a common and ignominious death. I cannot swim, and the gentleman sitting by my side had laid hold of my right arm, and — the colour of death upon his cheek — uttered in a ghastly and inarticulated manner: 'We are lost!' — 'Not yet' I replied, striving to disentangle myself from his spasmodic grasp, and at the same time apprehending that the boat might be driven obliquely into the fall, ordered the steersman to direct it down into the cascade headlong. A mournful silence succeeded this command, which, however was not obeyed, Captain Arabi being better acquainted than I with the locality; and now, indignated with the carelessness with which so many lives had been exposed to destruction, it was gratifying and more manlike to behold the exertions which were employed to make amends for it. Moved by a common impulse, most likely communicated by the vicinity of death, our men had taken up their paddles, and opposing all the strength they had to dispose of to an impetuous element, they managed the boat across the river. We reached the opposite shore at the distance of a man's length from the face [of the falls], and would have been drowned, if the foremost of our Negroes had not had the presence of mind to grasp at the solitary branch of a tree, which, happily, proved to be faithful.[4]

Hostmann reached his official residence in May and found it to be 'an uninhabitable hut, defiled by reptiles'. Most of his food supply was spoilt by the wet and he fell sick. He quit Anka in July, returned to Paramaribo and resigned his commission, but none the less avowed to continue to collect and agreed to Hooker's terms, possibly fifteen guilders per 100 specimens.

Hostmann sent further specimens and wrote to Hooker, by then Director of the Royal Botanic Gardens, Kew, in June, July and October 1842. His letters suggest that he had only received one, dated 12 January 1842, in return. Hostmann also wrote to Hooker in April and, apparently for the last time, in August 1843.

Abandonment of an expensive occupation

I received your letter [of] February 15 and must confess that your compliments, about the bad condition of the plants of the second envoy, did not come quite unexpected. Dried plants should never be kept in this country above three months. If, therefore, I had only known, in ... time, that my first envoy had pleased you, if, consequently, these, which had been collected since, had been shipped immediately after being collected, you may depend upon it that everyone of these plants would have reached you in the best condition. I leave it to you to decide whether this is my fault, but at all events, I feel extremely sorry that I failed in answering your expectations ...

I returned sick from my last excursion; I engaged an assistant, who proved to be of no use; I lost one of my men, — and getting no answer about the plants I had sent, finally resolved, to abandon so ungrateful and expensive an occupation as to collect plants ...

Though I am not a single moment at a loss what to do with my time, and with the burden of almost half a century on my shoulders, I must confess, that in preference to any other occupation I would have spent the remnant of life in the service of botany, if only I could have depended on that assistance, without which it would be a mere chimera to attempt the exploration of a country like Surinam. I am now forced to stick to some agricultural pursuit, which though prosaic and less gratifying to the mind, may prove more satisfactory to my financial affairs. It is a small estate situated at the upper part of the Surinam, between this and the Para River, where I shall give a trial to the tobacco culture. The forests of this solitary retreat extend for several hours in each direction, varieated [*sic*] by large plains, and watered by small rivulets. A fine field for botanising in my leisure hours, if only you and but a few of your friends in England could assist me.[6]

Hostmann is commemorated in the names of about twenty species of plants.

T. L. BRIDGES *(1844–1845)*

Thomas L. Bridges, born in England in 1807, collected plants and animals for various societies and wealthy individuals in Europe. For some years he resided in Chile, maintaining a botanical garden near Valparaiso. After losing his property in Chile through flooding, he emigrated to California in, or about, 1853. He collected objects of natural history in the Bolivian Andes, and on the headwaters of the Amazon and La Platte, he collected specimens for the Earl of Derby. He also collected in the district of Chiriqui in northern Panama. The following accounts relate to collecting trips in Bolivia during 1844–1845.[1]

Cacti and other plants

I shall now make an attempt to give you a brief idea of what I have done in this singular and (in some parts) interesting country. On the 13th of September [1844], I landed in Cobija, the only commercial port which the Republic possesses, and during the few days I remained there, I made an excursion up the dry, lofty and arid mountains which run parallel with the coast nearly the whole length of the Desert of Atacama. Along the coast and at the base of those mountains scarcely a plant exists. It is not possible for a person, who has not seen this place, to picture to themselves a spot so awfully barren. The only vegetation that is to be seen at a distance is a tall erect species of [the cactus genus] *Cereus*, which, if I am not mistaken, is the *C. coquimbensis* of Molina, for I have found the same species at Coquimbo. There are two distinct species found about Coquimbo with enormous long spines. Although in this respect they agree, in their seed-vessels they are widely different. The Cobija plant produces a large pear-shaped fruit, covered with long green or greyish hair, which are termed 'pasas canas' by the natives, and, in certain seasons of the year, form the food of the chinchilla. The other species alluded to yields a round smooth seed-vessel destitute of hair. After having ascended this ridge of mountains to the elevation of 1,500 feet to my greatest surprise I discovered a variety of plants and amongst them growing on some stunted bushes a beautiful new species of *Tropaeolum*, somewhat similar to

T. brachyceras, but with a more expanded flower, twice the size, and the plant altogether much more robust. I obtained fine tubers and specimens of this plant but unfortunately from what I learn, they have been lost on their passage to Valparaiso.

Having procured mules in Cobija for myself and two Chilian servants, we took the road to Potosi, and in three days reached the little town of Calama, 40 leagues distant from Cobija, situated in the desert of Atacama. It was within 13 leagues of this place, that I had the pleasure of finding in February the beautiful [cactus] *Pilocereus*. In my last letter from Valparaiso I gave you a few remarks also [about] the habitat of this interesting plant. Since then I have seen more of its habits and therefore I shall again trouble you with the following observations. It is generally found on the slopes of bold, rugged mountains whose aspect is towards the north where it enjoys plenty of sun in a dry sandy soil. Frequently 20 or 30 stems proceed from the same root, the outer ones partly lying on the ground forming a curve upwards. The inner stems grow erect and are those which are most hairy. They seldom reach the height of four feet, and from the older stems in the centre proceed the flowers, which are a beautiful dark red, about the size of *C. flagelliformis*. The seed-vessels are round or rather oval, smooth and shining on the surface, hollow within and void of a pulpy substance. The seeds are round and of a blackish colour. The place where I found it most abundantly, was near the vicinity of the city of Potosi at an elevation of 12,000 feet. Therefore you may judge from this it is frequently exposed to frost. In the language of the Quichuan Indians, it is called quchuallo, pronounced ke-wal-yo. The other enormous species of *Cereus*, which I mentioned, grows in the same localities and often attains the height of 20 feet. The flowers proceed from the top and are of a dark red colour situated in a ring. When viewed from a distance one might imagine that a flower of a *Paeonia* had been artificially placed on the plant. The stems are often 18 inches in diameter. The natives use the dried stems for rafters to their houses, also for doors, being the only timber the country produces in those parts. I possess in Valparaiso a piece of this wood which on my return I will forward for the purpose of giving you an idea of its size and structure.

From Calama, by regular stages, I arrived at Potosi, 158 leagues from Cobija. We travelled on the summit of the Andes after leaving Calama, 20 leagues, often at an elevation of 13,000 feet, till we arrived at Potosi. During the whole of this long journey, I did not collect a single specimen, as few plants exist and those we saw were not in flower, it then being the dry season. [Were] a traveller to pass the same road at the present time, he would be more fortunate, and might obtain many curious alpine plants ... I remained only a few days in Potosi, and from thence directed my way to Chuquisaca ... Before we arrived at Chuquisaca we crossed what may be termed head-waters of the river Pilcomayo. On the mountains on either side of this river there is a very interesting vegetation. Here I found a most beautiful tree belonging to the Bignoniaceae. It grows to a height of 20 feet and is completely covered with panicles of splendid dark blue flowers the size and shape of *Gloxinia speciosa*. I verily believe, on many trees, there were at least 10,000 flowers. I have preserved many specimens of this fine plant, accompanied with the seed-vessels. Therefore you will, when you receive them, soon find the genus to which it belongs. On the banks of the river, under the shade of trees, I met with a few plants of a *Gesnera* new to me, with a large tuberous root and pale red flowers. The commonest tree in the neighbourhood of Chuquisaca [is] the *Schinus molle*, which grows to a large size and is very ornamental when the long racemes of fruit are ripe which are a pink colour. On the large trees we saw many parasitical species of *Tillandsia*, and a few species of Orchidaceae, but not in flower. The Cacteae are very numerous in this part of the country and I found about 12 species of *Cereus* and *Echinocactus*, many with very fine flowers and all different from those in Chile. I have forwarded plants to Valparaiso and I hope by the time you receive this they may have arrived in England. From the nature of some of them I fear they will not stand the long voyage to Europe.[2]

The giant water lily

Bridges was not the first botanical collector to procure the giant water lily (*Victoria amazonica*, not *V. regia* as used below), but undoubtedly was one of the most ecstatic to have gathered this plant from the wild.

During my stay at the Indian town of Santa Anna, in the province of Moxos, Republic of Bolivia, during the months of June and July, 1845, I made daily shooting excursions in the vicinity. In one of these I had the good fortune (whilst riding along the woody banks of the river Yacuma, one of the tributary rivers of the Mamore) to come suddenly on a beautiful pond, or rather small lake,

A small girl seated on a leaf of Victoria amazonica. *(Source and copyright: Royal Botanic Gardens, Kew)*

embosomed in the forest, where, to my delight and astonishment, I discovered, for the first time, 'the Queen of Aquatics', the *Victoria regia*! There were at least 50 flowers on view, and Belzoni could not have felt more rapture at his Egyptian discoveries than I did in beholding the beautiful and novel sight before me, such as it has fallen to the lot of few Englishmen to witness. Fain would I have plunged into the lake to procure specimens of the magnificent flowers and leaves; but knowing that these waters abounded in alligators, I was deterred from doing so by the advice of my guide, and my own experience of similar places. I now turned over in my thoughts how and in what way flowers and leaves might be obtained, and I clearly saw that a canoe was necessary, and therefore promptly returned to the town, and communicated my discovery and wants to the Correjidor or Governor, Don Jose Maria Zarate, who with much kindness immediately ordered the Cacique to send Indians with a yoke of oxen for the purpose of drawing a canoe from the river Yacuma to the lake. Being apprised that the canoe was in readiness, I returned in the afternoon, with several Indians to assist in carrying home the expected prize of leaves and flowers. The canoe being very small, only three persons could embark; myself in the middle, and an Indian in the bows and stern. In this tottering little bark we rowed amongst magnificent leaves and flowers, crushing unavoidably some, and selecting only such as pleased me. The leaves being so enormous I could find room in the canoe for but two, one before me and the other behind; owing to their being very fragile, even in the green state, care was necessary to transport them; and thus we had to make several trips in the canoe before I obtained the number required. Having loaded myself with leaves, flowers, and ripe seed-vessels, I next mused how they were to be conveyed in safety; and determined at length upon suspending them on long poles with small cord, tied to the stalks of the leaves and flowers. Two Indians, each taking on his shoulder an end of the pole, carried them into the town; the poor creatures wondering all the while what could induce me to be at so much trouble to get at flowers, and for what purpose I destined them now they were in my possession ...

The leaves are round, varying considerably in size, the largest about four feet in diameter. They float on the surface of the water; the colour is a very light green, in age inclining to yellow, some of them even when young possess a yellow hue. The margins of the leaf are turned upwards, giving the leaf a singular appearance, somewhat like a floating dish; this margin and the under surface of the leaf are of a dark brown colour. The spines incline to the interior of the leaf, and in some leaves are nearly white ...

The *Victoria* grows in four to six feet of water, producing leaves and flowers, which rapidly decay and give place to others. From each plant there are seldom more than four or five leaves on the surface, but even these in parts of the lake where the plants were numerous, almost covered the surface of the water, one leaf touching the other. I observed a beautiful aquatic bird (*Parra* sp.?) [a jacana or lily-trotter] walk with much ease from leaf to leaf, and many of the Muscicapidae [Old-world flycatchers] find food and a resting place on them. The plant occupies almost exclusively the water, with the exception of a few floating aquatics of small dimensions, amongst which I saw a beautiful *Utricularia*.

The blossoms rise six to eight inches above the surface, expanding first in the evening, when they are pure white; changing finally (and by exposure to the sun) to a most beautiful pink or rose colour, flowers may be seen, at the same time, partaking of every tinge between the two hues, the recently expanded being pure white and the adult rosy, almost sinking under water to ripen its seed and produce a new race of plants when required. The largest flowers I saw measured from ten inches to one foot in diameter.

I had an opportunity of experiencing the fragrance of the flowers. Those I collected for preserving in spirits were unexpanded, but on the point of opening; on arrival at the Government House, in the town, I deposited them in my room, and returning after dark, I found to my surprise that all had blown and were exhaling a most beautiful odour, which at first I compared to a rich pineapple, afterwards to a melon, and then to the *Cherimoya*; but indeed it resembled none of these fruits, and I at length came to the decision that it was a most delicious scent, unlike every other, and peculiar to the noble flower that produced it ...[3]

Bridges died at sea in September 1865, while returning to California from a collecting expedition to Nicaragua.

R. SPRUCE *(1852–1854)*

Richard Spruce, born in Yorkshire in 1817, was for a few years a schoolmaster, but from 1844 he dedicated himself to botanical pursuits. He collected in the Pyrenees (1845–1846) and for many years in South America (1849–1864). The cost of Spruce's work in the latter was initially defrayed by a group of botanists, including William Hooker and George Bentham, and subsequently funded through the sale of botanical specimens. His published botanical works were primarily concerned with the classification of mosses and liverworts, but Spruce made thousands of collections of flowering plants and ferns which greatly increased the knowledge of the South American flora. Cartographic skills also enabled him to make a significant contribution to the understanding of the inland waterways of the Amazon Basin. He also made important observations on ethnobotany and presented economic botany collections to Kew. In 1860, much of his time was spent collecting seed and young plants of *Cinchona succirubra*, the plant from which antimalarial quinine is produced, for the Indian Government.[1, 2, 3] The following is a description of working conditions and pests encountered during a stay in and around São Gabriel, Rio Negro, in 1852.

Stocked with rats, vampires, scorpions and cockroaches

I found it a great advantage travelling in my own canoe. I had it fitted up so that I could work comfortably and stow away my plants when dried, besides being able to dry my paper on the top of the cabins when it was inconvenient to stop in the middle of the day. I was also master of my own movements; could stop where and when I liked, save that it was necessary to keep the Indians in good humour. When the weather was cool they did not like to be interrupted in pulling, but when they were toiling under a hot sun they rather liked a stoppage now and then. Towards the end of the voyage they got into the habit of peering into the trees as we went along in the hot afternoons, and would call out to me — busy among my papers in the cabin — 'O patrão! aikué potéra poranga' ('Patron! here's a pretty flower'). I of course turned out to see if it was anything new, as it often proved to be ...

Richard Spruce. (Source and copyright: Royal Botanic Gardens, Kew)

It is not very pleasant work here to be always among cataracts in my excursions. I have been once the whole length of the falls and up again. I was out four days, but two of them were lost time. I made my station at the house of the pilot of the falls, at the foot of the latter, and arrived just in time to see the commencement of one of their great festas. Much against my will, I was compelled also to see the end of it, for no one would stir until after two days of drinking and two nights of dancing. I was interested to hear the legend of the discovery of the mandioca-root sung in the Barré language, but this was poor consolation for such a loss of time; and you may imagine how I fretted in my imprisonment on a small rocky island, begirt with foaming waters, where I could not find a single flower that I had not already gathered. In returning, with four men, we passed all the falls without accidents until reaching the great fall above-mentioned; here, in dragging the boat up the rocks, it filled with water and a large parcel of plants in paper, about three feet high, was so completely soaked that two men could scarcely carry it. Two large vasculae full of fresh specimens floated out, but we secured them, and I lost only a few plants that were loose in a basket. I was much fatigued, having been on the water from six in the morning till five in the afternoon, yet I had now the soaked parcel to open out and the plants to transfer to dry paper, which occupied me until midnight. To some of them the mischief was already done — the leaves had begun to disarticulate — but you must take the specimens as they are, as I shall probably not find the same again. Whatever advantages São Gabriel may have as a station, on account of its interesting vegetation, it has disadvantages so great that if I had commenced my South American collections here I daresay I should have given them up in despair. The house I am in is very old; the thatch is stocked with rats, vampires, scorpions, cockroaches, and other pests to society; the floor (being simply mother earth) is undermined by sauba ants, with whom I have had some terrible contests. In one night they carried off as much farinha as I could eat in a month; then they found out my dried plants and began to cut them up and carry them off. I have burnt them, smoked them, drowned them, trod on them, and, in short, retaliated in every possible way, so that at this moment I believe not a sauba dares show its face inside this house; but they demand my constant vigilance. Then the termites, which are more insidious in their approaches, have covered ways along every post and beam. They have already eaten me up a towel and made their way into a deal packing-case, where fortunately they found nothing to eat. But the greatest nuisance at São Gabriel is one I had not foreseen. Almost the sole inhabitants are the soldiers of the garrison, and do you know how the armies of Brazil are recruited? When a man commits a crime which entitles him to transportation, he is enlisted and marched off to one of the frontier posts. Thus, of the fourteen men composing the garrison of São Gabriel, there is not one who has not committed some serious crime, and at least half of them are murderers. Judge with what security I can leave my house for a few days. It has already been twice entered during my absence, and about two gallons of spirits, a quantity of molasses and vinegar, and some other things stolen from it.

I have in the house with me two Indians — [a] hunter and a fisherman. One at least is an absolute necessity to prevent me dying of hunger, for here nothing is to be bought, not even an egg or a banana. For farinha I have had to send to the Rio Uaupés. The hunter I brought with me from the Barra. He is an excellent shot, and keeps me mostly well supplied with game. He is also useful to me for climbing trees and rowing, at both of which he cannot be excelled. But he is a terrible fellow for cachaça, like most of his race. I induced one of the Uaupe Indians who came with me from Uanauaca to become my fisherman. He was with me about two months when the Commandant of the fort seized him for the service of the corréo (post) to the Barra. Indians to row the courier's canoe are obtained in this way. A detachment of soldiers is sent by night to enter the sitios and seize as many men as are wanted, who are forthwith clapped into prison and there kept until the day of sailing — in irons if they make any resistance. The voyage averages 50 days, and these poor fellows receive neither pay nor even food for the whole of this time. The Indian, however, never dies of hunger when his brother Indian has food, and these men call at the nearest sitio to replenish their supply of farinha from time to time. But such treatment is a disgrace to the Government, and it is not to be wondered at that the Indians hide themselves in the forests when they get wind that the courier is about to be dispatched. Within these few days I have been fortunate enough to engage another fisherman. It is worth my while to keep these two men solely for the sake of accompanying me in my excursions, for it is not safe to venture among the falls with fewer than two oars.[4]

Bats, cats and bachelors

Sao Gabriel is terribly infested with vampires, and my house, which has an old, decayed roof, has more than its share of them. When I entered it there were large patches of dried-up blood on the floor which had been drawn from my predecessors by those midnight blood-letters, and my two men were attacked the first night, one of them having wounds on the ends of four toes, three on one foot and one on the other. The same has happened every night since, and the bats do not stop at the toes, but bite occasionally on the legs, fingers' ends, nose and chin and forehead, especially of children ...

A curious circumstance occurred to the family of my next neighbour since I arrived here. The children were much tormented by vampires, being bitten in various parts night by night. A cat was observed to be very expert at killing bats in the doorway at nightfall. One night, by accident, the cat was allowed to remain in the house, and whenever a bat alighted on the children's hammocks she pounced upon it. When morning came they had not once been bitten, and now the cat is their constant nocturnal guard. She also evidently knows her office, for as regularly as the children lie down at night to sleep she takes up her station by their hammocks. Poor Pussy! the good deeds of those who call thee 'ungrateful' and 'perfidious' seldom shine with such lustre on a naughty world! From my youth up I have been a lover of cats, and sagacious dames have at divers times foretold of me that for that reason I should die a bachelor, which, if I live not to get married, is likely enough to come true.[1]

Spruce recorded the following attack by ants on 15 August 1853.

Ant attack

Yesterday I had the pleasure for the first time of experiencing the sting of the large black ant called tucandéra in Lingua Geral ...

I had gone after breakfast to herborise in the caapoera north of San Carlos, where there were a good many decayed trunks and stumps. I stooped down to cut off a patch of a moss (*Fissidens*) on a stump, and remarked that by doing so I exposed a large hollow in the rotten wood; but when I turned me to put the moss in my vasculum I did not notice that a string of angry tucandéras poured out of the opening I had made. I was speedily made aware of it by a prick in the thigh, which I supposed to be caused by a snake, until springing up I saw that my feet and legs were being covered by the dreaded tucandéra. There was nothing but flight for it, and I accordingly ran off as quickly as I could among the entangling branches, and finally succeeded in beating off the ants, but not before I had been dreadfully stung about the feet, for I wore only slippers without heels and these came off in the struggle. I was little more than five minutes' walk from my house (for I was returning when the circumstance occurred), and I wished to walk rapidly but could not. I was in agonies, and had much to do to keep from throwing myself on the ground and rolling about as I had seen the Indians do when suffering from the stings of this ant. I had in my way to cross a strip of burning sand and then to wade through a lagoon, partly dried up and not more than two feet deep. Both these increased the torture: I thought the contact with the water would have alleviated it, but it was not so.

When I reached my house I immediately had recourse to hartshorn. No one was near but an Indian woman (my cook), and she, without my telling her (though I was about to do it), bound a ligature tightly above each ankle. After rubbing for some time with the hartshorn, and experiencing no relief, I caused her to rub with oil, and then with oil and hartshorn mixed. None of these seemed to have any effect; when the oil was made hot it relieved me a little, but very little indeed, and the wounds which were least rubbed, ceased to pain me the soonest, one that had not been touched being the first cured.

It was about two p.m. when I was stung, and I experienced no alleviation of the pain till five. During all this time my sufferings were indescribable — I can only liken the pain to that of a hundred thousand nettle-stings. My feet and sometimes my hands trembled as though I had the palsy, and for some time the perspiration ran down my face from the pain. With difficulty I repressed a strong inclination to vomit. I took a dose of laudanum at 4, and I think this did more than anything to lull the pain ...

My vasculum and one slipper were left on the field of battle. To obtain the former, which is to me a priceless article, I ventured today to revisit the spot, and cautiously picking my steps, I succeeded in drawing away with a long hooked stick both shoe and vasculum, nor did I disturb a single tucandéra.[1]

Spruce published a paper detailing his encounters with a variety of venomous reptiles and insects in South America. The following notes are recorded in his published journal.

Fierce little animals

On the Casiquiari, when we were one day hooking along my piragoa against the rapid current, one of the hooks caught a branch on which was a large wasps' nest. The wasps sallied out in thousands, and the men threw down their hooks and leaped into the river. I was at work in the cabin, and had just time to throw myself flat on my face, when the fierce little animals came buzzing in, and settled on me in numbers, but not one of them stung me. The boat drifted down the stream, and in a few minutes all the wasps had left it, when the man clambered on board and pulled across to the opposite bank. Another day I had got on the top of the cabin to gather the flowers of a tree overhead, and the first thing I hooked down was a wasps' nest, which I kicked into the river, and then went on gathering my specimens — battling all the while with the wasps and getting severely stung — for I saw the tree was new (it is *Hirtella casiquiarensis* n. sp. hb. 3196), and was determined not to leave it ungathered.[1]

Caterpillars and bad medicine

Leguminous trees are peculiarly liable to become infested with stinging caterpillars. Children who play under the tamarind trees at Guayaquil often get badly stung by hairy caterpillars that drop on them. I had always made light of caterpillars' stings until one evening at Tarapoto, in gathering specimens of an *Inga* tree, I got badly stung on the right wrist, at the base of the thumb; and when the pain and irritation at the end of half an hour went on increasing, I applied solution of ammonia pretty freely, and it proved so strong as to produce excoriation. The next morning the wound (for such it had become) was inflamed and very painful, but I tied a rag over it and started for the forest, accompanied by three men. We were out 12 hours, and had cold rain from the sierras all day; and when I reached home again my right hand was swollen to twice its normal size, and the swelling extended far up the arm. That was the beginning of a time of the most intense suffering I ever endured. After three days of fever and sleepless nights, ulcers broke out all over the back of the hand and the wrist — they were 35 in all, and I shall carry the scars to my grave. For five weeks I was condemned to lie most of the time on a long settle, with my arm (in a sling) resting on the back, that being the easiest position I could find. From the first I applied poultices of rice and linseed but for all that the ulceration ran its course. At one time the case looked so bad that mortification seemed imminent, and I speculated on the possibility of instructing my rude neighbours how to cut off my hand, as the only means of saving my life. I attributed my sufferings almost entirely to the ammonia — or rather abuse of it — and to the subsequent chill from exposure to wet; for had I not been impatient of the pain of the sting, I have little doubt it might soon have subsided of itself.[1]

Thwarted murder

In November 1854, toward the end of his five years' exploration of the Rio Negro, the Upper Orinoco, and some of their tributaries, Spruce recorded a plot to kill him.

Nov. 23 (Thursday). — This day about noon I left San Carlos. My crew consisted of four Indians; two of them were sons of the pilot (Pedro Deno). On the same day at 4 p.m. we reached the pilot's cunúco, a little within a narrow cano on the left bank, and stayed the night. Here a plot was laid to kill me. There were several people at the cunúco, including the pilot's wife, other sons and daughters, a son-in-law, etc. They were engaged in distilling bureche, and my men on arrival began to test its quality, which, though not of the best, sufficed to turn their heads and set them vomiting, all except their son-in-law (Pedro Yurébe), who drank enough to make him noisy but not to render his movements unsteady.

The cunúco consisted of two sheds, open at the sides, in one of which the still was at work. The port where the canoe was anchored was perhaps some 80 yards distant, down a rather steep descent. I had my hammock taken up and fastened under one of the sheds, and when night fell, after eating a small quantity of the forequarter of an alligator which I bought off Yurébe, I turned in. The Indians were very noisy, but as nothing is more tiresome than the conversation of these people when intoxicated, I paid little attention to it, save that I noticed one of the pilot's sons was inviting his brother-in-law Yurébe to make the voyage with us to Barra. After a while I heard them talk so much about 'heinali' ['the man'; that is, Spruce] that I could not help listening attentively to what they said, and it was well I did so.

Pedro Yurébe owed some 43 pesos to the Comisario of San Carlos and others, but he had no scruple to leave this unpaid till his return from the Barra, and a brilliant idea had struck him. 'The man', he said, was going to his own country, whence he would return no more. In the morning he (Yurébe) would offer his services for the voyage and get the pay beforehand (according to custom); they would then embark, and on reaching the mouth of the river Guasié, which they might do in three or four days, they would take the montaria while I was sleeping and make their way up that river, whence they could at any time return to their own territory, as it is but a short cut (a day overland) from the upper part of the Guasié to several tributaries of the Guainia. They would thus shirk the long, tedious voyage for which they had already received pay. This was largely discussed and approved by all. It then entered Yurébe's head to ask if 'the man' had much merchandise with him. 'Hulasikali! Wala!' ('He has plenty. He has everything') was the reply. But they deceived themselves, for most of my boxes were filled with paper and plants, and not with woven goods as they supposed. 'Then,' said he, 'we must not leave him without carrying off as much as we can of his goods, and for this purpose it will be necessary to kill him.' This also was approved of and the consequences discussed at length, it being considered that if they remained four months in the Guasié (where there were plenty of fugitives to bear them company) the affair would be quite forgotten. His genius seemed to expand as he talked the matter over and finally conducted him to what might be considered a climax. 'Why should we not kill the man now?' said he; 'we have him here sleeping in the midst of the forest, far removed from all observers. When he left San Carlos everyone knew him for a sick man, and no one will be surprised to hear of his death.' 'Hena nu camisha' ('I have no shirt'), 'and no sign will remain of violence having been used.' (In fact, his only clothing was a strip of bark between his legs.) This he repeated a great many times, and all his companions applauded the idea. Three questions remained for them to discuss: the disposal of the body, of the goods, and of themselves. The first offered no difficulty, for on account of the climate the dead are mostly interred at the end of 24 hours, and they could say 'the man' had died of his illness and they had buried him. As to the goods, they would leave a few in each box so as to give the latter the appearance of not having been disturbed. As to what they would do themselves there were various opinions; but at length they concluded that a better way than hiding themselves in the forest would be to present themselves boldly before the Comisario of San Carlos, tell their tale, and there would be an end of it, for 'the man' was a foreigner a long way from his country and had no relations here to make an inquiry as to the mode of his death. It may be supposed that I listened to all this with breathless attention, and I could hardly believe that their acts would be conformable with their words, till I heard them begin to lash themselves into a fury by recapitulating all the injuries they had received from the white men, all of which they considered themselves justified in retaliating on my devoted head — though in my short intercourse with them I had shown them only kindness, and particularly to Pedro Yurébe, whose little daughter I had a short time before cured of a distressing colic, which for many consecutive days and nights had allowed her no rest. I had on me a slight attack of diarrhoea — this is mostly the case with me on the first day I embark, when the excessive heat causes me to drink a great deal of water — and I had been obliged to leave my hammock two or three times since nightfall. It was now past midnight, and just as I lay down the last time I heard them deciding that the best way would be to strangle me as soon as I should be asleep again, which Yurébe undertook to do, and one of the others undertook to ascertain when I had fallen asleep. The fires had gone out and only the dim light of the stars illuminated the interior of the cabins. Though reclining in my hammock, I kept my feet on the ground ready to spring up should I be attacked. The darkness prevented their noticing this, and as I kept perfectly still for some time the man who had placed himself to watch me reported I was sleeping. I heard them all whispering one to the other, 'Iduali! Iduali!' ('Now it is good — now it is good'), and as Yurébe hesitated a moment, I got up and walked leisurely towards the forest as if my necessities had called me thither again; but instead I turned when I got a few paces and walked straight down to the canoe, unlocked the door of the cabin, which I entered, and having fortified the open doorway by putting a bundle of paper before it, I laid my double-barrelled loaded gun, along with a cutlass and knife, by my side, and thus awaited the attack which I still expected would be made. At intervals I could hear angry exclamations from the Indians, wondering that I did not return to my hammock; and it may be imagined in what state of mind I passed the rest of the night, never allowing my eye and ear to relax their watchfulness for a moment. However, they did not once stir to see what had become of me, and at length the break of day relieved me partly from my anxiety, but not entirely, for in that lonely place the dark deed contemplated might have been done almost as secretly by day as by night; and when shortly afterwards Pedro Yurébe came to offer to accompany me to the Barra, I took care while conversing with him never to move out of reach of my gun. Of course I declined his offer, excusing myself on the supposition that the Commandant of the Brazilian frontier would not allow him to pass on account of his name not being entered in the passport along with the others.

Though Pedro Yurébe was left behind, I took care throughout the rest of the voyage that the Indians should never approach me unarmed, and I never spent a gloomier time.[1]

The 'sagacious dames' proved correct. Spruce remained unmarried. He spent the last year of his life settled in Yorkshire, suffering from ill health but continuing his botanical studies. He was supported during these years by Government pensions, the actions of a fraudulent bank clerk having resulted in the loss of his savings, nearly one thousand pounds, from a South American bank. Spruce died in 1893.[1,2]

OCEANS & ISLANDS

J. D. HOOKER (1841–1842)

Son of William Jackson Hooker, Joseph Dalton Hooker (1817–1911) was born at Halesworth, Suffolk, in 1817. In 1820, the Hooker family removed to Glasgow, where William had been appointed to the University's Chair of Botany. Born to a botanical family, Joseph's interests also turned to natural history and he was to become one of the most eminent botanists of his time.

At fifteen years of age, Joseph entered Glasgow University and ultimately studied medicine. His botanical knowledge also continued to develop and, in 1839, with the help of his father, Hooker secured a position with the Government's Discovery Expedition, under the command of Captain James Clark Ross, to the Antarctic. This expedition consisted of two ships, *Erebus* and *Terror*. As one of the main objectives was to ascertain the position of the South Magnetic Pole, each ship was strengthened so as to withstand the pressure of pack-ice. Hooker was Assistant Surgeon on *Erebus* and was responsible for the botanical collections. The ships reached Kerguelen Island in May 1840.[1]

Kerguelen Island

The first plants to be seen, on landing, are, of course, seaweeds and lichens on all the rocks; then come a long grass, an *Agrostis*, a little *Ranunculus*, and more abundantly than either, a Composite plant [a daisy; the family Compositae or Asteraceae], forming small turfy slopes and ledges, of a bright green hue, among a mass of black bog-earth, covered with a *Callitriche* and portulaceous plant. Conspicuous amongst all these, is 'the CABBAGE', throwing out its thick round roots, one to two inches [in] diameter and exposed from a few inches to two or three feet, along the ground, bearing at its extremity, large cabbages, sometimes 18 inches across, of obconical or spathulate, rounded, concave, green, coriaceous leaves, enfolding a white heart, which eats like coarse, tough mustard and cress. From the sides of the heads, issues one, or more, long leafy stems, bearing such spikes of seed-vessels as my specimens, sent to the Admiralty, will show. The root tastes like horse-radish, the seeds like those of

cress; but the leaves are the grand fresh provision, and were so extremely relished by the sailors, that during the whole of our sojourn in that barren land, they were always boiled with the ship's company's beef, pork, or pea-soup. They taste to me very like stale cabbage, with a most disagreeable essential oil, which resides in cavities in the parenchyma of the leaves, and which are very conspicuous on making a transverse section of the heads of leaves. This oil gives to this vegetable a curious anti-heartburn property. Altogether, I consider this cabbage a most invaluable antiscorbutic, which few persons do not like, or cannot bring themselves to eat. Near the sea it grows in great abundance, and ascends to the tops of the hills, 1,500 feet high, where it is small and hairy, but retains all its properties.[2]

The Kerguelen Island cabbage is *Pringlea antiscorbutica* and, as its common name suggests, is a member of the family Cruciferae (or Brassicaceae).

The next most remarkable plant is a little tufted umbelliferous one. It forms long brown patches on the shores, the banks and rocks; sometimes covering many acres of land with deep cushions, on which you may, from their elasticity, lie with comfort, though, at other times, you sink up to the middle. The tap-roots of old tufts strike many feet into the soil which its own self has formed (owing to its property of shooting annually upwards) from the withered tops of the previous years' shoots, like *Bryum ludwigii*. The flowers are scarce and very inconspicuous. It has no smell, nor any essential or other oil; but is remarkable as one of a group of Umbelliferae, peculiar, I believe, to the southern hemisphere, and there only found in exceedingly alpine or Antarctic regions.

The seasons are evidently late on this island, and the winter comparatively mild. We have had frequent hail and snowstorms, but these seldom lasted more than a few hours on the low ground, the sun, wind, and rain soon removing the snow, with apparently slight injury to vegetation. There was but one strictly aquatic plant, and one entirely confined to dry land, all the rest, so far as I could discover, preferring a moist and peaty soil. Of Jungermanniae and mosses there was a considerable number of species, all belonging to alpine or Arctic forms; especially the genus *Andraea*, and another, approaching *Scouleria* in characters. The lichens appear to form a much larger component part of the vegetation at Kerguelen's Island than is the

OPPOSITE:

Pringlea antiscorbutica *by Walter Hood Fitch, being plate 90/91 of Hooker's* Flora antarctica, *which was published in 1845. (Source and copyright: Royal Botanic Gardens, Kew)*

case, comparatively, in other parts of the world; especially when it is remembered that, from the absence of trees, there can be no parasitic species. The rocks, from the water's edge to the summit of the hills, are apparently painted with them; their fronds, in general, adhering so closely to the stones, that it is only with difficulty they can be detached; in other cases, they seem to form part of the rock, which, from its excessive toughness and hardness, almost defies any attempt to procure such specimens as shall be at all satisfactory. At the top of the hills they assume the appearance of miniature forests on the black rocks, and nothing can be prettier than the large species, with broad black apothecia, which covers all the stones at an elevation of from 1,000 to 1,500 feet. A smaller kind, like a little oak tree, grows in spreading tufts (also upon stones), and is of a delicate lilac colour. Near the sea, the plants of this tribe are generally more coriaceous; especially a yellow one, that there forms bright patches on the cliffs. In the caves, also, on the coast, a light red species is so abundant as to tinge such situations with that hue, and many other sorts inhabit the rocks and their crevices.

Seaweeds are in enormous profusion; especially two large species, the *Macrocystis pyrifera* and *Laminaria radiata* (?). The former forms a broad green belt to the whole island so far as seen, of 20 or 30 yards, within 20 feet or so from the shore. Here the branches are so entangled, that it is sometimes impossible to pull a boat through the mass; and should any accident occur outside this girdle of seaweed, its presence would form an insurmountable obstacle to the best swimmer's ever reaching land. On the beach, the effect of the surf, beating it up and down, affords a very pretty appearance, but not so striking as is the view, from a slight elevation, of the Bay, with this olive-green band running round it. The sea-birds, when on the water, always fly over or dive under it, to re-appear on the other side. The *Laminaria* hangs down from every rock within reach of the tide; its digitate fronds, of a very thick coriaceous consistence and of great weight, are perpetually in movement from the lashing of the surf, and yet, thanks to their sliminess and strength, always uninjured. It protects thousands of limpets, that would otherwise be exposed to the attacks of the gulls and other sea-birds. To collect our food of Patellae was often hard labour, as we had to remove the tough and heavy masses of this weed to get at them.

During my stay at Kerguelen's Island, I devoted all my time to collecting everything in the botanical way. The Captain kindly took off all restriction, permitting me to go on shore whenever I liked. My rambles were generally solitary, through the wildest country I ever beheld. The hills were always covered with frozen snow, and many of my best lichens and mosses were obtained by hammering at the icy tufts, or sitting on them till they thawed. The days were so short, and the country so high, snowy and barren, that I never could go to any great distance from the harbour, though I several times tried for it, by starting before daylight. As far as I proceeded, the vegetation did not differ from that of the Bays. A boating excursion was undertaken to explore to the southward of the island. I volunteered to accompany it, but was advised to wait for a second, and my superior officer, the surgeon went. The party returned after some days, without having accomplished anything; the officer who led them found it impracticable for loaded men to travel by land, over rocks, round bays, and through snow-drifts; and when they took to the boat, the furious gales almost drove them out to sea. I went [on] several boating excursions, and on one was dismasted and nearly swamped, so Capt. Ross would allow no more to be sent.

I did my best to collect everything the Kerguelen's Island afforded, not neglecting the most insignificant plant, often walking on the beach, gathering seaweeds, my feet in the water, and wet to the skin with the dashing surf; I left not a hole unsearched, or stone unturned, and on those days when violent gales and snowstorms forbade all communication with the shore, I spent my time, and happily, too, in drawing, making analyses, and describing the specimens which I had brought on board. There is some danger, however, that inaccuracies may have crept into my work, for the rolling of the ship often obliged me to hold on, while thus employed, and to have my microscope lashed to the table, which renders dissection, under the glass, peculiarly difficult.[2]

The Discovery vessels reached Hobart in August 1840 and during the following weeks Hooker studied the Tasmanian flora. In November, sailing via the Auckland and the Campbell islands, they headed south. The expedition returned to Tasmania in April 1841 and then paid a short visit to Sydney before embarking for New Zealand where Hooker made large collections with the aid of William Colenso (*see* pp. 137–149). Near the year's end the *Erebus* and *Terror* again departed for the south.[1]

Icebergs and collision of ships

From the Bay of Islands [New Zealand], it had been Captain Ross's intention to proceed as far as 150th degree of west longitude, and then to go south. The winds were at first favourable, and the weather fine, though occasionally thick fogs came on, which, during their continuance, obliged us to be constantly firing muskets, beating gongs, and tolling bells, to keep company with the *Erebus*. On the 13th of December, we reached the parallel mentioned, and proceeded south, encountering the Pack ice in lat. 62½° and long. 147° W, which was considerably to the northward of where we made it last year. We pursued our way through it very well, till the 23rd, when the ice became thick and heavy, and we were unable to get on, except a few miles now and then, by boring and shoving along with poles. We crossed the Antarctic circle on the 31st, both ships made fast, at the same time, to one floe. We saw the old year out and the new year in, on the ice between the vessels; and on the evening of the 1st, had a ball there, and kept up the dancing till three in the morning. So you see that, while blocked up by frost on every side, we had some fun; but that was the first and the last of it. We cast off occasionally, but were obliged to make fast again.

On the 18th of January, we cast off, and on the 20th, encountered a very heavy gale with a tremendous swell, which rendered our situation for 36 hours truly perilous; it was more like the effect of an earthquake, than being tossed about by the sea; the immense blocks of ice threatening, as it were, to grind us to powder. Indeed, no ordinarily built ship could have stood it for an hour. Soon after the commencement of the gale, the *Erebus* had her rudder rendered useless, by the head of it being wrung, and ours was completely torn from the stern-post, although the fastenings were the same size as those used in line-of-battle ships. There we were, two ships in an unknown sea, drifting about at the mercy of the winds and, I may say, of the ice, without being in the slightest degree able to assist ourselves. Fortunately, the gale moderated and the swell went down so rapidly, that the next day we were enabled to make fast and repair damages. We had a spare rudder, and after great difficulty, succeeded in shipping it, although only half so secure as it was before. We experienced no other damage of consequence; a great deal of copper was stripped off, though some of it was thrice the thickness of that generally used; also, everything that in the least protruded from the sides, was torn away. However, in a couple of days, we set all to rights, and were enabled to proceed; and to our great delight, on the 2nd of February, got into open water, having been upwards of six weeks in the Pack ...

On the 5th of March, we re-crossed the Antarctic circle, and saw but a few icebergs. On the night of the 12th, or rather morning of the 13th, for it was a little after midnight, the night being pitch dark and stormy, with a heavy sea, in lat. 60°, we were running east, wind scarcely aft, when suddenly we found ourselves close to a chain of huge icebergs; and in hauling up to clear them (each ship doing so on opposite tacks), we came into unavoidable and, as it proved to be, exceedingly fortunate contact, striking most violently; our starboard bows met. This ship carried away jib-boom, cat-head, anchor, yard-arms, boom, and a boat. But the loss experienced by the *Erebus* was much greater; her bowsprit close off to the bows, fore-top-mast, cat-head, anchor, and a number of small spars gone. Nothing but their extraordinary strength prevented both ships being cut down to the water's edge; as it was, our consort smashed our strengthening pieces outside, while her bulwarks forward, were levelled with the deck. All the time we were foul, we continued helplessly drifting towards the icebergs, and thought ourselves inevitably lost; but on the ships clearing, we saw one part of the bergs darker than the rest, and happily it was an opening. Immediately after clearing the other ship, we were rushing close past an immense iceberg, and passed between two of these huge masses, through an opening not more than twice the breadth of our vessel, the foam caused by the sea against them, breaking over us on each side!

I have neither time nor inclination to dwell on the events of that dreadful night, which it even now makes me shudder to think of; but, some day, if it please God, through whose merciful interposition we were saved, I will give you an account when sitting over the fireside. The crippled state of the vessels prevented Captain Ross from performing all he had originally intended; which was, after reaching lat. 60°, long. 125° W, ... to have again proceeded south, if possible, as far as Cook's *ne plus ultra*, and then to this place. As it was, we made the best of our way, and with the exception of losing one man overboard, off Cape Horn, arrived here (Berkeley Sound, Falkland Islands), in safety, without an individual on the sick list in either ship, on the 6th of April [1842].[2]

As well as the Falkland Islands, the expedition visited Tierra del Fuego and Hermite Island before making a third trip to the south and subsequently returning to England in September 1843. The botanical results of this journey were largely published by Hooker in three volumes; that is, *Flora antarctica, Flora novae-zelandiae* and *Flora tasmaniae*. In 1847, he left for India (*see* pp. 57–69).

W. G. MILNE *(1855–1856)*

Born in Scotland, William Grant Milne trained as a gardener at the Royal Botanic Garden in Edinburgh. He was subsequently appointed as a botanical collector on the surveying voyage of HMS *Herald*, under Captain Henry Mangles Denham, to the South Seas.[1,2] Milne's position was largely funded by Kew. A most thorough account of the voyage of the *Herald*, including the scientific results, has been published by David.[3] The following account by Milne relates to time spent in the Fiji Islands in December 1855.

A hearty Scottish song

We are about getting underway for Norfolk Island and the Feejees ... It is my intention this time to spend as much of my time upon the large land Naviti Levue [= Viti Levu]. Until that island is properly examined the flora of the Fiijiis [*sic*] will rest upon doubts. I am almost satisfied [that there are] several more new *Pinus* on that large land. [In] my travels up those fine rivers last December I ascended up one of the main rivers upwards of 40 miles in a canoe with two natives. Nothing could be grander; as we reached the mountains it was one dense mass of vegetation. Towering above each other the mountains rising thousands of feet above the level of the sea, nothing could be finer than those picturesque [?ravines]. I could relate many amusing anecdotes which came under my notice while travelling amongst those island savages. I will only relate one. When about eight or ten miles from the bottom of the first range of mountains, in taking a turn of the river there [were] about 200 natives dancing and singing around a large fire. They desired us to bring our canoes close to the bank. To speak the truth, for the first time, a trembling came over my whole frame. I did not like the appearance of so many naked savages, their skins all covered with paint of various hues. I could see there was no chance of retreat. I was solely in their power. From [the] experience of the Feejee character [I knew] it would not do to appear afraid. I boldly went into the heart of them, holding out my hand to the chiefs. They shrank from [me] as if I had been a serpent. I gave them pipe and tobacco. Then they became very friendly. I gave them a hearty

Scottish song which created much laughter. To keep them in good humour I joined in the dance. I thought for a time those shouts and laughter would open up the heavens. From that moment I was in safety. They [gave] me as much yams and taro as I could eat. I told them I was [an] English chief and belonged to a Britannia man-of-war. Nothing was too good they could give. At first I thought it was a feast. I soon came to understand they were about to make presents to several of the neighbouring towns of portions of taro. They would not allow me to depart until the division took place. In about half an hour between 300 and 400 men made their appearance coming along the margin of the river, one man deep, each with a portion of the vegetable on his club ... To my astonishment one [portion] was laid aside for Queen Victoria, and in Her Majesty's name I received it, much to their satisfaction, and no less mine. At last we were allowed to pursue our journey, taking away their good wishes.[4]

The following accounts pertain to Milne's journey in Fiji during August 1856.

Turmeric and picturesque views

In my last letter from Sydney, dated the 21st of May, I mentioned that I anticipated another journey into the interior of [Viti Levu]. A party was formed by Captain Denham, consisting of Dr [Macdonald], the Reverend Mr Waterhouse, and [Dagwell], the Captain's coxswain. We finally left the ship, in one of our own boats, on Friday, the 13th of August, well supplied with calico, hatchets, knives, etc. to clear all expenses with the natives of the interior. The first day we arrived at Bau.

Saturday 14 Aug. — We left Bau in a large double-canoe, having a single-canoe and a small dingy in company. As we entered the river, the country was flat and somewhat undulating, and more or less in a state of cultivation. On ascending the stream, nothing could be more enchanting; both sides were one mass of mangrove-bushes, with their adventitious roots hanging to the surface of the water. Here and there were breadfruit trees, showing their incised foliage, with the fruit in a state of formation. Much more striking were the cocoa-nut, and a stately palm, a species of *Areca*. We called at several towns, visited their heathen temples, [and] obtained a great deal of information in regard to the residence of their gods. To dwell upon such topics would

OPPOSITE: Melastoma denticulatum, *a shrub less than 2 m tall, is common throughout Fiji. Watercolour by Walter Hood Fitch. (Source and copyright: Royal Botanic Gardens, Kew)*

not be botany ... I must restrict myself as much as possible to the vegetation of the country. As we ascended the stream, the features of the land continued much the same; at intervals the fresh-water fish and the wild-ducks rippled the surface of the water. We reached the Christian town of Navuso, where we found the chief, [Komai] Naitasiri, the highest chief in the district.

Monday 16 Aug. — We left [Navuso] for Naitasiri, being the next Christian town on the river. We had a ship's long-boat, called the *Victoria*, belonging to the Reverend Mr Moore; it formerly belonged to the ship *Lady Franklin*, at the time a mutiny broke out close to the Feejee Islands, when a number of convicts escaped from the ship in the above boat: it was retaken by Captain Denham at Ovalau. The small dingy and a single-canoe formed our armada. In passing along I saw great clumps of tree-ferns, belonging to the genus *Cyathea*. The *Areca* palm was becoming more frequent; the fruit at all times is from five to six feet from the apex, encircling the stipes. It is not unfrequent to see large clumps of these beautiful trees upon the face of the banks. Several species of *Convolvulus* now adorned the sides with their white, pink, and blue flowers, and a species of *Crinum*, with white flowers, are frequent in woody places along the banks; so that, what with Gramineae and Cyperaceae, there was ample scope for a collector; but I was somewhat confined in my researches, being in charge of the boat, and, owing to the intricate navigation, with all our caution more than once we got aground. At 8.30 we arrived at our place of destination, and found Dr [Macdonald], with Mr Waterhouse, quartered at the teacher's house.

Tuesday 17 Aug. — The weather being somewhat unfavourable, we did not prosecute our journey. I went out collecting with the chief, [Komai] Naitasiri, through a fine woody country, and found several interesting shrubs, which fortunately were in flower. One belonged to Scrophularineae (in this instance there were only two stamens, as in *Veronica*), and another tree belonging to Leguminosae. It was past flowering. I only saw one seed-pod. There were several other species of shrubs, and a number of ferns. Two of the latter in particular attracted my attention; one with broad, compound fronds, the indusium somewhat reticulated, and having young plants proceeding upon the points of the fronds; the other, I think, belongs to the genus *Dicksonia*, if I may judge from the nature of the indusium; however there is no room for description here. I collected a number of other things, but nothing I had not found in December, 1855.

Wednesday 18 Aug. — We left this place and ascended the river, leaving the *Victoria*, and taking a number of smaller canoes instead of the larger ones. As we passed along the stream, the country became a flat plain, in a state of cultivation, having all along the sides of the banks great numbers of shaddock trees (mole of the natives), large trees of *Calophyllum* (damue of the natives); patches of yams and taro were frequent; coco-nuts and breadfruits were less numerous. We arrived at a town called Tausa, where we remained for the night, and started the following morning up that branch of the river called Wai [Ndina]. The country thus far still continued to be flat. In passing along we came to a place where we found several women manufacturing turmeric, and upon the sides of the river were large quantities of refuse. In a small house close to the water there were two pits, eighteen inches deep, lined with banana leaves, and made water-tight; also a number of posts set in the ground, having rough bark, to be used as graters. When a quantity is grated, it is committed to the pits, where it remains for some time, and is afterwards carried to a canoe, then strained through a close-worked basket lined with fern leaves, and then put into short bamboos, where it remains for four nights and four days, when it is fit for use, and forms one of the principal articles of food, made into puddings, mixed with grated sugar-cane. It is used also for covering children after birth, and painting the bodies of women previous to strangulation. There was a species of *Ficus* in great abundance, with small foliage, all along the high grounds, and a number of other plants which I did not recognise, owing to the distance; but it was evident the features of the country were fast changing. Here and there were deep ravines, the sides of the banks lined with vegetation of a different aspect. At the same time the river became more tortuous; at times we were going south, at other times we were steering due north. It was with great difficulty we made any progress, owing to the force of the rapids. On coming to a sudden turn of the river, immediately to the right was a bamboo-forest, and right ahead was the mountain of Ambuga Levue [? = Mbuggi Levu], and a number of other detached conical peaks bearing to the south, intersected with deep craggy ravines, and thickly covered with vegetation. Here is a fine panoramic view, in fact one of the finest in the whole course of the river. The scenery was picturesque in the extreme. On the banks was abundance of what the natives called lololalo, or native fig [probably *Ficus vitiensis*], with large clusters of fruit covering the stems, and another tree which the natives call nelawa, and which bears great quantities of fruit.[5]

Stinging nettles

For some days we had incessant rain, but on Thursday I was determined to make the best of the day, whatever the nature of the weather might be. Accompanied by two natives, I took to the woods ... Owing to the unfavourable state of the day, it was with some difficulty I could prevail upon the natives to remain, and without them I could have made no progress. I found a young plant belonging to [the] Coniferae, with leaves like a *Taxus* (kau solo of the natives), and soon I saw one tree growing to 60 to 70 feet in height, and eight feet in circumference, perfectly straight. It was in vain I could tempt these people to ascend for specimens; they declared it was impossible. I have however a specimen in my possession; it was taken in a young state, and I enclose part for your examination. On my way through the woods, I found a number of fine mosses in fruit, but have collected the same species at Ovalau. In descending a deep ravine there were large plants of *Marattia*, their long fertile fronds covering a large space of ground. Many of them were formed into trees; and I think there are two species of *Marattia* in Feejee. On coming to a considerable mountain stream I got two species of parasitical orchids. After securing them in my box a few minutes walk brought me upon the margin of that beautiful river which is only to be found in the interior of [Viti Levu]. The branches of the trees were hanging over the water, literally covered with mosses and lichens; a large tree was in flower, of exquisite beauty, belonging to a [family] unknown to me; another tree was in flower of a cream colour, family Myrtaceae. Both sides of the banks were lined with ferns, such as *Asplenium, Aspidium, Dicksonia, Davallia* etc. There is a species of Urticaceae [called *Dendrocnide harveyi*], which the natives are very much afraid of; and well they may be, for if you should be so unfortunate as to sting yourself, you will feel the consequence for some months. I am at this moment suffering from its effects, from an accident which occurred a month ago. There is no eruption, but it is most painful when exposed to the influence of water. In some places this nettle is called kau tambua; it is best known as salato.[5]

In the branches of the shaddock trees ...

Wednesday 25 August — The weather being more settled, it was thought advisable to prosecute our journey. We reached the town of Nondravu, where we remained for the night, in the Burasau, and started the following morning, Thursday, and reached the town of

Suvian, where we found boiling springs: they were indeed boiling springs, unbearable to the touch. There was no time for collecting. We always left the towns early in the morning and had late arrivals. The features of the country had changed considerably. There was mountain after mountain rising above each other, with their bold, craggy precipices; there were the grey rocks, covered with lichens; and large, noble specimens of [?*Dammera*], covered with leaves of a rich green. We arrived at the town of Namosi on Friday the 28th, and we were met by a white man called by the whites of Feejee 'Harry the Mountain'; his proper name is John Humphrey [Danford]; he has been fifteen years amongst the inland tribes, and to that man we were much indebted. Namosi is a large town between two mountains. As we entered this place it was disgusting to see great quantities of human bones in the branches of the shaddock trees, as one would think on purpose that the odoriferous blossoms might overpower the odour from the human flesh in a state of putrefaction. There were also great numbers in the branches of a species of *Barringtonia*. These two last-mentioned trees seem to be their favourite ones for that purpose. There were some hundreds of small stones, neatly set into the ground, every stone indicating a murder. We were informed by Harry that six men had been killed by the chief Nelua Nelua on the coast, and a part of the bodies sent to the chiefs of Namosi, as their share of the food. A portion of this revolting food was brought for inspection. I visited the grave of the late chief, and found a number of skulls and other human bones. They worship the spirits of their fathers; at all times portions of food are to be seen upon the graves to feed the supposed spirits. One of our party saw a man's hand overhanging the fire-place, in the smoke, in one of the chief's houses. The day before we left this place a man and a woman were strangled.[5]

Shaddock is the common name of *Citrus maxima*, one of several species from which various important citrus fruits have been derived through hybridisation.

Milne remained with the *Herald* until 1859, when he resigned following pressure from Sir William Hooker, who felt that Milne's output as a botanical collector was wanting.[3, 6] After his voyage to the South Seas, Milne returned to Edinburgh and subsequently worked for a time as gardener at Glasgow Botanic Gardens. However, he was soon to venture to West Africa to collect objects of natural history (*see* pp. 37–44).

B. C. SEEMANN *(1860)*

Berthold Carl Seemann, born in Germany in 1825, was educated at the University of Göttingen. He subsequently trained at Kew Gardens and in 1846 was appointed naturalist to HMS *Herald*, employed at that time on a surveying expedition of the Pacific. He returned to England in 1851 and published several books, including the *Botany of the Voyage of HMS* Herald (1852–1857), before travelling to Fiji in 1860. There, over a period of about eight months, he collected approximately 800 plant species and recorded the customs of local tribes. In 1862, Seemann published a general account of his Fijian exploits and this was followed by the beautifully illustrated *Flora vitiensis* (1865–1873).[1,2] The following accounts pertain to his visit to Fiji.

To the summit of Somosomo

On the 30th of May, we ascended for the first time the summit of Somosomo [on the island of Taveuni]; Captain Wilson, Mr Coxon, and several men kindly sent from the mission at Wairiki, accompanied us, carrying baskets, for making collections. The Queen of Somosomo, hearing of our intention, joined the expedition with her whole court. At daybreak we found her train waiting for us, on the banks of a river, all fully equipped for the occasion. A few strokes of the pen will describe their dress. The Queen wore two yards of white calico around her loins, fern-leaves around her head, the purple blossom of the Chinese rose in a hole pierced through one of her ears, and a bracelet made of a shell. No other garment graces her stately person, and yet she looked truly majestic. Her attendants dispensed with the calico altogether, and were simply attired in portions of banana and coco-nut leaves fresh from the bush, which was so far convenient to them as they were ordered to push ahead, make a road, and shake the dew and rain from the branches, obstructing the way. In our European clothes, we stood no chance in keeping up with them. They were always a long distance ahead, waiting for our coming up, and enjoying themselves in opening coco-nuts, and smoking cigarettes, made with dry banana leaves instead of paper.

The ascent was rather steep, and Mr Stork [Seemann's assistant] had the misfortune to hurt himself rather seriously from falling down a considerable precipice, just when in the act of gathering some botanical specimens. The road was very bad, the forest being so thick that no glimpse of the sun could fall upon a soil saturated with excessive moisture. Large trees and abundant underwood of small palms and tree-ferns produced a solemn gloom, and made us long for a look at the sky. Wild pigeons of a brown colour, and in very good condition for eating, there abounded, and a number were brought down by our guns. As we were pushing on, collecting all that came in our way, and now jumping over rivulets, now climbing over rocks, we suddenly arrived at an open space, exhibiting a beautiful view of the whole Straits of Somosomo …

After another hour's scramble we reached the summit, and found it to all appearance a large extinct crater filled with water, and on the

Berthold Seemann. (Source: Frontispiece of volume 10 of the Journal of Botany, British & Foreign (1872). Reproduced with permission from the archives of the Royal Botanic Gardens, Melbourne)

north-eastern part covered with a vegetable mass, so much resembling in colour and appearance the green fat of the turtle, as to have given rise to the popular belief that the fat of all the turtles eaten in Fiji is transported hither by supernatural agency, which is the reason why on the morning after a turtle-feast the natives always feel hungry. This jelly-like mass is several feet thick, and entirely composed of some microscopic cryptograms, which, from specimens I submitted to the Reverend M. J. Berkeley, a weighty authority on such matters, proved to be *Hoomospora transversalis* of Brebisson, and the representative of quite a new genus, named *Hoomonema fluitans* Berkl. A tall species of sedge was growing among them, and gave some degree of consistency to the singular body. We were not aware until it was too late that these strange productions were only floating on the top of the lake and forming a kind of crust, or else we should not have ventured upon it. On the contrary, we took it to be part of a swamp, that might safely be crossed, though not without difficulty, for we were always up to our knees, often to our hips, in this jelly. All this caused a great deal of merriment. A little hunchback, who carried a basket swinging on a stick, looked most ludicrous in his endeavours to keep pace with us. Now and then, when one or the other was trying to save himself from sinking into inextricable positions, he had to crawl like a reptile, and the others were not slow to laugh at his expense. The first symptoms of danger were several large fissures which occurred in the crust we were wading through. The water in them was perfectly clear, and a line of many yards let down reached no bottom. These fissures became more and more numerous as we advanced, until the vegetable mass abruptly terminated in a lake of limpid water full of eels. The border was rather more solid than the mass left behind, and all sat down to rest, from the great exertion it had required to drag ourselves for more than a mile and a half through one of the worst swamps I ever crossed. As it was getting quite a fashionable hour for dinner, and our appetite was becoming more keen every minute, we determined not to postpone it any longer; cold yams, taros, and fowls, washed down with a bottle of Australian wine mixed with water from the lake, constituted our meal.[2]

Perfect mantle of scarlet and blue

At Nagadi the river branches off in two different directions: the eastern branch is not navigable even for small canoes ... We finally abandoned our canoes at Wai nuta, to proceed on foot to Namosi — there being no horses, mules, or any other mode of conveyance.

On stepping on shore I was shown the largest snake I ever saw in Fiji. It was only six feet long, two inches in diameter, of a light brown colour, and with a triangularly-shaped head. I was very desirous of obtaining it for my zoological collection; but the natives said that [Chief] Kuruduadua had just seen it and ordered them to prepare it for his supper on his return from Namosi. As he had passed on, I could not get the order revoked; and the reptile having been put alive in a bamboo, which was corked up at the ends, the boys, much to my regret, trotted off with it.

Climbing at once commenced. The paths being very narrow, we walked in single file, Kuruduadua taking the lead, and showing us the sites of the various towns which he or his fathers had taken when their victorious army gradually fought its way from the interior of Viti Levu to its southern coast. The soil appeared everywhere of the richest kind. We saw no plains of any size, but series after series of undulating ranges of no very great height, well suited for growing coffee, tea, and cotton. Now and then there was a fine bird's-eye view of the country, which Kuruduadua was always careful to point out, evidently enjoying our expressions of delight on these occasions. I saw a good many plants that interested me, and their collection ultimately isolated me and Soromato, henceforth my shadow, from the rest of the party.

I had just been speculating on the cause of the Fijian, in common with other insular floras, being poor in gay-coloured, and rich in green, white, and yellow flowers, when, lo! a look in the valley revealed bushes covered with a perfect mantle of scarlet and blue, thrown up to great advantage by the bright rays of the sun. I saw my travelling companions had made a halt near the very spot where nature had condescended to refute a deeply-rooted generalisation. I clambered down the hill as fast as the condition of the ground would admit, and for awhile lost sight of the gay display by intervening objects. A few more steps and I stood before a startling sight — Colonel Smythe's artillery uniform hung up to dry in the sun![2]

Salt is not forgotten

Naulumatua was the half-brother of Kuruduadua, and only died a short time previous to our visit, and the court was still mourning for him, which was the reason of our not having either dance or song. His head-wife took me to his grave, and lamenting his death, said that he might still be alive if he had only abstained from eating human flesh, and that both she and Danford [*see* p. 311] had done all in their power to convince him that he was ruining his constitution systematically by that indulgence. For it appears that human flesh is extremely difficult to digest, and that even the strongest and most healthy men suffer from confined bowels for two or three days after a cannibal feast. Probably, in order to assist the process of digestion, 'bokola', as dead men's flesh is technically termed, is always eaten with an addition of vegetables, which it may be ethnologically important to notice; since, thanks to a powerful movement amongst the natives, the influence of commerce, Christian teaching, and the presence of a British Consul, Fijian cannibalism survives only in a few localities, and is daily becoming more and more a matter of history.

There are principally three kinds which, in Fijian estimation, ought to accompany bokola, — the leaves of the malawaci (*Trophis anthropophagorum* Seem.), the tudauo (*Omalanthus pedicellatus* Benth.), and the boro-dina (*Solanum anthropophagorum* Seem.). The two former are middle-sized trees, growing wild in many parts of the group; but the boro-dina is cultivated, and there are generally several large bushes of it near every Bure-ni-sa (or strangers' house), where the bodies of those slain in battle are always taken. The boro-dina is a bushy shrub, seldom higher than six feet, with a dark, glossy foliage, and berries of the shape, size, and colour of tomatoes. This fruit has a faint aromatic smell, and is occasionally prepared like tomato sauce. The leaves of these three plants are wrapped around the bokola, as those of the taro are around pork, and baked with it on heated stones. Salt is not forgotten.

OPPOSITE:
*An illustration by
Walter Hood Fitch
of boro-dina. Named*
Solanum anthro-
pophagorum *by
Seemann, this name
is now considered to
be a synonym of*
S. uporo. *(Source
and copyright:
Royal Botanic
Gardens, Kew)*

Besides these three plants, some kinds of yams and taro are deemed fit accompaniment of a dish of bokola. The yams are hung up in the Bure-ni-sa for a certain time, having previously been covered with turmeric, to preserve them, it would seem, from rapid decay: our own sailors effecting the same end by whitewashing the yams when taking them on board. A peculiar kind of taro (*Caladium esculentum* Schott. var.), called kurilagi, was pointed out as having been eaten with a whole tribe of people. The story sounds strange, but as a number of natives were present when it was told, several of whom corroborated the various statements, or corrected the proper names that occurred, its truth appears unimpeachable. In the interior of Viti Levu, about three miles NNE from Namosi, there dwelt a tribe, known by the name of Kai-na-loca, who in days of yore gave

Solanum anthropophagorum

Taro, Colocasia esculenta, is pantropical by introduction and its natural range is uncertain. It is photographed here in a billabong in the Arafura Swamp region of the Northern Territory, Australia.

great offence to the ruling chief of the Namosi district, and, as a punishment of their misdeeds, the whole tribe was condemned to die. Every year the inmates of *one* house were baked and eaten, fire was set to the empty dwelling, and its foundation planted with kurilagi. In the following year, as soon as this taro was ripe, it became the signal for the destruction of the next house and its inhabitants, and the planting of a fresh field of taro. Thus, house after house, family after family, disappeared, until Ratuibuna, the father of the present chief Kuruduadua, pardoned the remaining few, and allowed them to die a natural death. In 1860, only one old woman, living at Cagina, was the sole survivor of the Na-loca people. Picture the feelings of these unfortunate wretches, as they watched the growth of the ominous taro! Throughout the dominions of the powerful chief whose authority they had insulted, their lives were forfeited, and to escape into territories where they were strangers would, in those days, only have been to hasten the awful doom awaiting them in their own country. Nothing remained save to watch, watch, watch, the rapid development of the kurilagi. As leaf after leaf unfolded, the tubers increased in size and substance, how their hearts must have trembled, their courage forsaken them! And when at last the foliage began to turn yellow, and the taro was ripe, what agonies they must have undergone! what torture could have equalled theirs![2]

The specific epithet, *anthropophagorum*, used for two of the species mentioned, reflects the fact that these plants were eaten with human flesh. As well as being used as a pot herb, *Solanum anthropophagorum* — now known as *S. uporo* — is used medicinally, not only in Fiji but also in other Pacific islands. Traditional uses include eating fruit to treat urinary disorders, rubbing crushed fruit and leaves mixed with capsicum on parts of the body affected by rheumatism, and drinking an infusion made from the leaves to reduce swellings caused by parasitic worms.[3]

The accepted name for taro is *Colocasia esculenta*, not *Caladium esculentum*. At one time the corms of taro probably provided the most important food for the people of Polynesia, 300 variants of taro being cultivated in Hawaii alone.[4]

Seemann visited Venezuela in 1864 and again collected in Central America in 1866. Soon after, he became managing director of a gold mine in Nicaragua and managed a sugar plantation. In 1871, when forty-seven years old, this prolific author (of several thousand articles on general literature and politics, and of about seventy botanical works[4]) succumbed to fever during a visit to Nicaragua.

Seemann is accredited with the introduction of a number of plants to British gardens; for example the creeper *Tecoma valdiviana*, the grape *Vitis chontalensis*, and many palms.[5]

APPENDICES

PLANT NAMES

Binomials

Common names of plants are frequently confusing, as they may vary from region to region and from language to language. This problem, plus the fact that the Latin names in use by naturalists at the time were mostly short, descriptive phrases, led in 1753 to the Swedish naturalist Carl Linnaeus introducing a consistent Latin binomial, or two-word system, of plant naming. In such names the first name is the generic name, the second is the specific epithet. For example, the swamp bloodwood, a tree of northern Australia, was first given the scientific name of *Eucalyptus ptychocarpa* F. Muell. Written in this form, the name tells us that the swamp bloodwood is a member of the genus *Eucalyptus* and has the specific name *ptychocarpa*. The 'F. Muell.' is the name of the person, in this case Ferdinand Mueller, who first validly named the species. In scientific papers it is common practice to include the name of the author(s) of a plant's name when it is first mentioned in the text. The authority is an abridged reference to the place and date of original publication of the name. This information is important to taxonomists concerned with ascertaining which names should be used for an organism. However, although used briefly below to explain name changes and the concept of a new combination, citation of authors is thought by some to be unnecessary for anything but strictly taxonomic works. That view is taken here.

The International Code of Botanical Nomenclature

The binomial naming system was readily accepted and today there are many Principles and Articles that govern the formal scientific naming of plants, these being set out in an *International Code of Botanical Nomenclature*,[1] a work that is followed and regularly reviewed by plant taxonomists.

Theoretically, if there was agreement as to the classification of all plants, and if the *Code* was consistently interpreted there would be no name changes. This is far from reality. Names commonly change both as the result of previous non-compliance with the *Code* and as the result of taxonomic decisions. In the latter case it is common for botanists familiar with a group of plants to find that a current classification is not a good reflection of the circumscription and relationships of plant taxa (a taxon is a taxonomic group such as a genus or species; pl. taxa). For example, many botanists believe that the bloodwoods, commonly placed in the genus *Eucalyptus*, should be removed from that genus and placed in their own genus, *Corymbia*. Thus, *Eucalyptus ptychocarpa* F. Muell. is sometimes referred to as *Corymbia ptychocarpa* (F. Muell.) K. D. Hill & L. A. S. Johnson, in this example Hill & Johnson being the authors who first made what is referred to as a 'new combination' under *Corymbia*.

Synonyms

Under the *Code*, with the exception of a few specified cases, provided that there is taxonomic agreement with the circumscription, position and rank, a taxon can only have one correct name. All other names which apply to the taxon are termed synonyms (commonly abbreviated as 'syn.'). For example, if it is accepted that the genus *Corymbia* should be recognised, then the name *Eucalyptus ptychocarpa* is a synonym of C. *ptychocarpa*. Conversely, if this is not accepted, then C. *ptychocarpa* is a synonym of E. *ptychocarpa*. Although there may be taxonomic dispute as to the genus in which it should be placed, the circumscription of the species is not problematic and its name is fixed by the rulings of the *Code*.

If it is accepted that *Corymbia ptychocarpa* should be used in preference to E. *ptychocarpa*, then the latter name is known as a nomenclatural (or homotypic) synonym, both names being based on the same type specimen, the type specimen being that material on which the name of a taxon — in this case a species — was first named.

Frequently the synonym is a taxonomic (or heterotypic) synonym, where the name is based on a type specimen which is different to the type specimen of the accepted name. For example, in 1837 when Robert Schomburgk found the plant we now know as *Victoria amazonica*, he sent specimens to England where John Lindley used them to describe and validly name the species. Lindley believed that not only was the species new but that it was also generically distinct from the genus *Euryale*, naming the taxon *Victoria regia* after the then reigning Queen Victoria. Unbcknown to him, Eduard Poeppig had seen other material (not Schomburgk's specimen) of this species and had in 1832 validly named it *Euryale amazonica*. It was subsequently agreed that Lindley was correct in placing the species in the genus *Victoria* but, with Poeppig's species name being the earlier of the two, the combination *Victoria amazonica* (Poeppig) Sowerby was later published, the name *E. amazonica* becoming a nomenclatural synonym, the name *V. regia* becoming a taxonomic synonym.

Taxonomic ranks

The above notes deal with generic and species names but there are a number of taxonomic ranks, the principal of which, in ascending order, are: species, genus, family, order, class and division. For the purposes of this book there is no need to elaborate, although some family names, which with the exception of a few accepted alternative names terminate in the ending '-aceae', do appear in the text. (In the case of *Corymbia ptychocarpa*, it belongs to the family Myrtaceae.) Various infraspecific names for naturally occurring entities are often applied, the most commonly used being subspecies (subsp.) and variety (var.), for example, *Corymbia ptychocarpa* subsp. *aptycha* and *Apium prostratum* var. *prostratum*.

Cultivars

The naming of cultivars, types of plants that are used for agricultural, horticultural or forestry purposes, is governed by *The International Code of Nomenclature for Cultivated Plants*.[2] Here the generic name or the binomial is followed by the cultivar name given in one of two ways; for example, *Grevillea* 'Robyn Gordon' or *Grevillea* cv. Robyn Gordon, *Grevillea alpina* 'Grampians Gold' or *Grevillea alpina* cv. Grampians Gold.

HERBARIA

History

The term 'herbarium' (plural, 'herbaria') was originally applied to a book about medicinal plants but during the eighteenth century it began to be used as an equivalent for the term *Hortus siccus*; that is, a collection of pressed and dried plants that are kept as a botanical record.[1] The practice of making herbaria commenced during the sixteenth century during the time when Luca Ghini, an Italian physician and botanist, taught botany in Bologna and Pisa. Although he apparently sent dried specimens of plants to pupils, Ghini himself seems not to have made a herbarium for his own use, teaching botany from living plants.[2]

Public herbaria

Initially most of these plant collections were privately owned but eventually their deposition in public, often purpose-built, herbaria became commonplace. In 1990, it was recorded that world wide there were 2,639 public herbaria distributed in 147 countries and holding, together, an estimated 273 million specimens.[3]

Function

The herbarium is the basic reference source, or data bank, for plant taxonomists — those people involved in the classifying, description and naming of plants. As such, herbaria and their associated taxonomists play a pivotal role in the documentation of biodiversity.

Most specimens housed in herbaria are usually dried specimens mounted on cartridge paper, although additional collections of pollen (mounted on glass microscope slides), specimens in liquid preservative, and bulky fruit, seed and wood samples may also be stored in an assortment of jars, plastic bags and cabinets. This may suggest that the bulk of taxonomic work is simply descriptive, the taxonomists confining themselves to describing morphological, and sometimes anatomical, features of plants. Although this is very often the case, given the opportunity most taxonomists will carry out extensive field work, examining plants *in situ* and thus observing aspects that are not evident from herbarium specimens. This can be extremely informative; for example, it may lead to a greater understanding of floral structures that are associated with pollination syndromes and this, in turn, may lead to a better classification. Taxonomists may also determine chromosome numbers and examine chromosome morphology. Some taxonomists study the chemistry of plants, examination of secondary metabolites such as flavonoids, often yielding data of much use in resolving the taxonomy of plant groups. Most recently the advent of DNA gene sequencing has begun to revolutionise the study of plant relationships.

Collecting herbarium specimens

As noted in several extracts, it was common practice for plant collectors on their rambles to place specimens in a vasculum. In this day and age, plastic bags and an assortment of backpacks are more likely to be used for keeping plants fresh before they are converted to herbarium specimens. Some botanists will also use portable day-presses for preliminary pressing before plants are transferred to a larger press for drying. In some cases, when critical features of flowers and fruit will be lost on pressing, specimens may also be preserved in spirit. A common preservative in use is composed of 70% ethanol, 29% water and 1% glycerol.[4]

Typically, plant specimens are dried by placing them between sheets of paper and these, in turn, are placed between pieces of cardboard. The resulting stack of plants, paper and cardboard is then placed into a press to keep them flat. Pressure is usually maintained for a period of several days to a week; that is, until the plants are dry. To avoid fungal damage, damp paper is often replaced with dry every day or two.

Newspaper is ideal for drying specimens, a tabloid sheet folded in half being a good size. The ease with which paper is obtainable today is in marked contrast to the experiences of Boissier (*see* p. 200) and many other early collectors.

Artificial drying of specimens is common practice in herbaria where often specially constructed drying cupboards, with fan-forced heated air, are used for that purpose. Specimens are dried over a period of several days, with temperatures deliberately kept low (about 50–55°C), as higher temperatures and rapid drying result in brittle specimens.

Field-driers that employ heat from gas burners are frequently used by professional collectors. This must be done with care. As with Forbes (*see* p. 105), today's collectors have occasional mishaps. In dry areas, specimens are readily dried by having the presses (tightly tied!) on roof racks of moving vehicles.

All professional collectors have field note books in which information concerning the specimens gathered is recorded. Basic facts such as locality, habitat and flower colour, that is, data that may not be apparent once the specimens are dried, are noted. Today, it is common to see noted on specimens, the latitudes and longitudes that have been determined using a Global Positioning System — a far cry from many early collections which may be labelled with no more than a note stating the country of origin. Each specimen is also usually given its own number as this facilitates reference to collections; for example when specimens are sent to a taxonomist for naming.

Private collectors may leave their dried plants in folders of newspaper but in public herbaria it is normal practice to mount each specimen on cartridge paper, placing with it a typed label containing notes about the collection. These specimens are then filed away in cupboards, often being arranged alphabetically by name — firstly by family name, then by genus and then species. Alternatively, they may be arranged following a phylogenetic system; that is, one in which supposed related families (and within them the subordinate taxa) are arranged together.

THE WARDIAN CASE

Transport of plants on long voyages was a problem for early collectors, potted plants succumbing readily to salt-water spray, extremes in temperature and lack of water. The Wardian Case, essentially a portable, more or less airtight greenhouse or glass box, usually solved such problems. A key point is that the boxes are sealed enough to keep the moisture from evaporating. Today such a solution may seem obvious (particularly to anyone familiar with terrariums) but when the concept was first put forward by Nathaniel Bagshaw Ward (1791–1868), a London physician, William Hooker was moved to publish a letter from Ward in his *Companion to the Botanical Magazine*. In it, Ward explained just how he came to develop the case.

> My Dear Sir,
> I have lately heard that you wish for some information respecting my new method of growing plants without exposure to air. As I do not intend to publish at present a detailed account, and as much misrepresentation exists upon the subject, I feel great pleasure in furnishing you with the principal facts, of which you may make any use you please.
>
> The depressing influence of the air of large towns upon vegetation, had, for many years, engaged my attention.
>
> The science of Botany, in consequence of the perusal of the works of the immortal Linnaeus, had occupied me from my youth up, and the earliest object of my ambition was to possess an old wall, covered with ferns and mosses. Compelled by circumstances to live surrounded by, and enveloped in, the smoke of numerous manufactories, all my endeavours to keep my favourites alive, proved sooner or later unavailing. I was led, however, to reflect a little more deeply upon the subject, in consequence of a simple incident, which occurred about seven or eight years ago. I had buried the chrysalis of a Sphynx [moth] in some moist mould, which was contained in a wide-mouthed glass bottle, covered with a lid. In watching the bottle from day to day, I observed that the moisture which during the heat of the day arose from the mould, condensed on the internal surface of the glass, and returned from whence it

A Wardian Case. (Source: As shown on p. 71, On the growth of plants in closely glazed cases, *second edition, by N. B. Ward, published in London in 1852. Reproduced with permission from the archives of the Royal Botanic Gardens, Melbourne)*

came, thus keeping the mould always equally moist. About a week prior to the final change of the insect, a seedling fern and grass made their appearance upon the surface of the mould.

After I had secured my insect, I was anxious to watch the development of these plants in such a confined situation, and accordingly placed the bottle outside my study window. The plants continued to grow, and turned out to be the *Poa annua* and *Nephrodium filix-mas* [= *Dryopteris filix-mas*]. I now commenced a series of experiments upon other plants, principally ferns, selecting those that were most difficult of culture, such as *Hymenophyllum*, etc. My method of proceeding was as follows : — Keeping nature always in view, I endeavoured to imitate the natural condition of the plants as much as possible, as regarded the exposure to light, solar heat, moisture, etc. Thus, if ferns were the subject of experiment, they were planted in the mould most congenial to them, well watered, but all the superfluous water allowed to drain off, and then placed in a situation having a northern aspect. If, on the contrary, I wished to grow cacti, they were planted in a mixture of loam and sand, suspended from the roof of the case, and fully exposed to solar heat. Upon this part of the subject I need not, however, dilate any further, and will therefore confine myself to the results obtained.

1st, That the depressing influence of the air of large towns upon the vegetation depends almost entirely upon the fuliginous matter with which such an atmosphere is impregnated, and which produces the same effect upon the leaves of plants as upon the lungs of animals.

2ndly, That, owing to the quiet state of the atmosphere surrounding the plants in my inclosed cases, the plants, like human beings, will bear extremes of heat and of cold, which under ordinary circumstances would be fatal to them. It is well known, from the experiments of Sir C. Blagden, and others, that man will bear great degrees of heat with impunity, provided the atmosphere be undisturbed, and it is equally a matter of fact, that the extremest cold of the Arctic Regions produces no bad effect, when the air is quite still. Mr King, who has recently returned from Capt. Back's Expedition, informed me that the greatest degree of cold he experienced was nearly 70° [Fahrenheit] below zero; that no inconvenience was felt at that low temperature, owing to the perfectly calm state of the air; but that if the wind arose, although the thermometer would likewise rapidly rise with the wind, the cold then became insupportable.

These facts I have proved in the one case, by the exposure to sun of *Hymenophyllum* and *Trichomanes*; and in the other by growing without heat, *Aspidium molle*, *Phoenix dactylifera*, *Rhapis flabelliformis*, *Dendrobium pulchellum*, *Mammillaria tenuis*, etc., etc.

3rdly, That owing to the prevention of the escape of the moisture contained within the cases, plants will grow for many months, and even for years, without requiring fresh supplies of water. Thus, in the first experiment, the *Poa* and *Nephrodium* grew for four years, without one drop of water having been given to them during that period, and would, I believe, have grown as many more, had they not accidentally perished in consequence of the rusting of the tin lid covering the bottle, and the admission of rain-water.

4thly, That the degree of development to which the plants attain, depend mainly, *cæteris paribus* [other things being equal], upon the volume of air contained within the case, and upon the quantity of light and solar heat received by the plants. Thus to revert to the first experiment. The *Poa* and *Nephrodium*, being contained within a small bottle — the one flowered but once during its confinement, while the other did not produce any capsules. Both ferns and grasses, in my larger cases, flower and fruit well. Phaenogamous plants, for instance, such as *Ipomoea quamoclit* and *coccinea*, will not flower in a case exposed to the North, while in the same case, fully exposed to the South, these very plants come up from seed, and flower very well.

To sum up all, in every place where there is light, even in the centre of the most crowded and smoky cities, plants of almost every family may be grown, and particularly those which have heretofore been found the most difficult to cultivate. I have now, in a wide-mouthed bottle, simply and loosely covered with a tin lid, the following plants: — *Hymenophyllum tunbridgense* and *wilsonii*, *Trichomanes brevisetum*, *Hookeria lucens*, and other mosses, *Jungermannia juniperina* and *reptans*, etc., etc. These plants have been inclosed for twelve months, and are growing most vigorously, although they have not once been watered during that period. In my other cases, the ferns, palms, orchids, grasses, many monocotyledonous plants belonging to the families of Scitamineae, Bromeliaceae, etc. etc. grow very well; while on the contrary, the continued humid state of the atmosphere is unfavourable to the development of the flowers of most of the exogenous plants, excepting those which naturally grow in moist and shady situations, the *Linnaea borealis*, for instance, which I have had for more than two years, and which flowered twice last year in a situation where, without my protecting cases, the London Pride (*Saxifraga umbrosa*) ceases to exist after twelve or eighteen months.[1]

Ward then acknowledged the help of the nursery firm of Messrs Loddiges, who had supplied him with plants for his experiments and then proceeded:

I come now to the most important application of the above facts: that of the conveyance of plants upon long voyages. Reflecting upon the causes of the failure attending such conveyance, arising chiefly from deficiency or redundancy of water, from the spray of the sea, or from the want of light in protecting them from the spray, it was, of course, evident that my new method offered a ready means of obviating all these difficulties, and in the beginning of June, 1833, I filled two cases with ferns, grasses, etc., and sent them to Sydney under the care of my zealous friend, Captain Mallard, copies of whose letters I have enclosed.

The cases were refilled at Sydney, in the month of February, 1834, the thermometer then being between 90° and 100° [Fahrenheit]. In their passage to England, they encountered very varying temperatures. The thermometer fell to 20° in rounding Cape Horn, and the decks were covered a foot deep with snow. In crossing the line the thermometer rose to 120°, and fell to 40° on their arrival in the British channel, in the beginning of November, eight months after they were enclosed. These plants were not once watered during their voyage, received no protection by day or by night, but were yet taken out at Loddiges' in the most healthy and vigorous condition. The plants chiefly consisted of ferns, among them *Gleichenia microphylla* never before introduced alive, and the *Hymenophyllum tunbridgense*. Several plants of *Callicoma serrata* had come up from seed during the voyage, and were in a very healthy state. As this experiment was made chiefly with ferns, I will briefly give you an account of one other experiment, in which plants of a higher order of development were the subject of trial. Ibrahim Pacha being desirous to obtain useful and ornamental plants for his garden near Cairo, and at Damascus, commissioned his agents in this country to send them. I was requested by his agents to select them, and they were sent out in August, 1834, in the Nile Steamer, to Alexandria. They were about two months on their passage ... Various other trials have been made to other parts of the world, as Calcutta, Para, etc. etc., and with the same success.[1]

Ward then responded to an inquiry as to the advisability of taking glazed boxes to Brazil:

I should imagine that these may be easily procured at Rio, and various other places; but if glass cannot be obtained, or is very dear, then a number of small panes might be carried, for use, as occasion requires.

It may be as well to state, once for all, that the success of my plan is in exact proportion to the admission of light to all parts of the growing plants, and to the due regulation of humidity of the mould wherein they grow. It is safer, in all instances, to give rather too little than too much water.[1]

Although there were occasional casualties, Wardian Cases revolutionised the transport of plants between far-flung countries. Robert Fortune used them to transport 20,000 tea plants from China to India. They were also used in the introduction of the quinine tree from South America to India and Java, rubber trees from South America to Malaya and Java, bananas from south-east Asia to other tropical regions, and coffee from Africa to the New World. In England, the development of the case also ushered in an early-Victorian craze for the cultivation and display of ferns.[2]

The arrival of the aeroplane eventually put an end to their use, although the Royal Botanic Gardens, Kew, continued using Wardian Cases up to World War II.[3]

REFERENCES & NOTES

Note: Letters examined in the Library and Archives of the Royal Botanic Gardens, Kew, are mainly part of the Directors' Correspondence, herewith abbreviated as 'Dir. Corres.', and are published with the kind permission of the Trustees of the Royal Botanic Gardens, Kew.

INTRODUCTION

1. Kimber, R. G. (1990). 'Flint, Ernest Ebenezer Samuel'. *In* Carment, D., Maynard, R. & Powell, A. (eds). *Northern Territory Dictionary of Biography. Volume One: to 1945.* (Northern Territory University Press: Casuarina). pp. 101–103.
2. Gregory, A. C. & Gregory, F. T. (1884). *Journals of Australian Explorations.* (Government Printer: Brisbane).
3. *Colonel Warburton's Explorations, 1872–3.* (Report No. 28 to South Australian Parliament, including extracts from Warburton's subsequently published journal.)
4. Willis, J. H., Pearson, D., Davis, M. T. & Green, J. W. (1986). 'Australian Plant Collectors: Collectors and Illustrators 1780s–1980s'. *Western Australian Herbarium Research Notes* 12: 1–111. A tally of data from this work showed c. 1,030 men and c. 135 women collected plants prior to 1901.
5. Hamersley, M. J. (1981). 'Botany and society in the Swan River Colony'. *In* Carr, D. J. & Carr, S. G. M. (eds). *People and Plants in Australia.* (Academic Press: Sydney). pp. 259–279.
6. Bassett, M. (1981). 'Augusta and Mrs Molloy'. *In* Carr, D. J. & Carr, S. G. M. (eds). *People and Plants in Australia.* (Academic Press: Sydney). pp. 357–373.

AFRICA
J. R. T. Vogel

1. Treviranus, L. C. (1846). 'Memoir of the life of Dr J. R. T. Vogel ... followed by Dr Vogel's Journal of the Voyage up the Niger ...'. *London Journal of Botany* 5: 600–644; 6: 79–106. Translated from the original German by the Rev. M. J. Berkeley; memoir first published in *Linnaea* 16. 533–560 (1842).
2. Extract from letter dated 30 June 1841, ibid.
3. Extract from letter dated 9 Aug. 1841, ibid.
4. Extract from letter dated 18 Sept. 1841, ibid.
5. Extract from letter dated 22 Oct. 1841, ibid.
6. Extract from letter dated 22 Nov. 1841, ibid.
7. McWilliam, J. O. (1843). *Medical History of the Expedition to the Niger During the Years 1841–2.* (John Churchill: London).

R. W. Plant

1. Gunn, M. & Codd, L. E. (1981). *Botanical Exploration of Southern Africa.* (A. A. Balkema: Cape Town).
2. Extracts from Plant, R. W. (1852). 'Notice of an excursion in the Zulu country'. *Hooker's Journal of Botany and Kew Garden Miscellany* 4: 257–265.

C. Barter

1. Anon. (1859). 'Obituary notices'. *Proceedings of the Linnean Society of London* 1859: xx–xxi.
2. Letter from W. B. Baikie to W. J. Hooker, written on board the S. S. *Dayspring* off Rabba, dated 22 Sept. 1857 (Dir. Corres. 59: 32). Published in *Gardeners' Chronicle* 1858: 37.

3. Letter to W. J. Hooker, written near Jeba, River 'Quorra', dated 30 Oct. 1857 (Dir. Corres. 59: 46). Published in *Gardeners' Chronicle* 1858: 54–55.

4. Letter to W. J. Hooker, written near Kétsa, River Kworra, dated 3 July 1858 (Dir. Corres. 59: 69). Published in *Gardeners' Chronicle* 1859: 170.

5. Letter to W. J. Hooker, written from Jeba, River Kworra, dated 18 Sept. 1858 (Dir. Corres. 59: 71). Published in *Gardeners' Chronicle* 1859: 218.

6. Letter to W. J. Hooker, written aboard the *Rainbow*, dated 2 Jan. 1859. Published in *Journal of the Proceedings of the Linnean Society, Botany*. 4: 17–23. Original not located.

F. M. J. Welwitsch

1. Trimen, H. (1873). 'Friedrich Welwitsch'. *Journal of Botany, British and Foreign* 11: 1–11.

2. Dyer, R. A. & Verdoorn, I. C. (1978). 'Science or sentiment: the *Welwitschia* problem'. *Taxon* 21: 485–489.

3. Extract from a letter from Welwitsch to W. J. Hooker, written from S. Paulo de Loando, dated 16 August 1860, and published in the *Journal of the Proceedings of the Linnean Society, Botany* 5: 182–187 (1861).

J. T. Baines

1. Gunn, M. & Codd, L. E. (1981). *Botanical Exploration of Southern Africa*. (A. A. Balkema: Cape Town).

2. Baines, [J.] T. (1866). 'The great-tree-aloe of Damara Land, S.W. Africa'. *Nature & Art* Dec. 1866: 200–204.

3. Van den Eynden, V., Vernemmen, P. & Van Damme, P. (1992). *The Ethnobotany of the Topnaar*. (Universiteit Gent: Gent, Belgium). p. 78.

W. G. Milne

1. Moore, D. (1866). 'The late Mr Grant Milne'. *Gardeners' Chronicle* 1866: 731.

2. Anon. (1866). 'Notice of the death of Mr William Grant Milne'. *Transactions of the Botanical Society, Edinburgh* 8: 485–486.

3. Letter to J. Sadler, sent from Creek Town, Old Calabar, dated 29 June 1863. Published in *Transactions of the Botanical Society, Edinburgh* 8: 71–73 (1864).

4. Letter to J. Sadler, sent from Creek Town, Old Calabar, dated 1 July 1863. Published in *Transactions of the Botanical Society, Edinburgh* 8: 72–73 (1864).

5. Letter sent from Gaboon, dated 22 March 1865. Published in *Journal of Botany, British and Foreign* 3: 193–195 (1865).

6. Letter to David Moore, sent from the Cameroons River, dated 28 June 1865. Photocopy provided by Dr E. C. Nelson. Partly published in Nelson, E. C. & McCracken, E. M. (1997). *The Brightest Jewel. A History of the National Botanic Gardens, Glasnevin, Dublin.* (Boethius Press: Kilkenny). p. 164.

7. Letter to David Moore, sent from Fernando Po, Cameroons River, dated 26 July 1865. Photocopy provided by Dr E. C. Nelson. Copy of original published in Nelson, E. C. & McCracken, E. M. (1997). *The Brightest Jewel. A History of the National Botanic Gardens, Glasnevin, Dublin.* (Boethius Press: Kilkenny). p. 165.

8. Letter to David Moore, sent from Fernando Po, Cameroons River, dated 26 Nov. 1865. Photocopy provided by Dr E. C. Nelson. Also published in Nelson, E. C. & McCracken, E. M. (1997). *The Brightest Jewel. A History of the National Botanic Gardens, Glasnevin, Dublin.* (Boethius Press: Kilkenny). p. 163.

ASIA

J. Arnold

1. Bastin, J. (1973). 'Dr Joseph Arnold and the discovery of *Rafflesia arnoldii* in west Sumatra in 1818'. *Journal of the Society for Bibliography of Natural History* 6: 305–372.

2. Brown, R. (1822). 'An account of a new genus of plant, named *Rafflesia*'. *Transactions of the Linnean Society of London* 13: 201–234. Includes letters from Raffles to Banks and from Arnold to Turner.

3. Beaman, R. S., Decker, P. J. & Beaman, J. H. (1988). 'Pollination of *Rafflesia* (Rafflesiaceae)'. *American Journal of Botany* 75(8): 1148–1162.

4. Meijer, W. (1997). 'Rafflesiaceae'. *Flora malesiana*. Series I, 13: 1–42.

G. W. & A. W. Walker

1. Burkill, I. H. (1965). *Chapters on the history of botany in India*. (Botanical Survey of India: Calcutta).

2. Extract from letter published in *Companion to the Botanical Magazine* 1: 3–14 (1835). Original not located.

3. Letter to W. J. Hooker, sent from Colombo, and dated 4 Jan. 1837. (Dir. Corres. 53: 133).

J. D. Hooker

1. Desmond, R. (1999). *Sir Joseph Dalton Hooker. Traveller and Plant Collector.* (Antique Collectors' Club: Woodbridge, Surrey).

2. *Hooker's Journal of Botany and Kew Garden Miscellany* 1: 1–14, 81–89, 113–136, 161–175, 226–233, 274–282, 301–308, 331–336, and 361–370 (1849). Under the title 'Calcutta to Darjeeling in Sikkim-Himalayah'.

3. Mabberley, D. J. (1990). *The Plant-book*. (Cambridge University Press: Cambridge).

4. *Hooker's Journal of Botany and Kew Garden Miscellany* 2: 17–23, 52–59, 88–91, 112–118, and 145–151. Under the title 'Excursion from Darjeeling to Tonglo, a Mountain on the Frontier of Nepal. May 1848'.

5. Hooker, J. D. (1891). *Himalayan Journals; or, Notes of a Naturalist in Bengal, the Sikkim and Nepal Himalayas, the Khasia Mountains, &c.* (Ward, Lock, Bowden & Co.: London).

R. Fortune

1. Van Steenis-Kruseman, M. J. (1950). 'Robert Fortune'. *Flora malesiana*. Series 1, 1: 179–180.

2. Fortune, R. (1850). 'Notes of a traveller. No. VII. The bamboo, and the uses to which it is applied in China'. *Gardeners' Chronicle*, 1850: 70.

3. Fortune, R. (1855). 'Leaves from my Chinese note book: No. 8. — A journey in search of a new cedar or larch, called *Abies kaempferi*'. *Gardeners' Chronicle*, 1855: 242.

4. Walter, K. S. & Gillett, H. J. (1998). *1997 IUCN Red List of Threatened Plant Species.* (IUCN Publication Services Unit: Cambridge, U.K.).

J. Motley

1. Van Steenis-Kruseman, M. J. (1950). 'James Motley'. *Flora malesiana*. Series 1, 1: 373.

2. Letter to W. J. Hooker, written from Banjarmasin, dated March 1855, and published in *Hooker's Journal of Botany and Kew Garden Miscellany* 7: 257–269.

3. Corner, E. J. H. (1993). *Botanical Monkeys*. (Pentland Press Ltd: Edinburgh).

4. Burkill, I. H. (1918). 'The circumstances attending the murder in 1859 of the botanist James Motley'. *Journal of the Straits Branch of the Royal Asiatic Society* 79: 37–38.

F. W. Burbidge

1. Britten, J. (1906). *Journal of Botany, British and Foreign* 44: 80.

2. Burbidge, F. W. (1880). *The Gardens of the Sun: or a Naturalist's Journal on the Mountains and in the Forests and Swamps of Borneo and the Sulu Archipelago.* (John Murray: London).

H. O. Forbes

1. Gibbney, H. J. (1972). 'Forbes, Henry Ogg'. *In* Pyke, D. (general ed.). *Australian Dictionary of Biography. Vol. 4: 1851–1890. D–J.* (Melbourne University Press: Carlton). pp. 195–196.

2. Forbes, H. O. (1885). *A Naturalist's Wanderings in the Eastern Archipelago, a Narrative of Travel and Exploration from 1878 to 1883.* (Sampson Low, Marston, Searle & Rivington: London).

3. Huxley, C. R. (1998). 'The tuberous epiphytic Rubiaceae — the Hydnophytinae'. *In* Hopkins, H. C. F., Huxley, C.R., Pannell, C. M., Prance, G. T. & White, F., *The Biological Monograph. The Importance of Field Studies and Functional Syndromes for Taxonomy and Evolution of Tropical Plants.* (Royal Botanic Gardens, Kew). pp. 81–92.

G. Forrest

1. Cooper, R. E., Curle, A. O. & Fair, W. S. (eds.) (1935). *George Forrest, V.M.H. Explorer and Botanist who by his Discoveries and Plants Successfully Introduced has Greatly Enriched our Gardens. 1873–1932.* (The Scottish Rock Garden Club: Edinburgh).

2. Cowan, J. M. (ed.). (1952). *The Journeys and Plant Introductions of George Forrest V.M.H.* (Oxford University Press: London).

3. Forrest, G. (1910). 'The perils of plant collecting'. *Gardeners' Chronicle*, May 1910: 325–326, and 344.

4. Extract from letter cited in Cooper R. E., Curle, A. O. & Fair, W. S. (eds.) (1935). *George Forrest, V.M.H. Explorer and Botanist who by his Discoveries and Plants Successfully Introduced has Greatly Enriched our Gardens. 1873–1932.* (The Scottish Rock Garden Club: Edinburgh). p. 28.

5. Desmond, R. (1987). *A Celebration of Flowers. Two Hundred Years of Curtis's Botanical Magazine.* (The Royal Botanic Gardens, Kew).

AUSTRALIA & NEW ZEALAND
R. W. Lawrence

1. Lawrence, R. W. (1834). 'Notes on an excursion up the Western Mountains of Van Diemen's Land'. *Journal of Botany (*ed. by W. J. Hooker*)* 1: 235–241.

2. Hooker, W. J. (1836). 'Contributions towards a flora of Van Diemen's Land'. *Companion to the Botanical Magazine* 1: 272–277.

3. Letter from R. C. Gunn, cited by W. J. Hooker in *Companion to the Botanical Magazine* 1: 272 (1836).

4. Hooker, W. J. (1840). *Lawrencia spicata. Hooker's Icones Plantarum* 3: t. 261–262.

5. Buchanan, A. M. (1990). 'Ronald Campbell Gunn (1808–1881)'. *In* Short, P. S. (ed.). *History of systematic botany in Australasia.* (Australian Systematic Botany Society Inc.). pp. 179–192.

6. Hooker, J. D. (1859). *The Botany of the Antarctic Voyage of H. M. Discovery Ships, Erebus and Terror, in the years 1839–1843, under the command of Captain Sir James Clark Ross. Part III. Flora tasmaniae.* (Lovell Reeve: London). Vol. 1, p. cxxv.

J. Drummond

1. Erickson, R. (1969). *The Drummonds of Hawthornden.* (Lamb Paterson: Perth).

2. Nelson, E. C. (1990). 'James and Thomas Drummond: their Scottish origins and curatorships in Irish botanic gardens (ca 1808–ca 1831)'. *Archives of Natural History* 17: 49–65.

3. Letter to W. J. Hooker dated June 1839. Published in *Journal of Botany (*ed. W. J. Hooker*)* 2: 344–345 (1840). Original not located.

4. Postscript to letter to W. J. Hooker, dated 3 Sept. 1840. Published in *Journal of Botany (*Ed. W. J. Hooker*)* 4: 79–86 (1842). Original not located. A letter of the same date is at Kew but the subject matter is different.

5. Cameron, J. M. R. (1977). 'Poison plants in Western Australia and coloniser problem solving'. *Journal of the Royal Society of Western Australia* 59: 71–77.

6. Oliver, A. J., King, D. R. & Mead, R. J. (1977). 'The evolution of resistance to fluoroacetate intoxication in mammals'. *Search* 8: 130–132.

7. Letter to W. J. Hooker, sent from the Swan River, dated 2 July 1841 (Dir. Corres. 76: 10). Published in *London Journal of Botany* 1: 215–217.

8. Letter to W. J. Hooker, sent from Cape Riche, dated 16 Jan. 1847 (Dir. Corres. 73: 144), edited and published in part in *Botanical Magazine* 74, *Companion*: 1–3 (1848). Drummond's account of this journey was first published in *The Inquirer* (7 and 14 April 1847) and that text has been republished in its entirety in *Nuytsia* 11: 1–9 (1996).

9. Letter to W. J. Hooker, dated 27 December 1847 (Dir. Corres. 74: 62). Published in Erickson, R. (1969). *The Drummonds of Hawthornden.* (Lamb Paterson: Perth). p. 118.

10. Undated manuscript (Dir. Corres. 74: p. 66). Published in *The Perth Gazette* (23 April 1852) and in *Hooker's Journal of Botany and Kew Garden Miscellany* 5: 118–122 (1853).

11. Fisher, L. J. (ed.). (1869). *Memoir of W. H. Harvey, M.D., F.R.S. ...* (Bell & Daldy: London). pp. 269–270.

W. Colenso

1. Hector, J. *et al.* (1899). Minutes of Annual General meeting of the Wellington Philosophical Society. *Transactions and Proceedings of the New Zealand Institute* 31: 722–724 (1899).

2. Lièvre, A. le. (1990). 'William Colenso, New Zealand botanist: something of his life and work'. *The Kew Magazine* 7: 186–200.

3. Colenso, W. (1884). *An Account of Visits to, and Crossing over, the Ruahine Mountain Range, Hawke's Bay, New Zealand; and of the Natural History of that Region; Performed in 1845–1847: cum multis aliis.* (Daily Telegraph Office: Napier, New Zealand).

F. W. L. Leichhardt

1. Aurousseau, M. (ed.). (1968). *The Letters of F. W. Ludwig Leichhardt.* (Cambridge University Press for the Hakluyt Society: Cambridge).

2. Leichhardt, L. (1847). *Journal of an Overland Expedition in Australia, from Moreton Bay to Port Essington, a Distance of Upwards of 3000 miles, During the Years 1844–1845.* (T. & W. Boone: London).

3. Jackes, B. R. (1990). 'Retracing the botanical steps of Leichhardt and Gilbert in June 1845'. *In* Short, P. S. (ed.). *History of Systematic Botany in Australasia.* (Australian Systematic Botany Society). pp. 165–169.

4. Leichhardt in letter written from Camden, dated 20 May 1846, to G. Durando. Published in Aurousseau, M. (ed.) (1968). *The Letters of F. W. Ludwig Leichhardt.* (Cambridge University Press for the Hakluyt Society: Cambridge). pp. 868–872.

5. McLaren, G. (1996). *Beyond Leichhardt. Bushcraft and the Exploration of Australia.* (Fremantle Arts Centre Press: South Fremantle, Western Australia).

6. Webster, E. M. (1980). *Whirlwinds in the Plain; Ludwig Leichhardt — Friends, Foes and History.* (Melbourne University Press: Carlton).

F. Mueller

1. Short, P. S. (1990). 'Politics and the purchase of private herbaria by the National Herbarium of Victoria'. *In* Short, P. S. (ed.). *History of Systematic Botany in Australasia.* (Australian Systematic Botany Society). pp. 5–12.

2. Home, R. W., Lucas, A. M., Maroske, S., Sinkora, D. M. & Voight, J. H. (eds). (1998). *Regardfully Yours. Selected Correspondence of Ferdinand von Mueller. Volume 1: 1840–1859.* (Peter Lang: Bern).

3. Birman, W. (1979). *Gregory of Rainworth. A Man in his Time.* (University of Western Australia Press: Nedlands).

4. Letter to W. J. Hooker, written from Melbourne, dated 14 Jan. 1857 (Dir. Corres. 74: 155). Published in *Hooker's Journal of Botany and Kew Garden Miscellany* 9: 165–173 (1857).

W. E. P. Giles

1. Feeken, E. H. J., Feeken, G. E. E. & Spate, O. H. K. (1970). *The Discovery and Exploration of Australia.* (Nelson: Melbourne).

2. Giles, E. (1875). *Geographic Travels in Central Australia. From 1872 to 1874.* (McBarron, Bird & Co.: Melbourne).

3. Lazarides, M. (1997). 'A revision of *Triodia* including *Plectrachne* (Poaceae, Eragrostideae, Triodiinae)'. *Australian Systematic Botany* 10: 381–489.

4. Giles, E. (1889). *Australia Twice Traversed.* (Sampson, Low, Searle & Rivington: London).

5. Forrest, J. (1875). *Explorations in Australia.* (Sampson Low, Marston, Low & Searle: London).

D. Sullivan

1. Willis, J. H. (1949). 'Botanical pioneers in Victoria — III'. *Victorian Naturalist* 66: 123–128.

2. Sullivan, D. (1882). 'Native plants of the Grampians and vicinity'. *Southern Science Record* 2: 51–54.

3. Sullivan, D. (1882). 'Victorian Leguminosae'. *Southern Science Record* 2: 249–251.

W. B. Spencer

1. Spencer, B. (1896). 'Through Larapinta Land'. *In* B. Spencer, (ed.). *Report on the Work of the Horn Scientific Expedition to Central Australia. Part I.* (Melville, Mullen & Slade: Melbourne and Dulau & Co.: Soho Square). pp. 1–136. [A facsimile copy of this work was published by Corkwood Press, Bundaberg, Queensland, in 1994.]

2. Mulvaney, D. J. (1990). 'Walter Baldwin Spencer'. *In* D. Carment, R. Maynard & A. Powell, (eds). *Northern Territory Dictionary of Biography. Vol. One: to 1945.* (Northern Territory University Press: Casuarina). pp. 268–270.

3. Morton, S. R. & Mulvaney, D. J. (eds). (1996). *Exploring Central Australia. Society, the Environment and the 1894 Horn Expedition.* (Surrey Beatty & Sons: Chipping Norton).

F. J. Gillen

1. Morton, S. R. & Mulvaney, D. J. (eds). (1996). *Exploring Central Australia. Society, the Environment and the 1894 Horn Expedition.* (Surrey Beatty & Sons: Chipping Norton, NSW).

2. Letter from Gillen to Spencer, dated 12 October 1894. Original letter from the Spencer Papers, Box 2/2, Manuscript Collections, Pitt Rivers Museum, Oxford. This extract mostly cited in Mulvaney, D. J. (1996). ' "A splendid lot of fellow": achievements and consequences of the Horn Expedition'. *In* S. R. Morton & D. J. Mulvaney, (eds). *Exploring Central Australia. Society, the Environment and the 1894 Horn Expedition.* (Surrey Beatty & Sons: Chipping Norton, NSW). pp. 3–12. The full letter has been published in Mulvaney, J., Morphy, H. & Petch, A. (eds). (1997). *'My Dear Spencer': the letters of F. J. Gillen to Baldwin Spencer.* (Hyland House: Melbourne). pp. 53–57.

M. Koch

1. Short, P. S. (1990). 'Politics and the purchase of private herbaria by the National Herbarium of Victoria'. *In* Short, P. S. (ed.) *History of Systematic Botany in Australasia.* (Australian Systematic Botany Society Inc.). pp. 5–12.

2. Audas, J. W. (1929). 'The botanical activities of Max Koch'. *Journal of the Royal Society of Western Australia* 15: 83–86.

3. Letter to W. Thiselton-Dyer, Kew, sent from Mt Lyndhurst, dated 6 March 1899. (Dir. Corres. 172: 36).

4. Letter to the Director, Kew, sent from Pemberton, dated 5 March 1924. (Dir. Corres. 169: 443–445).

5. Letter to the Director, Kew, sent from Pemberton, dated 30 Sept. 1924. (Dir. Corres. 169: 446–447).

6. Letter to W. Laidlaw, dated 24 January 1925. Library, National Herbarium of Victoria, Melbourne.

W. A. Michell

1. Letter to William N. Winn, sent from Whim Creek, dated 20 Sept. 1903 (Dir. Corres. 170: 340–341).
2. Unpublished lists and letters in the Library and Archives of the Royal Botanic Gardens, Kew. (Plant lists. Australia & New Zealand 1897–1916, 51: 88–91).
3. Farmar, L. (1905). 'Contributions to our knowledge of Australian Amarantaceae'. *Bulletin de l'herbier Boissier* 5: 1085–1091.

EUROPE
P. E. Boissier

1. Anon. (1886). Obituary notices. *Transactions of the Botanical Society, Edinburgh* 16: 308–309.
2. Lièvre, A. le (1994). 'A review of Edmond Boissier'. *The Kew Magazine* 11: 131–143.
3. Extracts from the part of Boissier's *Voyage Botanique dans le Midi de l'Espagne* published in *London Journal of Botany* 4: 157–166, and 385–393 (1845).

J. H. Balfour

1. Balfour, I. B. (1913). 'A sketch of the Professors of Botany in Edinburgh from 1670 until 1887'. *In* Oliver. F. W. (ed.). *Makers of British Botany*. (University Press: Cambridge).
2. Balfour J. H. (1844). 'Account of a botanical excursion to the Mull of Cantyre, and the Island of Islay, in August, 1844'. Reprinted from the *Proceedings of the Philosophical Society of Glasgow*.
3. Rendall, V. (1934). *Wild Flowers in Literature*. (The Scholartis Press: London).
4. Baker, J. G. (1881). 'In memory of Hewett Cottrell Watson'. *Journal of Botany, British and Foreign* 19: 257–265.
5. Balfour, J. H. (?1869). *Account of Botanical Excursions made in the Island of Arran During the Months of August and September, 1869*. (Edinburgh).

NORTH AMERICA
T. Drummond

1. Nelson, E. C. (1990). 'James and Thomas Drummond: their Scottish origins and curatorships in Irish botanic gardens (ca 1808–ca 1831)'. *Archives of Natural History* 17: 49–65.
2. Coates, A. M. (1969). *The Quest for Plants; a History of the Horticultural Explorers*. (Studio Vista: London).
3. Drummond, T. (1830). 'Sketch of a journey to the Rocky Mountains and to the Columbia River in North America'. *Botanical Miscellany* 1: 178–219.
4. Berlandier, J.-L. (1980). *Journey to Mexico during the Years 1826–1834*. (Texas State Historical Association: Austin, Texas). Cited in Davidson, A. (1999). *The Oxford Companion to Food*. (Oxford University Press: Oxford).
5. Hooker, W. J. (1834). 'Notice concerning Mr Drummond's collections, made in the southern and western parts of the United States'. *Journal of Botany (*ed. W. J. Hooker*)* 1: 50–60.
6. Letter to W. J. Hooker, sent from Apalchicola, Florida, dated 9 Feb. 1835 (Dir. Corres. 62: 75). Published in *Companion to the Botanical Magazine* 1: 39–49 (1835).
7. Hooker, W. J. (1835). '*Phlox drummondii*'. *Botanical Magazine*, t. 3441.

D. Douglas

1. Hooker, W. J. (1836). 'A brief memoir of the life of Mr David Douglas, with extracts from his letters'. *Companion to the Botanical Magazine* 2: 79–182.
2. Douglas, D. (1959). *Journal kept by David Douglas During his Travels in North America 1823–1827*. (Antiquarian Press: New York). [First publ. 1914.]
3. Harvey, A. G. (1947). *Douglas of the Fir*. (Harvard University Press: Cambridge, Massachusetts, U.S.A.).

4. Morwood, W. (1973). *Traveller in a Vanished Landscape. The Life and Times of David Douglas.* (Gentry Books: London).

5. Extract from Douglas's journal, partly published in the *Companion to the Botanical Magazine* 2: 79–182.

6. Letter to W. J. Hooker, sent from Monterey, dated 23 Nov. 1831 (Dir. Corres. 61: 104). Published in the *Companion to the Botanical Magazine* 2: 79–182.

7. Notes accompanying Hooker's description of the moss *Neckera douglassii* in *Botanical Miscellany* 1: 131–132, t. 35.

A. Gray

1. Stafleu, F. A. & Cowan, R. S. (1983). *Taxonomic Literature. A Selective Guide to Botanical Publications and Collections with Dates, Commentaries and Types.* 2nd edn. (Bohn, Scheltema & Holkema: Utrecht). Vol. 1, pp. 983–993.

2. Gray, A. (1842–1844). 'Notes on a botanical excursion to the mountains of North Carolina etc.; with some remarks on the botany of the higher Alleghany [*sic*] Mountains'. (In a letter to Sir W. J. Hooker, by Asa Gray, M.D.) *London Journal of Botany* 1: 1–14, 217–237; 2: 113–125; 3: 230–242.

3. Krebs, C. J. (1972). *Ecology. The Experimental Analysis of Distribution and Abundance.* (Harper & Row: New York).

4. Carefoot, G. L. & Sprott, E. R. (1967). *Famine on the Wind.* (Angus & Robertson: London). Cited in *Fungi of Australia* 1A: 292 (1996).

5. Warnement, J. (1997). 'Botanical libraries and herbaria in North America, 3. Harvard's botanists and their libraries'. *Taxon* 46: 649–660.

C. Geyer

1. Letter from H. G. Reichenbach to J. D. Hooker, published in *Hooker's Journal of Botany and Kew Garden Miscellany* 7: 181–183.

2. Geyer, C. A. (1845–1847). 'Notes on the vegetation and general character of the Missouri and Oregon territories, made during a botanical journey from the State of Missouri, across the south-pass of the Rocky Mountains, to the Pacific, during the years 1843 and 1844'. *London Journal of Botany* 4: 479– 492, 653– 662; 5: 22– 41, 198–208, 285–310, 509–524; 6: 65–79.

CENTRAL AMERICA & SOUTH AMERICA

G. U. Skinner

1. Bateman, J. (1867). *Gardeners' Chronicle* 1867: 180–181.

2. Letter to W. J. Hooker, sent from Guatemala, dated 16 May 1837 (Dir. Corres. 67: 180).

3. Letter to W. J. Hooker, sent from Guatemala, dated 5 June 1837 (Dir. Corres. 67: 180A).

4. Letter to W. J. Hooker, sent from Guatemala, dated 17 Feb. 1838 (Dir. Corres. 68: 121).

5. Letter to W. J. Hooker, sent from Guatemala, dated 2 April 1841 (Dir. Corres. 69: 312).

6. Stafleu, F. A. & Cowan, R. S. (1979). *Taxonomic Literature. A Selective Guide to Botanical Publications and Collections with Dates, Commentaries and Types.* 2nd edn. (Bohn, Scheltema & Holkema: Utrecht). Volume 2, p. 70.

F. W. Hostmann

1. Letter to W. J. Hooker, sent from Paramaribo, dated 21 Nov. 1838 (Dir. Corres. 68: 490).

2. Letter to W. J. Hooker, sent from Paramaribo, dated 14 Dec. 1840 (Dir. Corres. 69: 124). Highly edited and published in *London Journal of Botany* 1: 97–106.

3. Letter to W. J. Hooker, sent from Paramaribo (Dir. Corres. 69: 123). Dated, in part, as 23 April 1841 but its content and the letter of 10 May 1841 suggest that most of it was written, but not sent, in the previous year. Highly edited and published in *London Journal of Botany* 1: 97–106.

4. Letter to W. J. Hooker, sent from Paramaribo, dated 10 May 1841 (Dir. Corres. 69: 125). A highly edited version published in *London Journal of Botany* 1: 605– 626.

5. Dr W. Wüster, University of Wales, pers. comm., dated 17 June 2000.
6. Letter to W. J. Hooker, sent from Paramaribo, dated 10 Aug. 1843 (Dir. Corres. 69: 131).

T. L. Bridges

1. Anon. (1866). Untitled, being a notice of the death of Thomas Bridges as reported in an unnamed Californian paper. *Transactions of the Botanical Society, Edinburgh* 8: 434–435.
2. Letter to W. J. Hooker, sent from Cochabamba, dated 3 April 1845 (Dir. Corres. 70: 9). Published in *London Journal of Botany* 4: 571–577 (1845).
3. Letter cited in Curtis's *Botanical Magazine* 73: t. 4275– 4278 (1847).

R. Spruce

1. Spruce, R. (1908). *Notes of a Botanist on the Amazon & Andes ... Edited and condensed by Alfred Wallace ...* (Macmillan & Co., Ltd: London). Two vols.
2. Anon. (1895). 'Obituary notices'. *Proceedings of the Linnean Society of London* May 1895: 35–37.
3. Seaward, M. R. D. & Fitzgerald, S. M. D. (1996). *Richard Spruce (1817–1893). Botanist and Explorer.* (Royal Botanic Gardens, Kew).
4. Letter to G. Bentham, sent from Sao Gabriel, Rio Negro, dated 15 April 1852. Published in Spruce (1908), *Notes of A Botanist on the Amazon & Andes ... Edited and condensed by Alfred Wallace ...* (Macmillan & Co., Ltd: London). Vol. 1, pp. 290–298.

OCEANS & ISLANDS
J. D. Hooker

1. Desmond, R. (1999). *Sir Joseph Dalton Hooker. Traveller and Plant Collector.* (Antique Collectors' Club: Woodbridge, Surrey).
2. Hooker, W. J. (1843). 'Notes on the botany of H. M. Discovery ships, *Erebus* and *Terror* in the Antarctic Voyage; with some account of the Tussac Grass of the Falkland Islands'. *London Journal of Botany* 2: 247–329.

W. G. Milne

1. Moore, D. (1866). 'The late Mr Grant Milne'. *Gardeners' Chronicle* 1866: 731.
2. Anon. (1866). 'Notice of death of Mr William Grant Milne'. *Transactions of the Botanical Society, Edinburgh* 8: 485– 486.
3. David, A. (1995). *The Voyage of HMS* Herald *to Australia and the Southwest Pacific 1852–1861 under the Command of Captain Henry Mangles Denham.* (Melbourne University Press: Carlton).
4. Letter to W. J. Hooker, sent from Sydney, dated 10 May 1856 (Dir. Corres. 74: 109). This letter also published by David (ibid., p. 210) but without corrections to spelling.
5. Letter to W. J. Hooker, dated 7 Oct. 1856, and published in *Hooker's Journal of Botany and Kew Garden Miscellany* 9: 106–115. Original not located and the changes indicated by square brackets are the result of checking in David (1995). Milne's dates are not changed although they are apparently incorrect; for example, Friday 15 August, not 13 August.
6. Letter of resignation to Captain Denham dated 1858 (Dir. Corres. 74: 115).

B. C. Seemann

1. Anon. (1872). 'Berthold Seemann'. *Journal of Botany, British and Foreign* 10: 1–7 (1872).
2. Seemann, B. [C.] (1862). *Viti: an Account of a Government Mission to the Vitian or Fijian Islands in the years 1860–61.* (MacMillan & Co.: Cambridge).
3. Cambie, R. C. & Ash, J. (1994). *Fijian Medicinal Plants.* (CSIRO: Melbourne, Australia).

4. Croat, T. B. (1990). 'Colocasia'. *In* Wagner, W. L., Herbst, D. R. & Sohmer, S. H. *Manual of the Flowering Plants of Hawai'i.* (University of Hawaii Press: Hawaii). Volume 2, pp. 1356–1357.

5. Gardiner, B. G. (2000).' Berthold Carol [*sic*] Seemann'. *The Linnean*16(2): 6–12.

APPENDICES
Plant names

1. Greuter, W., McNeill, J., Barrie, F. R., Burdet, H. M., Demoulin, V., Filgueiras, T. S., Nicolson, D. H., Silva, P. C., Skog, J. E., Trehane, P., Turland, N. J., & Hawksworth, D. L., (eds). (2000). *International Code of Botanical Nomenclature (St Louis Code).* (Koeltz Scientific Books: Königstein, Germany).

2. Trehane, R. P., Brickell, C, D., Baum, B. R., Hetterscheid, W. L. A., Leslie, A. C., McNeill, J., Spongberg, S. A. & Vrugtman, F. (eds). *The International Code of Nomenclature for Cultivated Plants — 1995.* (Quarterjack Publishing: Wimborne, U.K.).

Herbaria

1. Stearn, W. T. (1957). 'An Introduction to the 'Species Plantarum' and Cognate Botanical Works of Carl Linnaeus.' (Prefixed to the Ray Society facsimile of Linnaeus, *Species Plantarum*, vol. 1). (London).

2. Stafleu, F. A. & Cowan, R. S. (1976). *Taxonomic Literature. A Selective Guide to Botanical Publications and Collections with Dates, Commentaries and Types.* 2nd edn. (Bohn, Scheltema & Holkema: Utrecht). Volume 1, p. 939.

3. Holmgren, P. K., Holmgren, N. H. & Barnett, L. C. (1990). *Index Herbariorum. Part I: the Herbaria of the World.* (New York Botanical Gardens).

4. Forman, L. & Bridson, D. (eds). (1989). *The Herbarium Handbook.* (Royal Botanic Gardens, Kew).

The Wardian Case

1. Ward, N. B. (1836). 'Letter from N. B. Ward, Esq. to Dr Hooker, on the subject of his improved method of transporting living plants'. *Companion to the Botanical Magazine* 1: 317–320.

2. Porter, D. M. (1971). 'Mr Ward's portable greenhouse'. *Missouri Botanical Garden Bulletin* 69: 16–20.

3. Desmond, R. (1987). *A Celebration of Flowers. Two Hundred Years of Curtis's Botanical Magazine.* (Collinridge: London).

INDEX

Page numbers in **bold** refer to illustrations.

A

Acacia catechu 59
accommodation
    boat & ship 4, 7, 62, 301
    huts 53, 56
    sinister 63
    Spanish hostelries 205
Aciphylla colensoi 148, 149
Acrostichum 83, 268
Adam's Peak 51–54, 56
Aegiceras majus 77
African, west
    housing 6
    native markets 5, 39
    servants 7
algae 24, 26, 300
Allegheny Mountainsns 238
Allocasuarina decaisneana **163**
Aloe dichotoma 33, **34**–36
Aluta maisonneuvii **163**, **164**
Amelanchier canadensis 245
American chestnut 243
Andalusian women 199, 200
Andersson, C. J. 32
Anka, district of (in Surinam) 273–277
ant plants 101, 102
ants 39
    as food 252
    attack by 101, 289
    fire 265
Arctomys ludovicianus 248, 250, 251
Armeria maritima **212**
Arnold, Joseph 47, **48**–50
    discovery of *Rafflesia arnoldii* 47
Arran (Is.) 211–214
Artemisia 251, 252

B

Baikie, William Balfour 19, 22, 23, 25
Baillie, Zerub 37
Baines, J. Thomas 31–36
Balfour, Isaac 211, 214
Balfour, John Hutton 206, **207**–214
bamboo 68, 79, 80, 106, 112, 113, 309, 315
    fish trap 80
    general uses 70–72
    part of tiger trap 104
Banksia 128–130
Barter, Charles 19–26
Bateman, James 263, 265, 267

Baudin, Captain Nicolas 179
bear, attack by 220–222
beaver **236**
beetles 32, 39
binomial system of plant-naming 323
bird nests, pendulous 88
blackboy (see *Xanthorrhoea*)
blight, of American chestnut 243
blue-bottle fly 143
Boissier, P. Edmond 199–205
    paper and trouble with customs 200
Bolivia 279–284
Borassus aethiopum 21
Bourdonnec, Père 110, 113
Bower, Colonel 242
brandy, medicinal 44
bridge, living **69**
Bridges, Thomas L. 279–284
    account of *Victoria amazonica* 281, **282**–284
Brown, Harry 151
Brown, Maitland x
bulbs 18
bullocks (see oxen)
Burbidge, Frederick William 90, **91**–99
    ascent of Mt Kinabalu 90–95
Burton, David vii
bushmaster 274
Bushmen 36
Butea frondosa 58
butter, as an emetic 179

C

cacti 265, 279–281
Calabar chop 38, 39
California 235
Calvert, Mr 153
camass 230, 256, 257
camels vii
    advantages compared to horses 178, 186
    poisoned 178–180
    qualities 184–189
Campbell, Mr 208
Campbelton 206
camping conditions 41, 42, 92, 161–163, 166, 224, 244, 257
cannibals 311, 315, 316, 318, 319
Carey, John 238
Carmichaelia 140
Castanea dentata 243
catechu 58, 59
caterpillars, irritant 36, 291
cats 89, 288, 289
Cattleya skinneri 268

Cereus 279–281
Chakoong 66, 68
Chapman, James 31
Charley (with Leichhardt) 153–155, 158
Chatfield, Mr 265
chestnut blight 243
Chinese tea, introduction to India 70, 334
cholera 263, 266
Citrus maxima 311
Clianthus formosus vii–ix
clothing, wear and tear 157
Coelogyne 93
Colenso, William 137, **138**–149, 301
  blue-bottle flies 143
  plant specimens carried in clothing 148
  tussle with *Aciphylla* 148, 149
Colocasia esculenta 39, **318**, 319
Columbia River 217, 220, 223, 229, 235, 254
Constable, J. 238
coolies 51–54, 56
Cope, H. M. 266
corn 13, 20
Corner, E. J. H. 87
Corylopsis spicata **71**
Corymbia ptychocarpa 323–325
Corysanthes 140
Crabbe, George 210
crocodiles 58, 86
Crowther, Reverend 21
Cryphonectria parasitica 243
cultivars, definition of 325
Cunningham, Richard vii
Curtis, Reverend A. 238
cushion plants **122**, 123
cycads, consumption of 154–157
Cycas arnhemica **155**

D
Dalton, Mr 21
Damaras, impersonating lion 32
Dampier, William viii
Danford, John Humphrey 311, 316
Darwinia 130
Davis, Mr 21
Dease, Mr 231
Dendrobium hookerianum 66, **67**
Dendrocnide harveyi 310
Denham, Henry Mangles 305, 307, 308
Derby, Earl of 279
Deschamps, Louis Auguste 50
diseases, high mortality from 8, 22
Douglas, David 225, 226, 229–**231**, 232–237, 248
  discovery of the sugar pine 233–235
  eating lichens 230
  hostile Indians 234, 235
  letters from home 233
  shooting prowess 229, 230

Douglas fir 236
Drake, Miss S. A. 265
Drummond, James 124, **125**–136, 225
  description of 135
  fungi 128, 129
  Hakea victoria 130, **131**, 132
  ophthalmia 132
  poisonous plants 126, 127
  Verticordia grandis 132, **133**–136
Drummond, Thomas 217–**219**, 220–228
  attack by grisly bear 220–222
  cold weather 222
  lonely existence 220
  snow blindness 223
  storm in Hudson Bay 225, 226
  winter camping and provisions 224
Dubernard, Père 108, 114
Dun-naomh-aig Fort 208
durian (*Durio zibethinus*) 95–**97**, 98, 99
dysentery 8, 26, 44

E
Echium vulgare 240
Eells, Mr 260
elephants, riding 57
emus, as food 154
Endothia parasitica 243
Epacris impressa 181
Epilobium angustifolium 207, **209**
Eucalyptus
  baxteri **183**
  coccifera **120**
  ptychocarpa 323–325

F
Falconer, William 276
Felle, Mr 60
Fernando Po 6, 41–44
ferns 42, 83, 84, 86, 144, 145, 147, 265, 268, 271,
  308, 310, 330–334
fever (see specific diseases)
Ficus elastica **69**
Fiji 305–319
Finlay, Mr 231, 232
fireflies 24, 87
fish
  diversity in Sumatra 81
  poison 38
fishing (in Sumatra) 79, 80
Fitch, Walter Hood 54, 65, 66, 299, 307, 316
flies
  abominable Australian 171
  as pollinators 50
Flint, Ebenezer vii, ix
food, priority over collections 158
Forbes, Henry Ogg 100–106
  ants and ant plants 101, 102

destruction of forests in Java 102
  encounter with tigers 102–105
  specimens lost in fire 105, 106
forests, destruction of 102
Forrest, George 107–116
  hunted by lamas 107–114
  loss of collections 114
  seed collections 114, 116
Forrest, John 164
Fort Assinaboyne 218, 222
Fort Colville 254, 256, 258, 259
Fortune, Robert 70–76, 334
  search for the golden larch 72–76
  value of bamboo 70–72
Franklin, John 217
Fumaria corymbosa 203
fungi, luminescent 128, 129

G
Ganges River 61, 62
Gardner, George 269
Gastrolobium calycinum **126**, 127
Genetyllis 130
Geum radiatum 244
Geyer, Carl Andreas 248–260
  congregation of rattlesnakes 252–254
  hardship of winter travel 254–260
  tobacco to stave off hunger 257
giant water lily 281, **282–284**, 324, 325
Gibson, Alfred 173–178
Gilbert, John vii, 157–159
  killed by Aboriginals 152–154
Giles, W. Ernest P. 167, **168**–180
  description of flies 171
  discovery of palm 168–**170**
  loss of Gibson 174–178
  mallee fowl eggs 173, 174
  poisoned camels 178–180
  Triodia and damage to horses 172, 173
Gillen, Francis James 190, 191
Glendinning, Mr 73
Glover, Lieutenant 23
golden larch 72–76
Goldie, Reverend & Mrs 39, 40
Grampian Ranges (Australia) 181, 183
Grandfather Mountain 244, **247**
grappler or grapple plant 32, 33
grasshoppers (*Gryllus*), eating of 252
Gray, Asa 238, **239–247**
Gregory, Augustus Charles 161, 163
Gregory, Francis Thomas vii, viii, x
Grevillea eriostachya **135**
Gryllus 252
Guatemala 263–268
Gunn, Ronald Campbell 123
gutta-percha 87
Gyrostemon ramulosus 178, **179**, 180

H
Hakea victoria 130, **131**, 132
Harpagophytum procumbens 32, 33
Harris, Joseph 127
Hartweg, Carl Theodor 267, 268
Harvey, William Henry 135
hat, made from *Helonias tenax* 230
Helichrysum incanum var. *alpinum* **165**
herbaria 326–328
  collecting specimens for 327, 328
  function 326, 327
  history of development 326
Hooker, Joseph Dalton 31, 57–58, **59–69**, 92, 123, 297–304
  hunting for tiger 60
  icebergs and collision of ships 302, 303
  India 57–69
  leeches 66
  on Kerguelen Island 297–301
  on the Ganges River 61, 62
  riding elephant 57
  ticks 65
Hooker, William Jackson x, 19, 51, 56, 69, 123, 226, 228. 229, 263, 269, 297, 329
Horn Scientific Expedition 184, 190, 191
horses
  as food 158
  as pack-animals 158, 161
  crashing through scrub 173
  drowned 158
  eating plant specimens 190, 191
  excessive heat fatal for 9
  injury from *Triodia* 172, 173
  suffering from thirst viii
  water requirements 178
Hostmann, F. W. 269–278
  encounter with venomous snake 273, 274
  near drowning in rapids 275, 276
  vampire bats 274
Howitt, Alfred William 188
Hudson Bay 224–226
Hudson's Bay Company 218, 220, 222, 223, 236, 248, 252
human flesh, accompaniments with 316
Hutchinson, Henry 32
Hutchinsonia 32
Hydnophytum 101, 102
  formicarum 101
Hylobates concolor 86

I
Impatiens walkeri **55**
Insect(s)
  attracted to light 7
  collection lost due to tribal warfare 18
  damage to plant collections 8
  odiferous 61

pests 7, 8, 61, 65, 66, 82, 143, 171, 251, 263, 287, 289–291
Islay (Is.) 208–210

J
Java 100–102
Jefferson 242, 243
Jungermannia 221, 222

K
Kangchenjunga **64**, 65
karang, source of lime 78
Kennedya nigricans 132
Kerguelen Island 297, 299–301
Kerguelen Island cabbage 297, **298**, 299
Kildaton church 209
Kintyre 206, 207
Klée, Mr 263
Kobes (with Forbes) 105
Koch, Max 192–195
Krause, K. 194
Kuruduadua, Chief 315, 318

L
Lachesis muta 274
Laelia superbiens **264**, 265, 267
Lagerstroemia regina 88
lamas, brutality of 113, 114
Laminaria 300
Lash, Mr 101
Latta, Mr 40
Lauche, Mr 43
Lawrence, Robert William vii, 119–123
Layard, E. 32
Laycock, C. 188
Lechenaultia macrantha **194**
leeches 66
Leichhardt, Friedrich Wilhelm Ludwig vii, 150–160, **151**, 163
    clothing problems 157
    death of John Gilbert 152–154
    loss of transport and specimens 158, 159
Leipoa ocellata 173, 174
lemon orchid **134**
letters
    burnt 43
    detained 18, 19
Leucochrysum albicans subsp. *alpinum* **165**
lichens 299, 300, 310
    eating 230, 231
Ligusticum actaeifolium 243
Lindley, John 135, 324, 325
Linnaeus, Carl 323
lions 10, 18, 31, 32
liverworts 221
Livistona mariae 168–**170**
Low, Hugh 92

M
Macaca nemenstrina 87
Macdonald, Chief-factor 254
McDonald, Mr 222
McMillan, Mr 220
Macrocystis pyrifera 300
magnolias in brandy and whiskey 241
Malaga 199, 200
malaria 21, 22
Mallard, Captain 333
Mangles, James 135
mallee fowl 174
Mann, Gustav 26
Melastoma 43
    denticulatum **306**, 307
men-of-the-sea 78–81
Menzies, Archibald
Michaux, André 238
Michaux, Francois 238
Michell, W. A. 196
milk, delights of sour 242
Milne, William Grant 37–44, 305–311
    burnt letter 43
    camping conditions in west Africa 41, 42
    Fiji 305–311
    health and teetotalism 44
    ingredients of Calabar chop 38, 39
    murderous class in west Africa 39, 40
    Scottish song to natives 305, 307
    west Africa 37–44
    witchcraft in west Africa 41
Mimosa farnesiana 199
missionaries 12, 107–109, 137, 237, 248, 260
Molloy, Georgiana xii
monkeys
    as food 39, 275
    of Sumatra 86
    pig-tailed 87
    trained to gather plants 86, 87
monofluoroacetic acid ('1080') 127
Moore, Reverend 308
mosquitoes 82, 263
mosses 120, 144, 145, 299, 310
Motley, James 77–89
    description of venomous ray 81
    pendulous bird nests 88
    the men of the mud 78–81
Motleyia 89
Mt Kinabalu 90–95
Mt Patteh 5
Mueller, Ferdinand J. H. 161, **162**–166, 167, 169, 189
    daily routine on A. C. Gregory's expedition 161–163, 166
Murray, Stewart 229
Musa (with Burbidge) 92
mutiny, state of 23

Myrmecodia 101, 102
  tuberosa 101

N
names, scientific 323–325
Namibia 31, 33
natives
  hostile 152–154, 162
  knowledge of natural history 100
Nepenthes 90–92
  edwardsiana 91, 92
  lowii 90
  rajah 91
  villosa 92
nettles 209, 210
Niger River 3, 19, 20, 37
nipa palm 82–84, **85**
North American Indians
  Bannacks 252
  Chenook (Chinook) 229
  Clatsop 229
  Eutaws 252
  Iroquois 220
  Sayelpies 260
  Shoshonies (Snake) 252
North Australian Expedition 161–163, 166
North, Marianne xi
Nymphaea 41, 150–152
  as food 151, 152
  macrosperma **152**
Nypa fruticans 82–84, **85**

O
Oenothera drummondii **225**
Oleandra nodosa 25
Onesimus (with Baines) 35, 36
ophthalmia 132
orchids 12, 14, 15, 25, 38, 65, 84, 86, 90, 101, 134,
    140, 263, 266–268, 271, 281, 310
  culture of African terrestrial 14
  Dendrobium hookerianum 66, **67**
  Schomburgkia superbiens **264**, 265
  Thelymitra antennifera **134**
oxen (bullocks) 32, 36
  dead and sickly 15, 16, 158
  pack-animals 9, 11, 158
  riding 9

P
Pacheem 63
pack-animals (*see* oxen, horses)
palanquin (palankeen) 51–53
Palm Valley **170**
palms 14, 20–22, 40, 61, 168, 271, 275, 307, 308
  cabbage **168**–170
  nipa 82–84, **85**
Pandanus 40

  spiralis **156**, 157
paper for drying plants 158, 161, 220, 233
Papyrus 40
Paritium tiliaceum 87
Parnell, Richard 206
pea, Sturt's desert vii–ix
Phalangium quamash 230, 231
Pheidole javana 101
Phlox drummondii 222, 226, **227**
Pinus lambertiana, discovery of 233–235
pitcher plants 90–92
plant collecting
  an expensive occupation 277
  to alleviate boredom xii, 181
plant specimens
  breakage of 161
  burning of 105, 106
  carried in clothing 130, 148
  cost of collecting 267
  drying 3, 105–106, 233, 270, 285
  lost through conflict 17
  eaten by horse 190, 191
  insect pests 8, 24
  lost in shipwreck 20
  lost through lack of transport 16, 158, 159
  mouldy 263
  payment for xii, 192
  prickly 196
  purchase by subscribers 226
  soaked in water 286, 287
  thrown overboard 266
Plant, Robert W. 9–18
  loss of collections 16–18
plants
  alpine **122**, 147, **165**, 212
  ant 101, 102
  antiscorbutic 297, **298**, 299
  churchyard 209–211
  cushion **122**, 123
  native names 100
  native food 151, 152, 156, 157
  poisonous 126, 127
  profusion of 147
  subalpine 144, 145, 210
  wounding and drawing blood 148, 149
Platte River 248
Port Essington 150
prairie dogs (prairie marmot) 248, 250, 251
Primula 114, 116
Prince's Island (Principe) 24
Pringlea antiscorbutica 297, **298**, 299
Pseudolarix amabilis 72–76
Pseudotsuga menzeisii 236
Ptilotus rotundifolius x

Q
quiver tree 33, **34**–36

R

Raffles, Lady 47
Raffles, Stamford 47–50
Rafflesia arnoldii 47–**50**
Ranunculus anemoneus **165**
rays, venomous 81
Red-Deer River 218, 219
rhinoceros 36
Rhododendron 65, 90, 91, 112, 114, 116
  maximum 245
  sulfureum 114, **115**
Ribes 231, 232
Richardson, John 217, 223
Richea scoparia **122**
Roan Mountain 244, 245
Robinson, Alec 171
Rocky Mountains sheep 244, 245
Roper, Mr 153
Ross, James Clark 297, 301, 303
Rowan, Ellis xi
Ruahine Range 137–149
Rulingia loxophylla **164**

S

Sabine, Joseph 229, 233
sage-cock 251
Sanderson, John 17
Sargent, Oswald H. 192
scarlet feather-flower 132, **133**–136
Schomburgk, Robert 269
Schomburgkia superbiens **264**, 265, 267
Schön, Frederick 4
Schroeder, Mr 12
Scilla esculenta 230
sea snakes 81
seaweeds 300
seed
  amount of 114, 116
  price of 192
Seemann, Berthold Carl 312, **313**–319
  cannibalism 315, 316, 318, 319
Senecio gregorii **163**
service tree 245
shaddock tree 311
ships
  collision of *Erebus* and *Terror* 302, 303
  desertion of crew 22, 23
  life aboard 4, 7, 301, 302
  loss of ship (*Dayspring*) 19, 20
Ships
  Acteon 265
  Albert 6
  Dayspring 19, 22
  Erebus 297, 301, 302
  Hebe 267
  Henry 128
  Herald 305, 311, 312

  Lady Franklin 308
  Soudan 6
  Sulphur 266
  Sunbeam 22
  Terror 297, 301
  Wilberforce 6
Sieber, Franz vii
Sierra de Mijas 204
Skinner, George Ure 263–268
skunk, as food 223, 224
Smythe, Colonel 315
snakes
  antidote to bite 247
  bushmaster 274
  rattlesnake 247, 250, 252–254
Snelling, Lilian 114
snow blindness 223
Solanum anthropophagorum (= *S. uporo*) 316, **317**,
  319
Somosomo, Queen of 312
Spain 199–205
Spencer, Walter Baldwin 184–191
Spinifex 173
spinifex (misapplied to *Triodia*) viii, 173
Spruce, Richard 285, **286**–294
  attacked by ants 289, 290
  attacked by wasps 290
  lover of cats 288, 289
  plot to kill him 291–294
  stings from caterpillars 291
Stanhopea 266
Stapelia gigantea **17**
stinging tree 310
Stewart, Mr 206
Stork, Mr 313
Stuart, John McDouall 164
Sturt, Charles viii
Sullivan, Daniel 181, **182**, 183
Sumatra 47, 77–89
superstitions 37, 39
Surinam 269–278
  difficulties of travelling in 269–270
Swainsona formosa vii–**ix**
synonyms, definition of 324, 325

T

taro 309, **318**, 319
  accompaniment with human flesh 316
Tasmanian alpine vegetation **122**
Tasmanian snow gum **120**
Tasmanian tiger 121
Tate, Ralph 184, 191
taxonomic ranks 325
tea, introduction to India 70, 334
Thelymitra antennifera **134**
Theobald, Mr 60
Thomas, Reverend 38

thrift **212**
Thryptomene maisonneuvii **163**, **164**
Thylacinus cyanocephalus 121
ticks, extracting 65
Tietkens, William Henry 173, 175, 177
tiger
  attack by a 102, 103
  hunt for 60
  trap for 103–105
tobacco
  as a reward 232, 234
  for barter 230
  for removing leeches 66
  to stave off hunger 257
Tribulus forrestii **164**
Trigonocephalus rhombeatus 274
Triodia **172**, 173
  puncturing legs of horses 172, 173
Tropaeolum aff. *brachyceras* 279, 280
Trophis anthropophagorum 316
Tugela River 9, 10
Tupaia tana 100
Turner, Dawson 47
twins, killing of 39, 40

U
Urtica pilulifera 210, 211

V
vampire bats 274, 287, 288
vasculum 222, 286, 289
Veitch, Peter 90, 94, 95
Verticordia 132, 136
  grandiflora 134
  grandis 132, **133**–136
Victoria amazonica 281, **282**–284, 324, 325
Vogel, J. R. Theodor 3–8

W
Wailes, Mr 266, 267
Walcott, Pemberton x
Walker, Mr (missionary) 260
Walker, George Warren & Mrs A. W. 51–56
Wallace, Alfred Russel 96, 99
Wang-a-nok, Mr 74
Warburton, Peter Egerton viii
Ward, Nathaniel Bagshaw 329
Wardian Case 19, 70, 74, **330**
  development of 329–334
wasps, attack by 90
water lilies 150–**152**, 281, **282**–284, 324, 325
Watson, Hewett Cottrell 210, 211
weeds, vile 240
Welwitsch, Friedrich Martin Josef 27, **28**–30
Welwitschia mirabilis 27–**29**, **30**, 31, 35
west Africa, mortality of Europeans 8, 22
Whitfield, Edward 134

Willdampia formosa vii–**ix**
Williams, Mr (with Hooker) 57
Wilson, Captain 312
Winn, W. N. 196
witchcraft 41
wreath plant **194**

X
Xanthorrhoea 124, 125
  australis 181, **183**
  used to start fires 124, 125

Y
yams 7, 39
yellow fever 268
York Road poison **126**, 127
Yunnan 107
Yurébe, Pedro 292–294

Z
Zulus 12